W9-DDL-333

MACHIAVELLI AND REPUBLICANISM

IDEAS IN CONTEXT

Edited by Richard Rorty, J. B. Schneewind, Quentin Skinner and Wolf Lepenies

The books in this series discuss the emergence of intellectual traditions and of related disciplines. The procedures, aims and vocabularies generated will be set in the context of the alternatives available within the contemporary frameworks of ideas and institutions. Through detailed studies of the evolution of such traditions, and their modification by different audiences, it is hoped that a new picture will form of the development of ideas in their concrete contexts. By this means, artificial distinctions between the history of philosophy, of the various sciences, of society and politics, and of literature, may be seen to dissolve.

Ideas in Context is published with the support of the Exxon Education Foundation. For a full list of titles in this series, please see end of book.

MACHIAVELLI AND REPUBLICANISM

EDITED BY

GISELA BOCK

QUENTIN SKINNER

MAURIZIO VIROLI

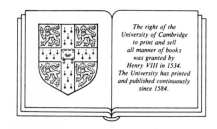

The right of the
University of Cambridge
to print and sell
all manner of books
was granted by
Henry VIII in 1534.
The University has printed
and published continuously
since 1584.

CAMBRIDGE UNIVERSITY PRESS

CAMBRIDGE

NEW YORK   PORT CHESTER   MELBOURNE   SYDNEY

Published by the Press Syndicate of the University of Cambridge
The Pitt Building, Trumpington Street, Cambridge CB2 1RP
40 West 20th Street, New York, NY 10011, USA
10 Stamford Road, Oakleigh, Melbourne 3166, Australia

© Cambridge University Press 1990

First published 1990

Printed in Great Britain at The Bath Press, Avon

British Library cataloguing in publication data
Machiavelli and republicanism – (Ideas in context).
1. Republicanism. Theories of Machiavelli, Niccolò,
1469–1527
1. Bock, Gisela 11. Skinner, Quentin 111. Viroli,
Maurizio 1v. Series
321.8'6'0924

Library of Congress cataloguing in publication data
Machiavelli and republicanism / edited by Gisela Bock, Quentin
Skinner, and Maurizio Viroli.
p.   cm – (Ideas in Context)
ISBN 0-521-38376-5
1. Machiavelli, Niccolò. 1469–1527 – Contributions in political
science. 2. Machiavelli, Niccolò. 1469–1527 – Contributions in
republicanism. 3. Republicanism – Italy – Florence – History – 16th
century. 4. Florence (Italy) – Politics and government – 1421–1737.
5. Republicanism. 1. Bock, Gisela. 11. Skinner, Quentin.
111. Viroli, Maurizio. 1v. Series.
JC143.M4M317 1990
321.8'6–dc20 89-22329 CIP
ISBN 0 521 38376 5

CONTENTS

LIST OF CONTRIBUTORS

Robert Black is Lecturer in Modern History in the University of Leeds. He is the author of *Benedetto Accolti and the Florentine Renaissance* (1985) and of articles on humanist historiography, on school and university education in the Renaissance and on Machiavelli's chancery career. He is now completing a book on education, society and humanism in Florentine Tuscany, 1350 to 1500, as well as a register of unpublished documents regarding the University of Arezzo in the Middle Ages and Renaissance.

Gisela Bock is Professor of History at the European University Institute (Florence) and at the University of Bielefeld (Federal Republic of Germany). Between 1987 and 1989 she was Director of the European Culture Research Centre at the European University Institute, in the framework of which the conference 'Machiavelli and Republicanism' took place. Her publications include books and articles on Tommaso Campanella (1974), Niccolò Machiavelli (1986), on women's history in the United States and Italy and on women and racism in National Socialist Germany (1986).

Elena Fasano Guarini is Professor of Modern History at the University of Pisa, Italy. She is the author of *Lo stato mediceo di Cosimo I* (1973) and of many articles on the constitutional history of Tuscany as well as being editor of *Potere e società negli stati regionali italiani del '500 e '600* (1978) and *Prato – storia di una città* (1986).

Martin van Gelderen is Assistant Professor of History at the Technical University of Berlin. He is preparing a volume of texts from the Dutch Revolt for the series 'Cambridge texts in the history of political thought'. A monograph on *The Political Thought of the Dutch Revolt (1555–1590)* is forthcoming from Cambridge University Press.

Eco Haitsma Mulier is Jan Romein Professor of the History of Historiography and Political Ideas at the University of Amsterdam. His publications include *The Myth of Venice and Dutch Republican Thought in the Seventeenth Century* (1980) and numerous articles on the historiography of early modern Europe. *A Dictionary of Dutch Historians (1500–1800)*, written in collaboration with G.A.C. van der Lem, is forthcoming with the Netherlands Historisch Genootschap.

Werner Maihofer is Professor Emeritus of Law at the University of Bielefeld, External Professor of Law and Honorary Principal of the European University Institute at Florence. His publications include *Recht und Sein* (1954), *Vom Sinn menschlicher Ordnung* (1956), *Rechtsstaat und menschliche Würde* (1968), 'Hegels Prinzip des modernen Staates' (1969), 'Rechtsstaat und Sozialstaat' (1972), 'Gesetzgebungswissenschaft' (1981), 'Gesellschaft, Staat, Recht' (1986), 'Die Einheit der Kultur Europas in der Vielfalt der Kulturen Europas' (1987). He is co-author of the *Alternativ-Entwurf eines Strafgesetz-*

buches (1966) and a member of the executive board of the Internationale Vereinigung für Rechts- und Sozialphilosophie.

Michael Mallet is Professor of History at the University of Warwick, and is currently editing vols. 5–7 of the *Carteggio di Lorenzo de' Medici*. Earlier publications include *The Florentine Galleys in the Fifteenth Century* (1967), *The Borgias* (1969), *Mercenaries and their Masters: Warfare in Renaissance Italy* (1974), and, with J.R. Hale, *The Military Organisation of a Renaissance State: Venice, c.1400–1617* (1984).

John M. Najemy is Associate Professor of History at Cornell University. He is author of *Corporatism and Consensus in Florentine Electoral Politics, 1280–1400* (1982) and essays on Florentine history and Machiavelli. He is completing a book on the Machiavelli–Vettori correspondence of 1513–15.

Nicolai Rubinstein is Emeritus Professor of History of the University of London. He is the author of *The Government of Florence under the Medici (1434–1494)* (1966) and of many articles on Italian medieval and Renaissance history and the history of political ideas. He is the general editor of the letters of Lorenzo de' Medici and has edited volumes 3 and 4 (1977, 1981) of the *Lettere*.

Judith Shklar is John Cowles Professor of Government at Harvard University where she teaches political theory. Her most recent books are *Ordinary Vices* (1985) and, in the Past Masters series, *Montesquieu* (1987). A new book, *The Faces of Injustice*, is currently in press.

Giovanni Silvano is Ricercatore in the Department of History of the University of Padua. He is the author of *'Vivere civile' e 'governo misto' a Firenze nel primo Cinquecento* (1985), and the editor of a new critical edition of Donato Giannotti's *Repubblica fiorentina* (1989).

Quentin Skinner is Professor of Political Science in the University of Cambridge and a Fellow of Christ's College, Cambridge. He has helped to edit a number of books, including *The Cambridge History of Renaissance Philosophy* (1988) and is the author of *The Foundations of Modern Political Thought* (2 vols., 1978), *Machiavelli* (1981) and *Meaning and Context*, ed. James Tully (1988).

Maurizio Viroli is Assistant Professor of Politics at Princeton University and is currently a member of the School of Social Science at the Institute for Advanced Study. He has published *L'etica laica di Erminio Juvalta* (1988) and *Jean-Jacques Rousseau and the 'well-ordered society'* (1989).

Blair Worden is a Fellow in Modern History at St Edmund Hall, Oxford. His publications include *The Rump Parliament* (1974) and a series of essays on the politics, religion and literature of seventeenth-century England.

ACKNOWLEDGEMENTS

My own part in editing this volume has mainly been to co-operate with the officers of the Cambridge University Press in seeing the manuscript into print. I welcome the opportunity this gives me of paying tribute to my two co-editors for the much more substantial efforts they have put into our project. Maurizio Viroli conceived the idea of holding a conference on the theme of Renaissance republicanism in the city of Machiavelli's birth. He drew up our original list of prospective contributors, and is thus responsible for the basic plan of this book. Gisela Bock revised and improved the original scheme, in addition to undertaking what proved to be the enormous task of organising the conference itself. This took place at the European University Institute (Florence) in September 1987 under the auspices of the European Culture Research Centre. Professor Bock corresponded with the scholars we wished to invite, persuading virtually all of them to attend. She also took charge of the arrangements in Florence, ensuring that the conference was a source of enjoyment as well as instruction to everyone who took part in it.

I should also like to express our appreciation to those who helped Professor Bock mount the conference. Kathinka Espana provided secretarial assistance well beyond the call of duty. The group named Interpreti di conferenza issued simultaneous translations of our discussions, a superbly skilful as well as indispensable service. The Banca d'Italia, the Banca Toscana and the Monte dei Paschi di Siena contributed generous grants towards our expenses. More recently, Valeria E. Russo gave further assistance in helping to put our proceedings into publishable form.

Among our friends in Florence, however, our chief debt is owed to Professor Werner Maihofer, who was at that time President of the European University Institute. He provided the facilities that enabled Professor Viroli to work at the Institute while helping to prepare the conference. He allowed us to hold our meetings in the spectacular and highly appropriate setting of the Villa Schifanoia at San Domenico, now the Conference Centre of the Institute. He also arranged the funding which enabled us to attract the international group of experts who met to discuss our chosen theme. For all these kindnesses and signs of trust, as well as for his own contributions to our proceedings, we offer him our warmest thanks.

We also wish to express our gratitude to those who took part in the conference. Some forty scholars attended, all of whom contributed valuably to our three days of debate. Above all, our thanks are due to those who delivered the main papers. Most of these have subsequently been revised – and in some cases entirely rewritten – in the light of the discussions we held. We are greatly indebted to those who undertook such revisions; they were completed in every case with evident cheerfulness and impressive punctuality.

Finally, a word of thanks to those connected with the Cambridge University Press. I am pleased to have persuaded my fellow editors of *Ideas in Context* to accept our book for their series, and thank them for their support. I am also most grateful for the help and encouragement I have received at all stages of production from the officers of the Press. I wish in particular to offer my thanks to Dr Jeremy Mynott, the Editorial Director, who originally encouraged me to submit our manuscript to Cambridge; to Richard Fisher, who brought to bear his exemplary skills and patience as our editor; and to Margaret Jull Costa, our subeditor, who worked on every chapter with the greatest meticulousness, thereby improving the presentation of our book in very many ways.

As our book goes to press, I am delighted to learn that there is still time to express our appreciation to Fiona Barr for compiling the index.

Quentin Skinner
Cambridge, September 1989

PART I

Machiavelli and the republican experience

1

Machiavelli and Florentine republican experience

NICOLAI RUBINSTEIN

Florence, wrote Machiavelli in 1519 or 1520 in his *Discursus* on the reform of the Florentine government, has never been a 'repubblica . . . che abbi avute le debite qualità sue'[1] – an observation which recapitulates the statement made a few years earlier in his *Discorsi sopra la prima deca di Tito Livio* that 'per dugento anni che si ha di vera memoria', Florence had never possessed a 'stato, per il quale la possa veramente essere chiamata republica'.[2] In the *Discorsi*, he attributes this to the fact that before acquiring its independence from the Hohenstaufen Empire, Florence had always lived 'sotto il governo d'altrui'. That it had never been a true republic, he states in the *Discursus*,[3] is borne out by the regime, the *stato*, it had had since 1393, when under Maso degli Albizzi's leadership the city became a 'repubblica governata da ottimati' and thus acquired an oligarchical regime, which lasted until 1434, when it was replaced with the Medici regime. Its 'difetti' were the excessive power, and yet insufficient 'reputazione', of the Signoria, the long intervals between the electoral scrutinies which qualified citizens for office-holding, the influence which private citizens exercised over the decisions of the government through their membership of advisory bodies, the *pratiche*, the lack of institutional safeguards against the formation of factions or *sètte* – 'le quali sono la rovina di uno stato' – by great citizens, 'uomini grandi'. But the worst of these 'disordini', the one 'che importava il tutto', was the virtual exclusion from the regime of the people, 'il popolo', which 'non vi aveva dentro la parte sua'. These criticisms, which reflect Machiavelli's disapproval of government by *ottimati*, as well as his passionate concern for a true 'ordine civile', contrast with the praise his friend Francesco Guicciardini had lavished, about ten years earlier, on the aristocratic regime of the early fifteenth century, of which 'meritamente si dice che . . . è stato el più savio, el più glorioso, el più felice governo che mai per alcuno tempo abbi avuto la città nostra'[4] – a judgement which echoed the nostalgia which that regime had evoked, later in the fifteenth century, among *ottimati*.[5] Florence, it

---

[1] *Discursus florentinarum rerum post mortem iunioris Laurentii Medices*, ed. M. Martelli, Niccolò Machiavelli, *Tutte le opere* (Florence, 1971), p. 24.   [2] *Ibid.* I, 49, p. 131.   [3] *Ibid.*
[4] *Storie fiorentine*, ed. R. Palmarocchi (Bari, 1931), pp. 2–3.
[5] Cf. N. Rubinstein, 'Florentine constitutionalism and Medici ascendancy in the fifteenth century' in N. Rubinstein, ed. *Florentine Studies* (London, 1968), p. 460.

was said, was then ruled by citizens who 'non dovriano dirsi inferiori a quei più savi Romani così celebrati dall' antichità'[6] and who placed the common good before private interest; Niccolò Soderini, one of the leading opponents of Medici ascendancy in 1465–6, declared that 'chi non governò innanzi al 33, non sa governare'.[7]

By way of criticism, as well as of praise, the regime under which Florence was governed in the early fifteenth century was thus considered by later generations the most significant manifestation of republican government the Florentines had experienced before the establishment, in 1494, of the Great Council. In this chapter on republican experience in fifteenth-century Florence, I shall therefore concentrate on the period before 1434, and then briefly discuss the changes which that experience underwent under the Medici, and after their expulsion in 1494.

This is a large subject, and in order to do it a modicum of justice, I propose to distinguish, in what must perforce be very general observations, the following three aspects of that experience: the concept contemporaries formed of Florence's republican institutions; the ways in which the working of these institutions affected Florentine citizens; and the extent to which they actively participated in the government of Florence.

If we want to ask how the Florentines conceptualised their republic, we have to go back to the fourteenth, and even the thirteenth century, when the rise of the Signoria in Northern and Central Italy brought about, in the surviving Italian city republics, the perception of a fundamental antithesis between despotic rule and the 'popoli che vivono in libertà',[8] the 'libertas populi',[9] a term which, in the fifteenth century, the humanists replaced with the classical one for commonwealth, *res publica*. According to Cicero's definition, as explained by St Augustine,[10] 'omnino nullam esse rem publicam, quoniam non esset res populi'; and, in his translation of the *Politics*, Leonardo Bruni rendered Aristotle's term for the third true constitution, *politeia*, with *res publica*.[11] The chief difference between the republican and the despotic regime was to concern the contrast between the absolute and arbitrary exercise of government and its limitation by law and the will of the people.

---

[6] Luca della Robbia, in his life of Bartolomeo Valori composed around 1500, ed. P. Bigazzi, *Archivio Storico Italiano*, 4, 1 (1843), pp. 239–40.

[7] That is before the victory of the Albizzi faction, which, after Cosimo de' Medici's return from exile in 1434, was followed by the establishment of Medici ascendancy. Ed. G. Pampaloni, 'Nuovi tentativi di riforme alla Costituzione Fiorentina attraverso le consulte', *Archivio Storico Italiano*, 120 (1962), p. 572 (*pratica* of 8 July). For a contemporary narrative of the crisis of the Medici regime in 1465–6, see M. Phillips, *The Memoir of Marco Parenti. A Life in Medici Florence* (Princeton, 1987 and London, 1989), chs. 7, 9, 10.

[8] See e.g. Matteo Villani, *Cronica*, IX, 87, ed. F.G. Dragomanni (Milan, 1848) VI, p. 275.

[9] E.g. Ferreto de' Ferreti, *Historia*, ed. C. Cipolla (Rome, 1908–20), II, p. 11.

[10] *De civitate Dei*, II, 21; cf. Cicero, *De re publica*, I, 25.

[11] *Politics*, 1279a: 'Cum autem multitudo gubernet ad communem utilitatem, vocatur communi nomine rerumpublicarum [πολιτειῶν] omnium, respublica [πολιτεία]', Aristoteles, *Libri omnes quibus tota moralis philosophia . . . continetur* (Lyons, 1579), V, p. 571.

Bruni was the first humanist to attempt, in his *Laudatio Florentinae urbis* of 1403,[12] an analysis of the republican constitution of Florence; but, largely owing to the panegyrical nature of this work, his analysis is incomplete and necessarily biased; while his later, more objective account, in his short Greek treatise on the Florentine *politeia*,[13] suffers from his attempt to apply Aristotelian constitutional theory, in the form of the mixed constitution, to Florence. What does, however, stand out in these analyses are a number of basic principles, which are conceived by Bruni as fundamental to an understanding of the Florentine system of government: for the executive, the Signoria, a strict limitation, by a variety of means, of its almost regal authority, and its dependence, in the last resort, on the will of the people, as voiced in the legislative councils of the People and of the Commune; for the citizens, liberty under the law, and an equality which implied, among other things, as Bruni pointed out in 1428 in his funeral oration for Nanni Strozzi, equal opportunity to rise to high office;[14] for the social classes, as he states in his constitutional treatise about ten years later, a balance between the patricians and the people which, while tilted towards the former, took no account of the extremes of private power and of poverty, whose representatives were excluded from government. How far did the political experience of Florentine citizens conform to these principles?

The overriding experience the average Florentine citizen had of his republic must have been the power, and indeed the majesty, of the Signoria, with its eight Priors and the Gonfalonier of Justice, a power which Gregorio Dati described, at the beginning of the century, as 'grande sanza misura'.[15] Decisively reasserted in 1382 after the Ciompi revolt of 1378,[16] it included the authority to initiate legislation, as well as the right to intervene in criminal jurisdiction when the public interest might demand it. But the Signoria, which deliberated jointly with its two Colleges, the Sixteen Gonfalonieri di compagnia and the Twelve Buonuomini, was not the only magistracy which the citizens would regard as the governing body of the republic. The Otto di Guardia, set up after the Ciompi revolt to protect the security of the state, had acquired extensive powers in policing it, the Dieci di Balìa were, after 1384, in times of war, in charge of military operations and diplomatic negotiations, the Ufficiali del Monte administered the funded debt and had become the central financial magistracy of the Commune. The increasing range of the powers and competence of the executive branch of government was part of the political experience of the Florentines from the 1380s onwards; it was largely due to the

---

[12] *From Petrarch to Leonardo Bruni*, ed. H. Baron (Chicago and London, 1968), pp. 217–63.

[13] 'Leonard Bruni's Constitution of Florence', ed. A. Moulakis, *Rinascimento*, 2nd series, 26 (1986), pp. 141–90. It was probably composed in 1439 or 1440: *ibid.* pp. 154–5.

[14] *Miscellanea*, ed. E. Baluze and G.D. Mansi, 4, (Lucca, 1764), p. 3.

[15] *Istoria di Firenze*, ed L. Pratesi (Florence, 1904), p. 148.

[16] See N. Rubinstein, 'Il regime politico di Firenze dopo il Tumulto dei Ciompi' in *Il Tumulto dei Ciompi* (Convegno Internazionale di Studi 1979) (Florence, 1981), pp. 105–24.

traumatic effects of the Ciompi revolt and its aftermath and of the wars against Giangaleazzo Visconti, and to the aggrandisement and reorganisation of the city's territorial dominion. But there were limits to this development. A permanent commission of eighty-one composed almost entirely of members of the executive branch, with full powers to hire mercenaries and levy taxes for this purpose, which had been set up in 1393,[17] was for all practical purposes abolished eleven years later, and a contemporary diarist commented: 'il populo ne fu molto lieto'.[18] It was significant of this reluctance to increase the powers of the executive even further, that when in 1411 a new council, of 200, was created, without whose assent no military action was to be undertaken, it consisted only partly of official members, and its decisions required in their turn the assent of the councils of the People and the Commune.[19] Indeed, these two ancient councils of the republic, whose membership totalled over 500,[20] provided the most important of the checks to the powers of the executive. They could be seen to represent the broad foundation of the republican structure of government. As Bruni puts it in his *Laudatio*, in terms derived from Roman law, 'quod enim ad multos attinet', must be decided by the many.[21]

Bruni points out that another check to the great power of the Signoria was the short term of their office. All public offices were held for short periods, mostly for six months, those of the Signoria for two months only. This, as well as the proliferation of offices since the second half of the fourteenth century, provided the citizens with a wide range of opportunities to hold office, and consequently to participate directly in government and administration. This extensive availability of public office was thus a major aspect of the republican experience of the citizens, and thus of the Florentine *libertas*;[22] another concerned the methods by which this availability was translated into fact, in other words, the methods by which citizens were actually elected to office.

Since early in the fourteenth century, election to public office was based on periodical vetting for eligibility in so-called scrutinies (*squittini*), which were carried out by specially convened commissions consisting of the Signoria, its two Colleges, a number of other ex officio members, and eighty additional members elected by the Signoria and the Colleges, which gave the executive a key role in determining the composition of the commission.[23] Actual

[17] See A. Molho, 'The Florentine oligarchy and the "Balìe" of the late Trecento', *Speculum*, 43 (1968), pp. 31ff.
[18] Giovanni di Pagolo Morelli, *Ricordi*, ed. V. Branca (Florence, 1956), pp. 426–7. Cf. G. Guidi, *Il governo della città-repubblica di Firenze del primo Quattrocento* (Florence, 1981), II, p. 146.
[19] Law establishing the council of 200, *Sulla repubblica fiorentina a tempo di Cosimo il Vecchio*, ed. F.C. Pellegrini (Pisa, 1880), Appendix, pp. ix–xiii.
[20] Cf. Guidi, *Il governo*, II, pp. 140, 142.
[21] *Laudatio*, as above, n. 12, p. 260. *Codex*, 5, 59, 5, 2. Cf. Rubinstein, 'Florentine constitutionalism', p. 446, n. 1.
[22] See N. Rubinstein, 'Florentina libertas', *Rinascimento*, 2nd series, 26 (1986), pp. 13, 15.
[23] On this and the following, see N. Rubinstein, *The Government of Florence under the Medici (1434 to 1494)* (Oxford, 1966), pp. 56ff.; Guidi, *Il governo*, I, pp. 283ff.

appointment to office followed on the extraction of the names of eligible citizens from the pouches in which they had been placed after the scrutinies. There were separate pouches for different offices or groups of offices, and of these the most prestigious contained the names of the citizens who had been made eligible for the so-called three highest offices, the Signoria, the Sixteen Gonfalonieri di compagnia, and the Twelve Buonuomini. Scrutinies – that of the Tre Maggiori Uffici was separate from that of all the other public offices – were to take place every five years (in fact, the intervals were usually longer), and votes were cast on nominations by the Gonfaloniers of the ancient militia companies, who could be assumed to be well acquainted with the citizens of their sixteen districts;[24] and both the identity of the voters and the results of the vote were kept strictly secret. This meant that citizens who had been nominated would not know whether they had been made eligible until their names were extracted from the pouches prior to the filling of a vacancy. This was a matter of particular importance for the three most prestigious offices, which included the Signoria; accordingly, even if a citizen, though eligible to them, was temporarily barred from being elected (for instance, because he had held the same office recently), he was now known (*veduto*), as were those who were actually elected to office (*seduti*), to have been qualified for government. This gave the group of *veduti* and *seduti* a preferential position not only in subsequent scrutinies, but also when it came to electing the membership of councils, such as that of 200, which were endowed with special responsibilities and powers, and hence affected the participation of citizens in political life.

The secrecy which was an essential feature of the Florentine electoral system conformed to that which surrounded the working of both the executive and the legislative organs of the republic; it formed an essential part of the republican experience of Florentine citizens. Just as the deliberations of the Signoria were meant to be kept secret – an obligation which was physically reflected in the separate location of their living quarters on the second floor of their palace – so the vote in the councils was by secret ballot. This concern with secrecy was underlined by the lengths to which the government would go in trying to prevent the formation of caucuses, as in the temporary suppression of religious confraternities, which were banned, for instance, in 1419, on the grounds that some of them encouraged factionalism; later in the century citizens who, as *veduti* or *seduti*, were known to be eligible to government, were forbidden to attend meetings of confraternities while electoral scrutinies were in progress. But there were ways of evading such prohibitions; we know of at least one of the more prestigious confraternities which, around the middle of the century,

---

[24] D.V. and F.W. Kent, *Neighbours and Neighbourhoods in Renaissance Florence: the District of the Red Lion in the Fifteenth Century* (Locust Valley, New York, 1982), pp. 17–19.

had special sponsors, *sollecitatori*, to support weaker members in the ongoing scrutiny of 1454.[25]

In fact, while the secrecy of the electoral system was, on the whole, effective, the same did not apply to the independence of the scrutinies from outside influence. It was quite usual for citizens to canvass members of scrutiny commissions to nominate them; there was even a technical term for this, *pregheria*, and family *ricordanze* would record such *pregherie* and the sense of obligation they involved. Gregorio Dati's *Libro segreto* throws a vivid light on this practice, as well as on the ways in which Florentine citizens experienced the intricacies of their electoral system. On 3 May 1412 Dati records that his name had been drawn for the office of Gonfaloniere di compagnia for his district; until then, he says, he had not been sure that his name was in the pouches for the Colleges, but for the sake of his own honour and of that of his descendants, 'pur lo disiderava'; 'onde', he continues, 'per non esser ingrato né volendo usare lo insaziabile appetito, che quanto più ha più disiderano, mi sono proposto e diliberato che da ora inanzi per ufici di Comune che s'abiano a fare o a squittinare mai non debo pregare alcuno, ma lasciare fare a chi fia sopra ciò . . .'.[26]

The desire to hold public office was, in fact, one of the most striking characteristics of the republican experience of Florentine citizens. A number of the offices in the administration of the dominion were sought not only for *onore* but also for *utile*, and could indeed bring considerable financial advantages to their holders; the honour which membership of the Signoria, whose salary was only intended to cover expenses, brought with it, could also mean social advancement and political influence for oneself and one's family. While the holding of public office was extolled by humanists such as Matteo Palmieri as the duty of the citizen who placed the common good above private interest and who knows 'essere commessa in lui la publica degnità et il bene commune essere lasciato nella sua fede',[27] others castigated the 'ambitio officiorum', the 'volere gli ufici', as the cause of 'tutto ciò che di male è stato nella benedetta città di Firenze';[28] while Alberti, in a famous passage, has Giannozzo deride the citizens' scramble for public office, which makes them into nothing better than 'publici servi': it was far preferable to 'vivere a sé, non al comune'.[29] Some

---

[25] See J. Henderson, 'Le confraternite religiose nella Firenze del tardo Medioevo: patroni spirituali e anche politici?', *Ricerche storiche*, 15 (1985), pp. 77–94, and also Rubinstein, *The Government of Florence*, p. 119.

[26] *Mercanti storici. Ricordi nella Firenze tra Medioevo e Rinascimento*, ed. V. Branca (Milan, 1986), pp. 550–1. [27] *Vita civile*, ed. G. Belloni (Florence, 1982), p. 132.

[28] Rinaldo degli Albizi in a *pratica* of 1431 (Pellegrini, ed., *Sulla repubblica fiorentina*, p. xxxiii): 'Causa vero [discordiarum] est ambitio officiorum'; Marchionne di Coppo Stefani, *Cronaca fiorentina*, ed. N. Rodolico, *Rer. Ital. Script.*, 30, 1 (Città di Castello, 1903 – Bologna, 1955), rubrica 923, p. 413 (*ad* 1382).

[29] Leon Battista Alberti, *I libri della Famiglia* in *Opere volgari*, C. Grayson, ed. (Bari, 1960–73), I, pp. 179–82.

citizens would agree, Giovanni Rucellai, for example, during his time in the political wilderness after Cosimo's return from exile and before being accepted, nearly thirty years later, into the Medici regime.[30] For the vast majority, however, high office represented the peak of their republican experience. The memoirs of fifteenth-century Florentines clearly show the role office-holding played in their lives. The 'cursus honorum' might begin with the election to the consulate of one of the guilds; communal offices would follow, until finally successful citizens would reach the plateau of the top offices of government and administration, which included, first of all, the Signoria and their Colleges, but also such powerful and prestigious magistracies as the Dieci di Balìa, the Otto di Guardia, and the Ufficiali del Monte.

The citizens who had reached this plateau, after having been made eligible for the government, constituted what the Florentines called the *reggimento*; after the scrutiny of 1411, it amounted to just over 1,000 citizens; by the time the scrutiny of 1433 had completed its business, it had risen to over 2,000.[31] While this shows a remarkable degree of social mobility, it should be added that only a fraction of these men (185 and 327 respectively) belonged to the craft guilds, although these contributed a quarter of the members of most offices: evidently because only a very small section of the lower classes were considered fit for positions in the government. Another significant feature of these figures is the prevalence of single families: of the 1757 citizens of the greater guilds who were made eligible to the three highest offices in 1433, just under 100 were individually successful, the rest belonged to 227 families. Among these a very small group was represented with far greater numbers than the average of 7.3 per family – such as the Capponi with 20 and the Strozzi with no less than 40 members. The *reggimento*, it has been said, has to be seen 'as a constellation of families rather than as an aggregate of individuals'.[32]

Nor was the elitist tendency in the access to high public office, and hence to a high level of political participation, confined to the procedure of qualification for these offices. The methods by which the results of the electoral scrutinies were used in the final stage of the electoral process, that is the extraction from the pouches which had been filled with the names of the successful candidates, included in their turn an element of selection. The Signoria comprised, besides the eight Priors, the most prestigious and influential member of the government, the Gonfalonier of Justice, and, to make appointment to this office exceptionally difficult, there had always been a separate pouch for it. To select

---

[30] See *Giovanni Rucellai ed il suo Zibaldone*, I: *'Il Zibaldone Quaresimale'*, ed. A. Perosa (London, 1960), pp. 39–43; cf. p. 122.

[31] For this and the following, see D. Kent, 'The Florentine reggimento in the fifteenth century', *Renaissance Quarterly*, 28 (1975), 575–638; see also A. Molho, 'Politics and the ruling class in early Renaissance Florence', *Nuova Rivista Storica*, 52 (1968), 401–20.

[32] Kent, 'The Florentine *reggimento* in the fifteenth century', p. 587.

names to be placed in this pouch from among those who were eligible to the Priorate, was the job of the officials who were in charge of the technical aspects of the scrutinies of the Tre Maggiori Uffici; but from 1387 onwards, these officials, the *accoppiatori*, could also place the names of those citizens into a special pouch for the Priorate, the *borsellino*, which, owing to the smaller number of name tickets it contained, provided their owners with greater opportunities for being actually elected to office.[33]

Even so, on the eve of the establishment of the Medici regime, the citizens who were eligible to government represented a sizeable part of the population of Florence, which in 1427 amounted to about 37,000 persons.[34] Of these, well over one half were men (*c.* 20,000); on the other hand, again according to the calculations of Herlihy and Klapisch, 46 per cent were under 20;[35] 25 was the minimum age for office-holding, 30 for the Priorate.

At the same time, one has to bear in mind that the Tre Maggiori Uffici represented only a fraction of the offices that had to be filled recurrently within the city and its territory. Only a few of the most sensitive of these were temporarily filled by way of direct elections, as were many of the minor ones, but here too the normal method was by sortition preceded by scrutiny. These scrutinies of the 'internal and external offices' concerned magistracies such as the Dieci di Balìa and the Otto di Guardia, whose importance could in some respects equal or even surpass that of the Signoria, as well as top offices of the territorial administration, such as those of the Captains of Pisa and of Arezzo, which combined great responsibilities with extensive powers; but the scrutinies also made citizens eligible for a host of minor administrative offices in the city and its territory. If republican experience, in terms of participation in government and administration, was to be based on eligibility to office, its range, despite all the gradations of that eligibility, was remarkably wide.

But if we define republican experience in terms of actual participation in decision-making, the picture is very different. Among the 3,000-odd posts, including membership of the councils, that had to be filled every year,[36] those which belonged to the executive branch of government were, at any given point in time, occupied by a small section of the citizens who were eligible for them. On the other hand, while participation in actual decision-making was restricted to a small group of citizens, this was counterbalanced by the rapid rotation of office. It was further compensated by the regular use, by the Signoria, of advisory committees, which consisted, apart from ex officio members, of citizens who at the time did not belong to the executive branch of government.

---

[33] Cf. *Cronica volgare di Anonimo Fiorentino*, ed. E. Bellondi, *Rer. Ital. Script.*, 27, 2 (Città di Castello, 1915 – Bologna, 1917), pp. 34–35.

[34] D. Herlihy and C. Klapisch-Zuber, *Les Toscans et leurs familles* (Paris, 1978), p. 183.

[35] *Ibid.* pp. 348, 375.

[36] Molho, 'Politics and the ruling class in early Renaissance Florence', p. 407.

Without any status in the constitution, the composition of these meetings, or *pratiche*, was determined by the choice of the Signoria, a choice which in its turn was based on convention. That eminent citizens should be summoned was long-established practice; under the regime established after 1382, the *pratiche* were the most reliable mirror of its aristocratic features. Since the Signoria seldom ignored their advice, they formed an essential, usually decisive, element in the process of decision-making. The new elitist style of politics is borne out by their increasing frequency and also by the shift, noticeable after the turn of the century, from advice being given by speakers on behalf of corporate bodies to being offered independently, or on behalf of other members.[37] The citizens who were regularly summoned to these consultative meetings represented the elite of the *reggimento*; in the early fifteenth century, they amounted to about seventy men.[38] In this inner circle of the regime, Maso degli Albizzi held, from 1393, a dominant position, in which he was succeeded, after his death in 1417, by his son Rinaldo. However, they shared this position with a few other prominent citizens, such as Rinaldo Gianfigliazzi and Niccolò da Uzzano, and their status within the *reggimento*, influential as it was, did not materially detract from its prevalently aristocratic character.

The aristocratic and elitist tendencies in the regime were counterbalanced by the role the legislative councils continued to play in it. Membership of these, and in particular of the council of the People, could be regarded, by way of the assent they had to give to the decisions of the government, as the most democratic feature of political participation within the regime, and hence of republican experience. But for the mass of Florentine citizens there was still another, more restricted sphere in which this experience could make itself felt. Dale and F.W. Kent have recently shown, in a seminal study, the role played in civic life by the *gonfaloni*, that is the sixteen districts into which the city was divided.[39] The *gonfaloni* had their own assemblies which were presided over by the Gonfalonieri di compagnia, who represented their districts in the electoral scrutinies by nominating residents for eligibility to office, and who helped the Commune in the distribution of the tax burden that had been allocated to their districts while the Catasto was not in force, that is, before 1427 and between 1434 and 1458. Meeting periodically in the principal parish church, they elected committees of residents to function as syndics for the tax assessments, and this provided a modicum of civic participation on the local level. Yet here too, appearances can be deceptive: in the district studied by these authors, Lion rosso, over a period of forty-six years about two-thirds of the citizens who attended these assemblies belonged to ten to fifteen families: the 'patrician families who ruled the city also provided leadership in the local world of the *gonfalone*'.[40]

[37] G. Brucker, *The Civic World of Early Renaissance Florence* (Princeton, NJ, 1977), pp. 284ff.
[38] *Ibid.* pp. 264ff.   [39] *Neighbours and Neighbourhoods*, pp. 17–19.   [40] *Ibid.*, pp. 77–8.

On an even more general level of republican experience the popular assemblies, or *parlamenti*, of all citizens were, like Marsilius of Padua's *legislator humanus*, considered to possess the ultimate political authority in the republic. However, they were summoned only on rare occasions to approve constitutional reforms or to grant full powers to decide on such reforms to specially elected councils (*balìe*).

Insofar as Florence's political system was based on direct participation, republican experience manifested itself in the membership of the legislative councils and of *pratiche* and in the holding of public office. This participation could, in a generalised fashion, be conceived ideally as representative; 'ogni buono cittadino', writes Palmieri, 'che è posto in magistrato dove rapresenti alcuno principale membro civile, inanzi a ogni altra cosa intenda non essere privata persona, ma rapresentare l'universale persona di tutta la città'.[41] Palmieri here reiterates pleas to set public over private interest, which were particularly frequent and emphatic during the years after 1426, a period which ended with the collapse of the regime by which Florence had been governed since the 1380s. Now the 'ambitio officiorum' became one of the major causes of the formation of two rival factions. Nothing shows better the extent to which the political fabric had been shaken than the creation, in 1429, of the new magistracy of the Conservatori di legge: their function was to exclude unqualified citizens from office-holding and to prosecute citizens who abused their public positions. This led to a flood of denunciations, but did little to restrain the sectarian spirit in the regime and, on the contrary, may have increased it.[42]

Machiavelli, who considered factionalism a deep-rooted disease of the Florentine body politic and a pervasive theme of the city's history, argues in the *Discursus* that one of the causes of the downfall of the aristocratic regime of the early Quattrocento was that 'non si era constituito un timore agli uomini grandi che non potessero far sètte, le quali sono la rovina di uno stato', that is of a regime.[43] But this had been precisely one of the aims the Conservatori di legge were meant to achieve. That the new office proved to be, in this respect, largely counterproductive, may be taken to show that, contrary to Machiavelli's belief, there was no institutional remedy of this problem – as there was none to stop the calumnies, notwithstanding his belief 'che se fusse stato in Firenze ordine d'accusare i cittadini, e punire i calunniatori, non seguivano infiniti scandoli che sono seguiti'.[44] But Machiavelli's overriding critique of that regime was that it

[41] *Vita civile*, p. 131.
[42] Cf. D. Kent, *The Rise of the Medici* (Oxford, 1978), pp. 201–2, 244–5; Brucker, *The Civic World*, pp. 490–2.
[43] *Tutte le opere*, p. 24. On the meaning of the word *stato*, see N. Rubinstein, 'Notes on the word *stato* before Machiavelli' in *Florilegium Historiale, Essays presented to Wallace K. Ferguson*, J.G. Rowe and W.H. Stockdale, eds. (Toronto, 1971), pp. 314–26.   [44] *Discorsi*, I, 8; *Tutte le opere*, p. 89.

was a 'repubblica governata da ottimati',[45] a form of government liable to turn into an oligarchy, which he condemned as corrupt.[46] Whether he gave a balanced account of it is a different matter. It could be argued that his analysis of its defects was profoundly influenced by his own experience of the working of a republican regime in Florence, which was in many respects a very different one from that of the early fifteenth century.

The new regime had been established after the expulsion in 1494 of the Medici, under whose dominance Florence had been governed for sixty years. The Medicean regime, 'lo stato di Cosimo', which replaced the preceding one in 1434, 'pendé', Machiavelli says, 'più verso il principato che verso la repubblica',[47] thus implying, correctly, that however effective and pervasive its institutional reforms and the dominant influence of Cosimo were, the new regime had by no means eliminated republican experience. What it did do was to modify it profoundly. I shall, before concluding this chapter, touch on a few major changes which that experience underwent after 1434.

The electoral system based on sortition and scrutiny remained in existence,[48] but scrutinies were held at increasingly long intervals by councils whose members were expected to be loyal to the regime, and, while the vast majority of offices continued to be filled as before by the drawing of names from pouches, the most sensitive and powerful ones, such as the Dieci di Balìa, were increasingly filled by way of election in Medicean councils. Above all, sortition was at first temporarily suspended, and then in practice abolished, for the Signoria. The Signoria was now elected *a mano* – in fact, by a kind of highly selective sortition – by the *accoppiatori*, who, from having originally been a technical office in charge of filling the pouches after scrutinies, had become a key institution of the regime, since they had to see to it that the Signoria, whose powers were legally undiminished, and who could theoretically overthrow the regime (as that of September 1434 had done by having Cosimo recalled from exile) was recruited from responsible supporters of the Medici. The regime retained, as far as its social structure was concerned, the upward, as well as downward, mobility of its predecessor. However, that mobility, and hence the share in political participation, was now increasingly determined from above. This created a new and expanding network of political patronage. Instead of *pregherie* being addressed to members of scrutiny councils, in order to obtain eligibility to public office, we now find appeals to the leaders of the regime, to have oneself or one's relative or friend elected to the Signoria, or at least to have their names drawn from the bags, so that they were, as *veduti*, known to be eligible, even if they were not appointed to the office (*seduti*). Under Lorenzo,

---

[45] *Discursus, ibid*, p. 24.
[46] *Discorsi*, I, 2; cf. *Istorie fiorentine*, VII, 3 and 4; *ibid.*, pp. 80, 794.
[47] *Discursus, ibid*, pp. 24–5.
[48] For the following see Rubinstein, *The Government of Florence*, pp. 56ff.

these pleas had reached such proportions that on at least one occasion he asked, in despair, to be left alone: 'de' Priori', he writes in 1485 to his secretary Niccolò Michelozzi, 'non mi advisate cosa nissuna, perché non voglo anchora questo carico. Io harei caro solamente che fusse de' Priori Filippo Carducci . . . Gl'altri faccino chi pare loro [i.e. the *accoppiatori*]. Levatemi le pregherie d'adosso, perché io ho più lettere di Priori che voglono essere, che non sono di nell'anno . . .'[49] As before, and even more so now, to have been *veduto* or *seduto* for the Tre Maggiori Uffici gave a citizen a privileged position in the *reggimento*, but within that group the men who had been *veduti* or *seduti* for the Gonfalonierate of Justice came to constitute the elite in a regime which was increasingly hierarchical. At the same time, the decline of the political influence and independent authority of the Signoria was bound to change the role it played in the political experience of the members of the *reggimento*. The same applied, to a much greater extent, to the legislative councils of the People and of the Commune, which were replaced, as the chief areas of political participation for the majority of the *reggimento*, first with the Medicean *balìe* and, from 1459, with the new council of Cento. Conversely, the consultative *pratiche*, which had been so prominent a feature of the aristocratic regime, gradually declined in importance, together with the Signoria whom they were designed to advise, and were for all practical purposes abolished under Lorenzo, their place being largely taken by informal meetings in the Medici Palace. As Alamanno Rinuccini put it in 1479, in a scathing critique of the regime: while previously 'viri graves de rebus agendis propositis sic in utramque partem libere disputabant, ut facile quid in quaque verum esset inveniretur . . . Nunc . . . cum paucissimos ad maximarum rerum consultationem adhibeant Catones nostri, ea plerunque decerni videmus quae postridie iidem ipsi . . . constituunt'.[50] The Settanta, which was created in the following year as the supreme council of the republic, while reaffirming Lorenzo's dominant position after the end of the war of the Pazzi conspiracy, also responded to such criticisms by being composed of the leading citizens of the regime. Its size bears a striking resemblance to the inner circle of the aristocratic regime of the early Quattrocento, but, unlike the loosely structured elite of the earlier *reggimento*, that of the Medici regime was institutionalised and headed by one man.

If, then, republican experience in terms of participation in government underwent profound changes under the Medici, the same applied to the citizens' perception of republican government itself. The awe with which they had regarded the power and majesty of the Signoria was now shifted to a large extent to the head of the regime who, unlike the Signoria, could dispense a vast amount of political patronage, and who was eulogised by humanists and

[49] Florence, Biblioteca Nazionale, Fondo Ginori Conti, 29, 129,1 (Bagno a Morbo, 17 April).

[50] *Dialogus de libertate*, ed. F. Adorno, in *Atti e Memorie dell' Accademia toscana di scienze e lettere 'La Colombaria'*, 22 (1957), p. 284.

courtiers as a sort of Platonic ruler, although Lorenzo himself insisted on his being a private citizen.[51] There were criticisms in the *reggimento* itself of the controls and restraints the Medici had imposed on the republican constitution, and in particular of the abandonment of the traditional methods of electing the government. These criticisms came to a head under Piero de' Medici in 1465, when elections *a mano* were in fact temporarily abolished. But the same patricians who played a leading role in the abortive republican reaction against Medicean controls would have agreed with Lorenzo that 'a Firenze si può mal vivere senza lo stato', that is without a prominent position in the regime.[52] They would witness, and reluctantly accept, a social mobility which was, owing to the manipulation of the electoral system, less open to free opportunity than it had been in the aristocratic regime at the beginning of the century. As Piero Guicciardini put it at the time of the last Medicean scrutiny, in 1484, 'continovamente viene su gente nuova, onde è necessario, che mettendosi nel reggimento tuttavia de' nuovi, a rincontro se ne cacci de' vecchi; et così si fa'.[53] As for the reaction of the people to the progressive emasculation of their share in the government of the republic, and thus of their republican experience in terms of participation, this is far more difficult to gauge. The violence of the uprising against Lorenzo's son Piero only two and a half years after his death suggests that the regime was not as universally popular as later apologists of it would imply, and the enthusiasm with which the Great Council was embraced after 1494, confirms this impression.

However great the changes which republican experience had undergone under the Medici, the experience still had much in common with that which prevailed in the early fifteenth century. One of these common features was the share in government through eligibility to office being provided by electoral scrutinies, another the elitist concentration of effective participation in decision-making in relatively small groups of citizens; a third the mobility within the social structure of the regime. The constitutional reform of December 1494 changed the forms of political participation, and hence of republican experience, to an extent which can be compared with the establishment of the Priorate in 1282. The 3,000-odd members of the Great Council became a virtually closed class that monopolised office-holding as well as legislation and, through electing to the Signoria and to other high offices, exercised an unprecedented control over the executive.[54] Admission to the Great Council

[51] See A. Brown, 'Platonism in fifteenth-century Florence and its contribution to early modern political thought', *The Journal of Modern History*, 58 (1986), 383–413; Rubinstein, *The Government of Florence*, pp. 226–8.

[52] *Ibid.* pp. 140ff.; *Ricordi* of Lorenzo de' Medici, ed. A. Fabroni, *Laurentii Medicis Magnifici vita* (Pisa, 1789), II, p. 42.

[53] Ed. Rubinstein, in *The Government of Florence*, p. 323.

[54] See N. Rubinstein, 'I primi anni del Consiglio Maggiore di Firenze (1494–99)', *Archivio Storico Italiano*, 12 (1954), 103–94, 321–47.

was based on the group of *veduti* and *seduti* appointed to the Tre Maggiori Uffici over three generations, although some additional admissions were provided for. Membership was, for all practical purposes, restricted to the citizens, or their forbears, who had been made eligible to government under the Medici regime. This continuity was characteristic of the social structure of politics in the Florentine republic, which was relatively little affected by the changes in its regimes.[55] The tensions and conflicts between aristocratic, oligarchical, and democratic tendencies were now played out within the Great Council in terms of extending, or restricting, participation in government and decision-making, and led to changes in the methods by which the Council conducted its elections and, finally, to the transformation of the Gonfalonierate of Justice into an office for life.[56]

The Great Council provided the framework for the republican experience of Machiavelli, who had just reached the minimum age required for office-holding when the new republican constitution was established. But that experience will be the subject of another chapter.

[55] See R. Pesman Cooper, 'The Florentine ruling group under the "*governo popolare*", 1494–1512', *Studies in Medieval and Renaissance History*, 7 (1985), 73ff., 92ff.

[56] Cf. Guicciardini, *Storie fiorentine*, pp. 136–7, 178–9, 242.

2

Machiavelli and the crisis of the Italian republics

ELENA FASANO GUARINI

It is impossible in Machiavelli's writings not to feel the pressure of the events of his time. His reflections and his political proposals refer directly to those events. Hence scholars, although using very different criteria for their interpretations, have often considered Machiavelli's major writings to be a direct and passionate response to the crisis of the republics or, on a wider plane, to that of the small Italian states – a crisis which he lived through without being able to witness its final outcome. This is the dominant theme in Federico Chabod's classic work on *The Prince*.[1] But this same general conception already underlies Pasquale Villari's and Oreste Tommasini's massive nineteenth-century biographies, in which the Florentine secretary's life, his writings and his 'times' are tightly interwoven.[2] This basic interpretation has recently been used, for instance, by Corrado Vivanti, who considers the *Discourses* to be not a theoretical work, but rather a concrete political proposal, a sort of manifesto for refounding the Italian republics in a political situation in which it was not yet clear what the final outcome would be.[3] 'Machiavelli and the crisis of the Italian republics' is hence much too broad and much too widely debated a problem for me to be able to discuss it without restricting it somewhat and without making some preliminary remarks.

Other scholars have given particular attention to the intellectual and ideological background from which *The Prince* and the *Discourses* emerged. One can see this emphasis in Felix Gilbert's now classic works.[4] For Gilbert, however, this side of the question is deeply linked to a general evaluation of the specific political and cultural situations that Machiavelli experienced. In other

[1] F. Chabod, 'Del *Principe* di Niccolò Machiavelli', (1925), in *Scritti su Machiavelli* (Turin, 1964).
[2] P. Villari, *Niccolò Machiavelli e i suoi tempi* (Milan, 1897), 3 vols.; O. Tommasini, *La vita e gli scritti di Niccolò Machiavelli* (Rome, 1881–1911), 2 vols.
[3] Introduction to N. Machiavelli, *Discorsi sopra la prima deca di Tito Livio*, Corrado Vivanti, ed. (Turin, 1983).
[4] F. Gilbert, 'The humanist concept of the prince and "The Prince" of Machiavelli' in *Journal of Modern History* (1939); 'Bernardo Rucellai and the Orti Oricellari: a study on the origin of modern political thought' in *Journal of the Warburg and Courtland Institutes* (1949); 'Florentine political assumptions in the period of Savonarola and Soderini', *Journal of the Warburg and Courtland Institutes* (1957), now in Gilbert, *Niccolò Machiavelli e il suo tempo* (Bologna, 1964). See also Gilbert, *Machiavelli and Guicciardini. Politics and History in Sixteenth-Century Florence* (Princeton, 1965; new edn New York and London, 1984).

more recent studies this emphasis on intellectual background has involved a radical change of perspective. Alberto Tenenti has pointed out the relevance of the basic concepts, of the 'mental tools' (what Lucien Febvre called the 'outillage mental') which shape political reflection, even though those very tools may come to be modified by the development of political thought. Thus Tenenti suggests that in Machiavelli's mental world a solid and complex communal heritage was at work along with an awareness of the decline of that heritage.[5] John Pocock and Quentin Skinner have tried to show that a republican 'language' had been elaborated around the concepts of *virtù* and *vivere civile*. Machiavelli was aware of working within this tradition in which *The Prince* and the *Discourses* represent an important turning point; nonetheless they can be considered neither its source nor its final result.[6] Along with the remarkable originality and novelty which distinguish Machiavelli's writings – which are given too exclusive an importance by those who believe that Machiavelli's work represents an immediate response to the crisis of his time – there are also numerous elements of continuity, numerous ties with the past.

Both these basic approaches can be useful in analysing the way in which Machiavelli considered his times and those specific historical processes which were then emerging. Here, however, I wish to pose a twofold question, and although it is not a new one, I think that it may yield some unexpected answers. How and to what extent did Machiavelli's political experience modify those paradigms and that political language which tradition had passed on to him? How did they survive in Machiavelli's works and how did they continue to define – or even to restrict – the broad span of his ideas, offering instruments of analysis, standards of judgement, and forms of expression?

In order to give a complete answer to these problems it would be of great interest to follow the path of lexical enquiry and semantic analysis. Many have already attempted to do so, but this line of enquiry has certainly not yet yielded all of its potential results.[7] And I too will have to try to define the meanings which terms such as *stato* and *città, libertà* and *vivere civile, popolo* and *grandi* assume in Machiavelli's works. Nevertheless I believe it is most fruitful to start

---

[5] A. Tenenti, 'La nozione di "stato" nell'Italia del Rinascimento' in Tenenti, *Stato: un'idea, una logica. Dal comune italiano all'assolutismo francese* (Bologna, 1987), pp. 53–97; A. Tenenti, '"Civiltà" e civiltà in Machiavelli', *ibid.* pp. 119–36.

[6] J. Pocock, *The Machiavellian Moment: Florentine Political Thought and the Atlantic Republican Tradition* (Princeton, 1975); Q. Skinner, *The Foundations of Modern Political Thought. I The Renaissance* (Cambridge, 1978). Still of importance is H. Baron, *The Crisis of the Early Italian Renaissance* (Princeton, 1966) (2nd edn).

[7] Lexical and linguistic analyses can obviously be found in many of the studies concerning Machiavelli's thought. For more specific approaches, besides the studies quoted in the previous two notes, see F. Chiappelli, *Studi sul linguaggio del Machiavelli* (Florence, 1952), and *Nuovi studi sul linguaggio del Machiavelli* (Florence, 1969). See nn. 39 and 49 for studies on particular terms.

from the different constitutional models[8] which appear in his works (whether as the object of careful examination or in the form of brief remarks) in order to discover how these models are presented and discussed, or at times compared. These, in fact, are the structures in relation to which political language assumes definite and concrete meanings and in respect to which it can be clarified.

The first decades of the sixteenth century were truly a time which encouraged political and constitutional comparison and discussion. In Florence the Italian wars were interwoven with the difficult and hard-fought transition from republican to princely government. More generally, the conflict with the great European powers brought to the fore new models for the state, at times accompanied by the prestige which surrounds victorious powers. The new European models were obviously completely different from the republican one, but they also had very little in common with the tyrannical model, which had been considered its opposite by the civic humanists according to Hans Baron and even earlier, by the medieval 'dictatores' according to Quentin Skinner. The European models were so alien to the composite Italian political world – because of their origin, their structure and the means by which they consolidated their legitimacy – that they were not and could not be considered imitable. They could, however, serve as stimulus to those who had the necessary ability to undertake new analyses and to elaborate comparative judgements. They could also, so far as was possible considering the weight of language and tradition, make Italians reflect on some crucial points of the republican political systems which, in that time of military conflict and confrontation of different political ideals, had come to appear quite fragile.

Notwithstanding the different political solutions which the two works propose, the troubled awareness which Machiavelli had of these problems emerges as a unifying motive in *The Prince* and the *Discourses*. It is perhaps one of the underlying themes which inspires both works. In Machiavelli's thought, the paradigms and the ideological contrasts typical of civic humanism are still vitally present. Nonetheless, we find that there is another world which lies beyond the range of those concepts. It is precisely this alien pole which seems at times to make Machiavelli look critically at the models and the values which had been transmitted by tradition, revealing weaknesses which although deep were hard to discern, and sharpening Machiavelli's awareness of their crisis.

2   An individual's biography sometimes suggests caution in reading his works but also what may be the proper perspective in which to do so. Thus,

---

[8] I here use 'constitution' and 'constitutional' in a very broad sense, similar to that used by A. Anzilotti, *La crisi costituzionale della repubblica fiorentina* (Florence, 1912) or by N. Rubinstein, 'Politics and constitution in Florence at the end of the fifteenth century' in *Italian Renaissance Studies*, E.F. Jacob, ed. (London, 1960).

although this aspect has been dealt with by others[9] and has been discussed here by Robert Black, it is perhaps best that I briefly recall what Machiavelli's role and functions were under the republic, both of which had such a lasting impact on him.

Florence was the centre of Machiavelli's life, as he wrote to Vettori in 1527, which he loved 'più dell'anima'. In his letters we see the city as the place to which he was bound by ties of affection, friendship and professional obligations. No less than Vettori, he loved, we might say – using words that his friend wrote to him in 1513 – 'generalmente tutti gli huomini . . . le leggi, i costumi, le mura, le case, le vie, le chiese et il contado' of Florence.[10] But, notwithstanding this visceral affection for his city, which reflects modes of existence and feelings typical of the communal world, 'compare Niccolò' – as the 'molto magnifico et honorando' Francesco Vettori called him – never had full rights of citizenship. Although he was descended from a family which had risen to major office in the fourteenth century, even under the *governo largo* of 1494 to 1512 he was not among those who had full civil rights and who could hope to be elected to the civic magistracies, that is, he was not one of the *beneficiati*. He was not, of course, of the aristocratic group, and furthermore, he was not included in the *popolo*. Other descendants of ancient families found themselves in the same situation, and it could be a very bitter one: it could even make a man decide to break away from the republican system – this was the case, for example, of Piero Vaglienti, author of an interesting *Storia dei suoi tempi*,[11] who found it a reason for hoping for the return of the Medici and the coming of a princely form of government.

We can perhaps feel Machiavelli's awareness of his exclusion from the citizenry in the particular arrogance with which he addressed the Florentine authorities in his *Discorso dell'ordinare lo stato di Firenze alle armi*: 'Voi della iustitia ne avete non molta e dell'armi non punto'.[12] In any case, as is well known, from 1498 on his path took him to the Chancery – the technical department which was supposed to assist the most important civil offices (the Signoria and the Dieci di Balia) in performing their political functions, recording their decisions, handling their correspondence, and carrying out missions and legations on their account. In the fifteenth century the Chancery was an office whose importance had to some extent been increasing in all states whether princely or republican. In Florence in particular, as Riccardo Fubini

---

[9] See R. Ridolfi, *Vita di Niccolò Machiavelli*, 7th revised edn (Florence, 1978), pp. 25ff. and especially N. Rubinstein, 'The Beginnings of Niccolò Machiavelli's career in the Florentine Chancery', *Italian Studies*, II (1956), 72–91 and 'Machiavelli and Florentine politics' in *Studies on Machiavelli*, M.P. Gilmore, ed. (Florence, 1972), pp. 3–28.

[10] N. Machiavelli, *Lettere*, ed. F. Gaeta (Milan, 1961), pp. 505, 285.

[11] P. Vaglienti, *Storia dei suoi tempi. 1494–1514* (Pisa, 1982), pp. 26–7, 32–3.

[12] In N. Machiavelli, *Arte della guerra e scritti politici mionori*, ed. S. Bertelli (Milan, 1961), p. 95.

has pointed out,[13] this office had been undergoing a process of consolidation at the same time as the ancient communal offices were losing their previous importance. Hence although he was not a *cittadino* by full right, Machiavelli was a public servant, a *uomo pubblico*[14] to use an expression Machiavelli himself applied, not without unstated pride, to another Chancellor. Because of his role he was excluded from any decision-making power, but he had responsible executive functions and he could exert some influence as an adviser, what today we would call an expert. Furthermore, until he lost office, he was well-informed about all public affairs (*faccende* and *segreti*), the ignorance of which was subsequently to be a heavy burden to him. Hence the *stato*, even though it was not his, was his *arte*, his profession.

From our point of view it is not very meaningful (as many have thought)[15] to discuss whether Machiavelli's role was largely a technical one or whether it was a completely political one. It is more interesting to point out the specific character of his office (very different from that of his predecessors, Chancellors in the humanistic mould) and the nature of the experience which he drew from it, and which we know about from his political correspondence and writings from the chancery period, where it is reflected earlier and more directly than in his later major works. This experience took place largely outside the city where nonetheless, as we have seen, Machiavelli's own strong original affections lay. Whether he had to visit those areas (such as Pisa) where rebellions threatened the state, or to travel around the countryside trying to recruit militia, he experienced at first hand the problems of the Florentine territorial state, of its *dominio*. Much of his time was also spent in dealing with Florentine relations with other powers. He became, we might say, an expert in military problems and international affairs: he was often involved in legations and diplomatic missions, in general accompanying the official *oratore*, the official ambassador, usually an important *cittadino*. He had not only to negotiate, carrying out specific orders, but also to collect information and transmit it, to evaluate trends, political relationships and forces, to try to foresee – as far as possible – future events, and to suggest appropriate action. From this experience perhaps, he acquired the habit of scrupulously searching out the *verità effettuale*, which would later mark his major works, even though he never relinquished his passion and his convictions.

---

[13] R. Fubini, 'Classe dirigente ed esercizio della diplomazia nella Firenze quattrocentesca' in *I ceti dirigenti della Toscana del Quattrocento* (Florence, 1987), pp. 117–91.

[14] Letter to a Chancellor in Lucca, from Florence, at the beginning of October 1499, in N. Machiavelli, *Lettere*, p. 48.

[15] S. Bertelli, in his introduction to N. Machiavelli, *Opere* (Milan, 1968), vol. 1, pp. xivff. ascribes great political importance to Machiavelli's activities in the Chancery; see also 'Petrus Soderinus Patriae Parens' in *Bibliothèque d'Humanisme et Renaissance. Travaux et documents*, 31 (1969), 109ff.; 'Machiavelli e la politica estera fiorentina' in *Studies on Machiavelli*, pp. 29–72.

This was the *arte* by which he first rose to be Piero Soderini's adviser, and at the same time both acquired great prestige and encountered violent hostility among the powerful in Florence.[16] Later, after his disgrace in 1512, Machiavelli felt he could honestly and loyally offer the same truly valid professional services to the Medici, and he was recommended to them by his friends the Vettori.[17] Nonetheless, his *arte*, deriving from his role in the Chancery, had a profound effect on certain aspects of his political ideology.

3   It is not surprising that Machiavelli, a 'public man' and not a party man, as Nicolai Rubinstein has pointed out, did not start to deal with constitutional problems connected with his city's political struggle until later, not until the years in which he was forced to leave public service.[18] It was following a different path that he became sharply aware of the crisis in the Florentine republic, and in the republican system in general. In 1513–14, in fact, the topics which impassioned Machiavelli and Vettori were the truce between France and Spain and its possible underlying political reasons, the possibility that war would break out again, the political choices open to the pope, the evaluation of the danger posed by the Swiss in the state of Milan, and the advantages and the risks of the possible return of the French. They were interested in the international situation, and they tried to imagine and even invent the possible framework of a new political balance, capable of preserving the *libertà* of the whole system of Italian states, as well as that of Florence. They did not discuss the possible forms of civil government; their primary concern was the survival of the *stato*. This was the way they reacted to the crisis. And these were the subjects that gave their correspondence at times the tone of a *ghiribizzo*, of a caprice, of a witty *divertissement*, and at times that of a discussion so intense that it seems to have brought them close to breaking off their friendship.

Nevertheless, explicitly or implicitly, Machiavelli does seem to examine the *ordinamenti*, the basic organisation, or rather the material structures of states, in several of his political writings dating from before 1512. However, he does this strictly on the level of his own professional interest, which is very different from the political level which interested most Florentine citizens. He is interested in the problems of governing the subject territories (*il dominio*), and behind his criticism of the Florentine ruling class's policies in that sector, one can often sense that he is worried about the city's constitution and that he feels – although not yet with perfect clarity – the need for a new basic constitutional framework. In the *Discorso dell'ordinare lo stato di Firenze alle armi* (1506), the persistent

---

[16] For example, letters addressed to Machiavelli by Biagio Buonaccorsi from 1499 onwards demonstrate both. See N. Machiavelli, *Lettere*. On Buonaccorsi, D. Fachard, *Biagio Buonaccorsi* (Bologna, 1976). See also J.N. Stephens and H.C. Butters, 'New Light on Machiavelli', *The English Historical Review*, 97, 1982, pp. 54–69.

[17] R. Devonshire Jones, *Francesco Vettori. Florentine Citizen and Medici Servant* (London, 1972).

[18] N. Rubinstein, 'The Beginnings', p. 16ff. See also R. Fubini's remarks, 'A proposito della relazione di N. Rubinstein', in *Studies on Machiavelli*, pp. 373–93.

restlessness of the Florentine district, the *distretto*, and the danger which the subject cities within it constitute as 'nidi grossi dove una provincia possa far testa' are contrasted with the calm of the *contado*, the countryside near Florence which was directly subject to the city. It is with respect to this contrast that the problems concerning the *ordinanza*, the utilisation of Florentine subjects for military service, are analysed, and the real military possibilities of the republic are measured.[19] The *dominio* is also the context which reveals Florence's inability to govern properly, making it appear a city without *armi* and without *giustizia*, which can neither defend nor punish her subjects, as Machiavelli had already written in his *Parole da dirle sopra la provisione del danaio*. From the fragility of its territorial system, badly guarded, exposed to external pressures, undermined internally by the presence of cities 'che desiderano più la vostra morte che la loro vita', emerge threats to its very survival. This is the plane on which the destiny of cities is played out, and those which are 'senza forze vengono al fine loro o per desolazione o per servitù'.[20] In Machiavelli's eyes, therefore, it is essential to consolidate the territorial state. And if in the first place that means reinforcing Florentine justice and its military system, it is also essential to modify internal relations in the subject territories, rewarding faithful subjects and punishing rebel cities so as to weaken them drastically. This is the most significant lesson to emerge from *Del modo di trattare i popoli della Valdichiana ribellati*[21] in which Machiavelli first comes under the spell of the Roman model. He approaches it by way of a passage from Livy concerning Camillus and the rebel peoples of Latium (VIII, 13, 11–18) which has particular importance, as we shall see, for the concept of *stato*.

In this early period of Machiavelli's work, we can find only limited considerations regarding the Venetian constitution. But in the dispatches which Machiavelli sent to the Dieci from Verona after Agnadello, when the Venetian republic, once a dangerously expansionistic power, seemed almost a symbolic example of the dissolution of a state, we find the same attention given to the problems of territorial government which we saw in the case of Florence. From Verona Machiavelli measures the vulnerability of the Venetian army: he observes the relationships between the ruling city and its subject city, he grasps the contrasting play of internal forces – the hostility of the Veronese aristocracy (*i gentiluomini*) towards Venice and the favour with which the *popolo* and the peasants regard it. From this outlying viewpoint on the Venetian *terraferma*,

---

[19] In N. Machiavelli, *Arte della guerra*, p. 96.

[20] *Ibid.* pp. 57–62. As an introduction to the writings of the Chancery period, besides the introductory note by S. Bertelli to N. Machiavelli, *Arte della guerra*, see J.J. Marchand, *Niccolò Machiavelli. I primi scritti politici (1499–1512)* (Padua, 1975). As to the possibility of considering them a true expression of Machiavelli's thought, even when written on behalf of others, see Marchand, 'Ambiguité du discours du pouvoir dans le premiers écrits de Machiavel' in *Le Pouvoir et la plume. Incitation, contrôle et répression dans l'Italie du XVIe siècle* (Paris; 1982), pp. 51–62.

[21] In N. Machiavelli, *Arte della guerra*, pp. 72–5.

Machiavelli seems to rediscover the problems of the territorial state and at times glimpses the complexity of the underlying social relationships which in other contexts appears to escape him.[22] As has been pointed out,[23] as regards Venice this was the beginning of that critical attitude towards its history and its constitution which was to be set forth later in broader and more substantial form in the *Discourses*, and subsequently in the *Histories*. It is an evaluation in which Machiavelli discards the myth of Venice and its peculiar balance of different civic forces and looks closely at the nature of its relationship with its subject territories.

Constitutional organisation and state structures, on the other hand, are amply treated in Machiavelli's works on France and on the empire, which were connected with his diplomatic activity. In Florence (unlike Venice) it was not necessary to present general reports at the end of a mission. Nonetheless, according to Machiavelli, it was advisable 'mettere innanzi agli occhi di chi lo manda tutto lo stato e l'essere di quella città e quel regno dove egli è oratore'. As he was to advise Raffaello Girolami many years later, when the latter was about to depart for Spain, taking the trouble to write general reports 'fa un grande onore a chi scrive ed un grande utile a chi è scritto'.[24] However, the *Rapporto* and the *Ritratto delle cose della Magna* (dated respectively 1508 and 1512) and the *Ritratto di cose di Francia* (dated 1510–11, according to J.J. Marchand),[25] are much more than simple general reports. Based, as the author himself says, not only on *cose udite*, but also upon material gathered in the courts and in the chanceries of the countries described,[26] the knowledge gained (which to be useful has to be 'objectively true' or *effettuale*) is organised in these works in such a way that it may be brought to bear on political issues. In 1508 Machiavelli's aims were perhaps eminently practical. He wished, that is, to explain – at the end of a very difficult legation, and in order to orient Florentine foreign policy – the otherwise incomprehensible fragility of the empire, and Maximilian's inability to carry out his planned journey to Italy. In later years his aims were broader and linked to more general reflections. The attention given to the political organisation of those countries in the broadest sense is the most outstanding characteristic of these works, and it is the aspect which most sharply differentiates them from Francesco Guicciardini's *Relazione di Spagna*[27] which

---

[22] N. Machiavelli, *Legazioni e commissarie*, S. Bertelli ed. (Milan, 1964), vol. III. pp. 1188–1205.

[23] I. Cervelli, *Machiavelli e la crisi dello Stato veneziano* (Naples, 1974), pp. 344–62.

[24] *Memoriale a Raffaello Girolami, quando ai 23 d'ottobre partì per Spagna all'imperatore* in *Arte della guerra*, pp. 285–6.   [25] J.J. Marchand, *Niccolò Machiavelli* pp. 246–79.

[26] See, for instance, the reference in *Rapporto delle cose della Magna* in *Arte della guerra*, p. 200, to the information gathered by 'Prè Luca' (Luca Rinaldi, Bishop of Trieste, who was one of Maximillian's most intimate advisers) and the reference to 'carte' on Germany sent to Machiavelli by Cesare Mauro, imperial Chancellor, in the letter from Cologne dated June 1508 in N. Machiavelli, *Lettere*, p. 186–7.

[27] F. Guicciardini, *Relazione di Spagna* in Guicciardini, *Opere*, ed. V. de Caprariis (Milan–Naples, 1953), I, pp. 27–44.

was written at the same time. As is well known, Machiavelli on the one hand drew a picture of a naturally powerful empire, abounding in 'men, wealth and arms', perfectly arranged so as to ensure the defence of every single community, but undermined by a 'disunione generale' between the single communities and the territorial princes, between the princes and the emperor, between the communities and the Swiss, and by the hostility of every power within the empire towards the 'grandezza dello imperadore'. This was a picture in which the various freedoms were presented as elements of weakness and obstacles on the road to centralisation and to power. That is the way Machiavelli saw both the dependency on themselves alone, the 'far capo da sé' of the free imperial cities, and the 'libera libertà' of the Swiss, who were the enemies of princes and nobles and opposed to 'distinzione veruna d'uomini fuor di quelli che seggono ne' magistrati'.[28] On the other hand, there was the image of a monarchy characterised by great *gagliardia* or vitality, supported by the Crown's wealth, and above all by an internal cohesiveness and a general deference to the king's will. Barons, once rebellious, were now *ossequientissimi*, linked to the Crown by tight and solid bonds; and 'Sono e popoli di Francia umili e ubbidientissimi, e hanno in grande venerazione il loro re'. *Libertà* and *civiltà* have no place here. The inhabitants of the land are in general 'commoners' – *ignobiltà* – who 'tanto stanno sottoposti a' nobili e tanto sono in ogni azione depressi che sono vili'. This is the reason for the poor quality of the French infantry. If the people are weak, the keynote of French society is the strong feudal structure. But the barons' power, and their 'autorità . . . mera' over their subjects clash with the sovereign's wide powers in the fiscal field and with his absolute authority in designating governors and lieutenants in the provinces and the lands of the kingdom, with the Grand Chancellor's *merum imperium*, with the royal offices' broad jurisdiction and with the Parlements' authority.[29]

If the writings concerning Florentine political problems and the rapid observations on the Venetian system had introduced themes which were unusual in civic republicanism, the three reports just considered take us completely outside that tradition. This is precisely why they are so important in the development of Machiavelli's works. The state models analysed are no longer considered within the 'freedom or tyranny' scheme characteristic of civic humanism. Nor do they suggest a simple contrast between the republican system and 'absolutism' (a historical category which in my opinion is inapplicable to the beginning of the sixteenth century).[30] Machiavelli compares

---

[28] *Rapporto delle cose della Magna* in *Arte della guerra* p. 203; *Ritratto delle cose della Magna, ibid.* p. 211. On Machiavelli's view of the Swiss communities, see E. Waldner, 'Machiavelli und die "virtù" der Schweizer', *Schweizer Beiträge zur Allgemeinen Geschichte*, 2 (1944), 69–128; Th. Brady, *Turning Swiss. Cities and Europe, 1450–1550* (Cambridge, 1985), pp. 18–22.

[29] *Ritratto di cose di Francia* in *Arte della guerra*, pp. 164–92.

[30] I do not think, for example, that one can speak of 'lotta . . . tra assolutismo e republicanesimo' as does G. Silvano in *'Vivere civile' e 'governo misto' a Firenze nel primo Cinquecento* (Bologna, 1985), pp. 13, 21.

the different models in a completely different context so as to throw light on a completely different problem – the problem, one might say, of the formation (in one case a success and in the other a failure) of the large state, the new protagonist of European politics.[31]

It is interesting to note that the use of language in these first reports also has a particular character, and that it differs in many ways from that prevalent in *The Prince* and the *Discourses*. This may be so because the aim of the earlier works is to gain knowledge rather than to support an ideological analysis, and because they refer to phenomena which were outside the Florentine humanistic tradition – and perhaps too because they are influenced by the oral and written sources of which Machiavelli made use. In the case of the *Ritratto di cose di Francia*, Machiavelli's prose has a particular juridical and institutional tone, which we can see in his use of technical Latin expressions ('merum imperium', 'etiam in capitalibus sine consensu regis', 'ut regibus placet'). In the writings on Germany Machiavelli's style is characterised by surprising distinctions and specifications (the Swiss 'libera libertà'), by categories rich in social connotation (the 'gentiluomini', the aristocracy or the nobles considered to be different in the Swiss communities and in the free cities of the empire). These terms and these categories are particularly significant because of their concrete meanings, and they will appear again in the later works (as for instance in chapter 55 of the first book of the *Discourses*) and will there become fundamental factors in distinguishing between the different constitutional models, and a key to understanding historical processes.

4   Maximilian's unsuccessful imperial structure does not have an important place in Machiavelli's mature works, which are much more markedly ideological than were his earlier writings. In the later works the empire is nothing more than a fragile framework under the emperor's mediation within which flourish 'tante diversità del vivere': the Swiss, the free cities, the princes, the emperor (*Discourses*, II, 19). Now the Swiss communities themselves become an autonomous model, as do the 'liberissime . . . città d'Alemagna', which now appear much more similar than they did in the *Relazione* and the *Ritratto*. They are provided with their own fortifications and arms, they have nothing to fear from the emperor or from any other power, and they are free because they are founded on 'equalità' among their citizens and deeply hostile to 'signori e gentiluomini'. They could seem an exemplary model of the ancient republican civic virtues, *bontà* and *religione*, acting to foster the common good (*The Prince*, 10; *Discourses* I, 55). But in their unsullied purity they have come to be a distant myth. That upright world and the 'corrupt' world of the Italian republics are too different. One thing is that constellation of cities without a dependent surrounding countryside which Machiavelli considers

---

[31] See G. Sasso's remarks in *Niccolò Machiavelli*, 2nd edn (Bologna, 1980), pp. 353–6.

(wrongly, some have said) to be a series of closed, static, archaic microcosms, devoid of contact with their neighbours, protected by the particular political conditions in the imperial area (*Discourses*, II, 19). The system of the Italian republics and principalities is something quite different. Of course they too are small states, but vastly more complex. They are involved in the struggle between the great new monarchies which is upsetting the European political balance. Threatened with dissolution, they (and especially Florence) are therefore compelled to try to expand in order to survive.

The positive image of France, unlike that of the empire, is confirmed and reinforced in *The Prince* and the *Discourses*. Aside from some contradictory elements (to which some scholars have perhaps attached too much importance),[32] Machiavelli's treatment of France has a basic inner coherence and shows us an image close to that of Claude de Seyssel's *Monarchie de France*.[33] Hence, in *The Prince*, where much is said about *virtù* and little about *ordini*, France is used as an example of a state whose sovereign possesses little *virtù* (see for instance the catalogue of errors committed by Louis XII in Milan [chapter 3]), but which is endowed with 'infinite costituzioni buone'. These are the source of 'la libertà e sicurtà del re' or 'la sicurtà del re e del regno' (chapter 19). If the king, unlike the Turk, 'è posto in mezzo d'una multitudine antiquata di signori' and cannot eliminate their *preeminenzie* except at his own risk, he possesses nevertheless the means of 'portare loro un freno in bocca'. In the first place there is the Parlement, a 'third judge', which limits and mediates the conflicts between the *popolo* and the *grandi*. The king, in this way, could remain aloof from the conflicting parties and act according to the golden rule which Machiavelli (reminding us in some ways of the idea of a mixed constitution) sees as the basis for a sound and well-balanced government: 'stimare e' grandi ma non si fare odiare dal popolo' (chapter 19). In the *Discourses* the judgement on the French kings is even more broadly negative. They are neither outstanding for their goodness nor for their wisdom (I, 58). They are considered weak because 'non stanno in su la guerra' (I, 19) and they are dependent on mercenary troops as the republican governments of Florence and Venice are, because they have chosen to disarm their *popolo* (II, 30). The country itself, like Spain, is partly corrupt (I, 55). But it lives 'sotto le leggi e sotto gli ordini più che alcun altro regno' (III, 1; see also I, 58). This pre-eminence of the law, imposed by Parlement on the nobles, and binding even on the kings who 'dell'armi e danaio [possono fare] a loro modo, ma d'ogni altra cosa non ne possono altrimenti

---

[32] G. Cadoni, *Machiavelli Regno di Francia e 'principato civile'* (Rome, 1974), pp. 81, 129, 148.

[33] Claude de Seyssel, *La Monarchie de France* (1518), ed. J. Foujol (Paris, 1961). A Spanish model does not emerge from the *Principe* or from the *Discorsi*, even though strong emphasis is laid on Ferdinand of Aragon; see M. Marietti, 'La Figure de Ferdinand le Catholique dans l'oeuvre de Machiavel: naissance et déclin d'un mythe', in *Présence et influence de l'Espagne dans la culture italienne de la Renaissance*, A. Rochon, ed. (Paris, 1978), pp. 1–54.

disporre, che le leggi si ordinassero,' is again the basis for the 'sicurtà di tutti i popoli' (1, 16).

Not even France, a hereditary monarchy based on 'ordini antichi,' is a model which can be imitated by the troubled Italian world of endangered republics and 'principi nuovi'. But in *The Prince* and the *Discourses* France is nonetheless an example to which one must refer in order to understand the processes which are taking place. Like Spain, but unlike Italy, it is a complete territorial state, a unified *provincia*, happy 'in ubbidienza di una repubblica o di uno principe' (1, 12).

The comparison with the French political system in which the laws and the institutions have power over the conflicting *umori dei grandi* and of the *popolo*, and even over the king, touches the very core of the 'republican language', modifying the meaning of important key expressions. Such is the case, for example, in one of the most complex chapters of the *Discourses* (1, 16), in which the French example is again explicitly and forcefully discussed. There the sharp contrast between the concepts of *libertà* and *sicurtà*, traditional in fifteenth-century debates on the respective merits of republics and principalities, seems to disappear – even though that contrast is very much present in other passages in Machiavelli's works, and we can see a new relationship emerging between the two terms. Certainly *vivere libero* is different, observes Machiavelli, from living under a prince; and he who has become a 'tiranno in patria' can only in part give freedom back to the *popolo* who desire it. But, he continues, developing themes which had already emerged in *The Prince* with regard to the *principato civile* 'una piccola parte di loro desidera di essere libera per comandare'. In all republics, in fact, 'in qualunque modo ordinate, ai gradi del comandare non aggiungono mai quaranta o cinquanta cittadini'. All the others instead 'desiderano la libertà per vivere sicuri'. And these, as the French example teaches, 'si sodisfano facilmente faccendo ordini e leggi dove insieme con la potenza sua si comprenda la sicurtà universale'. It would be no exaggeration to say that Machiavelli here appears to attribute a structurally and inevitably oligarchical character to republican power systems. *Libertà* here does not mean active participation in the government of the state as it did in the republican and communal tradition, but rather, as it will come to do more and more commonly in subsequent centuries, the passive enjoyment of a condition in which the security of single individuals is guaranteed by the law.[34]

5   These linguistic discontinuities, of which I could cite other examples,[35]

---

[34] For some similar remarks on the relation between *vivere civile* and *sicurtà* in Machiavelli, see J.H. Whitfield, 'On Machiavelli's use of Ordini' in *Italian Studies*, 10, 1955, 19–39. The distinction between active political freedom, based on participation, and 'modern' freedom which coincides with a guarantee of civil rights can already be found in J.Ch.L. Simonde de Sismondi, *Storia delle repubbliche italiane dei secoli di mezzo* (Capolago, 1844–6), vol. 10, pp. 370–1.

[35] See, for instance, *Discourses*, II, 2 where *vivere libero* means that all 'possono mediante la virtù loro diventare principi', but also that their 'patrimonio [non] gli sia tolto'.

are most significant. Nonetheless they are only discontinuities, not radical changes. Both in *The Prince* and in the *Discourses, libertà* and *vivere libero*, as well as *vivere civile* are used most often in the sense proper to republican humanism, whose terminology is very evident in Machiavelli's mature works.

It is not only in his remarks on France and Germany that one can see the influence on these works of Machiavelli's 'lunga esperienza delle cose moderne' acquired before 1512. This influence is evident not only in the importance given to the great new European states, but also in the continuing importance which Machiavelli (particularly in *The Prince*, but also in the *Discourses*) attributes to the international struggle, and hence to military organisation and to the size and wealth of the different territories. But, although the author continues to present himself as an 'expert', and not as a party man, *The Prince* and the *Discourses* are interwoven with the political debate and struggle which were taking place in Florence. The mature works take up the same constitutional themes: the fate of the regime in Florence, caught between *popolo* and *grandi*; the relations of the Medici with their 'parte' and with 'l'universale di Firenze'; the alternative between republic and principality.[36] They reflect the same culture and the same political language.

Historical criticism has given much attention in fact to Machiavelli's stance on the Florentine political struggle; in general his works have been interpreted in that light, although opinions diverge as to what his political attitude actually was. However, only rarely have historians observed the way in which he considers the problems of the territorial state.[37] Even more rarely have they tried to see how the two perspectives (the urban struggle and the territorial state) coexist, if they interact or react against each other. And yet it is precisely this coexistence which defines the perception which Machiavelli had of the crisis in the world to which he belonged, that of the small peninsular states and of republican Florence; it indicates the specific characteristics and the historical limits of that perception. To clarify its nature we can once again use some linguistic observations.

It is not necessary here to examine the question of whether there is an ideal continuity or discontinuity between *The Prince* and the *Discourses*. Nor shall I ask, as has been asked so often before, which of the two works is the authentic expression of the ex-Florentine secretary's thought. This question has seen ranged on opposite sides those who appreciate the republican Machiavelli, such

---

[36] For a general view besides A. Anzilotti, *La crisi costituzionale*, and R. von Albertini, *Das florentinische Staatsbewusstsein im Übergang von der Republik zum Prinzipat* (Berne, 1955), see G. Silvano, '*Vivere civile*'. On the political events of this period with particular reference to Machiavelli, J.N. Stephens, *The Fall of the Florentine Republic 1512–1530* (Oxford, 1983); H. Butters, *Governors and Government in Early Sixteenth-century Florence 1502–1519* (Oxford, 1985).

[37] See nevertheless G. Procacci's remarks in his introduction to N. Machiavelli, *Il Principe e Discorsi*, ed. S. Bertelli (Milan, 1960), pp. lxiii–lxviii and I. Cervelli, *Machiavelli e la crisi*, especially pp. 231ff.

as Felix Gilbert and Hans Baron, and those who prefer the Medicean and princely Machiavelli such as Carlo Dionisotti.[38] It seems to me, however, that among the significant differences between the two works which have not perhaps been mentioned often enough is the fact that *The Prince* speaks above all of *stati*, and begins precisely with the distinction between republican states and princely ones; whereas in the *Discourses* Machiavelli speaks particularly of *città*. And this from the very first chapter of the first book, dedicated to 'i principii di qualunque città'.

Historians have dedicated a great number of studies to the history of the word *stato* and to its semantic oscillations in Machiavelli's work, and more generally in Renaissance literature.[39] As a matter of fact, Machiavelli himself, when he uses the word at the beginning of *The Prince*, attempts to define it as if it were an unusual or not totally clear term. States, in that passage, are 'tutti e' dominii che hanno avuto et hanno imperio sopra gli uomini', that is all the forms of organisation of supreme political power, whether republican or princely. If I am not mistaken, no such studies have been dedicated, on the other hand, to the term *città*. Machiavelli himself does not feel the need to define it since it applies to a concrete reality, to the men and to the things which he loved. But it is also true that the use of the term, which is parallel to and often coincides with the term *republica*, rather than being modelled on the classical concept of *civitas*, takes us back to the world of the city republics and what was left of them within the fifteenth-century territorial states. It reminds us of the supremacy of the dominant city, where the power lay and where political conflict was acted out, and of the subjection of the territory – a passive object of government, for which at the very most citizens of the dominant city might propose (as Francesco Guicciardini did on occasion) a less unjust and harassing government, less influenced by the private interests of the *rettori*, the officials sent by the dominant city.[40] The spontaneous use of the term *città* to mean *repubblica* or *stato* without needing to define it, is connected with a language – the same

---

[38] H. Baron, 'Machiavelli. The republican Citizen and the author of the "Prince"', *English Historical Review*, 76, (1981), 217–53; F. Gilbert, *Machiavelli e Guicciardini*, pp. 133–71; C. Dionisotti, 'Dalla repubblica al principato', *Rivista storica italiana*, 83 (1971), pp. 227–63, now in Dionisotti, *Machiavellerie* (Turin, 1980), pp. 101–53.

[39] See, besides F. Chiappelli, *Studi sul linguaggio*, pp. 59–74, O. Condorelli, 'Per la storia del nome "stato" (il nome "stato" in Machiavelli)', *Archivio giuridico*, 89 (1923), 223–35 and 90 (1923), 77–112; J.H. Whitfield, *Machiavelli* (Oxford, 1947), pp. 92–3; F. Chabod, 'Alcune questioni di terminologia: Stato, nazione, patria nel linguaggio del Cinquecento' in *Alle origini dello Stato moderno* (Rome, 1957), now in Chabod, *Scritti sul Rinascimento* (Turin, 1967), pp. 630–50; J.H. Hexter, 'Il Principe and lo Stato', *Studies in the Renaissance*, 4 (1957), 113–38; F. Gilbert, *Machiavelli e Guicciardini*, pp. 271–3; N. Rubinstein, 'Notes on the word stato' in *Florilegium Historiale. Essays presented to W.K. Ferguson*, J.G. Rowe and W.H. Stockdale, eds. (Toronto, 1971), pp. 314–26; A. Marongiu, 'La parola "stato" nel carteggio Machiavelli–Guicciardini–Vettori', *Storia e politica*, 14 (1975), 333–44; A. Tenenti, 'La nozione di "stato"', and 'Archeologia medievale della parola Stato', in Tenenti, *Stato: un'idea*.

[40] F. Guicciardini, *Discorso del modo di riformare il governo per meglio assicurare lo Stato alla casa dei Medici* (1516), in Guicciardini, *Opere inedite*, ed. G. Canestrini, vol. II (Florence, 1858), p. 339.

language to which the paradigm *vivere civile* and *civilità* belongs – which has its first and most concrete reference point precisely in the *città*. It is no coincidence to find that a later political thinker from a very different society – Jean Bodin – thought that *cité* was a term which needed to be discussed critically.[41]

It would obviously be absurd to say that the use of the word *stato* in the sense that we have seen is limited to *The Prince*, and the term *città* to the *Discourses*. Both terms are used in both works. But the importance which *stato* assumes in the first and *città* in the second allows us to consider them, at least for the time being, as two key-words, which indicate two different points of view. That the first is essentially that of the brief 'treatise' or *institutio* of 1513, and that the other is that of the stratified body of reflections begun, according to the majority of scholars, before writing *The Prince* and completed several years later, depends no doubt in part on the external context in relation to which the two works were produced. The *institutio*, as many scholars have pointed out, was written for the Medici, and connected with the attention that Machiavelli gave to the project of founding a larger territorial state at the beginning of Leo X's pontificate. The great body of reflections which make up the *Discourses*, at least in their final phase, reflect instead just as important an outside influence: the republicans present with him in the Orti Oricellari. The existence of these two points of view, however, is connected in any event with some deep discontinuities in the way Machiavelli observed the political crisis of his time.

6 In *The Prince*, of course, we feel the impact of political events as well as of the broad territorial policy which Leo X was trying to implement. But the world which Machiavelli refers to is more generally the fragile and tormented world of the small Italian states. They do not have the necessary 'barbe e correspondenzie', they lack legitimate power, are very much subject to *fortuna*, and they rarely have leaders of great *virtù* such as would be essential for their survival. To Machiavelli this world seemed anything but closed off to outside influence: it was surrounded and penetrated by the great emerging states of which we have already underlined the importance in his political outlook. The crisis which threatens that world, in *The Prince* as in the works from the chancery years, is seen above all in relation to the international situation, taking into account the dimensions of the military conflict and the new forces which have come to have an influence on its outcome. Thus the central problem in that brief innovative *speculum* for new princes is how they can not only 'conservare lo stato', but also enlarge it, as was at that time necessary for survival – and reinforce it, endowing it with its own armed forces.

This does not mean that *The Prince* does not deal with the internal power struggle, nor that it does not give space (beyond that given to the rules of

[41] J. Bodin, *Les Six Livres de la République* (Paris, 1583; new edn, Paris, 1986), I, 6: 'Du citoyen et de la différence d'entre le subject, le citoyen, l'estranger, la ville, cité et République', pp. 68–100. See also Bodin, *Methodus ad facilem historiarum cognitionem* (Paris, 1566), p. 178ff.

behaviour toward one's subjects) to the *ordini*, to constitutions.[42] On the contrary, this level of reasoning is always implicitly present: giving good *ordini* is in fact the fundamental, palingenetic task of the prince, and *buone leggi*, along with *buone armi* are the 'principali fondamenti che habbino tutti li stati' (chapter 12). We have already seen how ample Machiavelli's comments on the German cities and particularly on France are in this connection. Machiavelli criticises Venice not only because it has abandoned the secure and glorious way of making war 'co' gentiluomini e con la plebe armata' which it had used in its maritime conquests and because of its dependence on mercenary troops for the conquest of its mainland territories in Italy. He also criticises its method of governing subject cities. He thinks that the Venetians' practice of supporting internal divisions in order to foster *differenzie* among the citizens of those cities so that 'non unissono contro di loro' is ill-advised (chapter 20). On the contrary he praises Cesare Borgia not only for wanting to have 'arme proprie', but also for his exemplary organisation of his subject territories. Here he refers to the particularly intelligent and practical plan for a process of centralisation tempered by recognition of the autonomy of each city. Under Borgia, the rule of the many tiny local lords, *impotenti*, quarrelsome and predatory, is replaced at first by a ferociously repressive use of justice and subsequently by the jurisdictional unification of the state through the founding of a supreme court, of 'uno iudicio civile nel mezzo della provincia' in which, however, 'ogni città vi aveva l'avvocato suo' (chapter 7). Florence too appears in *The Prince*, not only with regard to its subject territories, but also as a specific urban reality. It is difficult not to see, behind the celebration of the *principato civile*, founded on the *popolo* and against the *grandi* (chapter 9), the background of Florence's political struggle and the mark of the ex-secretary's complex relationship with the Medici. Indeed in the development of the brief treatise, this is a central point, a point in which we can observe Machiavelli's attempt to combine the princely model and the *vivere civile* tradition – perhaps with an implicit reference to the French model.[43]

These are examples which show the constant attention Machiavelli gave to the structural aspects of the state, in the first instance as regards its territorial problems. And yet, in *The Prince* we must note that this interest is instrumental. Whether he is dealing with hereditary, new, or mixed principalities, whether they are composed of provinces which have the same or different language, customs and institutions, whether they are already used to living under a prince, or used to being free, the basic question is still the one we have already stated:

---

[42] See J.H. Whitfield, 'On Machiavelli's use of Ordini', p. 35ff.

[43] See G. Sasso, *Niccolò Machiavelli*, pp. 346–57 and Sasso, 'Principato civile e tirannide' in *Machiavelli e gli antichi e altri saggi*, vol. II (Milan–Naples, 1988), pp. 351–490. For the reference to the French model see G. Cadoni, *Machiavelli*, pp. 75ff, whose argument, however, does not seem sufficiently proved.

how to maintain power and enlarge the *stato*. This is the problem with which the *virtù* of princes and the quality of the *ordini* must be measured.

7   The vaster body of reflections gathered together in the *Discourses* – formed over a long period, and according to recent studies the fruit of partial rewriting and reorganisation[44] – is also marked by a deep anxiety caused by the political upheavals of the time. In the *Discourses*, however, this anxiety takes two different forms. The 'variazioni de' governi' of which Polybius speaks are the keynote, but the cyclically determined succession of Polybius' six forms can be overturned by another more dramatic transformation, that is, by the state's becoming subject to 'uno stato propinquo che sia meglio ordinato'. And this, in reality, is the most probable outcome, for 'quasi nessuna republica può essere di tanta vita che possa passare molte volte per queste mutazioni e rimanere in piede' (1, 2). I do not intend here to reconsider the theoretical problems raised by the comparison between Polybius' text and the second chapter of the *Discourses*, which have already been amply analysed by Gennaro Sasso.[45] It is enough here to observe that the critical utilisation of Polybius' text offers a framework in which to express the awareness of a crisis which appears to involve both the constitutional foundations of the city-republics and their possibilities of survival as independent states. In the *Discourses*, that crisis is experienced, discussed and analysed from within the republican system and the central and recurring problems are how to reorder cities, how to renew the foundations of the *vivere civile*, creating an organisation which is 'fermo e stabile'. These problems appear to be strongly influenced by the Florentine experience. It is not by chance that references to both contemporary and long past events in Florentine history are frequent in the *Discourses*: Machiavelli even begins his long excursus on Polybius by mentioning the events of 1502 and 1512 as proof of how difficult it is to institute new constitutions except when forced to do so by extreme necessity, and of the danger that under those circumstances republics are likely to come to ruin before reform can be brought to completion.[46]

[44] P. Larivaille, *La Pensée politique de Machiavel. Les 'Discours sur la Première Décade de Tite-Live'* (Nancy, France: 1982). On the chronology of the *Discourses* Larivaille accepts the hypothesis of the pre-existence of a 'book of republics' proposed by F. Gilbert, 'The composition and structure of Machiavelli's Discorsi' in *Journal of the History of Ideas*, 14 (1953), pp. 136–56 (now in Gilbert, *Niccolò Machiavelli e il suo tempo*), but suggests a more complex succession of preparatory stages, on the basis of which he proposes a different arrangement of the different parts of the work. For example, Book 1, chapter 2 to which we will refer, may show traces of these various stages.

[45] G. Sasso, 'La teoria dell'anacyclosis' in Sasso, *Studi su Machiavelli* (Naples, 1967), pp. 161–222. See also Sasso, 'Polibio e Machiavelli: costituzione, potenza, conquista', *ibid.* pp. 223–80. For a detailed comparison of the two texts, see *The Discourses of Niccolò Machiavelli*, ed. by L. J. Walker (London, 1950), vol. II, pp. 6–15.

[46] 'Di che ne fa fede appieno la repubblica di Firenze, la quale fu dallo accidente d'Arezzo nel dua riordinata: e da quel di Prato nel dodici disordinata', N. Machiavelli, *Discorsi sopra la prima deca di Tito Livio*, ed. C. Vivanti (Turin, 1983), pp. 17–18. The reform of 1502, after the rebellions in Val di Chiana, consisted, as is well known, with the institution of the 'gonfalonierato a vita'. The 'disorder' in 1512, after the siege at Prato, was of course, the restoration of the Medici.

Compared to *The Prince*, the *Discourses* may at times appear to be a sort of withdrawal into a much more limited and traditional universe. As a matter of fact this is the work in which reference to the values of civic humanism is most systematic: Machiavelli often speaks (and often in a rather abstract way) of the *bene comune* and of *vivere civile*, of citizens' *virtù*, of *equalità* and *libertà*, of the *popolo* and of the *grandi*. But he does this in an obviously critical way, in two senses.

Referring to those values, using continual recourse to the example of Rome, allows Machiavelli to create an ideal republican model, with which he can contrast the reality of his time: the *corruzione* and the importance of *bene particulare*, of *inequalità*, *sette* and *divisioni*; the prevalence of *forze private* and *forze forestiere* over *forze ed ordini publici* (I, 7).[47] Machiavelli draws the parameters for judging the forms of power which prevail in Florence at that time from the republican tradition. To him, as an old *uomo publico*, these forms seem to be characterised (as he was to say using different and more direct language in his *Discursus florentinarum rerum* of 1520)[48] by a ruinous weakening of the institutions and of the 'maestà dello stato', by the overbearing force of 'luoghi transversali' and of 'uomini privati' to the detriment of the 'ordine politico'. Thus he uses the system's own ideological premises to criticise the way it works. On this basis he proposes putting an end to the 'migration of powers', as Stephens calls it, which has been going on since the beginning of the Medicis' predominance, by going back to the institutions in their broadest form, that is, to a government of the *popolo*.[49] But he also questions some of the fundamental premises of the city-state republican ideology. He declares his impassioned personal attachment to *vita civile*. But he feels that it can be implemented 'per via di regno o di republica'. Using Polybius and with France in mind, he distinguishes sharply between a principality which follows a system of *vivere politico* and 'potestà assoluta, la quale dagli autori è chiamata tirannide' (I, 25). Among the republics he contrasts Venice with Rome; clearly an anti-historical procedure (as Machiavelli's use of Roman examples in the humanistic style always is, of course), but one of great ideal value.

These two critical approaches in the *Discourses* are in reality so interwoven as to be almost inseparable. But it is best to distinguish them for the time being because they define two different planes of reflection and they lead back to the two points of view which we have tried to define. In the first in fact Machiavelli

---

[47] See on some of these topics A. Bonadeo, *Corruption, Conflict and Power in the Works and Times of Niccolò Machiavelli* (California, 1973).

[48] *Discursus florentinarum rerum post mortem iunioris Laurentii Medices* in N. Machiavelli, *Arte della guerra*, pp. 261–77.

[49] On the term *popolo* see A. Bonadeo, 'The role of the people in the works and times of Machiavelli' in *Bibliothèque d'Humanisme et Renaissance*, 32 (1970), 351–77. Even though single points of his analysis are not totally convincing, the impossibility of giving the term a precise socio-political meaning is thoroughly demonstrated. On the *grandi* see Bonadeo, 'The role of "Grandi" in the political world of Machiavelli', *Studies in the Renaissance*, 16, 1969, pp. 9–29.

appears to be completely immersed in a city-state attitude, and he proceeds in almost communal fashion. This is why he writes at such length about the play of the different forces within the city and he sees the explanation of the flourishing of republics and their decline in the two ever-present 'umori diversi', of the *popolo* and the *grandi*. In his eyes the city is the principal place where the political choices which he so desires and the reforms designed to create *buoni ordini* can be made. From his second point of view, however, as we shall now see, to some extent he criticises precisely the city-based character of the Italian republics, their still recognisably communal matrix. This is the level on which Machiavelli seems farthest from the republican tradition, although he remains a man of his time and does not make a radical break with it.

8   The memory of the events which at the turn of the sixteenth century had upset Florence's territorial state is vividly present in the *Discourses*, as it was in *The Prince*. This is not surprising, considering that Machiavelli had been personally involved in the problems which arose at that time. In *The Prince* he concedes the honours of war to Pisa: when Pisa rebels a hundred years after the first Florentine conquest, it becomes the example of a city 'consueta a vivere libera' which does not forget 'el nome della libertà e li ordini antiqui sua' (chapter 5). In the *Discourses* the story of Pisa is one of those which prove that fortresses are useless (II, 24), whereas Pistoia (II, 21 and 25), which threw herself 'spontaneamente . . . in le braccia a Firenze', proves the usefulness not only of fostering internal divisions in other cities but also of behaving like 'fratelli'.[50] The rebellion of Arezzo and of the Val di Chiana – which reintroduces into the *Discourses* the passage from Livy already used in the 1503 treatise – is used to prove how pernicious it is to adopt a 'via di mezzo' (II, 23). If, therefore, the fulcrum of the *Discourses* is the city, attention is also given in them to the subject cities, to the territorial dimension of the state. At least in one case, indeed, the *provincie* come to the fore: when Machiavelli finds in the presence of *gentiluomini* who 'comandano a castella' in the Kingdom of Naples, the Papal states, Romagna and Lombardy and in their absence in Tuscany, the basis for the *equalità* and the *disequalità* which favours the formation of republics in the latter area and of principalities in the former (I, 55).[51]

It has been correctly pointed out that it is precisely with regard to Venice's way of ruling the mainland territories that Machiavelli develops his negative judgement of that city. To Machiavelli – as to most ardent Florentine admirers of the myth of Venice[52] – it ranks 'intra le moderne republiche . . . eccellente'

---

[50] It is well to remember that Pistoia under Florentine rule enjoyed (unlike Pisa and Arezzo), a favoured treatment, because it was not a 'subject, but an ally and confederate' ('non subdita, sed socia et confoederata').

[51] On this chapter see G. Sasso, 'Intorno a due capitoli dei Discorsi' in Sasso, *Studi*, pp. 111–59.

[52] On Machiavelli, Venice and its myth, see besides I. Cervelli, *Machiavelli*, F. Gilbert, 'The Venetian constitution in Florentine political thought' in *Florentine Studies. Politics and Society in Renaissance Florence*, N. Rubinstein, ed. (Evanston, ILL, 1968).

when he considers its central institutions, the great authority of the Dieci, the possibility of having recourse to the decisions of the Quarantia, the broad jurisdiction of the Great Council (1, 34 and 49). He praises Venice's ability to regulate the activities of the public councils in such a way as not to interrupt the functioning of the state (1, 50). But for Machiavelli, as for others who criticise the Venetian constitution in those years,[53] the fragile organisation of the mainland territories, Venice's *terraferma*, seems impossible to deny. And the battle of Agnadello, the tragic day on which, after having occupied 'gran parte d'Italia . . . non con guerra ma con danari e con astuzia', Venice 'come la ebbe a fare pruova delle forze sue perdette . . . ogni cosa' (1, 6), continues to furnish proof of its inadequacy when it comes to maintaining or expanding its power. Machiavelli's judgement takes into account the specificity of the city's history, torn between its two vocations, maritime and terrestrial, and has been prepared for by his earlier direct experience with Venetian affairs. However, it must be seen as part of an overall evaluation of the territorial aspects of the crisis of the republics of city-state origin. This theme is extremely important in the *Discourses* and its keystone is precisely the comparison between Rome and Venice.

'Acquistare', 'mantenere', 'ampliare' and 'fare augmenti' are recurring terms not only in *The Prince* but also to a certain extent in the *Discourses*. If in the case of principalities, and obviously of kingdoms, 'augumento' seems almost a natural vocation, in the republican world it seems more a necessity than a choice. It would be better in fact for a republic to be able to organise its institutions so as to 'mantenere' and not to acquire further territories; to be able to avoid expanding its domains without being attacked by other states. 'Potendosi tenere la cosa bilanciata in questo modo', Machiavelli writes,

[questo] sarebbe il vero vivere politico e la vera quiete d'una città. Ma sendo tutte le cose degli uomini in moto, e non potendo stare salde, conviene che le salghino o che le scendino, e a molte cose che la ragione non t'induce, t'induce la necessità. (1, 6)

In this picture of transformation and conflict – the same picture which we find in *The Prince* – the communities of Germany are the exception that proves the rule. If they can live 'contente del piccolo loro dominio' and 'unite dentro alle mura loro', they owe it only to the particular fragmentation of the region and to the high sovereignty of the emperor. But

se quella provincia fusse condizionata altrimenti, converrebbe loro cercare di ampliare e rompere quella loro quiete. E perché altrove non sono tali condizioni, non si puó prendere questo modo di vivere. (II, 19)

But 'ampliare' is a hard task and not very congenial to republican systems of city-state origin: the 'acquisti' themselves for 'republiche non ben ordinate' can

---

[53] See in particular, Claude de Seyssel, *La Monarchie de France*, pp. 107ff. For a comparison with Machiavelli, see I. Cervelli, *Machiavelli*, pp. 344ff.

be dangerous (*ibid.*). It is an enterprise for which even antiquity can furnish only a single example, that of Rome.

For Machiavelli it is important to expand – so much so that, as is well known, he measures the quality of the different possible constitutions for cities by how suitable they are to this end. A republic such as Venice or Sparta 'che le basti mantenersi' is one thing, 'una republica che voglia fare un imperio, come Roma' quite another. Thus the aristocratic character of the Venetian constitution, where the 'guardia alla libertà'[54] is in the hands of the *gentiluomini* and these alone have the right to administrative posts, has in fact guaranteed the city's *libertà* for a long time. And its 'stato fermo e terminato', the sharp distinction between original citizen and foreigners, is very suitable for a state which wishes to maintain the status quo and its internal peace and stability (I, 5–6). But in Venice the *plebe* was unarmed, and this was the origin of Venice's military deficiencies, the reason for using mercenary troops and hence for the Agnadello disaster. Rome was completely different. In Rome, the 'guardia alla libertà' was entrusted to the *plebe*, and the Roman people, necessary for empire-building, was 'numeroso e armato'. This is the reason why the Roman republic was unavoidably 'tumultuaria', and between the plebs and the Senate there was much 'disunione': whence the 'leggi e ordini in beneficio della publica libertà', and subsequently the 'potenza di Mario e la rovina di Roma' (I, 4–5). And it is also the reason for the practical interest in having 'abbondanza di uomini', necessary for the city to flourish and expand: hence on the one hand the practice of bringing the inhabitants of the conquered cities to live in Rome, and on the other that of keeping the 'vie aperte e sicure' for foreigners, ensuring easy access to citizenship and to honours (II, 3).

With regard to Venice, therefore, Rome represents the 'popular' solution to the alternatives offered by the mixed constitution which characterises both cities. But it seems to me there are other differentiating factors. Rome is also a different kind of city, open and dynamic, just as Venice is closed and static. Rome, even before it organised its military forces, was able to grow because it had a different relationship with what was outside, with its territory. This is why it became the centre of an empire. Venice, on the other hand, provides the negative image of a city-state which was possibly in decline because of the very nature of urban society, because of the rigid distinctions between the different categories of its inhabitants and because it was so sharply divided from its territory.

The comparison between the two, although linked to problems of the territorial state, does not directly involve the forms and conceptions of territorial rule. But in other passages in the *Discourses*, it is not difficult to find traces of Machiavelli's reflections on this specific theme. These reflections are

---

[54] Guicciardini rightly found this expression slightly unclear (*Considerazioni intorno ai discorsi del Machiavelli.* published as an appendix to N. Machiavelli, *Discorsi*, ed. C. Vivanti, p. 550).

unsystematic and even ambiguous, but they raise stimulating questions. This in fact is one of the central themes of Book II, which discusses the Romans' way of making war and their territorial empire.

Once again the Roman model assumes great value as an example and is used to criticise the political logic of the Italian states. In this context Machiavelli makes its importance very clear as a model to be imitated with explicit reference to the problems of his own time – just as he had done in the Preface to Book I.

Tanti ordini osservati da Roma, così pertinenti alle cose di dentro come a quelle di fuora, non sono ne' presenti nostri tempi non solamente imitati, ma non n'è tenuto alcuno conto giudicandoli alcuni non veri, alcuni impossibili, alcuni non a proposito ed inutili; tanto che standoci con questa ignoranzia, siamo preda di qualunque ha voluto correre questa provincia.

This passage is in the fourth chapter of Book II; here Machiavelli examines the three possible 'modi circa lo ampliare'. He contrasts the two methods of creating leagues and 'farsi compagni' with that of 'farsi immediatamente sudditi'. The last is 'al tutto inutile'; it is impossible 'se tu non sei armato e grosso d'armi . . . governare città con violenza, massime quelle che fussono consuete vivere libere'.[55] The first is good, although 'una republica disgiunta e posta in varie sedi', based on the equal participation of the various communities, has only limited possibilities of expansion. Used at that time by the Swiss and by the Svevian League,[56] and in the past by the Etruscans, it could probably be practised by their decendants, if they find it too difficult to imitate the Romans. The best way, however, is the second: the Roman way of making more and more allies, bound to the city by living 'in di molte cose con equali leggi', but in actual fact subordinated to the 'grossissima città', which always reserves for itself 'la sedia dello Imperio ed il titolo del comandare'. Best of all then is the structure of a dependent territory which is to some extent associative, but in which the ruling city continues to enjoy its central character and its political supremacy.

This, it seems to me, is one of the most complete expressions of Machiavelli's reflections on the overall organisation of the republican state as regards its territorial aspect. In these passages one can see a much sharper awareness of the basic problems than in Guicciardini's *Considerazioni intorno ai Discorsi*, which accept the present situation much more passively.[57] Nonetheless there are boundaries which not even Machiavelli is able to cross. For him too the central role of the city in a territorial state, the definite subjection of the conquered cities and lands, is a basic premise of the republican system. Only a tyrant can

---

[55] The same theme is found in *The Prince*, ch. 5.
[56] We can find many comments on the Swiss in the letters exchanged by Machiavelli and Vettori in 1513–14.
[57] See in particular the comments on Book II, chapter 19 in F. Guicciardini, *Considerazioni*, p. 576.

break that rule, refusing to subject newly acquired territories to the city of which he is the lord.

Il farla potente non fa per lui; ma per lui fa tenere lo stato disgiunto, e che ciascuna terra e ciascuna provincia riconosca lui. Talché de' suoi acquisti solo egli ne profitta e non la sua patria. (II, 2)

Machiavelli's vision was profoundly influenced by communal tradition. It is no coincidence that he seems unable completely to understand the meaning of Livy's passage about Camillus' policies towards the rebellious peoples of Latium – a passage which, as we have seen, Machiavelli used both in his work of 1503 on the Val di Chiana and in the *Discourses* (II, 23). Livy recounts that Camillus, after the peoples has been reconquered, decided how to treat them case by case: he rewarded some of them with exemptions and privileges, giving them citizenship and punished the others by destroying their 'terre', deporting the inhabitants to Rome and sending new colonies to their homelands. The story clearly shows not only the harsh methods of government often used by the Romans, but also the practice of conceding citizenship outside their own city which was one of the bases of their empire.[58] But in his early work Machiavelli basically uses the episode to criticise Florence's policy towards Arezzo as being too bland, and more generally in the *Discourses*, as a negative judgement on 'middle-of-the-road' solutions. He concludes: 'Quando si ha a giudicare cittadi potenti, e che sono use a vivere libere, conviene o spegnerle o carezzarle'. But he does not dwell on the nature of the *carezze* used by the Romans, almost as if it were impossible for him to attribute to his ideal Roman model characteristics so radically different from those of the city-states within whose horizons he remains, held back by his experience and by his *forma mentis*.

It is on the theme of the relationship between ruling cities and their subject territories – fundamental to the critical analysis of the characteristics of the republican systems of his age – that Machiavelli refers to objects of comparison which are closer to him in time even though they are ideologically more distant. Between *vivere libero* and *vivere servo* (that is, in subjection to others) he seems to find an absolute contrast in republics, a contrast in which there is no space for further possibilities. Just as the free city is rich and flourishing, so the subject city is destined to know impoverishment, decline and exploitation. A hard, inevitable fate because the aim of a republic (evidently once again identified with a ruling city) 'è enervare ed indebolire, per accrescere il corpo suo, tutti gli altri corpi'. It is only under a princely government that subjects may be able to attain a different status. If the prince is not 'barbaro, destruttore de' paesi e

---

[58] On Machiavelli's understanding of the Roman *concordia*, see A. Momigliano, 'Camillo e la concordia' in Momigliano, *Storia e storiografia antica* (Bologna 1987), pp. 273–4, which, however, refers only to *Discorsi*, I, 5.

dissipatore di tutte le civiltà degli uomini come sono i principe orientali', he loves 'le città sue suggette equalmente, ed a loro lascia l'arti tutte e quasi tutti gli ordini antichi, talché se le non possono crescere come libere elle non rovinano anche come schiave' (II, 2). Under princely government it seems that the territory can be enlarged on a basis of parity between the subject bodies.

In the *Discourses*, therefore, alongside the ideal model of the *grossissima città* of Rome with its empire, the real-life models of the great monarchies and of the principalities that embrace many cities once again come to the fore. And it is in the light of this double comparison that Machiavelli, from within the archaic republican and communal world to which he so deeply belongs, interprets and gives witness to the nature of its crisis.

3

Florentine republicanism in the early sixteenth century

GIOVANNI SILVANO

I

The overthrow of the Medici regime in Florence in 1494 marks a turning point in the history of Florentine republicanism. Although a vital presence since the thirteenth century,[1] only at the end of 1494 did republicanism inspire the reform of the city government to an extent that led eventually to the establishment of the Consiglio Maggiore.

One clear aim of the constitutional reforms carried out by the Medici regime from 1434 onwards was to have the Councils of the Popolo and of the Commune deprived of their traditional powers.[2] These were then bestowed upon the new Councils of the Cento and of the Settanta, thus making all the more apparent that the Medici's policy did depart significantly from Florentine constitutional tradition. This specific aspect of sixteenth-century Medicean constitutional reform has a great deal to do with the events of late 1494, and in particular with the establishment of the Consiglio Maggiore. This institution was, in fact, regarded as a reinstatement of the old city's councils.

The inability of Piero de' Medici to orchestrate an effective defence policy against Charles VIII, who had crossed the Alps at the end of August 1494, and his haste to surrender Pisa and Sarzana to the French king, led to his exile on 9 November 1494. As an immediate consequence a constitutional crisis developed and the conflicting factions fought bitterly in an attempt to direct the reform of the city government:

---

[1] This view has been proposed by, among many others, N. Struever, *The Language of History in the Renaissance. Rhetoric and Historical Consciousness in Florentine Humanism* (Princeton, 1970), p. 117, and more recently by Q. Skinner, *The Foundations of Modern Political Thought* (Cambridge, 1978), 2 vol. 1 *The Renaissance*, pp. 77–84. Less inclined to recognise a 'clear' articulation of the concept of liberty in the Middle Ages is R. Witt, 'The Rebirth of the Concept of Republican Liberty in Italy in *Studies in Honor of Hans Baron*, A. Molho and J.A. Tedeschi, eds. (Dekalb, 1971), pp. 175–99 and R. Witt, *Coluccio Salutati and his Public Letters* (Geneva, 1976), pp. 73–88. Of course all of these views have to be read keeping in mind H. Baron's major thesis that 'civic humanism' as a change in political thinking in Florence occurred at the beginning of the fifteenth century, and that Leonardo Bruni was a major figure in such a transitional moment. See H. Baron, *The Crisis of the Early Italian Renaissance. Civic Humanism and Republican Liberty in an Age of Classicism and Tyranny* (Princeton, 1966).

[2] See N. Rubinstein, *The Government of Florence under the Medici (1434–1494)* (Oxford, 1966), pp. 183–5.

E certo io credo che già un grandissimo tempo la città non fussi stata in maggiori travagli: drento, cacciata una casa potentissima e che sessant'anni aveva avuto el governo, e rimesso tutti gli inimici di quella; per la quale mutazione rimanevano alterati tutti e' modi del governo, stavano in sommo timore tutti quegli che avevano avuto autorità a tempo di Lorenzo o di Piero, tutti quegli e' quali, o e' maggiori loro, avevano in tempo alcuno offesi gli usciti o e' sua antecessori, tutti quegli che o per compere o per vie di pagamento o di rapine possedevano de' beni di chi era stato rubello.'[3]

An agreement, however, could not be found until King Charles left Florence on 28 November 1494 'e come fu partito, sendo la città disordinata, si volsono gli animi a riformare lo stato'.[4]

And indeed it is puzzling that although the political situation in Florence was very tense, nonetheless a 'compromise' was soon found and a reform bill presented for approval. The first step was to have the Parlamento summoned on 2 December to abolish all the laws made from 1434 onwards, along with the Council of the Settanta, the Dieci, and the Otto di Balìa, whilst the Councils of the Popolo and Commune were restored. The purses were also ordered to be locked and an election was to take place after a new *squittino*.[5] Those who had served in office during the past Medici regime struggled to retain the political power which, they thought, was never to be shared with the descendants of those who had been in the *reggimento* prior to 1434. But now these men had returned to the city claiming full Florentine citizenship, in opposition to the Act of 2 December which required that members of the Councils of the Popolo and Commune had to be *veduti* or *seduti* to the three highest offices and over 25 years of age. Under this Act, a rebel could never qualify!

Soon after the Parlamento had been dismissed, it became apparent that it would have been impossible to comply with the many resolutions the Parlamento had adopted. A way had to be found of extending Florentine citizenship to those excluded by the Act of 2 December. In this particular circumstance Girolamo Savonarola played a part in working out a compromise among the conflicting factions. Whether or not Savonarola was spurred to enter the Florentine political scene by the rivalry between Paolantonio Soderini and Piero Capponi is less significant than the fact that Savonarola was indeed called upon to bring about a *mutazione di stato*.[6]

[3] F. Guicciardini, *Storie fiorentine*, in Guicciardini, *Opere*, ed. E. Lugnani Scarano (Turin, 1970–81), 3 vols., I, p. 126.

[4] *Ibid.*, p. 131. 'E a dì 28 di Novembre 1494, venerdì, si partì el Re di Firenze, dopo desinare, e andò albergo alla Certosa . . . E dissesi che fra Girolamo da Ferrara, famoso nostro predicatore, andò al Re, e dissegli che non faceva la volontà di Dio, allo stare, e che dovessi partire', L. Landucci, *Diario fiorentino dal 1450 al 1516 continuato da un anonimo fino al 1542*, ed. I. Del Badia (Florence, 1883), p. 87.

[5] See L. Landucci, *Diario*, p. 89. The text of the Act is in Florence, Archivio di Stato (ASF), Consigli Maggiori, Provvisioni, Registri, 185, cc. 1–7.

[6] 'Maravigliossi la brigata che in questa elezione fussi rimasto adrieto Paolantonio Soderini, sendo uomo di grande autorità e stato urtato da Piero de' Medici, e fu attribuito fussi stato Piero

The target was the intent of the Parlamento to establish a governo stretto, by restricting the eligibility requirements. This would have led the conflicting factions into an open fight if:

Erano nella città molti che arebbono voluto percuotere Bernardo del Nero, Niccolò Ridolfi, Pierfilippo, messer Agnolo, Lorenzo Tornabuoni, Iacopo Salviati e gli altri cittadini dello stato vecchio; alla quale cosa si opponevano molti uomini da bene, massime Piero Capponi e Francesco Valori, parte mossi dal bene publico perché in verità si sarebbe guasta la città, parte dal privato loro. Perché sendo loro naturalmente e e' maggiori loro amici della casa de' Medici, e che nel 34 avevano rimesso Cosimo, dubitavano che spacciati gli altri dello stato vecchio, e' quali vulgarmente si chiamavano bigi, loro non restassino a discrezione degli offesi nel 34, che naturalmente erano anche inimici loro . . . quando venne un aiuto non pensato, da fra Girolamo.[7]

The real political problem emerging from this passage of Guicciardini's *Storie fiorentine* has to do with the political expectations of the enemies of the *stato vecchio* who, despite Piero's defeat, felt threatened by the many Medici partisans who were still in power.

At this point, then, a *governo largo* seemed to be the right political choice, the only one capable, at least in theory, of extending full citizenship to the struggling political groups, from the Mediceans to their political opponents. To recognise the need of a *governo largo* in Florence was a very important political decision that found its legislative expression in the fundamental law of 22–3 December 1494, the constitutional cornerstone of the Florentine republic.

Here again, as had happened in the Act of the Parlamento, the law of 22–3 December was very careful in setting down the requirements with regard to eligibility for the Consiglio Maggiore. Basically, eligibility in the Consiglio Maggiore was granted to those who are or were *veduti* or *seduti* to the three highest magistracies or to those whose ancestors had been *seduti* or *veduti* during the previous three generations. Furthermore, the *beneficio* was also to be granted to those who had qualified in the scrutiny of 1484,[8] and to a number of citizens who, although lacking the *beneficio*, would, however, show strong interest in it.[9]

On the one hand, then, the *provvisione* lays down the fact that eligibility to the Consiglio Maggiore is to be based upon a quasi-hereditary principle, and on the other, it recognises the need for flexibility in dealing with this matter. This law and its further amendments in fact provided a number of men who had been

---

Capponi, el quale poteva assai e era inimico suo; in modo che si disse poi publicamente che per questo sdegno Paolantonio, per mutare lo stato, persuase a fra Girolamo, e lo adoperò per instrumento a predicare, si facessi el governo del popolo', F. Guicciardini, *Storie fiorentine*, pp. 131–2. See also E. Gusberti, 'Il Savonarola del Guicciardini', *Nuova rivista storica*, 54 (1970), pp. 581–622, 56 (1971), 21–89.

[7] F. Guicciardini, *Storie fiorentine*, pp. 132–3.
[8] A full description of this *Squittino* is in N. Rubinstein, *The Government of Florence*, pp. 210–18.
[9] The text of the law is in ASF, Provvisioni, 185, cc. 9r–13v. Important sections of it have been printed in F. Guicciardini, *Opere inedite*, illustrate da G. Canestrini (Florence, 1859), vol. III, p. 228.

excluded from office in the past with the possibility of claiming full Florentine citizenship.[10] This had to be the case for many of the Medici opponents. The Act of the Parlamento of 2 December and the law of 22–3 December shared the same political concern in that they both aimed at establishing the membership of Florentine republican *reggimento* soon after the overthrow of Piero de' Medici. They differed dramatically, however, in addressing the crucial choice between a *governo stretto* and a *governo largo*.

Although Florentines may not have perceived fully the revolutionary, political and social significance of the *Provvisione* of 22–3 December which established the Consiglio Maggiore, the fact remains that this institution changed the course of Florentine constitutional history, and was to remain a central issue in the city's political and ideological life. Membership of the Consiglio Maggiore was now to be controlled by law, and no longer could a citizen qualify for office on the basis of a biased *squittino*.[11] The most revolutionary aspect of the legislation of late December 1494 was that for the first time in its history Florence attempted to define in strict juridical terms the social basis of its present and future *reggimento*. According to the same law, the composition of the *reggimento* was not expected to change dramatically from Medicean times and there was a great deal of continuity between the Medicean *reggimento* and that of the *governo popolare*.[12] If some *uomini da bene*[13] opposed this institution as forcefully as they could, they did so because of the fear that such an

---

[10] In February 1497 a *provvisione* was enacted that also extended the *beneficio* to those citizens who could get it in *linea transversale*. See N. Rubinstein, 'I primi anni del Consiglio Maggiore a Firenze (1494–99)', *Archivio storico italiano*, 112, 2 (1954), 151–94, p. 154. See also 321–47 for a clear exposition of the electoral procedures in the Consiglio Maggiore. For a more general overview of the problem of citizenship in Renaissance Florence, see L. Martines, *Lawyers and Statecraft in Renaissance Florence* (Princeton, 1968), pp. 119–24. J. Kirshner also has some interesting remarks in 'Paolo di Castro on 'cives ex privilegio': A controversy over the legal qualifications for public office in early fifteenth-century Florence' in *Studies in Honor of Hans Baron*, pp. 229–64.

[11] See N. Rubinstein, 'I primi anni', 155, where it is said that the *squittino* was maintained. It should, however, be stressed that the *provvisione* of 22–3 December 1494 permitted a *squittino* to be carried out only once, and not as a general rule.

[12] This view was first proposed by N. Rubinstein, 'Oligarchy and democracy in fifteenth-century Florence' in *Florence and Venice: Comparisons and Relations*, 2 vols., I *Quattrocento*, S. Bertelli, N. Rubinstein, C.H. Smyth, eds. (Florence, 1979–80), pp. 79–80. Very recently much archival evidence has been brought to light that illuminates Rubinstein's assumptions. See R. Pesman Cooper, 'The Florentine ruling group under the "governo popolare", 1494–1512', *Studies in Medieval and Renaissance History*, (1985), 71–181. In this fundamental study, the author argues that the establishment of the *governo popolare* did not alter the social composition of the Florentine ruling group if compared with the *reggimento* of the previous Medici regime – as it has been described by D. Kent, 'The Florentine reggimento in the fifteenth century', *Renaissance Quarterly*, 28 (1975), 575–638, and D. Kent, *The Rise of the Medici. Faction in Florence, 1426–1434* (Oxford, 1978). Pesman Cooper, furthermore, is right when she conceives of the establishment of the Consiglio Maggiore as a *serrata*, as the attempt at fixing the boundaries of the Florentine political class once and for all. More questionable is her thesis that the Consiglio Maggiore did not cause a broadening of Florentine citizenship. To say that only one-third of all members of the council did actually exercise their right of being *seduti* does not necessarily mean that the purpose of the law of 22–3 December 1494 had not aimed at broadening this number. The number of *case* admitted

institution could be politically manoeuvred only with great difficulty. The *primi cittadini* sitting in the Consiglio Maggiore, soon realised that the distribution of official republic posts would now be the result of a decision endorsed by the majority of the Consiglio's members. In this new constitutional framework, some of the *governo stretto*'s staunchest supporters feared that their interests would no longer be protected. This is why aristocratic criticism of the Consiglio Maggiore aimed always at bringing political power back to the *luoghi più stretti*. The *provvisione* of 22–3 December, however, had in fact enacted a republic or a *vivere popolare*, far removed from Medicean tradition. What was the Consiglio Maggiore if not the reinstatement of the old Councils of the Popolo and Commune?

An enquiry into Renaissance Florentine republicanism from the last years of the fifteenth to the first decades of the sixteenth-century can justifiably focus upon the perception among Florentines of the Consiglio Maggiore. Despite being abolished twice by the Medici, soon after their return in 1512 and 1530, the Consiglio Maggiore remained a central topic in many contemporary political and historical writings. In this large body of writings a favourable attitude towards this institution emerges. In time the Consiglio Maggiore, losing its original historical features, came to be conceived in a more mythical vein both among the *uomini da bene* and among the *popolani*. Following the story of this changing perception of the institution, commonly regarded as the embodiment of the republic, provides a better historical understanding of the Florentine debate over the *governo largo* and *governo stretto* or between *uomini da bene* and *popolani*.

to the council increased more than 50 per cent over the number of families which had made up the Medicean *reggimento*. Important remarks on the political meaning of the establishment of the Consiglio are in N. Rubinstein, 'Florentina Libertas', *Rinascimento*, 26 (1986), 20–1. Not only were the members of the Consiglio eligible to the city's offices, they were also entrusted with legislative and some executive power.

13 A political, economic and cultural leadership of elite groups has long been recognised in Florentine Renaissance society of the late Middle Ages. An outstanding work in this direction is G. Brucker, *The Civic World of Early Renaissance Florence* (Princeton, 1977). Important remarks on the functioning of Renaissance oligarchies are in L. Martines, *Power and Imagination. City-States in Renaissance Italy* (New York, 1979), pp. 148–161. In these and other works an attempt at defining socially and numerically the Florentine ruling group has been successfully carried out. However, historians have employed different terms to refer to the Florentine upper class than was customary in Renaissance Florence: *ottimati, primi cittadini, uomini da bene* were all synonymous terms identifying members of the most powerful *case*. The ruling group in Florence was never a legally closed body – with the partial exception of the time of the *governo popolare* – and only after the Duchy had been established by Cosimo I de' Medici did the perception of belonging to an elite group become more and more apparent. See S. Bertelli, *Il potere oligarchico nello stato-città medievale* (Florence, 1978), pp. 106–16 and F. Diaz, 'L'idea di una nuova "élite" sociale negli storici e trattatisti del principato', *Rivista storica italiana*, 92 (1980), 572–87, printed also in *Firenze e la Toscana dei Medici nell'Europa del '500*, vol. II (Florence, 1983), pp. 665–681. On this issue see also R. Burr Litchfield, *Emergence of a Bureaucracy. The Florentine Patricians 1530–1790*, (Princeton, 1986), pp. 13–51.

II

After the Medici had been driven out of Florence in 1494, Girolamo Savonarola was one of the Consiglio Maggiore's staunchest supporters. Even before these dramatic events, he had addressed himself to politics, when, in the 1480s, he worked on his *Compendium totius philosophiae* whose last book bears the title *De politia et regno*.[14] In this period, his political perspective was cast fully in the Aristotelian and Thomist pattern of thought. The basic assumption is the belief that man is a social animal whose end consists in living together with other men. Therefore the next step is to find out which form of government would best serve this goal. Here Savonarola betrays his monarchical sympathies, based mainly on the apparent resemblance between monarchy and the divine government of the universe.[15] Finally, the duties and virtues of the good king are thoroughly discussed. A piece of orthodox Thomist political philosophy, this tract does not address any political issue of the time, but rather stems from Savonarola's philosophical education in the Dominican schools.[16]

While retaining his inner philosophical beliefs, as soon as Savonarola faced the constitutional crisis Piero de' Medici's exile had provoked in Florence, he set himself the task of intervening in the historical situation in as effective a way as possible. As a preacher with a large following, he had a chance to advocate a reform of the city government from the pulpit, and he did so in the Advent sermons of 1494. Never before had the friar entered the Florentine political scene in such an open way.

In the sermon of the second Sunday of Advent, on 7 December, he called for a deep moral renewal.[17] Only later did Savonarola speak of a political reform:

O Firenze, ora mi volto a te. Se tu vuoi renovarti, o città nuova, se tu vuoi esser nuova e se tu hai mutato nuovo stato, bisogna che tu muti nuovi modi e nuovo vivere, se tu vuoi durare, e se tu vuoi reggere [. . .] La prima cosa che tu debbia fare intra l'altre è questa: che tu facci tale legge, che nessuno più per l'avvenire possa farsi capo.[18]

---

[14] *Compendium totius philosophiae tam naturalis quam moralis, Reverendi patris Fratris Hieronymi Savonarolae de Ferraria ordinis praedicatorum, nunc primum in lucem editum* (Venetiis, MDXXXIIII). See also E. Garin, 'Ricerche sopra gli scritti filosofici di Girolamo Savonarola. Opere inedite e smarrite' in Garin, *La cultura filosofica del Rinascimento italiano* (Bari, 1961), p. 208.

[15] 'Bonum multitudinis est pax et unitas quae multo melius potest per unum fieri quam per plures . . . et hoc regimen est magis naturale, ut pote magis simile regiminis totius universi et partium eius . . .', Savonarola, *Compendium*, p. 223.

[16] On this work see D. Weinstein, *Savonarola and Florence. Prophecy and Patriotism in the Renaissance* (Princeton, 1970), pp. 290–4.

[17] 'Così dico a te, Firenze: rinuovati lo intelletto, che par tu l'habbi perduto, ricorri a Dio in ogni tua cosa . . . Firenze, escludi da te ogni superstizione e *a signis coeli noli metuere*, come dice la Scrittura . . . renuovate la vita vostra in buoni costumi, riducetivi al culto divino, cacciate via gl' incantatori e le superstizioni e divinatori . . .', G. Savonarola, *Prediche sopra Aggeo*, ed. L. Firpo (Rome, 1965), p. 129.

[18] *Ibid.*, p. 132.

In keeping with a long tradition of thought going back to Bartolus of Sassoferrato and Coluccio Salutati,[19] Savonarola endorses the view that tyranny is the worst form of government. He could not make a more direct allusion to the Medici regime.[20] In this sermon Savonarola addresses the issue of political reform in Florence only in very general terms; there is no mention of any specific reform, the foremost concern being the absolute necessity of establishing a government capable of checking any attempt at tyranny.

A week later, on 14 December, Savonarola managed to propose to his audience some reforming thoughts in more technical terms. Taking great care to convey the idea that: 'Dio ha voluto che tu vegga ed esperimenti la mia inettitudine, acciò che tanto più tu vegga e consideri che gli è lui e non io che fa el tutto',[21] Savonarola argues that, although theoretically government by one man is best, for Florence, government *dei più* is the most suitable. The friar implies that he is for an aristocratic form of government, because, according to his classification of the forms of governments, *i più* refers to the aristocracy.[22] At this point it seems that the Florentine aristocracy succeeded in enlisting Savonarola's support to its cause. Furthermore this would certainly be consistent with the two references he makes to the excellence of the Venetian government.[23] Although careful to provide details of a long-awaited fiscal reform in Florence, on the constitutional score, Savonarola does not go further than expressing his preference for the Venetian government. In this sermon there is no direct mention of the Consiglio Maggiore and only his calling upon the Venetian model could be interpreted as an unspoken but strong advocacy of the Consiglio Maggiore. Only later did Savonarola refer openly to the Consiglio Maggiore, and only dealt with it fully in 1498 in his *Trattato circa el reggimento e governo della città di Firenze*.[24]

This short treatise was composed at the request of the Signoria which was

---

[19] See R. Witt, *Hercules at the Crossroads. The Life, Works, and Thought of Coluccio Salutati* (Durham, NC, 1983), pp. 368–86, and D. Quaglioni, *Politica e diritto nel trecento italiano* (Florence, 1983).

[20] On this line see A. Rinuccini's 'Dialogus de Libertate', ed. F. Adorno, in *Atti e Memorie dell'Accademia Toscana di Scienze e Lettere 'La Colombaria'*, 22 (1957), 267–303 and L. Martines, *The Social World of the Florentine Humanists (1390–1460)* (Princeton, 1963), pp. 299–300.

[21] G. Savonarola, *Prediche*, p. 212.

[22] 'Alcuni si reggano per uno capo solo, alcuni per più persone, alcuni si reggano da tutto el popolo insieme', *ibid.* p.210.

[23] 'La forma che avete principiata non può stare, se non la riordinate meglio. Credo che non sia la migliore di quella de' Veniziani e che voi pigliate esemplo da loro . . .', *ibid.* p. 226.

[24] See *Le lettere di Girolamo Savonarola*, ed. R. Ridolfi (Florence, 1933), p. 95. The *Trattato* is quoted from G. Savonarola, *Prediche sopra Aggeo*, pp. 435–87 (hereinafter cited as *Trattato*). See A. Fuhr, *Machiavelli und Savonarola. Politische Rationalität und politische Prophetie* (Frankfurt am Main, 1985), pp. 97–102. A brief, though useful article is D. Weinstein, 'Machiavelli and Savonarola' in *Studies on Machiavelli*, Myron P. Gilmore, ed. (Florence, 1972), pp. 253–64. To be sure, Savonarola alluded to the Council on several occasions, and his thoughts on the institution must have been widely known in Florence. This fact comes to light in the writing of D. Cecchi's 'Riforma Sancta et Pretiosa' of 24 February 1497, ed. U. Mazzone, *'El buon governo'. Un progetto di riforma generale nella Firenze savonaroliana* (Florence, 1978), pp. 32–52; 185–6.

piagnona in its political feelings. Savonarola was expected to illuminate the inner political significance of the Consiglio Maggiore in Florentine history.[25] His intention was to make clear once and for all the true character of the reform of December 1494. At that time he had advocated it on the grounds that Florence had to pattern its government after the Venetian model. Now, four years later, the friar was no longer willing to recognise any Venetian influence in the making of the Florentine *governo popolare*.[26]

His starting-point in the tract is very philosophical. Man's nature requires him to live with other men and to set up a political community so as to promote the common good. While, absolutely speaking, monarchy is the best form of government, in more practical and historical terms, the character of the people, that is its history, determines choice among the different forms of governments. On these grounds, then, Savonarola argues for the *governo civile* in Florence. On the one hand, the nature of the people excludes the possibility of establishing a monarchy in the city,[27] and on the other, tradition is the foremost reason to be sceptical of the *ottimati*'s government:

Ora el popolo fiorentino, avendo preso antiquamente el reggimento civile, ha in questo fatto tanta consuetudine, che, oltre che a lui questo è più naturale e conveniente di ogni altro governo, ancora per la consuetudine è tanto impresso nella mente de' cittadini, che saria difficile e quasi impossibile a rimuoverli da tale governo. E avvenga che siano stati già molti anni governati da tiranni, nientedimeno quelli cittadini . . . non tiranneg-giavano per tal modo . . . ma con grande astuzia governavano el popolo, non lo cavando dal suo naturale e della sua consuetudine: onde lasciavano la forma del governo nella città . . .[28]

In Savonarola's view, the Consiglio Maggiore reinstated, institutionally, this traditional form of government. This council was the most suitable in Florence because it appeared to be the only possible solution to the problem of the city's civil strife.[29]

Florentine political community was divided by the ambition of the *grandi*: in Savonarola's judgement the return to Florence in 1494 of those who had been exiled in 1434 had made the political atmosphere so tense that only a *governo civile* could face it. In historical perspective Savonarola holds the view that the Consiglio Maggiore was actually founded to overcome any civil disorder

---

[25] 'Ma perché le Signorie Vostre mi richiedono, non che io scriva del governo de' regni e città *in generali*, ma che particularmente tratti del nuovo governo della città di Firenze . . .', *Trattato*, p. 435.

[26] See G. Savonarola, *Prediche italiane ai fiorentini*, ed. F. Cognasso (Perugia–Venice, 1930), vol, III, pp. 1–2, p. 56; p. 234.

[27] 'La natura dunque di questo popolo non è da sopportare el governo di uno principe, *etiam* che fussi buono e perfetto', *Trattato*, p. 447.   [28] *Ibid.*, p. 448.

[29] A number of essays are devoted to this issue in the volume *Violence and Civil Disorder in Italian Cities 1200–1500*, L. Martines, ed. (Berkeley–Los Angeles–London, 1972). See especially Martines' introduction, pp. 3–18.

arising from the presence in Florence of conflicting social groups. The *governo civile* in fact goes beyond factions by allowing a very large number of citizens in the Council. It therefore promotes the common good of the city in the most effective way:

> . . . e se fu divisa e piena di discordia nelli tempi passati per la ambizione e per li odii delli principali cittadini . . . essendo ritornati li cittadini, li quali furono scacciati in diversi tempi da chi ha governato, massime dal '34 in qua . . . il consiglio e governo civile, il quale fu in lei fundato non da uomini, ma da Dio, è stato instrumento . . . a mantenerla nella sua libertà.[30]

Savonarola's paramount concern is with the liberty of Florence. His basic assumption is that to promote and preserve a *governo civile*, no private citizen ever has the authority to bestow upon other fellow citizens honours and offices in the state. If this occurred, very likely all citizens would hasten to submit themselves to the one holding out promises of honours, thus paving the way to tyranny. The power of such distribution of honours ought then to remain with the people, to prevent any private citizen from becoming a tyrant.[31] 'Fatto dunque questo numero di cittadini, el quale si domanda Consiglio grande, e avendo lui a distribuire tutti li onori, non è dubbio che questo è il signore della città',[32] the only authority legitimising the distribution of honours in Florence. In Savonarola's view, the Consiglio Maggiore embodies a truly popular republic, capable of bringing to the city prosperity and freedom from tyranny.[33]

The fall of Piero de' Medici and the immediate return to Florence of his enemies, along with some internal divisions among the same Medici friends, had convinced the friar that only a republic – *governo largo* – would restore to Florence the much-awaited and needed unity. To this urgent demand Savonarola's answer was the Consiglio Maggiore. But what had some of the *uomini da bene* to say about the Consiglio Maggiore? Did they share Savonarola's belief in the unifying role of the Council?

In some interesting political memoranda written just before the *provvisione* of December 1494 was enacted, some *uomini principali* seemed to welcome the institution of the Consiglio Maggiore, aware, as they had to be, of the difficulty they would meet in establishing a *governo stretto*.[34] This comes to light in Piero

---

[30] *Trattato*, p. 449.

[31] ' . . . bisogna provedere che niuno cittadino abbia autorità, per modo alcuno, di potere dare li beneficii e officii e dignità della città, perché questa è proprio la radice che fa nelle città un tiranno . . . E' necessario dunque instituire, che l'autorità di distribuire li officii e li onori sia in tutto el popolo acciò che uno cittadino non abbia a risguardare all'altro, e ciascuno si reputi equale all'altro, e che non possi fare capo', *ibid.*, pp. 473–4.   [32] *Ibid.*

[33] See *ibid.*, pp. 481–7.

[34] Among the staunchest supporters of the *governo stretto* is to be counted Bernardo Rucellai whose political activity is described by F. Gilbert, 'Bernardo Rucellai and the Orti Oricellari: a study on the origin of modern political thought', *Journal of the Warburg and Courtauld Institutes*, 12 (1949), 101–31, now reprinted in Gilbert, *History. Choice and Commitment* (Cambridge, MA, 1977), pp. 215–46.

Capponi's answer to Domenico Bonsi's proposal on the institution of the Consiglio Maggiore. The new institution, although not perceived as the magical solution to the city's political future, is much respected. In keeping with the aristocratic viewpoint, Capponi asks that a senate be established:

Non fa mentione Messer Domenico di fare uno Consiglio di scelti, il quale è necessarissimo et per fare alchuna electione di più importanza et per fare alcune deliberationi come a Vinegia si costuma, et per adoperarlo più spesso come una pratica et consiglio della Signoria . . . Et questo Consiglio fia molto utile alla libertà nostra, perché la Signoria non oserà di fare cosa alchuna sanza questa pratica, nè potrà dare reputazione ai cittadini in chiamare più uno che un altro.[35]

It is all the more important to note that neither Savonarola nor Domenico Bonsi ever mentions the senate as an essential institution in their popular republic.

In the *grandi*'s view the Consiglio Maggiore, if essential in Florence, ought, however, to be helped in its functioning by a much smaller Council, like a senate. The allusion is here to the Venetian Consiglio dei Pregadi.[36] In Capponi's mind such a Council is to work as a *pratica* in such a way that only a very select group of influential citizens would actually have a voice in it.[37] Furthermore this Council was to check the power of the Signoria which would always act after the Council's deliberations. In Capponi's proposal, then, a small number of *uomini da bene* were to rule the republic, thus dramatically decreasing the prestige and the actual power of the Consiglio Maggiore. Capponi's interest in the Consiglio dei richiesti was to become a major political issue for the Florentine aristocracy for many years to come. And in fact in 1494 a smaller council than the Consiglio Maggiore was established. Such Consiglio degli Ottanta did not, however, fulfill the *grandi*'s demand for a permanent place in Florentine politics. In fact its members had to be elected every six months in the Consiglio Maggiore. Furthermore the Ottanta had very limited power, limited mainly to the election of ambassadors and commissaries.

At the end of the fifteenth century in Florence, supporters of the popular and aristocratic republic challenged each other on this very issue. From a constitutional viewpoint the former wanted all political power in the Consiglio

---

[35] *Ricordi di Piero Capponi*, pp. 162–3 ed. S. Bertelli in his article 'Constitutional reforms in Renaissance Florence', *The Journal of Medieval and Renaissance Studies*, 3 (1973), 139–55, documents, pp. 156–64.

[36] On the impact of the Venetian myth in Florence, see F. Gilbert, 'The Venetian constitution in Florentine political thought' in *Florentine Studies*, N. Rubinstein, ed. (London, 1968), pp. 463–500, now in Gilbert, *History*, pp. 179–214. Venetian in its inspiration is Piero Capponi's demand 'Et che si faccia uno libro, nel quale si scriva tutte le famiglie tanto d'artefici quanto delle arti maggiori, che hanno ad intervenire in detto Consiglio, le quali famiglie siano dichiarate pe' Signori et collegi presenti', *Ricordi*, p. 164.

[37] For the meaning of the *pratica* in Florentine political life, see F. Gilbert, 'Florentine political assumptions in the period of Savonarola and Soderini', *Journal of the Warburg and Courtauld Institutes*, 20 (1957), 187–214, and more recently G. Brucker, *Renaissance Florence* (Berkeley–Los Angeles–London, 1983) 2nd edn, pp. 134–5.

Maggiore, while the latter would have preferred a Consiglio Maggiore playing only a marginal part in the city's policy-making process, thus leaving the most relevant part to the senate. In Florentine constitutional language these two different perspectives on the republic were alluded to by the expressions *governo stretto* and *governo largo* which, however, do not advocate a totally different constitutional organisation of the city.[38] If the *popolani* praised the Consiglio Maggiore because it increased the number of Florentine citizens, the *uomini principali* praised it only to the extent that it proved to be an effective way of preventing any private citizen from becoming a tyrant, something they wanted to avoid at all costs. On this point, Francesco Guicciardini holds that if any citizen of a good republic expects to participate and enjoy the *benefici* the city can offer, it is of the greatest importance:

avere rispetto di non desiderare tanto lo allargare e volere tanto che ognuno partecipi, che ne seguiti qualche disordine o qualche danno al publico, che sia di più importanza che non è il bene che nasce dallo allargare.[39]

Even if a very technical issue regarding the election procedures in the Council is at stake here, Guicciardini, while making his point, expresses a political persuasion which was to become a cornerstone for many Florentine citizens: the quest for a *governo stretto*. Furthermore, Guicciardini, by holding the view that the Consiglio Maggiore was introduced in Florence after the Venetian model[40] sees the revolution of 1494 as an achievement by the *uomini da bene*.

During the first years of the republic, some of the city's *uomini da bene* expressed their criticism of the Consiglio Maggiore by pointing out the need to establish – through a senate – a *governo stretto*. In their government, however, the Consiglio Maggiore would have retained an important place among the many city's institutions, even if not the most prominent. It seems that the same political adversaries of the *governo popolare* in Florence did not dare to attack the Consiglio Maggiore directly: their strategy was to oversee it and to approach the question of the city's reform from an alternative perspective, and in this effort, a major victory was the establishment of the *gonfalonierato a vita* in 1502.

A number of reasons may account for this reform: Florence, threatened by Cesare Borgia's army,[41] was still to recover Pisa and was now also facing a dangerous revolt in Pistoia.[42] Furthermore, dissatisfaction and opposition

---

[38] The most recent allusion to this political terminology is P. Burke, *The Italian Renaissance. Culture and Society in Italy* (Princeton, 1987) 2nd edn, pp. 188–9.

[39] F. Guicciardini, *Discorso per appoggiare* . . . in *Opere inedite*, vol. III, p. 238.

[40] 'Non credete voi onorevoli cittadini, che a Vinegia, a esemplo della quale fu cominciato questo Consiglio grande . . .', *ibid.* p. 247.

[41] 'E però sendo tornato Valentino in Romagna e preparandosi alla impresa di Bologna, sentito che ebbono questo Vitellozzo e gli Orsini . . . considerando che se el Valentino pigliava Bologna, arebbono tutti a stare a sua discrezione, si ristrinsono insieme . . . così accendendosi uno principio di nuovo fuoco, la città diminuì assai la paura del Valentino, e così di Vitellozzo e degli altri', F. Guicciardini, *Storie fiorentine*, p. 196.   [42] See *ibid.* p. 193.

among the members of the Consiglio Maggiore which could not find an effective policy to return Florence to its traditional prosperity, was so serious that a constitutional reform seemed to many the only way out of the city's crisis of the 1500s. In 1501 and 1502 the idea of establishing a new Council – much smaller than the Consiglio Maggiore – was being debated, but it was never presented for approval in the Consiglio Maggiore since there was some fear that it would never have been passed.[43] This being so, the idea of a *gonfaloniere a vita* received more and more support from among the *cittadini principali* who felt confident the Consiglio Maggiore would not oppose such reform. And, in fact, on 26 August 1502 a law was approved establishing the *gonfalonierato a vita*.[44]

Although in recent years many different views have been put forward regarding this office,[45] the fact remains that this reform was patterned after the Venetian dogeship, and that, as such, it was easily thought of as a fulfilment, albeit partial, of the aristocracy's struggle for reform. In the opinion of those who, like the Salviati, had strongly supported the candidacy of Piero Soderini, the new *gonfaloniere* was expected to promote and protect the interests of his supporting group and eventually lay the foundations for an aristocratic republic. But things did not work out that way in the sense that:

Principalmente lui, o perché considerassi che se e' metteva el governo delle cose importanti nelle mani degli uomini da bene, che loro sendo savi e di autorità ne disporrebbono a modo loro e non seguiterebbono el suo parere . . . e così mosso da ambizione, o pure avendo preso sospetto contra ragione, che se gli uomini da bene pigliavano forze vorrebbono ristringere uno stato e cacciare lui di quello grado che aveva acquistato per opera loro . . . e così da ambizione mescolata con sospetto, cominciò a non conferire ogni cosa colle pratiche.[46]

---

[43] ' . . . ma pensare un modo che, mantenendosi el consiglio, si resecassino quanto più si poteva e' mali della città e loro; e' quali erano in somma, che le cose grave e importante si trattavano per mano di chi non le intendeva; e' cittadini savi e di qualità non avevano grado nè reputazione conveniente . . .'. A senate then was a necessity, but even if 'Questa conclusione piaceva assai, ma si dubitava che el popolo, per el grande sospetto che aveva che non si mutassi lo stato, come e' vedessi ordinare deputazione di cittadini non vi concorrerebbe', *ibid.*, p. 188. See also H.C. Butters, *Governors and Government in Early Sixteenth-century Florence 1502–1519* (Oxford, 1985), pp. 43–6.

[44] ASF, Provvisioni, vol. 193, cc. 50r–52r.

[45] For the beginning of Piero Soderini's career see R. Pesman Cooper, 'L'elezione di Pier Soderini a gonfaloniere a vita. Note storiche', *Archivo storico italiano*, 125 (1967), 145–85. This article has to be read together with 'Pier Soderini: aspiring prince or civic leader?', *Studies in Medieval and Renaissance History*, 1 (1978), 71–126, where the author argues that Piero Soderini intended his mandate to strengthen the *governo popolare*. In opposition to this view S. Bertelli is inclined to conceive of Piero Soderini more in terms of making a personal bid for supremacy in Florence. See 'Petrus Soderinus Patriae Parens', in *Bibliothèque d'Humanisme et Renaissance*, 31 (1969), 93–114; 'Pier Soderini 'Vexillifer Perpetuus Reipublicae Florentinae' 1502–1512' in *Studies in Honor of Hans Baron*, pp. 335–46 and 'Uno magistrato per a tempo lungo o uno dogie' in *Studi di storia medievale e moderna per Ernesto Sestan*, vol. II (Florence, 1980), pp. 451–94. Bertelli emphasises the role of France and of Cesare Borgia in Soderini's election and argues strongly that no sooner was the *gonfaloniere* elected than he tried to secure his personal position in the international and domestic political scene. Critical of Bertelli's interpretation is H.C. Butters, 'Piero Soderini and the Golden Age', *Italian Studies*, 33 (1978), 56–71.

[46] F. Guicciardini, *Storie fiorentine*, p. 216.

Despite growing opposition to the *gonfaloniere*'s government, culminating in the reconciliation of the Medici with the Strozzi,[47] Piero Soderini managed to maintain his office until 1512, when the Medici returned to Florence.[48] During these ten years no further constitutional reform took place. In particular, at this point, the Consiglio Maggiore was no longer at the centre of Florentine political and constitutional thinking.

The time for constitutional experimentation was now over in Florence. Another radical reform wave was to be witnessed only in the 1530s, when the Medicean lordship over Florence was institutionally formalised in the Duchy. But before that happened, in the 1520s and 1530s, while the Medici were struggling to have their pre-eminence in Florence recognised, the Consiglio Maggiore re-emerged not only in the writings of the great Florentine republicans, but also in the last Florentine republic. The Consiglio Maggiore had become an essential part of Florentine history, despite the fact that the Mediceans – especially after their return in 1512 – had done their best to destroy even the memory of the revolution of December 1494.

III

Niccolò Machiavelli describes the political situation in Florence after the Medici had returned to the city in 1512 as being potentially explosive:

Essendosi in quel tanto fatto certo nuovo ordine di governo, nel quale non parendo al viceré che vi fusse la sicurtà della casa de' Medici né della lega, significò a questi signori, essere necessario ridurre questo stato nel modo era vivente il magnifico Lorenzo, desideravano li cittadini nobili satisfare a questo, ma temevano non vi concorresse la moltitudine.[49]

Despite this fear, the reform was actually achieved: the Consiglio Maggiore was dismissed,[50] the *Gonfalonierato a vita* abolished, and the Council of the Settanta and Cento restored.[51] This *mutazione di stato* witnessed the clash between the Medici and the great majority of the city's *uomini principali* who had hoped to come to terms with the Medici, now thanks to Lorenzo's political leadership, moving further in the direction of the *principato*.[52]

---

[47] See Melissa M. Bullard, 'Marriage, politics and the family in Florence: The Strozzi–Medici Alliance of 1508', *American Historical Review*, 84 (1979), 668–87.

[48] Now available on Soderini's downfall is R. Pesman Cooper, 'La caduta di Pier Soderini e il 'Governo popolare'. Pressioni esterne e dissenso interno', *Archivo storico italiano*, 43 (1985), 225–60, where the *gonfaloniere's* weak response to the events of 1512 is considered a major reason for his defeat.

[49] Niccolò Machiavelli a una gentildonna, Firenze, post 16 Settembre 1512, in Machiavelli, *Epistolario*, ed. S. Bertelli (Milan, 1969), p. 233.

[50] See L. Landucci, *Diario*, p. 333.

[51] For more details, see G. Silvano, *'Vivere civile' e 'governo misto' a Firenze nel primo Cinquecento* (Bologna, 1985), pp. 23–6.

[52] See R. Devonshire Jones, 'Lorenzo de' Medici, Duca d'Urbino "Signore" of Florence' in *Studies on Machiavelli*, pp. 299–315.

Medicean lordship in Florence did not, however, go unquestioned since it took about two decades before the *principato* could be institutionally recognised.[53] It is hardly a surprise then that during this period the political and ideological debate on the best form of government for Florence reached its peak. In this context the Consiglio Maggiore was broadly discussed, despite the effort of the Medici to cancel its memory. In this debate, affinities and dissimilarities emerge among Florentine republicans, who could not agree on the political significance to be attached to this particular institution. This was a period of intensive thinking about politics, the age of Machiavelli, Guicciardini and Giannotti to mention only a few among the many.

During the last days of Piero Soderini's *gonfalonierato*, at the end of August 1512, Francesco Guicciardini wrote his *Discorso di Logrogno*, an important political document addressed to the broad issue of the best form of government for Florence. For the first time since the beginning of the sixteenth century this short treatise addresses at some length the issue of the Consiglio Maggiore. Regarded as the cornerstone of Florentine liberty, it is praised as the foundation of the *vivere civile*:

E però per fondamento della libertà bisogna el vivere populare, del quale è spirito e basa el consiglio grande, che abbi a distribuire e' magistrati e degnità della città. Tenendo fermo questo, si può fare uno difficilmente grande nella città, perché non sendo in mano sua dare stato e reputazione a persona, non ha chi si truova in magistrato cagione di ubidirgli o per paura o per speranza; levato questo non è la città libera, nè può essere, perché è necessario che la si empia di sette e fazione, e almeno con corso di qualche anno si riduca in mano di uno solo.[54]

Guicciardini maintains that the Consiglio Maggiore, by advocating the exclusive right to distribute the dignities in the state, makes it impossible for a private citizen to usurp power. Although he seems to endorse what looks like the Savonarolan view on the Consiglio Maggiore,[55] at the same time he advocates a privileged role in the political life of the republic for the city's *primi cittadini*. Willing to leave the task of electing the magistrates of the city with the Consiglio Maggiore on the grounds that the Council's choice would naturally fall upon men of great reputation and experience,[56] he is not anxious, for instance, to consult the Council on matters of financial policy requiring such experienced deliberations as may be found only 'nei luoghi più stretti'.[57]

[53] See G. Spini, *Cosimo I e l'indipendenza del principato mediceo* (Florence, 1980). In addition see N. Rubinstein, 'Dalla repubblica al principato' in *Firenze e la Toscana dei Medici nell'Europa del '500*, vol. 1 (Florence, 1983), pp. 159–76. Also interesting is C. Vasoli, 'Cultura e "mitologia" nel principato (considerazioni sulla "Accademia fiorentina")' in Vasoli, *La cultura delle corti* (Bologna, 1980), pp. 159–89. See also R. Cantagalli, *Cosimo I de' Medici granduca di Toscana* (Milan, 1985).

[54] F. Guicciardini, *Discorso di Logrogno*, in *Opere*, vol. 1, pp. 255–6.

[55] This, however, does not mean that F. Guicciardini may not have expressed a more critical view like 'E se bene con questa larghezza vi concorrino alcuni pazzi, molti ignoranti e molti maligni, nondimeno . . .', *ibid*. p. 256.   [56] *Ibid*. p. 257.   [57] *Ibid*. p. 259.

Guicciardini is sceptical of the Consiglio Maggiore's ability to handle those matters of republican life which require extensive experience as is the case of the election of ambassadors or the approval of financial legislation.

For this reason and to check the authority of the *gonfaloniere*

> . . . è necessario darli uno mezzo di uno consiglio di cittadini, a quella similitudine che sono ora li ottanta, el quale consiglio sia di uomini eletti e del fiore della città, con chi si consultino e deliberino tutte le cose importanti della republica. Il che serve a fare che le cose grande non si abbino a consigliare con la multitudine, di che nascerebbe, una soluzione populare . . .[58]

It seems all the more clear at this point how the senate should, in Guicciardini's view of the republic, be entrusted with the most crucial political acts of the state, thus keeping the Consiglio Maggiore far removed from the city's policy-making process. According to him, new legislation, because it affects the whole community, ought to be formally approved in the Consiglio Maggiore, but it should not be debated upon in the same Council: ' . . . venendo giù in consiglio digestite e discusse prima ne' luoghi più stretti e già presupposte utile, non è necessario che le si disputino . . .'[59] and the same holds true for legislation on financial matters which Guicciardini asks to be deliberated on by the very few.[60]

At the end of 1512 Guicciardini has thus laid down the main lines along which an aristocratic republic ought to be founded: between the Consiglio Maggiore – the many – and the Gonfaloniere – the one – there is the senate – the few – the *timone della città*, the expression of the *primi cittadini*'s political wisdom and experience.[61] 'E in effetto tutto 'l pondo del governo si riduce alla fine in sulle spalle di molti pochi, e così fu sempre in ogni republica e a' tempi antichi e a' moderni',[62] a belief which enlightens the oligarchic character of Guicciardini's republican feelings. If the Consiglio Maggiore is maintained, it is only to make it appear that the many have the final word in the city's politics,[63] an illusion the *uomini da bene* would be careful to maintain. From Savonarola's time when the Consiglio Maggiore was thought of as an institution through which more Florentines could become citizens than ever before, the meaning of the reform increasingly faded into shadow. To Guicciardini the Consiglio Maggiore was only the constitutional channel by which the many could approve the deliberations of the few.

A few years later in 1516, when the Medici were well established in power in Florence and the Consiglio Maggiore was no longer a reality, Guicciardini in his *Discorso del modo di assicurare lo stato alla casa de' Medici* allows no role for the

---

[58] *Ibid.* p. 260.   [59] *Ibid.* p. 264–5.   [60] *Ibid.* pp. 265–6.

[61] 'Con questi ha a essere una deputazione di cittadini che sieno el meglio della città; e se bene e' non sono molti quelli che si intendino tanto dello stato che meritino esservi, pure el numero vuole essere largo per conservazione della libertà, acciò che tanto pondo non si riduca tutto in mano di pochi' *ibid.* p. 276.   [62] *Ibid.*, p. 277.

[63] ' . . . avendo le legge a legare ognuno, che e' non si possa dire che le siano state fatte da pochi e sanza universale consenso', *ibid.*, p. 265.

Consiglio. Mentioning the *universale*, he does not regret that this large portion of Florentine citizenship no longer has institutional representation in the Consiglio Maggiore. He only suggests that at this time things would still be good, perhaps even better than during the previous republican regime, if only 'fusse stato possibile che il vivere e conversare con loro [Medici] fussi stato più civile e più equale, a uso di Lorenzo vecchio'.[64]

In this memorandum, Guicciardini points out that the previous republic had come close to the perfect republic during the first years of Piero Soderini's *gonfalonierato*.[65] In his memory it is likely that the reform of 1502 was more important, because more aristocratic in nature, than the reform of 1494. During Lorenzo de Medici's tenure of power the Consiglio Maggiore could no longer be a topic of discussion, given the character and trend of Medicean policy in Florence.

In these years, despite growing opposition to Lorenzo's policy, the Medici in Florence could still count on the powerful support of Leo X, whose worldly name was Giovanni de' Medici.[66] This alliance between Rome and Florence strengthened Medicean policy within and without the city's walls to an extent that only the sudden death of Lorenzo in 1519 and of Leo X in 1521 could shake it. Deprived of its head both in Florence and in Rome, the Medici family looked now to Cardinal Giulio de' Medici as heir to the pope's legacy. The future of Florence was now in the hands of a leader who, at the beginning of the 1520s, seemed anxious to restore the city to its republican past.[67] The reform of the state seemed to be his foremost concern and for this reason he asked that proposals on this issue be presented to him. Among the first who responded to his appeal was Niccolò Machiavelli.

On this occasion he wrote the *Discursus florentinarum rerum post mortem iunioris Laurentii Medices*, a tract in which he set down his thoughts on the reform of the city's government.[68] Aware of writing the *Discursus* for the Medici family whose

---

[64] F. Guicciardini, *Discorso V*, in *Opere inedite*, p. 336.   [65] See *ibid.*, p. 334.

[66] On the reception in Florence of the news of the election to pontificate of the first Medici pope, see G. Silvano, '*Vivere civile*', pp. 30–2.

[67] ' . . . fu costante opinione comunemente di ognuno che la nostra città sotto il reggimento de' Medici non fusse mai governata con maggiore apparenza di civiltà . . . che al tempo che essa fu governata da Giulio cardinale de' Medici', J. Nardi, *Istorie della città di Firenze*, ed. A. Gelli (Florence, 1858), vol. II, p. 64. The Latin oration *de republica* Alessandro de' Pazzi wrote for Giulio de' Medici illuminates this atmosphere of political expectation. See Appendix III in Silvano '*Vivere civile*', pp. 182–92.

[68] Printed in N. Machiavelli, *Opere*, ed. S. Bertelli, vol. II (Verona, 1979), pp. 393–418. For the date of composition see Bertelli's note following the *Discursus*, pp. 419–24 where the end of 1520 or the very beginning of 1521 is suggested. On this matter see also G. Guidi, 'Niccolò Machiavelli e i progetti di riforme costituzionali a Firenze nel 1522' in *Machiavellismo e Antimachiavellici nel cinquecento* (Florence, 1969), pp. 252–68.

[69] 'Vero è che, essendo venuta la cosa in termine, come è, per la morte del duca, che si ha a ragionare di nuovi modi di governi, mi pare, per mostrare la fede mia verso la Santità Vostra . . .', Machiavelli, *Discursus*, p. 396. S.N. Stephens has some interesting remarks on the relationship between the Medici and Machiavelli after 1512 in his 'Machiavelli's Prince and the Florentine revolution of 1512', *Italian Studies*, 41 (1986), 45–61.

benevolenza he had been struggling to obtain since 1513,[69] Machiavelli outlines a constitutional reform which the Medici could easily welcome. As is the custom in this kind of memorandum, the approach to the subject matter is historical: past Florentine history provides the ground to support the view that the city's government needs reforms. The first section of the *Discursus*, especially the part dealing with the *governo popolare*, which may give a sense of what Machiavelli would have said in his *Istorie*, had he covered the period,[70] brings the author into a close debate with his contemporaries. Here he criticises those reform projects which, patterned after the fifteenth-century Medicean model,[71] look back nostalgically to the past, and those which, looking at the beginning of the *governo popolare*, are for an indiscriminate broadening of the *reggimento*.

This criticism helps Machiavelli to present his reform project as the most suitable for Florence. He argues that, given the 'equality' existing among its citizens only a republic may be successfully established in the city: 'E per il contrario, a volere uno principato in Firenze, dove è una grandissima equalità, sarebbe necessario ordinarvi prima inequalità'.[72] From this general view of the social composition of the Florentine citizenry, the reform has to take into consideration that in Florence there are three sorts of people whose ambitions ought to be fulfilled in the government of the city.[73] The conclusion is that the *primi* should sit in the Signoria, the *mezzani* in the Consiglio degli scelti, and the *ultimi* in the Consiglio de' mille.[74]

In this constitutional reform project – very conventional in essence – there is an element of novelty in that Machiavelli makes it clear that the *imborsazione* for the city's magistrates has to be carried out by *accoppiatori* chosen for their loyalty to the Medici family.[75] Machiavelli is here for an oligarchic republic, certainly *più stretta* than Savonarola's *governo popolare* had been. His recommendation as to how members of the inner circle of the *reggimento* have to be selected shows how deeply Machiavelli perceived the political role of the *accoppiatori*, the magistrates who safeguarded Medicean pre-eminence in the fifteenth century. He now tries to make good use of these magistrates in a constitutional framework including the Consiglio Maggiore. In the 1520s, Machiavelli seems to disregard an essential aspect of the reform of 1494. He has no interest in the Council as a means of broadening Florentine citizenship, as was the case in 1494. In the *Discursus*, the Council is not the most important institution of the republic, and

---

[70] In this section of the *Discursus*, there is no direct mention of the Consiglio Maggiore.

[71] The most comprehensive study of the subject is E. Gusberti, 'Un mito del Cinquecento: Lorenzo il Magnifico', *Bullettino dell'Istituto storico italiano per il medio evo e archivio muratoriano*, 91 (1984), 183–279. [72] N. Machiavelli's *Discursus*, p. 403.

[73] 'Coloro che ordinano una R. P. debbono dare luogo ad tre diverse qualità di huomini, che sono in tucte le ciptà: cioè primi mezzani et ultimi,' Machiavelli, *Discursus*, p. 404.

[74] See *Discursus*, pp. 405–9.

[75] 'Et perché gli vostri amici si certificassino andando a partito del Consiglio, d'essere imborsati, deputassi V. S.tà otto accoppiatori, i quali stando al secreto, potessino dare il partito a chi e' volessino et non lo potessino torre ad alcuno. Et perché l'universale credesse che fussino imborsati quelli che lui vincessi, si permettessi che il Consiglio mandassi al securo dua ciptadini squittinati da llui per essere testimoni delle imborsazioni', N. Machiavelli, *Discursus*, p. 409.

its very existence responds largely to the Machiavellian wish to cast his reform thoughts in a form already traditional even among the *primi cittadini*.

Machiavelli's attitude towards the Council has to be placed in a context broader than the one offered in the *Discursus*. In a largely historical context, how did he look at the crucial events of late 1494? As is well known, Machiavelli expressed mixed feelings about Savonarola's doings,[76] and it is apparent that he never believed the friar could be counted among the great reformers of the past.

E però conviene essere ordinato in modo, che, quando non credono più, si possa fare credere loro per forza. Moisè, Ciro, Teseo e Romulo non arebbono possuto fare osservare loro lungamente le loro constituzioni, se fussino stati disarmati; come ne' nostri tempi intervenne a fra' Girolamo Savonerola; il quale ruinò ne' sua ordini nuovi, come la moltitudine cominciò a non crederli, e lui non aveva modo a tenere fermi quelli che avevano creduto, né a far credere e' discredenti.[77]

Machiavelli, while not acknowledging fully the friar's contribution to the establishment of the Consiglio Maggiore, seems anxious to point out the weakness of the *governo popolare* as it was established in 1494. Because Savonarola, as well as the *reggimento* as a whole, did not consider the defence of the new government by means of a *militia propria* the foremost political concern, his efforts were doomed to failure.

Savonarola overlooked what Machiavelli considered to be a cornerstone in the life of a healthy republic: the tight and vital relationship between the *buone armi* and the *buoni ordini*:

tutte l'arti che si ordinano in una civiltà per cagione del bene comune degli uomini sarebbono vani, se non fussono preparate le difese loro . . . i buoni ordini, sanza il militare aiuto, non altrimenti si disordinano . . .[78]

The truly popular republic provides for its defence, if not for its expansion. In Machiavelli's view the establishment of the Consiglio Maggiore is but one aspect, albeit extremely important, of a much more articulated constitutional reform project necessary to the foundation and preservation of a truly popular republic. After only a few years of service to the republic in the second Chancery, could Machiavelli, under the *gonfaloniere's* protection, engage in what proved to be the difficult task of providing the *governo popolare* with the appropriate military defence. He showed a quasi-religious commitment to the organisation of the *militia*. Furthermore when, between 1519 and 1521, he wrote *L'arte della guerra*, Machiavelli strongly defended his *ordinanza*, and the

[76] See N. Machiavelli's letter to Ricciardo Becchi of 9 March 1498 in N. Machiavelli, *Epistolario*, pp. 11–16.
[77] N. Machiavelli, *Il principe* in *Opere*, vol. I, ed. S. Bertelli (Milan, 1968), pp. 20–1.
[78] N. Machiavelli, *L'Arte della guerra* in *Opere*, vol. II, ed. S. Bertelli (Verona, 1979), p. 11.

idea that nothing expressed the vitality and perfect condition of the republic better than its ability to avoid corruption through the exercise of its military strength.[79]

The republic, as a product of human activity, is subject to ups and downs that will eventually lead it to face either a foreign threat or internal turmoil.[80] This being so, the republican *militia* is not only a valuable means of defence, but a display of its virtue. In the *Discorsi*, Machiavelli outlines a republic in which the question of citizenship goes beyond juridical considerations to the point where it involves a political issue. Machiavelli finds that the inner problem of the Florentine republic resides in the fact that those who are fully-fledged citizens and consequently members of the Consiglio Maggiore, call upon others – not Florentine citizens – to defend and possibly expand the limits of 'their' republic. If placed in this conceptual framework, Machiavelli's scant allusions to the Consiglio Maggiore may be taken not only as indirectly blaming Savonarola and the *primi cittadini*, but as an indication that for him the republic cannot be embodied only in the Consiglio Maggiore.[81]

Although in his correspondence and in his writings Machiavelli hardly mentions the Consiglio Maggiore, he does, however, maintain the belief that authority in the state must rest with the people. This fundamental assumption is articulated fully in the *Discorsi sopra la prima deca di Tito Livio*. Comparing the famous republics of Sparta, Venice and Rome, Machiavelli shows the superiority of the Roman republic on the grounds that the 'guardia della libertà' was in Rome entrusted to the *universale*, and not to the *grandi* because

a' legislatori di Roma era necessario fare una delle due cose, o volere che Roma stesse quieta come le sopradette republiche; o non adoperare la plebe in guerra, come i Viniziani; o non aprire la via a' forestieri, come gli Spartani.[82]

[79] 'Dunque lodate voi l'ordinanza? Perché, volete voi che io la danna?' N. Machiavelli, *L'arte della guerra* in *Opere*, p. 28. And again on the man's virtue 'in quale uomo debbe ricercare la patria maggiore fede, che in colui che ha a promettere di morire per lei', *ibid.* p. 11. 'E qualunque cittadino che ha in tale esercizio altro fine, non è buono; e qualunque città si governa altrimenti non è bene ordinata', *ibid.* pp. 21–22. For other Machiavellian writings on the issue, see *La cagione dell'ordinanza, dove la si truovi et quel che bisogni fare* in *ibid.* pp. 251–5; *Provisione prima per le fanterie del 6 Dicembre 1506* in *ibid.* pp. 259–82; and *Ghiribizi d'Ordinanza*, in *ibid.* pp. 359–63. Important remarks in J.G.A. Pocock, *The Machiavellian Moment. Florentine Political Thought and the Atlantic Republican Tradition* (Princeton, 1975), pp. 199–202. The Machiavellian blame for the 'businessman', held responsible for leaving the Florentine militia in a state of degradation, is described by M. Hulliung, *Citizen Machiavelli* (Princeton, 1983), pp. 65–6. On the *Arte della guerra* see also F. Gilbert, 'Machiavelli: The renaissance of the art of war' in *Makers of Modern Strategy from Machiavelli to the Nuclear Age*, P. Paret, ed. with the collaboration of Gordon A. Graig and F. Gilbert (Princeton, 1986), pp. 11–31.

[80] 'E sanza dubio credo, che, potendosi, tenere la cosa bilanciata in questo modo, che e' sarebbe il vero vivere politico e la vera quiete d'una città. Ma sendo tutte le cose degli uomini in moto, e non potendo stare salde, conviene che le salghino o che le scendino; e a molte cose che la ragione non l'induce, t'induce la necessità', *Arte della guerra* in *Opere*, p. 113.

[81] See *Discorsi*. I, 47, pp. 194–5 where he describes the events of 1494 without mentioning the institution of the Consiglio Maggiore. A little more in his *Storie fiorentine*, cxii, pp. 124–7; cxvii, p. 181. [82] N. Machiavelli, *Discorsi*, i. 61, p. 111.

At this point, then, it comes to light that the republic of the *Discorsi* and the republic of the *Discursus* are not quite the same. Defined in highly idealistic terms in the *Discorsi*, the republic of the *Discursus* is in Machiavelli's own words in fact a monarchy:

Parci, considerato tutto questo ordine come republica, e senza la vostra autorità, che non le manchi cosa alcuna, secondo che di sopra si è a lungo disputato e discorso: ma se si considera vivente la Santità Vostra e monsignore reverendissimo, ella è una monarchia.[83]

On the one hand, Machiavelli trusts the city's liberty to the Consiglio de' mille, for: 'Senza satisfare all'universale, non si fece mai alcuna republica stabile et non si satisferà mai all'universale dei ciptadini fiorentini se non si riapre la sala.'[84] On the other, he stresses that its power of electing the city's magistrates – with the important exception of the members of the Sessantacinque, Dugento, and Otto di balìa – must be politically controlled by the Medici, through their *accoppiatori.*

The *universale* of the *Discorsi* is something different from the *universale* of the *Discursus*.[85] Furthermore, in the *Discursus* a central theme of the *Discorsi* is somehow missing: the cyclic relationship between *buoni ordini* and *buone armi*.[86] It is all the more important to note that in the *Discursus*, Machiavelli avoids dealing at length with the issue of the *militia*, thus leaving the impression that this tract, because of the historical circumstances in which it was composed, reveals Machiavelli's republican persuasions only in a certain measure.

Alessandro de' Pazzi criticised Machiavelli's *Discursus* on the grounds that any attempt at departing from tradition in dealing with the reform of the city government is to be avoided:

E però io dico, ch'io fuggirei tutte le spezie di governi nuovi, delle quali so esserne date forme a V. S. Reverendissima, massime dal Machiavello: la qual forma non mi piace, perchè è insolita a questa Città, e stravagante . . .[87]

Alessandro de' Pazzi does not articulate his criticism of Machiavelli's *Discursus* in more detail, turning immediately to the issue of Florentine government

---

[83] N. Machiavelli, *Discursus*, p. 413.   [84] *Ibid.* pp. 409–10.
[85] See Machiavelli, *Discorsi*, I, 5. On this fundamental chapter are to be read F. Guicciardini's remarks in his *Considerazioni sui Discorsi di Machiavelli* in Guicciardini, *Opere*, I, pp. 617–19.
[86] 'Dove è buona milizia, conviene che sia buono ordine, e rade volte anco non vi sia buona fortuna', *Discorsi*, I, 4, p. 105. Also in *De principatibus, ibid.*, ch. XII, p. 38 it is said 'E, perché non può essere buone legge dove non sono buone arme, e dove sono buone arme conviene sieno buone legge.' An echo of this argument is in F. Guicciardini's *Dialogo del reggimento di Firenze*, in *Opere*, vol. I. Book II, p. 449: 'Voi avete laudato le arme de' Romani come meritatamente sono laudate da ognuno, e biasimato molto il governo di drento che ancora è secondo la opinione di molti; pure io ho udito disputare qualcuno in contrario, e le ragioni che loro allegano sono che ponendo quello fondamento che nessuno nega né può negare, che la milizia sua fussi buona, bisogna confessare che la città avessi buoni ordini, altrimenti non sarebbe stato possible che avessi buona disciplina militare.'
[87] Alessandro de' Pazzi, 'Discorso di Alessandro de' Pazzi al Cardinale Giulio de' Medici – Anno 1522', *Archivio storico italiano*, I (1842), 429.

reform. He proposes a mixed government, patterned after the Aristotelian paradigm,[88] and comprising a Prince, a senate, and the Consiglio Maggiore. The senate, whose members ought not to exceed 100 men and are expected to be life-members, is the soul of the republic, while the Consiglio Maggiore's authority is lessened dramatically. This institution is not to be trusted for in the past 'bisognava adulare al Consiglio Grande e ciurmarlo, volendo vincere cosa buona, ovvero invocare i nove cori delli angeli'.[89] In the constitutional reform project that Alessandro de' Pazzi addressed to Cardinal Giulio de' Medici, the Consiglio Maggiore remains, but the senate is considered the soul of the republic, as was common in the writings of the Florentine *uomini da bene*.

Among them, at about the same time and up to 1525, Guicciardini was working on the *Dialogo del reggimento di Firenze*, the masterpiece which, better than any other work, outlines the features of the aristocratic republic to be founded eventually in Florence. The *Dialogo* is not to be read as a utopian plan[90] for, deeply rooted in the past Florentine tradition of thought, it presents a constitutional reform which could be put into practice.[91] In the first book, one of the speakers, namely Piero Capponi, maintains that after Piero de' Medici's downfall in 1494, while some *uomini da bene* aimed at establishing a *governo stretto*, Savonarola, together with another group of influential Florentines, managed to establish the *governo largo* and the Consiglio Maggiore.[92] In the dialogue this institution, then, becomes the target of Bernardo del Nero's attack on the *governo popolare*. In essence the attack is made on the grounds that

avendo voi, o per dire meglio chi ha ordinato questo governo nuovo, rimesso al consiglio grande la elezione di tutti gli offici, che non si possa aspettarne altro che molti errori, perché el popolo non sarà buono giudice delle qualità degli uomini, nè misurerà con diligenza quanto pesi ognuno, anzi andrà alla grossa e si governerà più con certe opinioni che andranno fuora senza fondamento, e per dire meglio con certi gridi, che con ragione.[93]

Guicciardini makes Bernardo express here the view of the most radical among the *uomini da bene*, of those, like Bernardo Rucellai, who would never come to terms with the *governo popolare*.

---

[88] Translations of Aristotle's political and moral works had been available in Latin since the Middle Ages. It was, however, among Florentine humanists that Aristotle was recognised among the leading political theorists of the republican city-state. See G. Silvano, '*Vivere civile*', p. 169 and the fundamental C. Schmitt, *Aristotle and the Renaissance* (Cambridge, MA, 1983) where other relevant literature is discussed. To emphasise the presence of Aristotelianism in Renaissance Florence is not meant to neglect other sources of classical thought certainly vital in the same milieu, as is the case for Stoicism. On this point see Q. Skinner, *The Foundations*, vol. I, *passim*.

[89] Alessandro de' Pazzi, 'Discorso' p. 430.

[90] See V. de Caprariis, *Francesco Guicciardini dalla politica alla storia* (Bari, 1950), p. 81 and G. Sasso, *Niccolò Machiavelli. Storia del suo pensiero politico* (Bologna, 1980), pp. 628–44.

[91] 'Ma io non so se a noi è a proposito el procedere così, perché non parliamo per ostentazione e vanamente, ma con speranza che el parlare nostro possa ancora essere di qualche frutto,' *Dialogo*, II, p. 399. The same attitude is expressed in *ibid.*, pp. 419; 439.

[92] See *Dialogo*, I, p. 316.   [93] *Ibid.*, pp. 341–2.

But in the second book of the *Dialogo*, Bernardo del Nero attenuates his position to the extent that the Consiglio Maggiore is given a role in the new aristocratic republic. This apparent contradiction between the first and second book – between blame and praise for the Consiglio Maggiore – has often been pointed out and explained in different ways.[94] It may, however, be argued that Bernardo's change of mind about the Consiglio Maggiore can be understood by considering the different character of the two books: the first is a retrospective analysis of the revolution of 1494 and a comparison between the Medicean government and the *governo popolare*, whilst the second is a constitutional reform project. Although in historical perspective those *grandi* who were for a *governo stretto* might well regard the introduction of the Consiglio Maggiore as their political defeat, in more practical and political terms their attitude became more favourable towards this institution as they realised how the Consiglio Maggiore could serve their cause too, by preventing any private citizen from usurping power.

Bernardo himself seems to be aware of the difficulty in reconciling his opinions on the Council as expressed in the two books and perhaps for this very reason he states:

Però si ha a attendere non solo che el governo sia populare, ma ancora che sia bene ordinato, e per questo ho io discorso e' difetti di che io ho paura, per dare occasione di pensare a ricorreggergli. E' quali principalmente sono, che le cose importanti verranno in mano di chi non saprà deliberarle né governarle . . .[95]

This being so, Bernardo's outline of the constitutional role of the Consiglio Maggiore in his aristocratic republic is all the more important.

In Bernardo's view, the soul of the *governo popolare* is the Consiglio Grande, since it includes all qualified Florentine citizens. Full sovereign power rests with the Council which, then, has authority to bestow honours and distribute official state posts.[96] But this Council should not be entrusted with any important deliberation for 'Non bisogna mettere la salute dello infermo in mano di medico imperito, né in mano del popolo, per la incapacità sua.'[97] On this assumption – which is also Bernardo's point in the first book – the Consiglio Maggiore ought only to enact new legislation, leaving to much smaller bodies of citizens the

[94] See N. Rubinstein, 'Guicciardini politico' in *Francesco Guicciardini 1483–1983. Nel V Centenario della nascita* (Florence, 1984), pp. 161–89, and G. Cadoni, 'Per l'interpretazione del 'Dialogo del reggimento di Firenze' di Francesco Guicciardini', *Storia e Politica*, 22 (1983), 625–73. An important study of Guicciardini's *Dialogo* is G. Sasso, 'Sul Dialogo del reggimento di Firenze in Sasso, *Per Francesco Guicciardini. Quattro studi* (Rome, 1984), pp. 181–253. Finally, see Pocock, *The Machiavellian Moment*, pp. 219–271.

[95] *Dialogo*, II, p. 401.

[96] 'El fondamento principale adunche, e la anima del governo populare, è come avete fatto voi, el consiglio grande, cioè uno consiglio universale di tutti quegli che secondo gli ordini nostri sono abili a avere gli offici della città, e che hanno la età legitima di intervenirvi che debbe essere da' 24 anni in su; e questo consiglio ha a essere distributore di tutti gli uffici, onori e dignità, eccetti quegli pochi . . .' *ibid.*, pp. 401–2.   [97] *Ibid.*

discussion and formulation of the legislation itself.[98] In this sense, Bernardo asks that policy made by the few be approved by the many. Something of the popular government is thus retained, although in essence this republic is oligarchic. If Bernardo maintains that the Consiglio Maggiore is the *principe* of the city, this may well be due to Guicciardini's use of key political terms characteristic of the Florentine political vocabulary of his time.

For in Bernardo's judgement the real soul of government is the senate, since it numbers all the wisest and most politically experienced citizens of Florence. Bernardo's comparison between the governments of Florence and Venice must be read in this sense.

E se bene ha nome diverso da quello che vogliamo fare noi, perché si chiama governo di gentiluomini e el nostro si chiamerà di populo, non per questo è di spezie diversa, perché non è altro che uno governo nel quale intervengono universalmente tutti quegli che son abili agli uffici, né vi si fa distinzione o per ricchezza o per stiatte, come si fa quando governano gli ottimati.[99]

And indeed it was public knowledge that Venice was an aristocratic republic. No surprise, then, if Bernardo del Nero devotes several pages to the senate's role in the republic where the *uomini da bene*'s ethos emerges in its most refined formulation. In the senate sit only the *uomini da bene* whose wisdom is at the service of the city's needs. Furthermore senatorial authority will prove to be also a check on the *gonfaloniere's* power and a corrective to the Consiglio Maggiore's ignorance.[100] In Bernardo's constitutional thinking, then, the senate and not the Consiglio Maggiore is the most relevant agency of the state if

Questo senato ha adunche insino qui queste autorità: deliberare le cose importanti; di più vincere le provisione prima che vadino al consiglio grande, eleggere gli imbasciadori e commessari e lo ufficio de' dieci, oltre a qualche altra elezione di che io dirò de sotto.[101]

Before 1527, then, Florentine republicans did not advocate a totally different constitution for their city. There seems to be general agreement on the fact that the new republican constitution would have to be essentially articulated in three major institutions: the Consiglio Maggiore, the senate, and the *gonfalonierato*. Of course, as pointed out previously, differences do exist, but the essential fact remains that the same *cittadini principali* in the course of time did change their attitude towards the Consiglio Maggiore. In Guicciardini's or Alessandro de' Pazzi's writings the Consiglio Maggiore is something different, however, from the Consiglio Maggiore which had gathered in Florence at the end of the fifteenth century. From a position of absolute supremacy in 1494, the Council is

[98] Però allo intento nostro basta che el consiglio grande, che non è altro che el popolo, abbia queste condizioni [. . .] che non si possa fare leggi nuove nè alterare le vecchie sanza la approvazione di questo consiglio; non dico deliberazione, ma approvazione, perché il fare delle leggi nuove o correggere le vecchie ha a essere deliberato in consigli più stretti . . .,' *ibid.*

[99] *Ibid.*, p. 406.   [100] See *ibid.*, p. 419.   [101] *Ibid.*, p. 421.

now, in the 1520s, placed by the *uomini da bene* in an ancillary position to the senate. By the mid-1520s the Consiglio Maggiore had become essential in the political discourse of Florentine republicans.

IV

In May 1527 the Medici were once more overthrown,[102] and, as had happened in 1494 and in 1512, the city's *cittadini principali* did their best to secure a permanent place for themselves in the soon to be restored Florentine republic. In this atmosphere of political expectation among the city's republicans, the Consiglio Maggiore was intensively debated, and its restoration was very much hoped for. At this time in the Palazzo Vecchio the Venetian constitution was being widely discussed on the basis of a very recent and fairly accurate account of its institutions as provided by Donato Giannotti in his *Della republica de' viniziani*.[103] Giannotti immediately gained a great reputation among Florentine reformers of the last republic, and became a protégé of the *gonfaloniere* Niccolò Capponi to whom he addressed a brief *Discorso sopra il fermare il governo di Firenze*.[104]

In Giannotti's view the republic must fulfil the different ambitions of its citizens by granting the many liberty, the few liberty and honour, and the very few monarchical authority. In institutional terms, the Consiglio Maggiore, the senate and the *gonfalonierato* together with the Procurators were expected to satisfy these different ambitions. The *universale*, then, whose ambition is liberty, will sit in the Consiglio Maggiore, in fact:

Quel membro che ha a rappresentare la popularità, è necessario che sia uno aggregato di tutti li cittadini; cioè di tutti quelli che godono il benefizio: perché propriamente questi sono cittadini, essendo cittadino chi è partecipe di comandare e obbedire. E questo membro è quello il quale debbe essere il signore della città; perchè altrimenti non rappresenterebbe la città, se non fosse signore di far le leggi e distribuire i magistrati . . .[105]

This view echoes thoughts and ideas surrounding the first establishment of the Council in 1494. Although Giannotti seems not to share fully with Florentine

---

[102] The League of Cognac of 1526 between Francis I and Clement VII against Charles V was not successful and its defeat paved the way for the overthrow of the Medici in Florence after Rome had been captured. Among the many contemporary historical writings on these events see F. Vettori, 'Sacco di Roma. Dialogo' in Vettori, *Scritti storici e politici*, ed. E. Niccolini (Bari, 1972), pp. 275–96.

[103] On the *Republica de' Viniziani* see G. Cadoni, *L'utopia repubblicana di Donato Giannotti* (Milan, 1978).

[104] *Discorso sopra il fermare il governo di Firenze l'anno 1527. Indiritto al Magnifico Gonfaloniere di Giustizia Niccolò di Piero Capponi* in D. Giannotti, *Opere politiche e letterarie*, ed. F.-L. Polidori, 2 vols. (Florence, 1850), vol. 1, pp. 3–15. For a good introduction to Giannotti, see R. Starn's introduction to *Donato Giannotti and his Epistolae* (Geneva, 1968), pp. 1–58.

[105] *Ibid.*, p. 4.

uomini da bene the persuasion that the senate ought to be the *timone dello stato*, he does maintain, however, that the *universale* is only expected to enact what the senate has approved already. The Council is the foundation of the republic in that it would always act as a check on any attempt the few might make to have legislation harmful to the common good of the republic passed.[106]

Giannotti's position becomes even clearer if compared with what a *cittadino principale* like Niccolò Guicciardini had to say at about the same time. Between the two no disagreement exists on the need for a Consiglio Maggiore, a senate, and a Prince in a good republic. Substantial differences appear in that while Giannotti emphasises the pivotal role of the Council in the political life of the republic, Niccolò Guicciardini carefully warns that:

Et perché le nominationi cattive procedono in gran parte dalla qualità delli homini tracti al nominare, si potrebbe provedere che alla electione di ogni magistrato si trahessi dalla borsa de' senatori . . . E quali essendo homini di qualità, nominerebbono bene.[107]

The republican experiment of 1527, though, was soon to come to an end, without bringing to light any new view of the Consiglio Maggiore. The political expectations that had surrounded the Council in the fifteenth century were now, after thirty years, brought on to the scene again. In April 1529 Niccolò Capponi was deposed and Francesco Carducci and Raffaello Girolami took over his office. During this time the regime became increasingly more hostile to members of the city's past regime to the extent that a large number of them were either banished or convicted on political and not criminal charges.[108] During this attack on the men of the old state in August 1530, Florence surrendered to the joint papal and imperial troops after a long siege and a strenuous defence. Once more the Medici returned to the city, and once more a period of discussion on the best form of government for Florence was set to take place.

At this point, the *cittadini principali* could not but come to terms with the Medici family which was now expected to play a prominent role in the political life of the city, supported, as it was, by Pope Clement VII in Rome, in the world Giulio de' Medici. In this new context, F. Guicciardini's *Discorsi*, composed between 1531 and 1532, prove very interesting. The author believes the creation of a new Council – a senate – including all the Medici's friends and supporters, essential to the new state. He argues that 'noi non possiamo fare stato di molti, perchè lo universale non ci è amico, e perchè non ci è panno da abbracciare tanti'.[109] When writing for the Medici, F. Guicciardini is careful not to mention

---

[106] 'Il senato vorrebbe essere come di sopra è detto a vita: e la elezione sua si facessi dal Consiglio Grande per le più fave,' *ibid.*, p. 6.

[107] N. Guicciardini, 'Discursus de Florentinae Rei Publicae Ordinibus' in R. von Albertini, *Das Florentinische Staatsbewusstsein im Übergang von der Republik zur Prinzipat* (Berne, 1955), p. 379.

[108] See J.N. Stephens, *The Fall of the Florentine Republic 1512–1530* (Oxford, 1983), pp. 222–30.

[109] F. Guicciardini, *Discorso VII* in *Opere Inedite*, vol. II, p. 356.

the Consiglio Maggiore which would have soon been taken as a sign of open sympathy with the *governo popolare*. Other contemporary memoranda written on this topic by a number of *primi cittadini* like Ruberto Acciaiuoli, Francesco Vettori and Luigi Guicciardini share Francesco Guicciardini's disregard for the *governo popolare* and for the Council. Once more, Florentine *uomini da bene* were trying to safeguard their place in the new Medicean Duchy.[110]

In April 1532 a new constitution was enacted in Florence. Alessandro de' Medici was formally recognised as *Duca della repubblica fiorentina*, thus leaving no doubt about the political and constitutional destiny of the city.[111] The Consiglio Maggiore was never again to be a constitutional reality. Staunch republicans, however, died hard. Many *fuoriusciti* continued to fight what they regarded as the tyranny of the Medici, until they were defeated at Montemurlo in 1537.[112] Eventually only the memory of the Consiglio Maggiore survived the events, for Donato Giannotti in his *Republica fiorentina* and Francesco Guicciardini in his *Storia d'Italia* reconsidered this institution at some length in political and historical perspective.

In Book II of the *Republica fiorentina*, Giannotti brings to light in a highly suggestive and convincing way the many reasons why the two past Florentine republics of 1494 and 1527 were bound to collapse. Despite their being republics, their government was *stretto* 'quantunque a molti nostri savi ella paresse tanto larga'.[113] Giannotti maintains that the authority bestowed upon the city's magistrates far exceeded the power that any such magistrate ought to possess in a republic. Only theoretically, then, was the Consiglio Maggiore the foundation of the republic for 'la creazione de' magistrati sanza dubbio era in potere degli assai, perché tutta dependeva dal Gran Consiglio' but 'la deliberazione della pace e guerra era in potestà del magistrato de' Dieci', that is, in the hands of the few,[114] as were the administration of justice and the actual handling of the legislative procedures.

To amend, at least theoretically, the mistakes of the past, Giannotti in Book II describes in detail the constitutional form of a truly popular republic. In doing

---

110 See F. Gilbert, 'Alcuni discorsi di uomini politici fiorentini e la politica di Clemente VII per la restaurazione medicea', *Archivio storico italiano*, 93 (1935), 3–24. The memoranda here discussed are in *Archivio storico italiano*, 1 (1842), pp. 433–67.

111 See F. Diaz, *Il Granducato di Toscana. I Medici* (Turin, 1976), pp. 50–83. This is vol. 13, part 1 of the *Storia d'Italia* edited by G. Galasso. Also fundamental is E. Fasano Guarini, *Lo stato mediceo di Cosimo I* (Florence, 1973).

112 See R. Starn, *Contrary Commonwealth. The Theme of Exile in Medieval and Renaissance Italy* (Berkeley and Los Angeles, 1982). On the political activity of some *fuoriusciti*, see A. Stella, 'Utopie e velleità insurrezionali dei filoprotestanti italiani (1545–1547)', *Bibliothèque d'Humanisme et Renaissance*, 27 (1965), 133–61, documents, pp. 162–82.

113 I have prepared a new edition of Giannotti's *Republica fiorentina*, based on the autograph manuscript Magliabechiano xxx, 230 of the Florentine Biblioteca nazionale which is in press in the series Travaux d'Humanisme et Renaissance, Geneva. The following quotations are, however, from F. Diaz' reprint of Polidori's edition (Milan, 1974), *Opere*, vol. I, II, 10, p. 241.

114 *Ibid.*, p. 221.

so, he emphasises the role of the Consiglio Maggiore. Membership of the Council ought to be large enough to include, along with the *grandi* and *mediocri*, the *popolari*. They pay taxes to the city's treasury and therefore they may well expect to be considered citizens of the republic. This is Giannotti's political argument, but

perché noi dicemmo che non ci volevamo discostare molto da quello che si era usato ne' tempi passati; perciò lasseremo in dietro questi popolari, e ci contanteremo che ciascuno anno se ne mandi a partito buono numero, come si usava; persuadendosi ciascuno che quanti più ne saranno ammessi a' magistrati, tanto maggiore basa e miglior fondamento si farà alla republica. Dico adunque che in questo consiglio deono convenire tutti quelli che sono abili a' magistrati . . . e perché il detto Consiglio debbe essere il signore della Città (altrimenti la republica non inclinerebbe nel popolo) debbe avere in potestà sua quelle azioni le quali sono principali nella republica, ed abbracciano tutta la forza dello stato. Queste sono quattro: cioè, la creazione de' magistrati; le deliberazioni della pace e guerra; la introduzione delle leggi; e le provocazioni.[115]

Attachment and respect for tradition had always played a fundamental role in Florentine thinking about politics. This recalls Machiavelli's persuasion that any political reform ought to look and go back to the *principi*.[116] Nevertheless, although Giannotti does recognise the need to broaden the social basis of the Consiglio Maggiore, he is not willing to go too far in this direction.

The Council is to have the final word in any relevant political and juridical matter of the republic. On this score it is all the more important to note that, while leaving to the senate the handling of foreign policy, Giannotti is careful to point out that senators do depend on the Council for their election.[117] Machiavelli himself in the *Discursus* had seen the senate as an independent body from the Council. For Giannotti, the senate has to retain its traditional political power and prestige,[118] a position, however, which is never to surpass the political authority of the Consiglio Maggiore.

At the same time, Giannotti's theory of the Florentine republic involves more than the presence of the Council. In the *Republica fiorentina* the issue of the *militia cittadina* is carefully investigated. Giannotti argues for the *militia* on the assumption of the citizens' natural drive towards it. Only afterwards does he put the issue in political perspective by maintaining that a thorough conscription should be carried out of all suitable men, regardless of the fact that they may or may not have the *beneficio*.[119] In speculative terms, in Giannotti's

---

[115] *Ibid.*, p. 282.   [116] See Machiavelli, *Discorsi*, I, 25; III, 1.
[117] Giannotti, *Republica fiorentina*, p. 283.   [118] *Ibid.*, pp. 285–7.
[119] ' . . . che se si dovessino non solamente quelli armare che chiamiamo benefiziati, ma gli altri ancora, che abitano la città e son partecipi de' carichi di quella, possedendo in essa, o case, o possessioni; e non solamente vogliamo questi armare, ma eziandio il Contado e Dominio,' *ibid.*, IV, 1. A remarkable and suggestive glorification of the citizen military *virtù* is Giannotti's description of Francesco Ferrucci's behaviour during the siege in *ibid.*, IV, 5.

thinking the question of citizenship is linked not only to sitting on the Council, but also to active service in the militia.

In the *Storia d'Italia* F. Guicciardini deals with the Consiglio Maggiore from the historian's viewpoint. Describing the events of 1494 in Florence in two invented speeches made by Paolantonio Soderini and Guidantonio Vespucci, F. Guicciardini is able to put face to face supporters and critics of the revolution of 1494. Those who wanted the Council asked for a

governo dependente in tutto dalla potestà del popolo ma che sia ordinato e regolato debitamente: il che consiste principalmente in due fondamenti. Il primo è che tutti i magistrati e uffici, così per la città come per il dominio, siano distribuiti, tempo per tempo, da uno consiglio universale di tutti quegli che secondo le leggi nostre sono abili a partecipare del governo.[120]

Consequently if all magistrates' election have to take place in the Council only the management of foreign policy should be trusted to a much smaller Council – the senate – which is, however, elected in the Consiglio Maggiore.[121] In a less technical fasion, Paolantonio Soderini expresses the same view Giannotti had formulated in the *Republica fiorentina*.

Those who did not want the Consiglio Maggiore maintained that it would be totally foolish for a republic to rely on the political wisdom of the many who have never had direct access to politics. The *universale* would soon turn out to be tyrannical

perché e un popolo è simile a un tiranno quando dà a chi non merita, quando toglie a chi merita, quando confonde i gradi e le distinzioni delle persone; ed è forse tanto più pestifera la sua tirannide quanto è più pericolosa l'ignoranza, perché non ha né peso né misura né legge che la malignità, che pure si regge con qualche regola con qualche freno con qualche termine.[122]

Interestingly both Paolantonio Soderini and Guidantonio Vespucci call upon the Venetian model to prove their case! A different understanding of the Venetian constitutional history lies behind their argument: the former is inclined to esteem the Venetian Maggior consiglio highly as the embodiment of the city's citizenship thus kept united and determined to promote the common good, the latter sharply criticises this view which counts the establishment of the dogeship as the most important among the many reasons for the Venetian political stability.

V

The story of Florentine Renaissance republicanism defies schematisation. Machiavelli and Guicciardini, to mention only the two most important protagonists of this story, often hold conflicting ideas which may be partially

[120] F. Guicciardini, *Storia d'Italia*, in *Opere*, ed. E. Scarano, vols. II–III, (Turin, 1981), II, pp. 211–12.
[121] See *ibid.*, p. 212.   [122] *Ibid.*, p. 216.

understood only if placed in their historical context. There is no possibility of drawing a simple line marking the boundaries between different formulations of republicanism. In constitutional terms, the Consiglio Maggiore was central to any republican reform project and differences among them only come to light if the details of such reform projects are analysed.

On one issue *popolari* and *uomini da bene* hold different, if not conflicting views. The latter paid less attention to the question of the *militia*, while the former tended to place service in the *militia* among the highest duties of the citizen.[123] In regard to the Consiglio Maggiore, Florentine republicans agree on its fundamental role in the political life of the republic. The view of those *uomini principali* who, at the end of the fifteenth century, regarded this institution as a threat to their socially and politically pre-eminent position, in time became more favourable towards the Council. This change of attitude has been the major focus of this study. The *primi cittadini* had to learn how to face the revolution of 1494. In this way the Consiglio Maggiore became part of their thinking about politics, once the Council had secured an important place in Florentine political tradition.

Paradigmatic of this change of attitude is the persuasion that

è difficile trovare la medicina appropriata, perché bisogna sia in modo che medicando lo stomaco non si offenda il capo, cioè provvedere di sorte che non si alteri la sustanzialità del governo popolare, che è la libertà; e che per levare le deliberazioni di momento di mano di chi non le intende, non si dia tanta autorità a alcuno particolare, che si caggia o si avvii in una spezie di tirannide.[124]

The *uomini principali* tended to diminish the original political meaning of the Council – the broadening of Florentine citizenship – by stressing the pivotal role of the senate in governing the republic. They were driven to regard the Council with favour in the belief that this institution was the only constitutional check on a private citizen whose political ambition could prove to be harmful to the freedom of the city. The need for Florentine republicans to clarify this case spurred them to think and write about politics with as much vigour as they could. Their fight, political and ideological as well, had a common target: Medicean lordship over Florence, which would have transformed Florentine citizens of any social status into subjects. The Consiglio Maggiore was a safeguard against this danger. Being *signore*, the Council, by preventing any

---

[123] 'Il primo, che le deliberazioni importanti sono maneggiate da chi le intende, e non vanno nello arbitrio della moltitudine, che è il primo pericolo di che si teme in uno governo popolare; il secondo che, come ho detto, è uno freno a moderare la troppa autorità che potessi pigliare uno gonfaloniere a vita, e così vedete che questo consiglio di mezzo, quale vorrei che si chiamassi senato, è un temperamento tra la tirannide e la licenza popolare; il terzo, che questo è uno modo da tenere contenti i cittadini di più virtù e meglio qualificati, perchè riducere il governo in mano delle persone che vaglino, non solo serve perché le cose siano governate da chi ne è capace, ma ancora a tenere bene satisfatti quegli che sarebbe male che fussino male contenti', F. Guicciardini, *Dialogo.*, II, pp. 155–6. [124] *Ibid.*, p. 133.

private citizen from usurping power in the republic, promoted a sort of 'equality' among the city's citizens which alone would have been the basis of the republic.

Last but not least, the *uomini da bene* came round to the idea of the Council because it was difficult to form factions and divisions within it, in fact 'sarebbe bene che le numero del Consiglio fussi maggiore, perché quanto è più largo, meno vi possono le sette'.[125] The Council had changed a pattern in Florentine history. In the second decade of the fifteenth century, political success depended largely on Medicean patronage, while in the *stato popolare* the patron/client relationship was no longer essential to the political success of a citizen. The Consiglio Maggiore was expected to promote and protect a new kind of political relationship among the citizens of the city. Republicanism developed and became a political answer to the fear that someone – whether Medicean or not is less important here – might take over the state as his own possession.

This was a justifiable fear if one bears in mind that the Florentine republic was not yet a modern state. Political and historical theorists of the time had not formulated the concept of the modern state as an independent political and constitutional order which ought to be preserve⁵o be preserved and protected. To Florentine republicans, to Machiavelli or F. Guicciardini, to 'rule' and 'to possess' the state were largely the same thing in the sense that they thought the state comprised the rulers themselves.[126] In this historical context, the expressions *governo stretto* and *governo largo* are highly significant, and common in Florentine political and historical writings.[127] These expressions allude to the number of citizens allowed to participate in the government of the city and, therefore, to benefit from the many political and economic opportunities involved in service to the state.

---

[125] N. Guicciardini, *Discursus*, p. 380.

[126] See Q. Skinner, *The Foundations*, vol. I, pp. ix–x, vol. II: *The Age of Reformation*, pp. 349–58 and G. Silvano, '*Vivere civile*', pp. 170–1.

[127] A good example is in F. de' Nerli, *Commentari de' fatti civili occorsi nella città di Firenze dall'anno 1215 al 1537* (Trieste, 1859), p. 193.

4

◁ ══ ▷

Machiavelli, servant of the Florentine republic

ROBERT BLACK

From 19 June 1498 until 7 November 1512, Niccolò di Messer Bernardo Machiavelli served in the chancery of the Florentine republic. The Florentine chancery consisted mainly of a body of quasi-permanent officials who administered the republic's internal and external affairs, carrying out policies which had been determined by the city's magistrates and councils. The internal business of the republic was executed by a number of autonomous chancery departments: the notary of the Signoria looked after the day-to-day business of Florence's chief magistracy; the notary of the Tratte supervised elections to Florence's many magistracies; the notary of the Riformagioni administered the business of Florence's legislative councils. External policies were decided by the chief magistracy, the Signoria, as well as by a theoretically occasional magistracy, the Dieci di Balìa. The business of these magistracies was administered by one department, presided over by the first chancellor; second in command of this department of external affairs was the second chancellor. In theory, the first chancellor was in charge of administering Florentine relations with foreign states, while the second chancellor was meant to supervise Florentine business outside the city proper but within Florentine subject territories; in practice, however, there was considerable overlap in the responsibilities of the first and second chancellors.[1] On 19 June 1498 Machiavelli was elected second chancellor[2] and less than a month later, on 14 July 1498, he was given the additional task of serving the Dieci di Balìa.[3] Eight and a half years later, on 12 January 1507, Machiavelli was given a third chancery office as chancellor to the newly created Nove Ufficiali dell'Ordinanza e Milizia Fiorentina, in charge of administering the business of the newly created Florentine militia.[4]

---

[1] On the Florentine chancery, see D. Marzi, *La cancelleria della repubblica fiorentina* (Rocca San Casciano, 1910); A. Brown, *Bartolomeo Scala* (Princeton, 1979), pp. 135–92; R. Black, *Benedetto Accolti and the Florentine Renaissance* (Cambridge, 1985), pp. 115–83.
[2] N. Rubinstein, 'The beginnings of Niccolò Machiavelli's career in the Florentine chancery', *Italian Studies*, 11 (1956), 90.   [3] *Ibid.*, p. 73; Marzi, *Cancelleria*, p. 289.
[4] O. Tommasini, *La vita e gli scritti di Niccolò Machiavelli*, 1 (Rome, Turin and Florence, 1883), p. 367. Machiavelli's work with the Florentine militia has been analysed by N. Rubinstein, 'Machiavelli and the world of Florentine politics' in *Studies on Machiavelli*, M. Gilmore, ed. (Florence, 1972), pp. 5–16.

Like all other chancery officials, Machiavelli's principal duty was the preparation of written documents. For members of the chancery concerned with external affairs like Machiavelli, this mainly consisted of writing letters, on behalf of the Signoria or the Dieci, to foreign individuals and states, to Florentine diplomats and private citizens abroad, to Florentine officials serving in the subject territories or to citizens resident there, to military captains in the service of the Florentine government, to Florentine military commissioners supervising the military captains, and to Florentine subjects and subject cities. Machiavelli also shared in the general administrative work of the chancery, for example, preparing lists of citizens for elections or nominations, or minuting the meetings of the deliberative assembly, the *pratica*; Machiavelli also acted not just as letter writer for the Nove di Milizia but also worked as their general administrator, for example, supervising the recruitment of troops in the countryside. One of Machiavelli's most notable chancery duties was as a courier, negotiator and diplomat, often with the title of *mandatario*; as such, he undertook many missions, some long and important, not just in Florentine territory or elsewhere in Italy but abroad to France and Germany.[5]

In all these areas of chancery business Machiavelli was remarkably active in the fourteen and a half years of his public service. He devoted the same kind of intense energy to his official duties as he would later dedicate during his enforced retirement to his literary, political and historical writings. It is commonplace to stress Machiavelli's originality and unique qualities as a thinker and writer; much less consideration has been given to the question of Machiavelli's particular contribution as a public servant. It would be useful to know to what extent Machiavelli's career and activities in the service of the Florentine republic were shaped by his distinctive personality and intellect and how far his chancery service followed patterns and traditions well-established in the Florentine chancery. In considering these questions, it may be interesting to compare Machiavelli's career with the chancery service of some of his contemporaries and predecessors – the more so as this kind of comparative method has hitherto been very little used for the study of Machiavelli's biography. In particular, there are four main areas of Machiavelli's career as a public servant which I should like to examine: his work as a humanist, his role as a diplomat, his status as a bureaucrat, and his activities in the political affairs of the republic.

As a humanist, Machiavelli's service to the republic followed time-honoured traditions in the Florentine chancery. The basic service rendered by chancellors

---

[5] For the range of written documents and records prepared by Machiavelli personally, see his *Legazioni. Commissarie. Scritti di governo*, ed. F. Chiappelli (Bari, 1971–); for his administrative work, see R. Ridolfi, *The Life of Niccolò Machiavelli*, trans. C. Grayson (London, 1963), pp. 15–132 *passim*.

– letter writing – had been carried out in the humanist manner since the second half of the fourteenth century, when Coluccio Salutati first introduced a vast range of classical quotations, references, *exempla* and *sententiae* into the public letters of the Florentine chancery.[6] The *missive* composed by Florence's fifteenth-century chancellors are generally more modest compositions, lacking the enormous classical erudition of Salutati's letters, although Marsuppini and Accolti, who served in the middle of the century, did go some way to restoring the rich classical content of Salutati's *missive*. Nevertheless, the fifteenth-century chancellors went beyond Salutati in matters of style, introducing the orthography, syntax and eventually handwriting favoured by the new learning into their public letters. Moreover, as a result of the reforms of Benedetto Accolti, chancellor from 1458 to 1464, humanism penetrated even further into the chancery. Until the mid-fifteenth century, the influence of the *studia humanitatis* was noticeable only in the *missive* of the first chancellor; other chancery records – for example, the debates of the *pratiche* and ambassadorial records – were compiled with scant regard for the standards of humanist latinity. However, Accolti extended the sway of the *studia humanitatis* in the chancery, so that henceforth not only the *missive* but also *pratica* debates and records of formal diplomatic interchanges were composed in humanist Latin. Moreover, he insisted that all records of the first chancery were written in humanist italic script. It was therefore imperative to have assistants in the chancery with humanist training in order to ensure the maintenance of these new standards of style, orthography and script. Accolti was the first chancellor to appoint as his coadjutor a trained humanist – Bastiano di Antonio Foresi,[7] and he thus began a tradition which was rigorously continued by his successor, Bartolomeo Scala, who had as his subordinates such notable figures as Alessandro Bracessi, Niccolò Michelozzi, Bernardo Nuti and Cristoforo Landino.[8] By the end of the century, not only was the first chancellor himself a distinguished humanist but the chancery as a whole was a centre for humanist studies. A humanist background had become essential for chancery service, and it was with these qualifications that Machiavelli entered the chancery in 1498.

The chancery ambience in Florence, therefore, was by the end of the century undoubtedly thoroughly permeated with humanism. Nevertheless, there has been a tendency to regard Machiavelli as an outsider in this learned environment. Thus, for example, according to Capponi's *Storia della Republica di Firenze*, 'non ebbe il Machiavelli scienza bastante nemmeno dai libri',[9] a view which, despite the great weight of contrary evidence that has emerged in the last thirty or forty years, still lingers on. Indeed, as recently as 1986 one student of

---

[6] D. De Rosa, *Coluccio Salutati* (Florence: 1980), pp. 22–7; H. Langkabel, *Die Staatsbriefe Coluccio Salutatis* (Cologne and Vienna, 1981), pp. 29–47.
[7] Black, *Accolti*, pp. 138–72.   [8] Brown, *Scala*, pp. 187, 203, 204.
[9] G. Capponi, *Storia della repubblica di Firenze*, 2nd edn (Florence, 1876), III, 187.

early sixteenth-century Florence wrote, 'Unlike Bruni and Poggio and Alberti and Bernardo Rucellai, Machiavelli seems not to have been an expert in *studia humanitatis* . . . It may be that it was his somewhat different background, and somewhat different education, that enabled him to break loose from conventional methods.'[10]

Such an attempt to deny Machiavelli his humanist origins and to place him outside the traditions of the Florentine chancery must be questioned. In the first place, Machiavelli's training was the same as that received by a number of the Florentine elite, for whom a humanist education had become fashionable. From the age of seven, elementary reading and writing using the *Ianua* (*Donatello*) as a primer; from eight, the beginnings of Latin; from eleven, arithmetic or abacus training; from twelve, more advanced secondary study of Latin authors. A succession of various private teachers – beginning with a humble reading teacher, one Maestro Matteo, progressing to a clerical grammar teacher, one ser Battista da Poppi of the church of San Benedetto, culminating in lessons from a prominent humanist pedagogue, ser Paolo Sasso da Ronciglione, teacher of Pietro Crinito and Michele Verino, humanist colleague of Landino, Merula and Pontano.[11] All this was the pattern according to which many members of the Florentine patriciate had been educated since humanist studies had become the vogue in Florence at the beginning of the fifteenth century.[12] Similarly, there is little reason to doubt Paolo Giovio's testimony that Machiavelli finished his education by attending Marcello Virgilio Adriani's lectures in the humanities at the Studio Fiorentino – 'constat eum . . . a Marcello Virgilio . . . graecae atque latinae linguae flores accepisse'[13] – again following the established pattern whereby sons of the Florentine patriciate attended the Studio for lectures from such professors as Filelfo, Marsuppini, Landino, Argyropulos or Poliziano.[14]

Secondly, there is the evidence of Machiavelli's literary activity and study before and shortly after his election to the chancery in 1498. As a twelve-year-old, he probably studied Justin; in his teens, probably the *Decades* of Livy and Biondo.[15] Then there are the two poems, the *canzone a ballo*, 'Se havessi l'arco et le ale' and the *capitolo ternario*, 'Poscia che all'ombra sotto quest'alloro', recently studied by Martelli and dated to 1493–4, in which the currents of Laurentian humanist culture are evident.[16] There now seems general agreement that Machiavelli was in fact the copyist of Lucretius in Vatican Ross. 884, which, on

---

[10] J.N. Stephens, 'Machiavelli's *Prince* and the Florentine revolution of 1512', *Italian Studies*, 41 (1986), 49.

[11] Ridolfi, *Life*, p. 3; F. Gilbert, *Machiavelli and Guicciardini* (Princeton, 1965), pp. 321–2.

[12] C. Bec, *Les Marchands écrivains* (Paris, 1967), pp. 383–93; R. Black, 'Florence' in *The Renaissance in National Context*, R. Porter and M. Teich, eds., forthcoming from Cambridge University Press.

[13] Cited in Ridolfi, *Life*, p. 262, n. 17.

[14] See A. Verde, *Lo studio fiorentino*, vol. III (Pistoia, 1977), *passim*; A. Della Torre, *Storia dell'Accademia Platonica* (Florence, 1902), *passim*.   [15] Ridolfi, *Life*, p. 4.

[16] M. Martelli, 'Preistoria (medicea) di Machiavelli', *Studi di filologia italiana*, 29 (1971), 377–405.

the evidence of watermarks, is to be dated in the 1490s and about which Martelli remarks, 'è proprio in un lavoro di questo genere che si può scorgere uno di quei titoli letterari, che . . . erano indispensabili alla sua carriera di funzionario pubblico'.[17] Then there is his request to Biagio Buonaccorsi in October 1502 to procure a copy of Plutarch's *Lives* for him while he was on his mission to Cesare Borgia.[18]

Thirdly, Machiavelli's epistolary style from the very beginning of his public service bears the indubitable stamp of a humanist. His very first public letter from 14 July 1498 contains several figures of speech, including two litotes, a polyptoton, and an anadiplosis, not to mention two notable latinisms, 'irritato' and 'innovare', the first of which, according to Martelli, is 'di indubbia e preziosa rarità.'[19] Moreover, there is the evidence of orthography in his early autographs, from the years 1498 to 1500, in which he uses latinate diphthongs, indicated with the cedilla under the 'e', or more rarely written out fully.[20]

In his education, in his literary interests, in his technical command of language and style, Machiavelli was a fully-fledged humanist when he entered the chancery in the summer of 1498, a worthy successor to the pre-eminent figures who had previously filled the office of second chancellor. Indeed, it is hardly conceivable that the Florentines would have elected a man of limited education and learning to succeed Braccesi, Machiavelli's immediate predecessor, or Francesco Gaddi, whom Braccesi himself had followed. A notary, lawyer, banker and wool merchant, Gaddi was a cultivated amateur humanist,[21] following a pattern set for the Florentine patriciate at the beginning of the fifteenth century by Niccolò Niccoli and Palla Strozzi and confirmed in his own generation by the example of the Medici themselves. A follower of Ficino, Gaddi was befriended by the leading Florentine humanists of his day, including Landino, Scala, Poliziano, and Della Fonte;[22] a student of Latin, Greek and French, his library included more than 200 volumes, which he divided into five principal sections, of which the largest, consisting of 110 books and constituting more than half the collection, was made up 'di libri in humanità'; there was also a separate section of Greek books, consisting of two vocabularies, two primers and two grammar texts.[23] A selection of these books

---

[17] M. Martelli, 'L'altro Niccolò di Bernardo Machiavelli', *Rinascimento*, ser. 2, 14 (1974), 95.

[18] N. Machiavelli, *Lettere*, ed. F. Gaeta (Milan, 1961), p. 82.

[19] Martelli, 'L'altro Niccolò', 47–9.

[20] P. Ghiglieri, *La grafia del Machiavelli* (Florence, 1969), p. 300.

[21] See Della Torre, *Storia*, pp. 730–1; Marzi, *Cancelleria*, pp. 265–7; C. Bologna, *Inventario de'mobili di Francesco di Angelo Gaddi 1496* (Florence, 1883), nozze Bumiller–Stiller; A.M. Bandini, *Catalogus codicum latinorum Bibliotecae Mediceae Laurentianae* (Florence, 1774–8), IV, pp. iv–xiii; C. Bec. 'La biblioteca di un alto borghese fiorentino: Francesco Gaddi (1496)' in his *Cultura e società a Firenze nell'età della rinascenza* (Rome, 1981), pp. 197–207; L. Sozzi, 'Lettere inedite di Philippe de Commynes a Francesco Gaddi' in *Studi di bibliografia e di storia in onore di T. de Mariniis*, IV (Vatican City, 1964), pp. 205–62. [22] Della Torre, *Storia*, p. 730.

[23] Bec, 'La biblioteca'.

accompanied Gaddi on embassies abroad: for example, while at Milan in 1488 he had with him 'il Temistio, il Burleo, il Comento di S. Tommaso sopra la Fisica, l'Euclide, l'Etica coll'Argiropilo'.[24] Indeed, on that occasion in Milan he also had the company of Ermolao Barbaro, the Venetian ambassador, with whom, according to Ficino, he engaged in erudite discussion and study: 'Tu igitur, dilectissime Francisce noster, Hermolaum Barbarum imitatus interim in legatione philosophari non desinis'.[25]

Whereas Gaddi was a refined dilettante, Alessandro Braccesi, Machiavelli's immediate predecessor as second chancellor, was a humanist by profession. Braccesi's classical education is clear from his Latin letters, for which, at the age of twenty, he won the praise of Michelozzi, who pointed to his 'admirabilis in scribendis letteris disciplina' and his 'copiosissima scribendi elocutio'. In contact with leading representatives of humanist culture, such as Naldi and Campano, Braccesi achieved greatest distinction as a Latin poet, composing three books of Latin verse, under the influence particularly of Landino. He achieved fame as a translator too, particularly with his Italian version of Aeneas Silvius' *Historia de duobus amantibus*, but also with his vernacular translation of Appian's histories.[26].

In understanding Machiavelli's humanism, one problem has always been the obvious fact that, as an erudite, he cannot be classed together with the leading Florentine lights of his day, such as Poliziano, Landino or Ficino. According to such standards, however, the humanism of a Scala or a Michelozzi, for example, would be open to doubt. There has been a tendency in some recent research not to deny categorically a rudimentary knowledge of Greek to Machiavelli,[27] and this is probably all that either of his predecessors could boast of: the Greek books in Gaddi's library testify to an interest in learning the language, but there are no signs that he ever achieved any degree of proficiency;[28] the same was probably true of Braccesi, who relied on the Latin version of Pier Candido Decembrio for his translation of Appian.[29] With regard to Latin, there can be little doubt that Machiavelli's knowledge was competent, as is clear from two early compositions, the fragmentary autograph draft of a letter of 1 December 1497 and the dedicatory letter to the *Decennale Primo* of 9 November 1504. Thus, in the autograph *minuta, causae* is correctly spelled with a diphthong, although Machiavelli uses *oe* instead of the preferable *ae* in spelling *poenitebit*; however, he misses a common pitfall by spelling *ceteris* without a diphthong.[30] Moreover, there is more than a touch of humanist pedantry in the dedicatory letter of the *Decennale primo* to Alamanno Salviati, whom he addresses, using Latin on this

[24] Bandini, *Catalogus*, IV, p. xi.   [25] Della Torre, *Storia*, p. 731.
[26] A. Perosa, in *Dizionario biografico degli italiani* (henceforth *DBI*), XIII, pp. 602–8.
[27] Compare R. Ridolfi, *Vita di N. M.*, 7th edn (Florence, 1978), p. 7, with his *Life*, 3.
[28] Bec, 'La biblioteca', 207.   [29] Perosa, *DBI*, XIII, p. 605.
[30] Biblioteca Nazionale, Florence, Carte Machiavelli, I, 58bis.

occasion, in the second person singular, scrupulously following classical usage; indeed, his other surviving letter to Salviati, written in the vernacular, uses the second person plural, even though Salviati replies to him in the singular.[31]

This may seem a sparse Latin output for an aspiring chancery secretary, but there is also the long Lucretius transcription, which may indeed be regarded as something of an edition, showing variants close to those in the edition of Pier Candido Decembrio and in common with the anonymous corrections in *Laurenziano* xxxv, 32.[32] Moreover, comparison may again be relevant, as in fact a number of other chancery humanists produced few Latin compositions. Machiavelli's friend and colleague, Biagio Buonaccorsi, historian, poet (whose verse shows the influence of contemporary neo-Platonism), professional scribe, according to his recent biographer, Fachard, 'homme de lettres certainement doué de qualités d'humaniste', composed nothing in Latin at all.[33] An even closer parallel to Machiavelli's scholarly activities is provided by another minor figure, Bastiano Foresi, who served for twelve years as a chancery coadjutor from 23 February 1453 to 23 April 1465. A notary by profession, Foresi was a student of classical authors, borrowing copies of *De officiis*, Varro and Horace from Poggio in the mid-1450s. He was a competent Latinist, who aided Benedetto Accolti's reform of the chancery, not only with his excellent humanist chancery italic script, but also by correcting Accolti's own orthography and syntax. He was probably also a professional humanist scribe, and the likely copyist of twenty humanist manuscripts, from such authors as Petrarch, Sallust, Cicero, Varlerius Maximus and Plautus. His humanist interests are clear from his two long vernacular poems; by no means popular lyrics, these are weighty compositions, revealing a wide knowledge of ancient and humanist literature, history and philosophy. He was also a close personal friend of Ficino's and a correspondent of Sabellico's. However, like Machiavelli, Foresi's original Latin production is almost non-existent: in fact, only one letter, a dedication to Lorenzo de Medici, written in competent humanist Latin.[34] If Foresi and Buonaccorsi were true humanists – as they undoubtedly were – then there can be no denying that Machiavelli was a humanist as well. According to Martelli, 'in poche parole, tutto quel che sappiamo di Niccolò Machiavelli ci porta sulle orme di un letterato e di un umanista'.[35] One reviewer of Martelli's important work has rightly asked for further clarification: 'To say that Machiavelli *was* a humanist and that his intellectual formation was rooted in the literary humanism of the late Quattrocento is a somewhat more troublesome proposition. It must be acknowledged that Martelli does not really make clear

[31] *Lettere*, ed. Gaeta, p. 136; M. Luzzati and M. Sbrilli, 'Massimiliano d'Asburgo e la politica di Firenze in una lettera inedita di Niccolò Machiavelli', *Annali della scuola normale superiore di Pisa*, Lettere e filosofia, ser. 3, 16 (1986), 849–54.   [32] Martelli, 'L'altro Niccolò, 94–5.
[33] D. Fachard, *Biagio Buonaccorsi* (Bologna, 1976), p. 7.   [34] Black, *Accolti*, pp. 165–70.
[35] Martelli, 'L'altro Niccolò', 96.

what sort of humanist in his view Machiavelli was. Indeed, it may not be a very easy task to characterise Machiavelli's "humanism" . . .'[36] In answer to this question, it may be suggested that Machiavelli was a humanist of the type who had filled the subordinate ranks of the Florentine chancery since the mid-fifteenth century.

Machiavelli's service as a humanist thus followed the traditions of the Florentine republic, but making use of his classical learning to prepare written documents was not his only duty in the chancery. Machiavelli also had an extremely active diplomatic career, with more than forty missions to his credit during his fourteen years of public service. Traditionally chancery officials had served as diplomatic administrators in Florence; they issued instructions and corresponded with diplomats; they administered the details of embassies, recording the dates of departure and return and organising the payment of salaries and expenses; they spoke on behalf of the Signoria to foreign diplomats when members of the Signoria could not speak Latin (or more rarely French or Greek); they minuted the debates of the *pratica* meetings, which were largely concerned with diplomatic problems; they recorded formal diplomatic inter-changes.[37] Before the later fifteenth century, however, Florentine chancery secretaries were rarely used as diplomats. It is interesting that in this respect Florentine custom stood in contrast to the practice of the other great Italian fifteenth-century republic, Venice, where throughout the fifteenth century secretaries were frequently entrusted with diplomatic missions. An early example is the career of Jacopo Languschi, ducal secretary by 1410, who was

[36] J. Najemy, in *Speculum*, 52 (1977), 159. The extent to which humanism had penetrated the subordinate ranks of the chancery by the early sixteenth century is suggested by the library of one of its longest-serving minor officials, ser Girolamo di ser Griso Griselli. He was elected second coadjutor in the chancery of the Tratte on 11 October 1498 at an annual salary of 72 florins (Archivio di stato, Florence (henceforth ASF), Tratte Appendice, 5, fol, 78r), an office which he continued to hold until at least 31 March 1531 (ASF, Carte Riccardi, 816, inserto n. 58: for intervening reconfirmations, see ASF, Tratte Appendice, 5, fol. 120r; 6, fol. 49v, 124v; 7, fol. 16r, 104v, 189v; 8, fol. 86r, 177r; 9, fol. 48v, 125v; 10, fol. 25r, 139r; 11, fol. 62v; 13, fol. 68r; Marzi, *Cancelleria*, p. 324). The inventory of the books he left to his widow Fiammetta comprised 56 volumes, of which 25 were legal and notarial texts, and 6 were biblical and patristic texts. Most interesting was his large collection of classical works, including Cicero's orations, *De officiis* and *De oratore*; Aulus Gellius' *Attic Nights*; the complete works of Virgil; Ovid's *Metamorphoses* and *Fasti*; the bucolics of Calpurnius; the *Punica* of Silius Italicus; four volumes of Plutarch's *Lives*; Caesar's *Commentaries*; extracts from Livy's *Decades*; and some works of Suetonius. He also possessed Boethius' *Consolation* and Perotti's *De fortuna et virtute hominum*. The inventory, dated 28 October 1535, is found in ASF, Carte Riccardi, 816, fasc. a., n. 1, inserto 63; Griselli had made his will on 13 August 1534: *ibid.* inserto 62. I am extremely grateful to Dr E. Rosenthal for referring me to Griselli's papers. His father, Griso Griselli, had been secretary and chancellor to Giannozzo Manetti, from whose library some of these books may have derived. See Della Torre, *Storia*, 276ff., 332, 337, 343, 345, 422. For Griso Griselli's association with Marco Parenti and with Vespasiano da Bisticci, see Mark Phillips, *The Memoir of Marco Parenti* (Princeton, 1987), p. 44. For Griso's association with Luca Pitti, see Biblioteca Comunale di San Gimignano (Archivio storico communale), NN, 127, fol. 46v (15 June 1463).

[37] Black, *Accolti*, pp. 116–17, 164–5.

sent on a series of embassies to Genoa, Udine, Ferrara and Bologna from 1416 to 1419.[38] Another important humanist secretary with a diplomatic career in Venice was the Greek Niccolò Sagundino, who, having received the title of ducal secretary by 1455, was sent on missions to Naples and Rome between 1455 and 1458, and then in 1460 to Modon, Constantinople and Trebizond.[39] Perhaps the most active of these Venetian humanist secretaries in the mid-fifteenth century was Febo Capella, who had worked as a secretary from at least 1442. He served his diplomatic apprenticeship as secretary to Francesco Barbaro on his legation to Milan in 1443–4. In the 1450s he rose to the rank of ducal secretary, and was entrusted with a series of important diplomatic missions, to King René of Anjou in 1455, to Emperor Frederick III in 1459, to Florence in 1460.[40] The confidence which he inspired as a diplomat is shown by his difficult mission in 1463 to Florence, where he was given the almost impossible task of persuading the Florentines to interrupt their lucrative commerce with Constantinople during the forthcoming Venetian war with the Turks.[41] Venetians continued to call upon the diplomatic services of their humanist secretaries at the end of the fifteenth century, as is clear from the career of Antonio Vinciguerra, who became a ducal notary in 1459. Vinciguerra served his apprenticeship as secretary to Venetian ambassadors to Castile in 1468–9 and to the pope in Rome in 1470–1. In ensuing years, he was employed in almost continual diplomatic missions, most notably to Florence and Ferrara in 1474–6, Florence and Rome in 1478–9, Veglia in 1480–1 and again in 1488–9, Rome in 1486–7, and Bologna in 1495–9.[42]

Florentine chancery officials, such as ser Lapo Mazzei[43] and ser Benedetto Fortini,[44] had occasionally been used on diplomatic missions before the late Quattrocento, but it was only in the period of Lorenzo de' Medici's ascendancy that the practice became more regular. An early example was Alessandro Braccesi, coadjutor to the first chancellor, who was sent, as secretary to the ambassadors Iacopo Guicciardini and Pierfrancesco de' Medici, to Naples and Rome between August 1470 and March 1471.[45] Soon afterwards in September–October 1471 Niccolò Michelozzi, then also coadjutor to the first chancellor, accompanied Lorenzo himself on a mission to Rome.[46] Braccesi was probably sent on an embassy to Bologna and Ferrara in October 1471,[47] but it was only in the 1480s that chancery officials were frequent members of diplomatic legations or even ambassadors in their own right. One such figure was ser Franceso di ser Barone, who entered the chancery of the Otto di Pratica in November 1481, became chancellor of the Dieci di Balìa in September 1482

---

[38] M. King, *Venetian Humanism* (Princeton, 1986), p. 387.   [39] *Ibid.*, p. 428.
[40] *Ibid.*, p. 348–9.   [41] Black, *Accolti*, p. 255.   [42] King, *Venetian Humanism*, p. 443.
[43] Marzi, *Cancelleria*, pp. 134, 178.   [44] *Ibid.*, p. 154.   [45] Perosa in *DBI*, XIII, p. 603.
[46] R. Fubini, 'Note Machiavelliane' in *Studies on Machiavelli*, Gilmore, ed., p. 374.
[47] Perosa in *DBI*, XIII, p. 603.

and after 5 December 1483 was elected one of the six secretaries of the Signoria after the reform of the chancery in November 1483. His legations included missions to Pisa from 28 January to 25 February 1482, to Lunigiana from 27 September to 29 October 1482, to the Valdelsa between 17 and 21 February 1483, to Barga between 15 and 24 April 1483, to the Pistoiese hills from 15 to 22 May 1483, to Sarzanello from 19 March to 3 April 1484, to Rassina near Anghiari in June 1484 and to Lunigiana between September 1484 and February 1485 during the Sarzana War; his final missions were to Pisa from 28 July to 1 August 1485 and to Rassina in June 1489.[48] An even more important secretarial diplomat during the Laurentian period was Franscesco Gaddi, who himself describes his triple role as public ambassador, personal representative of Lorenzo, and chancery official; his chancery offices were secretary to the Dieci in 1478 and secretary to the Otto di Practica after 1488, while his embassies included Milan in September 1488 and Siena in September 1489. Gaddi's role as secretary and diplomat did not end with Lorenzo's death in April 1492, but continued with missions to Venice in December 1492 and to Rome in May 1493.[49] Similarly, Braccesi continued to serve as both secretary and diplomat under Piero, as he had done under Lorenzo, with missions to Città di Castello in 1490 and then to Siena in 1491, where he remained until the expulsion of the Medici in November 1494.[50] What is particularly interesting is that the use of chancery secretaries as diplomats did no cease with the fall of the Medici regime in 1494. Thus Gaddi, second chancellor under the reformed republic and chancellor to the Dieci, was sent as ambassador to the Duke of Urbino in 1495.[51] Even more active was the diplomatic career of Braccesi, who was re-appointed to the chancery at the end of 1494 and promptly despatched to Lucca and then several times to Perugia between the beginning of 1495 and July 1496. His most delicate mission, however, was to the papacy between 3 March 1497 and 8 June 1498, where he acted in favour of the Savonarolan party and clearly as personal emissary of Florence's leading *frateschi* as well as public ambassador, just as he had represented the Medici on his official missions before November 1494.[52]

It is clear, therefore, that Machiavelli's active diplomatic service as second chancellor was by no means unprecedented, although his diplomatic career did form part of a relatively new trend in the history of the Florentine chancery. As a diplomat, he was hardly more active than Braccesi or Gaddi had been, and, moreover, he was not the only chancery secretary to be sent on diplomatic missions outside Florence in the first decade of the sixteenth century. Biagio Buonaccorsi, who served in the chancery of the Dieci from August 1498 to 22

---

[48] G. Ristori, 'Ser Francesco di Ser Barone Baroni', *Archivio storico italiano*, 134 (1976), 231–80; R. Ristori, in *DBI*, xxiii, pp. 287–90.

[49] Bologna, *Inventario*, pp. 5–12; Bandini, *Catalogus*, iv, pp. vi–xii.

[50] Perosa, in *DBI*, xiii, pp. 605–6. [51] Bologna, *Inventario*, p. 12.

[52] Perosa in *DBI*, xiii, p. 606.

January 1500 when he was elected coadjutor to the first chancellor, went on four diplomat missions, to Pisa from June to July 1500, to France from September 1501 to July 1502, to Mantua in May 1503, and to Rome from November 1505 to June 1506,[53] while Agostino Vespucci, coadjutor to the second chancellor, was sent to Rome in summer 1501 and to Bologna in December 1506.[54] Nevertheless, it is true to say that Machiavelli was by far the most active diplomat among the chancery secretaries during his years of service from 1498 to 1512.

As a humanist and diplomat, Machiavelli's service in the chancery represents time-honoured practice, but it has been argued that as a bureaucrat he represented a new trend in the development of the Florentine state. Machiavelli was not a notary and so his term of office has been seen as signifying the growing separation of legal and political sectors of government, as well as enhancing Florence's position as a sovereign state. According to Riccardo Fubini,

è molto preciso un fatto negativo e ciò è che Machiavelli non sia notaio . . . Leonardo Bruni è il primo cancelliere di Firenze a non essere notaio come è scritto negli statuti cittadini. Ora, Machiavelli non è il primo cancelliere; però Machiavelli è tra le figure subalterne e non credo che prima di lui si riconoscano dei non notai. Ciò è significativo per il crearsi di un corpo di professionalità politica che naturalmente coincide poi con figure di letterati, di intellettuali . . . Ecco Machiavelli in questo senso credo che, se non innova in senso assoluto, dilata un uso che esce fuori dalle consuetudini statuarie fiorentine. Questo è un elemento abbastanza importante . . . Non è una questione di notaio perché più esperto. E' una questione che è notaio perché ha una capacità legale per autenticare l'atto, per produrre degli atti validi. E' per questo che lo statuto prescrive che il cancelliere deve essere notaio. Per estensione quindi tutto il personale di cancelleria. E' vero che poi compaiono dei giureconsulti, ma i giureconsulti sono dei notai potenziati. Viceversa Machiavelli è una figura fuori dell'ordine legale; questo è importante. Anche qui si potrebbero tracciare delle tendenze che tendono alla separazione dell'ordine politico dall'ordine legale.[55]

Fubini is here developing a theme earlier pursued by Alison Brown: the reforms of the Florentine chancery instituted by Bartolomeo Scala in the second half of the fifteenth century involved

transforming the status of its functionaries and the legal form of its documents to reflect Florence's position as a sovereign power. In theory, the city was still subject to the emperor and, although in practice her councils exercised sovereign authority within the state, their decrees and legal instruments were written as though they needed imperial authority (conferred by the attestations of imperial notaries) to be valid. According to

---

[53] Fachard, *Buonaccorsi*, pp. 70–105. [54] Machiavelli, *Lettere*, ed. Gaeta, pp. 62–8, 175–7.
[55] According to the transcription of Fubini's comments made at the Machiavelli conference where this paper was originally read; I am not aware that he has hitherto published his views on this theme.

the statutes, the chancellor as well as the notary of the Riformagioni had to be a notary by profession and all legal instruments had not only to be signed by all members of the ratifying body . . . but also subscribed by the . . . attestations of notaries. This procedure . . . implied that Florence still lacked the necessary authority to validate her own decrees. Scala saw this very clearly, and his most important reforms aimed at replacing the old notarial officers by secretaries without legal qualifications, who were quite simply the executive servants of the sovereign government they represented. Emulating the chanceries of France and England, they produced short letters and legal instruments authenticated by the communal seal and the subscription of the chancellor, who acted not as a notary but as the representative of the government . . . the fact that Machiavelli (like Bernardo Ricci before him) was appointed a member of this secretariat, although he had no legal qualifications, shows that Scala's reforms were not without effect.[56]

It is true that most chancery officials were notaries and the appointment of Machiavelli to the subordinate ranks of the chancery may therefore seem exceptional and noteworthy; however, it is difficult to know how to interpret the significance of such non-notarial chancery appointments. In the first place, the fact that Machiavelli was not a notary does not place him entirely outside the traditions of the Florentine chancery; as Fubini has observed, the first non-notary to serve in the chancery was Bruni, and after his time there were few first chancellors who were notaries. Moreover, beginning with Filippo Balducci in 1444, several lawyers lacking notarial qualifications – Leone Leoni, Niccolò Altoviti, Jacopo Modesti – became chancellors of the Riformagioni. Indeed, Machiavelli was not the first subordinate official in the chancery not to be a notary: earlier chancery secretaries had included Bernardo Nuti, Cristoforo Landino and Bernardo Ricci.[57]

The importance of such non-notarial appointments should not be exaggerated, as they hardly represented a decisive trend in the history of the Florentine chancery's subordinate positions. Machiavelli and his colleague, Buonaccorsi, were the only two non-notaries among the secondary staff of the chancery in the years 1498 to 1512, and when they were replaced it was with two notaries. Indeed, after 1512, the only non-notarial members of the chancery were the first chancellor and the chancellor to the Riformagioni, which was a return to the way in which the chancery had been staffed in the 1440s and 1450s.[58]

The fact remains, however, that after 1427 the chancery included some non-notaries who could not legally authenticate (*rogare*) documents. Fubini has

[56] Brown, *Scala*, pp. 162–3.   [57] Marzi, *Cancelleria*, pp. 603, 604, 606, 613.

[58] For the staffing of the chancery after Machiavelli's appointment in June 1498 and until 1515, see ASF, Tratte Appendice, 5, fol. 68r, 69r–70r, 78r, 119r–v, 120r–v, 124r–v; 6, fol. 49r–v, 58r–v, 121r–v, 124r–v, 139r–v; 7, fol. 13v, 16r–v, 29v–30r, 104r–105v, 114v–115r, 187v, 189v–190r; 8, fol. 13r–14r, 86r–v, 95v–96r, 176v–177v; 9, fol. 2v–3r, 48r–v, 64v–65r, 125v–126r, 136r–v; 10, fol. 24v–25v, 36v–37v, 114v, 131r, 138r–139v, 159r–v; 11, fol. 61v–63r, 83r–v, 178r, 179v–180r, 191v; 12, fol. 45v–46r, 149r–v, 154r–v; 13, fol. 66v–68r, 72r–v, 79v–81v, 85r–86r, 87v–89r, 174r–175r.

suggested that this represents a growing separation of the political and legal spheres of government, while Brown believes it was a landmark on the way to Florence's emergence as a sovereign state. Long before the fifteenth century, however, Florentine government had ceased to use the authentication of imperial notaries to validate its most important acts. Until 1349, it had been customary for notaries of the Riformagioni or their coadjutors to authenticate the volumes of laws approved by the commune with their notarial seals accompanied by their rogations, just as notaries did in the protocols of private notarial business. However, this practice was abandoned in 1349, not to be renewed again in the ordinary legislative provisions of the commune. Thus by 1350 the Florentine republic had taken the step of issuing laws on its own authority, without the legal sanction provided by the rogation of imperial notaries.[59] It is difficult to see how the appointment of a few non-notaries to the chancery after 1427 represented a significant constitutional step in the separation of political and legal spheres of government or in the growth of sovereignty, when Florentines had already been issuing legislation without imperial sanction for more than seventy-five years. Rather than an innovation in its own right, the appointment of non-notaries to the chancery would seem to represent a confirmation of existing constitutional practice.

The entire juridical development of the Italian city-states is in some sense the history of growing legal independence from imperial authority. Certainly the appearance of non-notaries and lawyers among the chancery staff was made possible by this legal and constitutional development, but this practice hardly represents a new vision or concept of communal bureaucracy, such as seems to be implied by Fubini and Brown. If there was a novel view of Florentine legal status, it was introduced by the notaries who began to issue legislation without imperial validation in the mid-1300s. Moreover, in practical terms a non-notarial chancellor such as Machiavelli was hardly a more flexible servant of the executive in a politically independent and sovereign state, untrammelled by the legal paraphernalia of Roman law, than were notaries such as Giovanni Guidi or Niccolò Michelozzi, who hardly felt much restraint in pursuing the interests of their political masters.

The practice of appointing non-notaries to the chancery clearly represented a desire to have public offices filled by men with the most up-to-date qualifications. By the fifteenth century, the laws of the Florentine commune had become increasingly technical and complex; when the communal statutes of 1415 were compiled the work was no longer entrusted to notaries but to a team

---

[59] The change in procedure occurred in the volumes, ASF, Provvisioni, Registri, 35 (17 August 1347–11 April 1348), which has notarial seals and rogations throughout the volume; *ibid.* 36 (23 August 1348–27 August 1349) with notarial seals and rogations on fol. 2r, 2v, 139v, 158v; *ibid.* 37 (11 September 1349–13 March 1349 ab inc.) with one seal and rogation only at the end, fol. 115r) and 38, 39, 40, etc. which have no seals or rogations.

of fully qualified lawyers. In the same way it made sense to have a fully qualified lawyer serve as legislative notary. Similarly, what was required for the first and second chanceries was humanist training in letter writing and public oratory, and so priority was given to humanists. All the non-notarial appointments to the chancery after 1427 were lawyers, such as Balducci, Leoni, Altoviti and Modesti, or humanists, such as Machiavelli, Buonaccorsi and Landino.

Therefore, just as his service as a humanist and diplomat represented normal practice in the Florentine chancery, so Machiavelli's bureaucratic status was hardly unprecedented or innovatory. Much more problematic, however, are Machiavelli's political activities during his period of public service. Traditionally, officials of the chancery, because they enjoyed *de facto* permanent or long-term tenure of office, were excluded from the arena of Florentine politics: thus, they were not called to speak at sessions of Florence's most important political forum, the *pratica*; they were usually not members of the politically active social class, the patriciate, but were either foreigners or drawn from the politically impotent notariate; they normally did not enjoy a *cursus honorum* of high political office, unlike members of the patriciate. The chancery followed this pattern for most of the fourteenth and fifteenth centuries, and it is no distortion to say that chancellors such as Chello and Naddo Baldovini, Salutati, Pietro di Mino, Marsuppini, Accolti and Poggio were hardly political activists. Neutrality was the norm in the Florentine chancery, but there were exceptional periods of constitutional innovation and intense political factionalism, when chancery officials entered the political arena: thus Ventura Monachi and his son Niccolò engaged in political activity in the mid-fourteenth century, as did Fortini and Martini in the 1420s, while Bruni enjoyed a very unusual *cursus honorum* from 1437 to 1444. The chancery returned to its more normal pattern after Bruni's death, but with the Medici consolidation of power in 1466 and the unprecedented series of constitutional innovations undertaken by Lorenzo, chancery officials such as Scala, Braccesi, Gaddi and Baroni and particularly Giovanni Guidi and Simon Grazzini were brought into the very heart of the regime. This intense political involvement continued after the fall of the Medici, with patricians such as Niccolò Altoviti and Piero Beccanugi serving in the chancery's highest posts and political activists such as Braccesi and Gaddi continuing to hold secretarial positions. However, as has been suggested in a recent article, the year 1498 marked a watershed in the history of political activism in the chancery; with the fall of Savonarola, not only was the chancery purged of *frateschi* but also of political activists altogether. The new chancery staff – Adriani, Antonio and Agostino Vespucci, Antonio della Valle, Francesco Ottaviani – were all men outside the arena of Florentine politics, foreigners or Florentines beneath the patrician class, and Machiavelli was successful in the elections for the chancery, not only because he was a critic of

Savonarola, but also because he had had no previous record of active political participation. After 1498 the chancery largely returned to the more normal pattern of pre-Laurentian Florence as is clear from the careers of the chancery officials elected in 1498, most of whom were just as happy to work under Piero Soderini after 1502 as they were to cooperate with the restored Medici regime after 1512.[60]

Machiavelli was of course no mere letter writer; he was deeply involved in the fortunes of the republic after 1498, in its foreign, diplomatic and military policy. The question remains, therefore, to what extent did he enter the internal political arena of the republic, how far was he involved in the factional conflicts in which Florentines were embroiled particularly during the years of Soderini's gonfaloniership. Did Machiavelli follow the lead of the two senior chancery officials, Adriani, the first chancellor, and Ottaviani, the chancellor of the Riformagioni, and keep well out of political intrigues, or did he follow the precedent of his two predecessors in the second chancery, Gaddi and Braccesi, and enter into the thick of the political fray? Felix Gilbert has articulated the problem with great clarity:

Nella qualità di impiegato alla Cancelleria [Machiavelli] avrebbe potuto restare politicamente neutrale al di fuori dalle lotte politiche. Bartolomeo Scala, capo della Cancelleria sotto i Medici, mantenne la stessa carica sotto la Repubblica. Il successore di Scala, Marcello Virgilio Adriani, conservò l'incombenza che gli aveva affidato la Repubblica anche dopo il ritorno dei Medici. Lo stesso si può dire di molti altri membre della Cancelleria. Esperti nella stesura di documenti legali e politici, erano quello che oggi noi chiameremmo 'pubblici ufficiali'. Invece Niccolò Machiavelli e Biagio Buonaccorsi, suo assistente e amico, furono rimossi dalla carica al ritorno dei Medici nel 1512. Ciò sta a indicare che Machiavelli non fu un funzionario governativo politicamente incolore, ma una figura di spiccato rilievo politico. Domandarsi quale sia la participazione di Machiavelli alle lotte di partito nella sua città è dunque giustificato; solo che non è facile fornire la risposta.[61]

Gilbert himself never gives a direct answer to this important question, and the reason for the continuing uncertainty about Machiavelli's political role is not hard to discover: in fact, unlike earlier or later chancery figures involved in

---

[60] R. Black, 'Florentine political traditions and Machiavelli's election to the chancery', *Italian Studies*, 41 (1985), 1–16. I should like to take this opportunity to correct two errors in this earlier article; I apologise for the inaccuracies, but I do not think the changes weaken the argument presented. First, Machiavelli was not defeated by the politically neutral Antonio della Valle in February 1498 (p. 11) but by the minor *fratesco*, Antonio Migliorotti. Nevertheless, the overall pattern of the February elections still remains as I described: mainly politically neutral candidates were successful, with a few minor *frateschi* still gaining office; this reflects Parenti's view that the *frateschi* were weakened but not yet powerless in February 1498. Second, Francesco di ser Barone re-entered the chancery in 1495 as a *fratesco* but by February 1498 he had joined the opponents of Savonarola (*DBI*, XXIII, pp. 288–9). Thus Machiavelli faced in June 1498 two rival *arrabbiati* (Gaddi and Baroni) and one *fratesco* (Romolo), not two *frateschi* and one *arrabbiato*, as I wrote on p. 12. Nevertheless, the point still stands that Machiavelli enjoyed a very low political profile compared to his three opponents.   [61] *Terzoprogramma*, 1 (1970), 10.

political factionalism, there is no absolute or positive evidence of Machiavelli's participation in partisan conflict during his years in public office. For Martini and Fortini in the 1420s, there is the evidence of the confession of Niccolò Tinucci, which is corroborated by the private letters of the Medici and the records of the *pratica*;[62] for Guidi, there is Piero Guicciardini's *ricordanza* of 1484[63] as well as the testimony of Parenti, who also vouches explicitly for Grazzini's, Gaddi's and Altoviti's involvement;[64] indeed, Parenti's declaration that Braccesi had 'operato in favore de' frateschi' is corroborated by his correspondence during his embassy to Rome in 1497–8.[65] And there can be no doubt that Machiavelli's replacement as second chancellor, Michelozzi, was at the heart of the new regime, in view of Giuliano de' Medici's correspondence and his instructions to his nephew Lorenzo.[66] But there is no such direct evidence for Machiavelli – no partisan statements or writings before the return of the Medici in 1512, no statement in any contemporary Florentine source that he engaged in factional activities.

A further difficulty is that the indirect evidence seems inconsistent. On the one hand, the most important piece of circumstantial evidence in support of his political involvement was his sacking in 1512, which suggests that he was identified with the old regime by Florence's new masters. This may be related to the disfavour which he had often encountered among the patriciate in the years after 1502. Soderini placed great confidence in Machiavelli, and his trust did not ingratiate Machiavelli with the opponents of his regime: hence, according to Cerretani, he was Soderini's 'mannerino' and for Alamanno Salviati, he was a 'ribaldo';[67] hence, possibly, the attempt to have him sacked as a tax debtor in 1509 and the two anonymous denunciations of him to the Otto di Guardia in 1510 and 1511.[68] Moreover, there is the undoubted hatred which Machiavelli showed for the aristocrats who had destroyed the Soderini government, a sentiment to which he gave vent almost immediately the Medici had returned to Florence. As Marchand has pointed out, the *Ricordo ai Palleschi*, which, so he argues, dates from between 1 and 7 November 1512, is characterised by

violenza di certi termini che si riferiscono al partito aristocratico: non si tratta più della maniera concreta di esprimere un sentimento, un comportamento o un concetto, usata spesso in scritti anteriori, ma della ricerca sistematica di espressioni più plebee e più violente.[69]

[62] D. Kent, *The Rise of the Medici* (Oxford, 1978), pp. 224–8; Marzi, *Cancelleria*, pp. 184–6; Black, *Accolti*, pp. 107–8.
[63] N. Rubinstein, *The Government of Florence under the Medici* (Oxford, 1966), pp. 318–25.
[64] *Ibid.*, 231; Marzi, *Cancelleria*, pp. 259–70; Black, 'Florentine political traditions', pp. 13–16.
[65] Perosa in *DBI*, XIII, p. 606.
[66] H. Butters, *Governors and Government in Early Sixteenth-Century Florence* (Oxford, 1985), pp. 208–9, 221–2.   [67] Ridolfi, *Life*, 99.
[68] *Ibid.*, pp. 112–13; J.N. Stephens and H.C. Butters, 'New light on Machiavelli', *English Historical Review*, 97 (1982), 57.
[69] J.-J. Marchand, *Niccolò Machiavelli, I primi scritti politici (1499–1512)* (Padua, 1976), p. 308.

Such evidence might suggest Machiavelli's political involvement, but there is equally weighty circumstantial evidence to the contrary. In diplomacy Machiavelli seems hardly to have played the role of a private diplomatic agent whose mission was not only to represent the official policy of the government but also the particular views and interests of a faction; a few earlier chancery diplomats such as Gaddi or Braccesi in fact worked on behalf of the Medici or the *frateschi* during their embassies, but the weight of evidence suggests that Machiavelli had no significant role as Soderini's personal political agent. In the first place, there is no real evidence that Piero Soderini actually conducted his own distinctive foreign policy: according to his biographer, Roslyn Pesman Cooper, 'the years [1510–1512] . . . are the most fully documented period, and from the evidence it seems that Soderini was not so much pursuing an independent policy as supplementing that conducted by the *Signoria* and *Dieci*';[70] her conclusion is supported by Humfrey Butters, who writes:

On several occasions Soderini was to find his views and those of a majority of the *Dieci* in conflict, and he may have been tempted in his dealings with Florence's ambassadors abroad to conduct his own foreign policy, but if he ever felt such an impulse, the two volumes of his correspondence [ASF, Minutari, 19 and 20, 1505–12], which contain many letters to ambassadors, show him manfully resisting it.[71]

Moreover, Machiavelli's conduct during his imperial legation of 1508 has been scrupulously analysed by Rosemary Devonshire Jones, who has demonstrated that there was no foundation for Cerretani's claim that Machiavelli on this occasion acted as Soderini's *mannerino*, having been sent by the gonfalonier 'not only to keep an eye on Vettori but to get him to write back what suited his ends'. Devonshire Jones shows that Machiavelli wanted to leave immediately he had delivered the new instructions to Vettori, who himself insisted that Machiavelli should remain; moreover, Soderini favoured a pro-French policy, but Machiavelli continued to take the German threat seriously, even after Vettori had become sceptical, so that the despatches in Machiavelli's hand were even more unfavourable to Soderini's policies than Vettori's.[72] It has also been argued recently that Machiavelli's secret mission on this legation was to secure the imperial vicariate for Soderini, but this theory rests on very thin ice indeed. The only evidence is the correspondence of the Pisan ambassador at the imperial court; his testimony, obviously hostile to Soderini, is unconfirmed by Florentine sources, many of whom of course would have leaped at the opportunity to smear Soderini.[73] The imperial vicariate, if in fact it was actually being sought, may not have meant more than a confirmation of the 'presente

---

[70] R. Pesman Cooper, 'Pier Soderini: aspiring prince or civic leader?', *Studies in Medieval and Renaissance History*, n. s., 1 (1978), 100.　　[71] Butters, *Governors*, p. 80.

[72] R. Devonshire Jones, *Francesco Vettori* (London, 1972), pp. 24ff.; R. Devonshire Jones, 'Some observations on the relations between Francesco Vettori and Niccolò Machiavelli during the embassy to Maximilian I', *Italian Studies*, 23 (1968), 93–113.　　[73] Butters, *Governors*, p. 124–6.

stato e dominio' of Florence, such as would be requested from the emperor in 1512.[74]

There are a few other occasions when Machiavelli might seem to have assumed the mantle of Soderini's private envoy. Thus in 1508 while on his imperial legation at Bolsano, Machiavelli wrote to Soderini, 'né scrivero più al pubblico'; this has led Ridolfi to suggest

Al 'pubblico', no. Ma evidentemente all'amico gonfaloniere, sì. E sono queste parole, e sopratutto il tono confidenziale della lettera, a darci una nuova conferma della intimità dei rapporti fra il primo magistrato della Republica e il suo secondo cancelliere.[75]

However, if the letter is read without a full stop after 'pubblico', it takes on a different meaning: 'né scrivero più al pubblico ma qua farò quel poco del buono intenderò, anchora che la stanza mia qui sia al tucto superflua'[76] – 'nor shall I write any more official letters, but I shall do here what little good I can, although my presence here is totally superfluous'. The letter was a plea to be recalled to Florence from what Machiavelli felt was a useless mission; Machiavelli thought he had nothing to contribute, either publicly or privately. Machiavelli was given an explicitly private mandate by Soderini only once – on his mission to the French court in the summer of 1510: this private commission was reinforced by Soderini's brother, Francesco, Bishop of Volterra, who wrote to Machiavelli with his approval of this personal mandate on behalf of the Soderini. Moreover, another source confirms that Machiavelli was the particular 'messo dil Confaloniere di Fiorenza e dil Cardinale di Volterra, suo fratello'. However, this hardly represented a sinister piece of independent diplomacy: during this mission Machiavelli reported to the Dieci as well, and Francesco Soderini declared that Machiavelli had been despatched 'per rispecto del publico et privato nostro'.[77] Machiavelli was evidently given the gonfalonier's own mandate to personalise and hence reinforce an otherwise official mission; the personal instructions from Soderini showed that the gonfalonier himself attached particular priority to this mission on behalf of Florence. It is true that on two formal occasions Machiavelli conveyed Soderini's personal respects to Cesare Borgia,[78] but such gestures have no unequivocal political implication, and so it must be concluded, in the light of available evidence, that Machiavelli's diplomatic activity did not have any noticeable partisan overtones.

During his term in the chancery, Machiavelli's principal domestic project was the militia; the most controversial aspect of the scheme was the

[74] Pesman Cooper, 'Pier Soderini', 103–4.   [75] Ridolfi, *Vita*, 7th edn, 618.
[76] G. Hurlmann, 'Une lettre "privée" de Machiavel à Piero Soderini', *La bibliofilia*, 74 (1972), 183.
[77] On this legation, see Pesman Cooper, 'Pier Soderini', 91 (n. 85), 101–3, and her 'Machiavelli, Francesco Soderini and Don Michelotto', *Nuova rivista storica*, 66 (1982), 354, and 'Machiavelli, Pier Soderini and *Il Principe*' in *Altro Polo. A Volume of Italian Renaissance Studies*, C. Condren and R. Pesman Cooper, eds. (Sydney, 1982), p. 123.
[78] S. Bertelli, 'Machiavelli and Soderini', *Renaissance Quarterly*, 28 (1975), 15.

appointment of Don Michele de Corella, Cesare Borgia's former henchman and the author of the massacre at Senigaglia, as its captain. This prospect terrified Soderini's aristocratic opponents, whose fears were articulated by Guicciardini:

Ebbononne e cittadini di qualità grande alterazione, dubitando che questa voglia di avere don Michele non fussi fondata in su qualche cattivo disegno e che questo instrumento non avessi a servire o per desiderio di occupare la tirannide o, quando fussi in qualche angustia, per levarsi dinanzi e' cittadini inimici sua.[79]

Guicciardini's testimony has been accepted at face value by Carlo Dionisotti, who has suggested that Machiavelli's ulterior motive here was to turn the *gonfalonier a vita* into a prince with the militia as his private army.[80] Dionisotti's lead has been followed by Sergio Bertelli,[81] but their interpretation has been definitively refuted by Pesman Cooper. She shows in the first place that there are no sinister overtones in the correspondence between the Soderini brothers and Machiavelli regarding Don Michele's appointment; the principal theme of their letters was discipline and, having seen Don Michele 'in action with the Romagnol peasants conscripted into Cesare Borgia's army', they felt he was ideally suited to recreate the *virtù* of the ancient Roman army. Pesman Cooper also carefully examines the texts of Machiavelli's *Discorso dell'ordinare lo stato di Firenze alle armi* and of the law of 6 December 1506 establishing the militia, which closely follows Machiavelli's *Discorso*; she shows that both documents 'went to considerable lengths to ensure that it would not become a private instrument'. She also points out that, in practice, these formal safeguards worked: Soderini's opponents were represented in both the magistracies which controlled the militia.[82] With regard to Machiavelli's personal role in the militia, there is little doubt that he himself was the originator of the project. As Nicolai Rubinstein shows, however, the realisation of the scheme is eloquent testimony to the limits of Machiavelli's political influence in Florence;[83] moreover, the most controversial feature of the project, the appointment of Don Michele, probably originated not with Machiavelli but with Francesco Soderini: Pesman Cooper points out that he was the first to float Don Michele's name in a letter to his brother on 26 August 1505 and that, according to Parenti, Don Michele's appointment ran into opposition in Florence because 'stimassi da Roma del Cardinale Soderini venisse tal ordine'.[84]

[79] F. Guicciardini, *Storie fiorentine*, R. Palmarocchi, ed. (Bari, 1931), p. 281.

[80] C. Dionisotti, 'Machiavelli, Cesare Borgia e don Michelotto' in his *Machiavellerie* (Turin, 1980), pp. 3–59.

[81] S. Bertelli, 'Petrus Soderini Patriae Parens', *Bibliothèque d'humanisme et renaissance*, 31 (1969), 93–114, and his 'Pier Soderini Vexillifer Perpetuus Reipublicae Florentinae: 1502–1512' in *Renaissance Studies in Honour of Hans Baron*, A. Molho and J.A. Tedeschi, eds. (Florence, 1971), pp. 347–57.

[82] Pesman Cooper, 'Machiavelli, Francesco Soderini and Don Michelotto', 350–2; and her 'Pier Soderini', 113. [83] Rubinstein, 'Machiavelli and the world of Florentine politics', 16.

[84] Pesman Cooper, 'Machiavelli, Pier Soderini', 140–1 (n. 37).

Another indication that Machiavelli was not a partisan during his years of public service was his circle of acquaintance and friendship, which was not limited to Soderini's supporters; indeed, he made constant efforts to extend his base of support to Soderini's opponents. Machiavelli's relations with the Salviati family were excellent in the early months of Soderini's regime: in October 1502 he successfully enlisted the aid of Jacopo Salviati in settling a tax problem and in December of that year, Alamanno Salviati allayed any doubts Machiavelli might have had about his impending reconfirmation to the chancery with a warmly eulogistic letter.[85] However, by the early months of 1504 a breach had opened between the Soderini and the Salviati,[86] who were to become the leaders of the aristocratic opposition to the regime; nevertheless, Machiavelli saw no reason to distance himself from Alamanno Salviati, to whom he dedicated the *Decennale primo* in November of that year.[87] This work contains a panegyric of an unnamed citizen whom Machiavelli portrays as the saviour of the republic. Most commentators are agreed that Machiavelli is referring here to Alamanno Salviati;[88] Pesman Cooper's attempt to identify this figure as Piero Soderini is doubtful for the simple reason that Machiavelli refers to him as then in charge of Florence ('che allora governava' vostro stato').[89] Salviati at that time was a member of the Signoria (literally the lords, 'signori' of Florence), whereas Soderini was only a member of the Dieci, who had authority ('balìa') but were not literally governing the state. Machiavelli's dedication and panegyric in the *Decennale primo* were an undoubted attempt to salvage his relations with the Salviati, an effort which failed in the short run, as is shown by Salviati's reference to him as a 'ribaldo' in 1506 and the omission of the dedication when the *Decennale* was printed in that same year.[90] Nevertheless, Machiavelli was not a man to give up hope: the successful effort to regain Pisa between March and June 1509 brought Salviati and Machiavelli into close cooperation in the camp of the besieging Florentine forces.[91] Machiavelli did not hesitate to ingratiate himself again with Salviati, to whom, now Captain of Pisa, he despatched a long and important letter in September 1509 after he had returned to his duties in Florence.[92] According to its editors, Machiavelli used particularly exaggerated forms with which to greet Salviati, not to mention a notably unctuous valediction.[93]

---

[85] Luzzati and Sbrilli, 'Massimiliano d'Asburgo', 836; Pesman Cooper, 'Machiavelli, Pier Soderini', 141 (n. 43).   [86] *Ibid.*

[87] Bertelli, 'Machiavelli and Soderini', 11–13; Butters, *Governors*, p. 72; Ridolfi, *Life*, p. 82; Pesman Cooper, 'Machiavelli, Pier Soderini', 125–8.

[88] Tommasini, *Vita*, 1, pp. 308ff; Dionisotti, 'Machiavelli' pp. 36ff; Bertelli, 'Machiavelli and Soderini', 11–12.

[89] Pesman Cooper, 'Machiavelli, Pier Soderini', 125–8. For the text, see Machiavelli, *Opera*, ed. M. Bonfantini (Milan and Naples, 1954), p. 1058.

[90] Ridolfi, *Life*, p. 95; Pesman Cooper, 'Machiavelli, Pier Soderini', 128; Luzzato and Sbrilli, 'Massimiliano d'Asburgo', 837.   [91] *Ibid.*, 839–40.   [92] *Ibid.*, 849–53.   [93] *Ibid.*, 841.

A close reading of Salviati's reply on this occasion will show that Machiavelli was yet again unsuccessful,[94] but he was still not entirely discouraged. He used his friendship with Luigi Guicciardini in 1509 to ask to be recommended to another aristocratic opponent of Soderini's, his brother, Francesco Guicciardini, Salviati's son-in-law.[95] Again he achieved little on this occasion, but he was much more successful with another patrician family notable for their opposition to Soderini. Machiavelli's friendship with Francesco Vettori originated during their mission to Germany in 1508; although Francesco did not share his brother Paolo's vehement hostility to Soderini, he was nonetheless hardly Soderini's political ally, advocating for example alliance with Julius II and the Spanish viceroy in 1512. His political affiliation was, in the words of Devonshire Jones, the '"constitutional" opposition to Soderini led by Jacopo Salviati which Nerli registers',[96] and so it is clear that with Vettori Machiavelli succeeded where he had failed with Salviati.

This kind of political fence-sitting was commonplace in the history of the Florentine chancery. Leonardo Bruni had had the closest relations with the opponents of the Medici, even to the point of marrying into the Castellani family, who numbered many of the most prominent exiles in 1434;[97] nevertheless, he also enjoyed the friendship of leading figures among Mediceans, including Agnolo Acciaiuoli and Cosimo himself,[98] and indeed his election as chancellor in 1427, according to Giuliano di Averardo de' Medici, pleased everyone.[99] Similarly, Benedetto Accolti had links with the growing opposition to the Medici in the 1460s, but he still dedicated his principal compositions to Cosimo and Piero in 1462–4.[100] The most artful political survivor in the history of the chancery, however, was surely Salutati: indeed, on 4 August 1378, at the height of the Ciompi's ascendancy, Salutati gave a positive verdict on the revolution in one private letter, but in 1383 after the fall of the popular regime he utterly condemned the revolt and the insane violence of the Florentine mob, a condemnation which he repeated later that year and again in 1385.[101] Salutati's flexibility was almost matched in Machiavelli's day by Francesco Ottaviani, the notary of the Riformagioni, who was given Florentine citizenship in 1509 by the Soderini government,[102] only to preside over the Parlamento of 16 September 1512 which established the Medici Balìa and to be qualified for inclusion by the *accoppiatori* in the electoral purses of the new

[94] See pp. 97–8 below. [95] Ridolfi, *Life*, 285, n. 10. [96] Devonshire Jones, *Vettori*, p. 63.
[97] L. Martines, *The Social World of the Florentine Humanists* (Princeton, 1963), pp. 199–210.
[98] Vespasiano da Bisticci, *Le vite*, ed. A. Greco (Florence, 1970–6), II, p. 169; L. Bruni, *Humanistisch-Philosophische Schriften*, ed. H. Baron (Leipzig and Berlin, 1928), pp. 146–7.
[99] Black, *Accolti*, p. 108. [100] *Ibid.*, pp. 184ff., 209–10, 277–85.
[101] A. Petrucci, *Coluccio Salutati* (Rome, 1972), pp. 43–53.
[102] Marzi, *Cancelleria*, p. 292. I apologise for misreading this date in my earlier article, 'Florentine political traditions', p. 10.

regime in March 1514.[103] Chancery officials wanted to keep their jobs despite changes in regimes, and the only difference in this respect between Machiavelli, and Salutati, Bruni, Accolti and Ottaviani, is that he failed.

His personal relations with Piero Soderini do not convincingly suggest a partisan role for Machiavelli on the Florentine political stage. Bertelli has attempted to characterise Machiavelli as Soderini's courtier,[104] but Pesman Cooper has shown that Soderini made little attempt to follow the example of the Medici and build up a personal power base of supporters, clients and family. Soderini's supporters hardly predominated in the Dieci, a magistracy which, according to contemporaries, provided the most frequent and obdurate opposition to his regime. If Soderini's allies were prominent as ambassadors, that was due to the frequent refusal of his opponents to serve on missions abroad. Soderini had the right, like other members of the Great Council, to nominate office holders, but Pesman Cooper has found that his candidates were not extraordinarily successful. Like other important men in Florence, Soderini was besought for favours by his relatives, but the Este ambassador in Florence considered him 'essere tanto timido e respettivo, ch'el non si ordinassi ad usare fora dell'ordinario per fare uno piacere', a view supported by one of Soderini's harshest critics, Cerretani. Moreover, Soderini's elevation to the gonfalonier-ship did not particularly enhance the diplomatic careers of his brothers, who, following in the footsteps of their father Tommaso (d. 1485), had already been virtual career diplomats since 1494. As far as Francesco Soderini's cardinalate is concerned, Bertelli himself points out that the prime mover here was not so much Piero Soderini as Cesare Borgia.[105] With regard to Machiavelli's own career, Pesman Cooper points out that the first chancellor, Marcello Virgilio Adriani, was made a member of the Great Council and hence eligible for political office in 1503, but that nothing similar was done for the second chancellor; Machiavelli had to wait until 1521 for the patronage of Soderini.[106] Machiavelli's personal feelings for the Soderini family were hardly strong or durable; the main reason he was hesitant to accept Vettori's invitation to Rome at the end of 1513 was his dread of having to see the Soderini again: 'Quello che

---

103 Butters, *Governors*, pp. 184, 232. Ottaviani ceased to be notary of the Riformagioni in November 1514 (Butters, *Governors*, p. 14) and Marzi wondered whether he had been sacked or had died (*Cancelleria*, p. 309). In fact, he died in office, showing that he successfully managed to retain the confidence of the new regime until the end of his life: ASF, Tratte Appendice, 13, fol. 80r: (10 January 1514 ab inc.) Messer Jacopo di ser Michele Modesti da Prato is elected chancellor of the Riformagioni 'loco ser Francisci Antonii de Aretio premortui olim cancellarii et officialis dicti loci'; see also *ibid.* fol. 85v: 'in locum ser Francisci Octaviani de Aretio premortui'. A stop-gap chancellor of the Riformagioni had been ser Bernardo Fiamingi da San Miniato, who had served until 3 January 1514 ab inc. (*ibid.* fol. 79r–v).

104 Bertelli, 'Machiavelli and Soderini', 1–16.

105 Pesman Cooper, 'Pier Soderini', 83–4, 109–10, 115–18.

106 Pesman Cooper, 'Machiavelli, Pier Soderini', 125.

mi fa stare dubbio è, che son costì quelli Soderini e' quali io sarei forzato, venendo costì, vicitarli et parlar loro.'[107]

Such divergent interpretations of Machiavelli's relations with Soderini, as have been put forward by Dionisotti, Bertelli, Pesman Cooper and Butters, in part result from differences in historical method. The years after 1494 offer an abundance of contemporary chronicle sources without precedent in Florentine history. The problem is how to use this rich material. Bertelli's views are founded largely on the basis of a literal reading of these chroniclers, supplemented principally by diplomatic correspondence and, to a lesser extent, by contemporary literary evidence. It is not surprising that he takes a sinister view of Soderini's and Machiavelli's role in Florentine politics, since that was the attitude of most of the contemporary historians – especially Parenti, Guicciardini and Cerretani. Pesman Cooper and Butters start from a different premise. Aware of the chroniclers' extreme prejudice against the Soderini regime, they have attempted to see to what extent other evidence corroborates the narrative testimony against Soderini. Not surprisingly, they have found that a rather different picture emerges from private letters, the debates of the *pratiche* and lists of office holders and nominations. Inexplicably omitting any refutation of Pesman Cooper, Bertelli has replied by accusing Butters of ignoring or performing a cosmetic operation on the evidence of contemporary witnesses.[108] The most cogent objection he makes to Butters' work – the failure to consider the growth of the Soderini clan and clientage network because of an artificial chronological starting point (1502)[109] – loses its force when it is realised that this question had already been explored by Pesman Cooper.[110] He erroneously accuses Butters of ignoring one of his own publications[111] and more importantly of 'voluta omessa utilizzazione di un testo fondamentale' – the *Ricordanze* of Giovanvittorio Soderini.[112] In fact, Butters cites this work several times in his text as well as in his bibliography;[113] it is not surprising that Butters does not use it more extensively, since it breaks off in 1498/9 and, more importantly, since the passages which Bertelli quotes at length do not so much show the growing power of an ambitious Soderini clan as illustrate the

---

[107] *Lettere*, ed. Gaeta, pp. 304–5. See Pesman Cooper, 'Machiavelli, Pier Soderini', 142, n. 57, where the letter is curiously interpreted as indicating Machiavelli's sense of personal attachment to Soderini.

[108] S. Bertelli, 'Di due profili mancati e di un bilancino con pesi truccati', *Archivio storico italiano*, 165 (1987), 579–610.   [109] *Ibid.*, 582.   [110] Pesman Cooper, 'Pier Soderini', 115ff.

[111] Bertelli, 'Di due profili', 607, n. 70. See Butters, *Governors*, p. 148, n. 71. According to Bertelli (581), Butters overlooked the fact that the *divieto* against immediate re-election to the Consiglio degli Ottanta was waived in 1494, but this comment is not entirely justified. The *divieto* was waived in 1494, introduced in 1498 and once again removed in 1502: see R. Pesman Cooper, 'The Florentine ruling group under the "Governo popolare", 1494–1512', *Studies in Medieval and Renaissance History*, n. s. 7 (1985), 92, 95; Butters, *Governors*, p. 48.

[112] Bertelli, 'Di due profili', 582.   [113] Butters, *Governors*, pp. 26, 36, 37, 44, 322.

desperate attempts of the family to survive politically after the fall of Savonarola, with whom the eldest Soderini brother, Pagolantonio, had been closely associated.[114] In the end, it comes down to this: if all contemporary evidence is of equal weight, regardless of prejudice or bias, then Bertelli wins the day; if, on the other hand, the court should consider not only the testimony of witnesses at face value but also assess their motives, then Pesman Cooper and Butters must prevail.

It is difficult not to see a predisposal to the conspiracy theory of history in Bertelli's efforts to see the sinister implications of every manoeuvre, to regard 'la politica soderiniana' as 'in tutto e per tutto una lezione machiavellica',[115] whereas the Anglo-Saxon belief in fair play and constitutionalism has possibly left its mark on Pesman Cooper's and Butters' view of Soderini as a 'civic leader', as a man 'who regarded his office in non-political terms, as above politics',[116] whose 'time in office was on the whole marked by a nice observance of the legal limits that defined his position in government'.[117] It would be satisfying to conclude that there was an element of truth in both views, but on this particular occasion Butters' and Pesman Cooper's sympathies do seem to approximate to historical reality more closely. The Florentine political world of the late fifteenth and early sixteenth centuries was one in which there were present strong currents of factionalism, favour, patronage, nepotism and corruption. Nevertheless, when Machiavelli came to office in 1498, followed by Soderini in 1502, Florence had just experienced a period of unprecedented political manipulation and clientage under the Medici, to be followed by four years of almost unimaginably bitter factional strife surrounding Savonarola. In these circumstances, it is not surprising that there emerged a politician who wished to turn his back on the immediate past and return to a mythical golden age of justice, peace and civic harmony; despite its humanist conventions, its Virgilian sources (the fourth Eclogue and *Aeneid*) and its encomiastic tone, Cipriano Bracali's poem which was recited at Piero Soderini's pre-inaugural banquet in 1502 probably reflects the gonfalonier's personal idealism.[118]

Machiavelli's instinct for political survival may have encouraged a somewhat more cynical approach to the political world, as is suggested by his egregious manoeuvring among the political factions in the years 1504 to 1512. John Najemy's view of Machiavelli as a man of independent mind who, carried away by his belief in himself and his own ideas, lost more friends than he won, is an important new insight into his complex behaviour in the years up to 1512.[119]

---

[114] Bertelli, 'Di due profili', 582–88.   [115] *Ibid.*, 597.

[116] Pesman Cooper, 'Pier Soderini', 121.

[117] Butters, *Governors*, p. 308. It should perhaps be pointed out that Pesman Cooper tends to see Soderini as a rather less worldly figure than Butters, who believes that Soderini had to enter the political fray to do the job of *gonfalonier a vita*.

[118] H. Butters, 'Piero Soderini and the Golden Age', *Italian Studies*, 33 (1978), 56–71.

[119] See below, chapter 5, esp. pp. 101–3, 117.

Nevertheless, however Machiavelli behaved in this period – and there is no reason to think he was more consistent than anyone else – his conduct as a public official had to conform to the norms laid down by his political masters. Under Piero Soderini's regime, that meant keeping himself out of the thick of partisan political strife. Moreover, some of Machiavelli's writings during this period of his life have as their theme or purpose political harmony, such as the *capitolo Dell'ambizione*, which was composed in the last months of 1509,[120] at the same time as the letter to Salviati, with its call not to resurrect the pro-imperial stance of 1507–8 and so to continue the unity of the regime which had achieved the reconquest of Pisa.[121] Even more specific were the lines eulogising Alamanno Salviati and Piero Soderini in *Decennale primo*: in his term as prior (July–August 1502) Salviati had pacified Pistoia, quelled the rebellion in Arezzo and the Val di Chiana, and dispelled confusion in Florence by initiating the moves for constitutional reform which culminated in the election of a *gonfaloniere a vita* (vv. 355–69). Piero Soderini, then installed in this office, 'was the bedrock' of Florentine peace, and no one should now detract from the harmony and good order which these two men – Soderini and Salviati – had achieved. Written after Salviati had begun to oppose Soderini, these lines were a call to return to the unity which had characterised the months of the new regime and had come so close to solving all of Florence's problems.[122]

If a close examination of the evidence from Soderini's term of office does not suggest a partisan involvement for Machiavelli, neither do a number of important documents and texts from the immediate aftermath of the fall of the regime. One is Machiavelli's letter of 10 December 1513 to Vettori in which he states that he has been a man of good faith for forty-three years. Martelli has argued that Machiavelli had an association with the Medici dating from before 1494 and that this letter is not merely a bland declaration of personal probity but also an affirmation that he had never acted against the interests of his early patrons, the Medici family;[123] if there are such implications in this letter, it would mean that Machiavelli was denying that he had engaged in partisan activity against the Medici or their supporters between 1498 and 1512. If he had not acted as an anti-Medicean under the popular government, this would make more credible his immediate recourse to the Medici after the fall of Soderini. This must remain speculation, but what is not speculative is the text of the confession of Giovanni Folchi from 1 March 1513 regarding the anti-Medicean conspiracy in which Machiavelli was implicated. Besides confirming that Machiavelli was not involved in subversive plots, Folchi declares that Machiavelli, even after his dismissal, was more preoccupied with the external

---

[120] N. Machiavelli, *Capitoli*, ed. G. Inglese (Rome, 1981), 101. See Luzzati and Sbrilli, 'Massimilano d'Asburgo', 846, n. 80. [121] *Ibid.*, 846.
[122] Machiavelli, *Opere*, ed. Bonfatini, pp. 1058–9. See Pesman Cooper, 'Machiavelli, Pier Soderini', 125–8. [123] Martelli, 'Preistoria (medicea)', 405.

position of Florence than with the highly unstable and faction-ridden internal politics of the city: 'Con Nicolò Machiavelli dixe havere parlato de' fatti del Ghonfaloniere . . . et alsì di Giovanbaptista Soderini, et più delle gherre che della città.'[124] It seems strange that a partisan, recently deprived of office for partisan activities, should be more concerned with external affairs than with the internal politics which had just cost him his job.

Most eloquent, however, is the *Ricordo ai Palleschi*. This text, written probably between 1 and 7 November 1512,[125] is of course directly focussed on partisan political issues: Machiavelli is telling the Medici, newly restored to power, how to maintain their position; above all else he warns, do not trust the aristocrats. What is particularly significant is the contrast between this tract and all Machiavelli's earlier political writings. Marchand draws this contrast with great clarity:

This text is profoundly different from those before: for the first time the subject is not the internal or external policies of Florence, the military organization of Tuscany or the structure of a European state, but the partisan struggles in the capital after the fall of the Soderini republic and their influence on the state and on the power of the Medici.[126]

Here Machiavelli's own writings testify that before 1512 his concerns were not with factional quarrels, and it was only his endangered position that focussed his attention, for the first time, on the problems of Florentine partisan politics. Moreover, Machiavelli's hatred for the aristocrats in the *Ricordo ai Palleschi* is not in itself evidence that he had acted against them in the years of the Soderini regime. In fact, the emergence of these views only in the *Ricordo* suggests that he had actually been restraining his political opinions in previous years. The contrast between the *Ricordo* and his earlier writings does not imply that he underwent some kind of profound change of outlook as a result of the fall of the Soderini government; indeed, the continuity and steady development of Machiavelli's thought in these early years seems beyond doubt.[127] What this contrast does demonstrate is that Machiavelli was actually exercising political restraint, that he was attempting to keep out of the internal politics of the republic in the years of his political service. All this was in keeping with the tone of the chancery at the beginning of the sixteenth century. Indeed, Machiavelli's colleague, Biagio Buonaccorsi, who also suffered dismissal by the new regime, has recently been shown by Fachard to have been a figure of almost complete political detachment, his writings largely devoid of political comment or prejudice.[128] In fact, even the Medici themselves were not at first keen to tamper with the tone of political impartiality which had been largely re-established in the chancery at the beginning of the sixteenth century. When Francesco

---

[124] Stephens and Butters, 'New light', 67. [125] Marchand, *Primi scritti*, pp. 298–301.
[126] *Ibid.*, 302. [127] See Marchand, *Primi scritti*, pp. 367–95.
[128] Fachard, *Buonaccorsi*, pp. 5, 22, 139.

Ottaviani died in office in November 1514, Galeotto de' Medici had been made caretaker of the city by Lorenzo, future Duke of Urbino; as a replacement, Galeotto wrote to Lorenzo recommending the appointment of one ser Bonaventura, whose suitability for the chancellorship of the Riformagioni was generally agreed, for he was a man 'con poche ho nissuna spezieltà, e finché nonn avere dipendenza da persona'.[129]

Of course, there remains the problem of Machiavelli's dismissal; if he was not a partisan, Najemy justifiably asks, why was he sacked?[130] In itself, the delay of a little more than two months between the fall of Soderini and Machiavelli's expulsion from the palace does not necessarily imply that he was free of political contamination; a similar gap was noticeable after the revolution of 1498, when the leaders of the *frateschi* were imprisoned in the Bargello in April whereas a minor *fratesco* in the chancery such as the notary of the Tratte, Bartolomeo Ciai, was allowed to remain in office until May and an even less prominent Savonarolan, Antonio Migliorotti, the second secretary, was not sacked until June.[131] What may be significant here is the difference between being perceived as a partisan and actually being a genuine activist. There is little doubt that aristocrats such as Salviati, Guicciardini and Cerretani regarded Machiavelli as politically compromised. As Pesman Cooper and Butters have shown, nevertheless, their perception of the leader of the fallen regime, Piero Soderini, was far from accurate and there is no particular reason to think they were any closer to the truth in their view of Machiavelli. He would not have been the first or last person to suffer unjust dismissal. The hatred which Machiavelli shows for the aristocrats in the *Ricordo ai Palleschi* may have been not so much a committed partisan's antipathy to his long-standing enemies as the resentment of an ordinary man, a *popolano*, directed against the inveterate prejudice and snobbery of his social betters. Machiavelli's own behaviour, as Najemy admirably demonstrates, could hardly have safeguarded his position in the volatile months after the fall of Soderini, and this aspect of his character is not only visible in the texts which Najemy discusses but also in the recently published correspondence between Machiavelli and Alamanno Salviati in 1509.

The editors of this new letter by Machiavelli highlight not only his efforts to ingratiate himself with Salviati but also his increasing egotism and self-assertion. This letter, with its categoric and exhaustive analysis of Florentine diplomatic prospects, is comparable, as they point out, with Machiavelli's earlier letter to Giovanni Ridolfi of 12 June 1506. What is particularly revealing is that, whereas in the earlier letter Machiavelli does not take personal credit for his analyses but declares them to be the opinions of 'citadini . . . più savi', now in September 1509 he flaunts his own views, openly revelling in the divergence

---

[129] Butters, *Governors*, p. 14. [130] See below, Ch. 5, p. 102.
[131] Black, 'Machiavelli's election', 11, 16.

between his personal analysis and 'la commune opinione'.[132] It is difficult not to see the growing arrogance of an intellectual, whose ego has recently been given an enormous boost by the success of his pet scheme, the militia, in the recapture of Pisa. Machiavelli was aware of his tendency to preach to his correspondents; he excuses himself here by calling his prolix discourse a 'badalucco', a 'plaything', whereas in the earlier letter he apologises for writing 'queste bibbie'.[133] Nevertheless, his egotism was thereby rendered hardly the more palatable, as is clear from Salviati's reply, which itself is laden with irony and sarcasm. Although praising the fine construction of Machiavelli's discourse, he refuses to accept or reject his conclusion. He is willing, clearly unlike Machiavelli, to defer to the experts, in this case, the captains of the Florentine force in Pisa, about the likely outcome of the imperial siege of Padua. Machiavelli's lack of religious faith, he jibes, must make it difficult to appreciate his own fatalism in the face of the improbable and inexplicable turn of events, 'cosa miracolosa più presto che naturale'. Machiavelli, his learned correspondent, 'mio dottore', must make up for his own intellectual shortcomings, and he closes on an even more sarcastic note, asking that 'Idio ti guardi'.[134] It would be hard to find a more eloquent testimony of the loathing which Machiavelli – in Salviati's view a godless, arrogant intellectual – inspired among the Florentine conservative patriciate.

Machiavelli's dismissal, therefore, may have had as much to do with his personal behaviour as with his Soderinian connections, just as, indeed, the chancellor, Paolo Fortini, was sacked in 1427 because of the 'gozaia', 'odio e nimicizia' which he inspired in one of the priors, Luigi Vecchietti.[135] Machiavelli's case even more closely resembles the fate of another fifteenth-century chancellor. In 1456 Poggio was not reconfirmed in office, at least in part because he was closely identified with Cosimo de' Medici at a time when the Medici regime was in deep crisis. He had lived away from Florence for more than fifty years and hardly understood the workings of Florentine government; he was in no position to exercise partisan influence on behalf of anyone, and yet he was sacked not least to embarrass the regime and particularly Cosimo. But like Machiavelli too, Poggio was unconventional, outspoken and arrogant, and he notably failed to ingratiate himself with the entire governing class of Florence.[136]

Nevertheless, Machiavelli was sacked together with another chancery official, his friend Biagio Buonaccorsi, a fact which suggests that something more than Machiavelli's personality was involved. Besides their identification with a fallen political leader, Machiavelli and Buonaccorsi shared a common

[132] Luzzati and Sbrilli, 'Massimiliano d'Asburgo', 842.   [133] *Ibid.*   [134] *Ibid.*, 853–4.
[135] Black, *Accolti*, p. 108.
[136] D. De Rosa, 'Poggio Bracciolini cancelliere della Repubblica Fiorentina', *Studi e ricerche*, 2 (1983), 217–50; Black, *Accolti*, pp. 88–98.

social position – they were both members of the chancery/notarial class. Pesman Cooper has shown that this social group had been particularly successful in climbing the Florentine social ladder in the fifteenth and early sixteenth centuries.[137] This kind of prominence of course invited reaction and resentment from the patriciate. Hence, the exclusion of notaries from the Signoria after 1434 observed by Martines, culminating in the legislation of March 1496 which required notaries to choose whether they would serve in notarial offices or ordinary political posts.[138] Hence, the invectives launched against the preferential treatment accorded to notaries and chancellors by Piero Vaglienti in his chronicle and in his 'Apologia alla Signoria' dating from around 1500, as well as Guicciardini's comment in his *Dialogo* that 'la authorità ed el pondo del governo è in cancelleri, personne villi e di pocca qualità'.[139] In view of such sentiments it is not surprising that a particularly prominent chancellor such as Machiavelli attracted the hostility of the patriciate, who at the same time sacked for good measure yet another chancery minion who had risen to prominence by clinging to Machiavelli's coat tails.[140]

Machiavelli was, of course, a figure of astounding individuality, and he made a remarkably energetic contribution to Florentine administration during his years as an official of the republic. Nevertheless, his public service – as a humanist, as a bureaucrat, as a diplomat, as a statesman – still very much followed the time-honoured traditions of the Florentine chancery. The 'quindici anni che io sono stato a studio all'arte dello stato' were not in themselves an extraordinary experience. What was astonishing was Machiavelli himself and what he made of his years as a civil servant; his originality becomes even more awesome when it is understood that he emerged from such a conventional background.

[137] Pesman Cooper, 'The Florentine ruling group', 84–6.
[138] L. Martines, *Lawyers and Statecraft in Renaissance Florence* (Princeton, 1968), pp. 47–50; Pesman Cooper, 'The Florentine ruling group', 85.   [139] *Ibid.*, 115 (n. 89), 118 (n. 125).
[140] On Biagio Buonaccorsi and Machiavelli, see G. Sasso, 'Biagio Buonaccorsi e Niccolò Machiavelli', *La cultura*, 18 (1980), 195–222, and Najemy, chapter 5 below.

5

The controversy surrounding Machiavelli's service to the republic

JOHN M. NAJEMY

At the origin – or very close to it – of Machiavelli's encounter with the traditions of republican history and thought lies his complex relationship to the Florentine republic that he served for fourteen years as chancellor and secretary. Machiavelli himself, in the dedicatory letters of both *The Prince* and the *Discourses*, emphasised the 'lunga esperienza' and 'pratica' of modern events together with the reading of ancient texts as the twin sources of his knowledge of politics. In fact most of the usual images of Machiavelli's years in the chancery derive from these and a few other famous sentences (mostly in the great letter to Vettori of December 1513) that he wrote after the fall of the republic and the Medicean restoration forced him out of office: the picture of the tireless and self-effacing public servant, full of good faith and honesty, who paid a heavy price for such devoted service. Clearly, these post-1512 representations by Machiavelli of his chancery years are coloured by the bitterness he felt over his dismissal and humiliation.

But what did that experience seem like during the years it unfolded, both to Machiavelli and to those with whom, in one way or another, he worked? And, in the light of what we can learn about his activities and experience before 1512, what can be said of its relationship to his later writings on republics? Robert Black reopens these questions (see chapter 4) by claiming that Machiavelli's public service followed the 'traditions of the Florentine chancery' in at least three important respects: his credentials as a humanist, his diplomatic activity, and his lack of identification with any faction in the turbulent politics of Florence between 1498 and 1512. The general thrust of Black's analysis is to normalise Machiavelli the public servant: to place him within the depoliticised context of institutional constraints and professional qualifications characteristic of chancery officials from at least the mid-fifteenth century. Here at least, in Black's view, Machiavelli was no revolutionary. Moreover, most of Machiavelli's attention in these years was directed to foreign and military policy, not to domestic politics. Thus, given the expectation – to which, if Black is correct, Machiavelli conformed – that chancery officials should stay clear of any involvement in partisan or factional politics, Black's approach appears to diminish the extent to which those 'quindici anni che io sono stato a studio all'arte dello stato' could really have been, as Machiavelli later presented them, the fountain of experience from which so much revolutionary theorising about republican politics flowed. Black sees the *Ricordo ai Palleschi* (probably of early November 1512) as a major break for Machiavelli: the moment in which, for the first time, he demonstrates interest in – or finally reveals his feelings about – the domestic political situation of the republic under Soderini. Until that moment, according to Black, Machiavelli had respected the conventions of the chancery by staying away from partisan politics and by cultivating friendships across party lines. Black's argument is not that Machiavelli had no opinions or feelings about such matters before 1512; it is rather that he recognised the need to mask those feelings over fifteen years in order to do his job well, indeed in order to keep his job at all.

But, as everyone knows, Machiavelli was dismissed from his posts just two months after Soderini and the republic fell. And the question we must ask is this: if, for fifteen years, Machiavelli did indeed conform to the norms and conventions of chancery service, if, by and large, he kept his opinions to himself and avoided involvement in partisan politics, why was he fired? Of all the chancery staff, only Machiavelli and his friend and colleague Biagio Buonaccorsi were removed from their posts. Obviously, Machiavelli's close relationship to Piero Soderini had much to do with his dismissal, but the curious time lag of two months between Soderini's ouster on 31 August and the firing of Machiavelli on 7 November suggests that the special relationship with the *vexillifer perpetuus* is not of itself a sufficient explanation for Machiavelli's removal, let alone for the disgrace and humiliation inflicted on him in February–March 1513. The fact is that Machiavelli had enemies – or at least people who disliked him enough to make sure that he would never again hold any significant position in Florentine government. Perhaps it was the *Ricordo ai Palleschi* – with its strong anti-*ottimati* sentiments – that did him in. But if that memorandum was indeed written in the days just prior to Machiavelli's dismissal, it seems odd that the secretary who, in Black's view, had been so cautious and restrained for nearly fifteen years should have taken such a risk in so precarious a moment – in the very days in which scores were being settled and in which both the Medici and the *ottimati* were willing to scapegoat the demoralised republicans in their contest for control of the city.

Machiavelli may have tried to suppress his political opinions during his years in the chancery. More problematic is whether he succeeded in this effort at self-control, and whether he was perceived by others as having done so. Letters written to Machiavelli by friends, chancery colleagues, and leading Florentine political figures[1] strongly suggest that he did not and that his attitude and tone

---

[1] The most useful editions of Machiavelli's correspondence are: Niccolò Machiavelli, *Tutte le opere*, ed. Mario Martelli (Florence, 1971), pp. 1009–1256, hereafter cited as M; and *Opere di Niccolò Machiavelli*, vol. III, *Lettere*, ed. Franco Gaeta (Turin, 1984), hereafter cited as G. The Gaeta edition includes a good introductory essay and useful explanatory notes and bibliography.

in the performance of his official tasks were frequently controversial, not because of any particular partisan stance – here again one can agree with Black – but because of a certain posture of independence, a tendency to stand apart from the political system and leaders he served and to subject them to criticism often mixed with more than a hint of contempt. His friends warned him that this posture was sometimes perceived as arrogance, that it was isolating him and might eventually leave him vulnerable.

Gennaro Sasso's excellent essay on Machiavelli and Biagio Buonaccorsi reminds us that Machiavelli's friendships were complex matters. In the case of Buonaccorsi, Sasso concludes that jealousy, envy, and the nagging doubt that his great admiration – even love – for Machiavelli were never reciprocated go far in explaining the subconscious motivations for the often bleak picture he painted of Machiavelli's situation – repeated warnings in which, according to Sasso, Buonaccorsi exaggerated, for psychological reasons of his own, the secretary's precarious position and unpopularity. Sasso sees Buonaccorsi as painfully aware of his own inferiority to Machiavelli and, consequently, needful of playing the role of the 'wise practical adviser' who saw the dangers of which Machiavelli took little notice. Thus, for Sasso, Buonaccorsi's warnings should not be taken at face value, especially in the light of the lavish praise that Machiavelli's work received from others.[2]

But Biagio was not the only one to warn Machiavelli of dangers stemming from the way he carried out his official duties. The very fact that Machiavelli's work frequently elicited expressions of both admiration and friendly criticism is an indication of its controversial nature and of the extent to which friends and colleagues often worried about the impression it would make on the Signoria, the Dieci, the Nove, and leading *ottimati*. The praise he received should perhaps be no more taken at face value than the dire warnings. Taken together and read in light of each other, however, they suggest that, while no one had any doubt about his remarkable abilities, Machiavelli's reluctance to respect the conventions and proprieties of the political system within which he worked – not its formal or constitutional aspects, but its unwritten rules of deference and hierarchy – was a source of much concern to those who admired him and wanted him to stay on the job.

So often did Machiavelli's friends tell him that his letters and dispatches met with approval and praise that one begins to suspect either that he needed such reassurance or that they were expressing some worry of their own. On 19 July 1499 Buonaccorsi told him that 'in my judgement you have until now carried out the mission entrusted to you [to Caterina Sforza] with great honour to yourself; I have taken and continue to take great pleasure in this' (M 1016a; G 79). A week later (27 July), Biagio mentioned that one of their friends 'has heard your letters being much praised' (M 1017a; G 82–3). On 23 August 1500 Biagio

---

[2] Gennaro Sasso, 'Biagio Buonaccorsi e Niccolò Machiavelli', *La Cultura*, 18 (1980), 195–222.

wrote that he did not want to omit mentioning 'how much your letters please [*satisfanno*] everyone; and believe me, Niccolò, for you know that adulation is not my trade, that when I read those first letters of yours [from the French court] to certain citizens, and indeed to some very prominent ones, you were most highly commended. This gave me great pleasure, and I tried with a few words of my own skilfully to confirm this opinion, demonstrating with what facility you did this' (M 1019b–1020a; G 88–9). Does this mean that Machiavelli's dispatches, even as they impressed the politicians back home, needed some explanation or justification? Another example of high praise that seems to allude to reservations in certain quarters comes from a letter of Niccolò Valori of October 1502, during Machiavelli's second mission to Cesare Borgia. Referring to the dispatch of 7/8 October (M 402b–405a), Valori wrote: 'your discussion and portrayal could not have been more approved, and people recognise what I especially have always recognised in you: a clear, apt, and forthright report, on which one can make a solid foundation' (M 1033a; G 120). The sense of Valori's comment must be that others were then beginning to see what he had always seen ('et conoscesi quello che sempre io in spetie ho cogniosciuto in voi'). Among the adjectives that Valori used to describe the special qualities of Machiavelli's dispatches ('una necta, propia et sincera relatione'), 'sincera' stands out as an important clue to the kinds of reactions provoked by Machiavelli's letters: he seems to be saying that they were candid, unreserved, sincere in the sense of hiding nothing, and showing little fear of possible consequences – precisely the sort of 'sincerity' that could make some people uncomfortable. A few days later Valori wrote again to say that 'your reports and analyses really could not be better or more approved. Would that it please the Almighty that every man conduct himself as you do, and fewer mistakes would be made' (M 1039b; G 135). Valori's point was obviously that few men 'conducted themselves' in the way Machiavelli did – here again, a hint of Machiavelli's distance from the normal and conventional discourse of politics and diplomacy. Two other letters from Valori during this same month of October 1502 similarly mix compliments with the intimation that there was dissatisfaction in some quarters with the secretary. On the 28th, after saying yet again that 'the reports that come from you could not be more approved', he added: 'but in order to discuss things as we are accustomed to doing, one would wish that you wrote more often' (M 1041b; G 139) – a criticism that Machiavelli would hear repeatedly. And on the 31st he assured Machiavelli that he had made efforts, 'both in public and in private to make known your services; even though they shine on their own, it will suit our purpose to reveal them . . . And in truth these last two letters you sent contain so much vigour and show such good judgement on your part that they could not have been more approved' (M 1042a; G 140). As Buonaccorsi had done in 1500, Valori was apparently trying to promote Machiavelli's reputation among people who mattered.

What was the problem? What was Machiavelli doing or not doing that called for such intervention on his behalf? One source of irritation was that Machiavelli apparently reported to his superiors when *he* thought it useful and necessary – and not when *they* did. His friends understood his reasons. On 4 January 1500 Roberto Acciaiuoli began a letter by saying that he accepted Machiavelli's explanations for the infrequency ('rarità') of his letters to him, 'both because you are so busy and because of the duty of silence [*l'officio del silentio*], for which you cannot be praised enough, for this is what is required of a good secretary' (M 1019a; G 86). But others reminded him that his official letters were expected on a regular basis. In November 1502 Piero Soderini himself expressed his pleasure in receiving Machiavelli's reports and then urged him to 'continue frequently and diligently to write' (M 1046a; G 148). Just a day later, Biagio Buonaccorsi informed him more pointedly that the Signoria 'has the impression that you have delayed writing, because a letter you enclosed on the 5th never arrived, nor perhaps did you ever write it' (M 1047a; G 151). At the end of the month Biagio told him that he could do more on behalf of Machiavelli's request for additional funds if he would send 'a hundred of these onions, for, by God, just this morning two committees asked me to write and tell you to send some letters with the first courier' (M 1049a; G 154–5). Three more times over the next few weeks Soderini urged him to keep writing: 'In the meantime you will write often, portraying as much as you can of these things, as you have done until now; about which, together with the other Signori, I am most satisfied: and when anything comes to your attention, you will let me know about it.' Again: 'I have nothing else to tell you except to commend you and urge you, for as long as you're there, to continue to keep me informed about events as they happen, in addition to what you will write to the Ten [Dieci].' And yet again: 'and you will continue in your task of keeping a close watch on things up there and writing often' (M 1049a–b, 1049b, 1051a; G 155, 156, 160). In January 1503 Biagio wrote to say that he didn't know which was greater, the worry over the fact that for some time no letters from Machiavelli had arrived or the sense of relief people felt in learning, when one letter finally came, that Machiavelli was still alive: 'for here we were not without some fear [about whether he was alive], seeing that for eight days after the event [Cesare Borgia's imprisonment and execution at Senigallia of the leaders of the Magione conspiracy] we had no letters from you, despite the fact that reports were pouring in from everyone else and from every direction' (M 1053a; G 166). The point in all this is not that Machiavelli was not writing: the surviving dispatches demonstrate that he wrote at length and in detail. But he seems to have preferred to write according to his own schedule, when he believed he understood events sufficiently to be able to send the kind of report that he thought his government needed. He defended himself on precisely these grounds. Writing from Imola on 13 November 1502, Machiavelli expressed some pique concerning the criticism that he wrote too infrequently. 'If your lordships [the Dieci] are surprised at not having received any letters from me [over a period of eight days], I am not, but I do regret that I couldn't and still can't do anything about it.' Evidently some letters had been delayed or lost, and Machiavelli asked to be excused on this account. But then he added that the Ten should take into consideration that 'things can't just be guessed at . . . and that if one doesn't wish to write fantasies and dreams [*ghiribizzi e sogni*], one has to verify matters [*bisogna che riscontri le cose*], and that verifying them takes time, and I am doing my best to use my time well and not waste it.' And later in the same dispatch he returned some sarcasm for what was, in his opinion, an unjust rebuke: 'Your lordships expect many reports from me, and I think I have fulfilled this expectation so far, if all my letters have been read' (M 443b–444a). It would only be surprising if there were no expressions of annoyance among the Dieci over a line like that.

The larger issue behind the sniping over the alleged infrequency of his dispatches was, to judge from a letter from Biagio Buonaccorsi of 28 October 1502, that some people felt that Machiavelli was advancing too many opinions and judgements when he ought to have limited himself to reporting the facts. 'Although you are wise and prudent', Biagio began, 'and it is presumptuous on my part to want to remind you how you should write, especially about those things that you have at each moment before you, nonetheless I will briefly tell you what I have to say, despite the fact that I've done my duty in all those places and with all those persons who have wanted to criticise you [*che vi havessino voluto dare carico*].' His first point was that Machiavelli should write more often 'because making people here wait eight days for every letter of yours does you no honour and does not please those who sent you there; and you have been reproved by the Signori and others for this, since, these being matters of the importance that they are, there is a great desire here to learn often at what point things are.' Buonaccorsi then came to the heart of the problem as it must have been perceived by Machiavelli's superiors: although the secretary had described in great detail the military forces of both Cesare Borgia and his enemies,

nevertheless you make too bold a conclusion [*tamen voi fate una conclusione troppo gagliarda*] when you write that by now [Borgia's] enemies can no longer harm him very much; and it seems to me – not that, as far as I know, anyone has criticised you for this – that you can't make such a firm judgement about such matters [*che voi non ne possiate fare iudicio così resoluto*].

Buonaccorsi's reasoning was that Machiavelli could not possibly have sufficiently accurate information about Borgia's enemies in his own camp, whereas in Florence there were plenty of reports concerning the strength of his enemies but little foundation for any 'good judgement' about Borgia himself. 'Thus, once you have prudently and in detail discussed everything you observe, as you have done, leave the judgement to others [*del iudicio rimetetevene a altri*]' (M

1040b–1041a; G 137–8). It seems unlikely that Buonaccorsi would have offered Machiavelli this kind of advice without having been urged to do so by persons in Palazzo Vecchio who wanted less of Machiavelli's own interpretation of matters and more frequent accounts of what was actually happening.

A year later, at the end of 1503, Machiavelli was still making himself unpopular in certain quarters with his opinions about Cesare (see Buonaccorsi's letter of 15 November 1503; M 1056a–b and G 174–5) and with his habit of not responding promptly to requests for regular reports of news and information. On 21 November, Agnolo Tucci, a member of the Signoria, wrote to Machiavelli, then in Rome, asking for an update on papal and Venetian policy in the Romagna (M 1059 a–b; G 181–2). Two weeks later Biagio let Machiavelli know that Tucci was furious over his failure to reply ('il quale . . . era alterato gravissimamente contro di voi, per non li havere mai resposto . . .'). Tucci inveighed against Machiavelli in a meeting of the Signoria with words 'che invero furono di mala natura', and the other Signori, according to Biagio, sat and listened, without getting upset over it, because of various strong feelings among them about Machiavelli: 'tutti li altri Signori stettano ad udire, che chi per una passione et chi per un'altra non si hebbono per male'. Biagio said he would save the details of these anti-Machiavellian *passioni* until the secretary returned: for the moment he should be aware that 'ci è di maligni cervelli' (M 1060 a–b; G 183–4). Here indeed is a case where we might imagine that Biagio was exaggerating, as Sasso claims he so often did, especially since Biagio goes on to say that he had defended and would continue to defend Machiavelli in any way he could – in ways, in fact, that would make Machiavelli realise that Biagio loved him more than he did himself. Perhaps. But when Machiavelli got around to answering Tucci, sometime before the end of December, he displayed the same kind of sarcasm to which he had treated the Dieci a year earlier. Machiavelli excused himself by pointing out that all the matters about which Tucci inquired had been communicated to him in official instructions, and that he had answered

so extensively that you can inform yourself on the basis of what I have already written [i.e., in official dispatches]; nonetheless, so as not to be remiss in my duty toward you who have asked me about these matters, I will repeat the same things; I will speak in the vernacular, just in case I may have communicated with the chancery in Latin, which I don't think I did.' (M 1060b–1061b; G 185–6).

Of course, Machiavelli never wrote his dispatches in Latin; he was flinging a little *cattiveria* at Tucci, saying in effect that if Tucci was unable to understand the official letters, which were available to him in the chancery, here were the same answers in simpler language – at the same time implying that, *if* those letters to the chancery had been written in Latin, Tucci certainly would not have been able to read them. It was a double insult of the sort that was sure not to win

Machiavelli many friends among the middle ranks of Florentine officeholders – Tucci was a paper seller (G 171, n. 1) – who, finding themselves elected to some major executive office for a short term, wanted to feel important and respected and to make their voices heard. The last thing they wanted was to be ridiculed by a chancery official who, for all his influence, international connections, and closeness to Soderini, was not even eligible for the political offices they held.

Over the next few years Machiavelli continued to be a controversial figure, and, if anything, even more so as a consequence of two particular issues: the project for the militia, or *Ordinanza*, that he promoted with Soderini's support against the opposition of many *ottimati*; and his disputed, and ultimately unsuccessful, appointment as ambassador to the imperial court in 1507. Much has been written about the political objections to the *Ordinanza*,[3] and here it will be enough to underscore the echoes of that opposition in letters from Machiavelli's friends and protectors. The Gonfalonier's brother, Cardinal Francesco Soderini, welcomed Machiavelli's 'disegno' (probably for the militia) as early as January 1504 (M 1061b; G 187); but by May of the same year (in a letter in which he told Machiavelli not to blame others for the scarcity of his correspondence), the cardinal was already alluding to accusations that the militia would be an instrument for the consolidation of his brother's, or family's, power: 'one should not be suspicious of a force created for public, and not for private, advantage' (M 1062b; G 191). He referred to similar objections again in October (M 1066b; G 200), and for those, including many prominent *ottimati*, who did perceive the whole idea in such sinister terms, Machiavelli – whose 'invenzione' the *Ordinanza* was generally thought to be[4] – must have become very suspect indeed. Early in 1506 his chancery colleague Marcello Virgilio di Adriano Berti conveyed Piero Soderini's encouragement to proceed with all diligence in the recruitment of troops from the *contado*, 'because here [in Florence] the idea is enjoying more favour every day' (M 1071b; G 211–12) – an acknowledgement that opposition was still strong when Machiavelli went beyond the planning stage to actual recruitment. And in October of that year Biagio mentioned that a recent letter from Machiavelli to the Dieci had resulted in increased support for the project: 'and so the matter is going ahead with much good favour; but the daily arguments about it are infinite: and yet it's getting better' (M 1090a; G 261). Writing a few days after the new magistracy of the *Nove ufficiali dell'Ordinanza* was approved on 6 December 1506 – a law whose text Machiavelli himself drafted – Cardinal Soderini wrote to congratulate the secretary: 'To us it really seems that this *Ordinanza* is from God, because it gains

---

[3] See especially Gennaro Sasso, 'Machiavelli, Cesare Borgia, Don Micheletto e la questione della milizia' in Sasso, *Machiavelli e gli antichi e altri saggi*, vol. II (Milan and Naples, 1988), pp. 57–117.

[4] Leonardo Bartolini to Machiavelli, 21 February 1506: 'Della nuova militia . . . gudico [*sic*] riuscirà cosa mirabile, che molto me allegrerò, quando la vedrò a perfetione, sì per il bene del publico, et etiam per essere inventione vostra'; M 1072a. Also G 213.

more support every day, despite the ill-will, etc. [*non obstante la malignità etc.*].'
His interpretation of the controversy over the militia seems to have been
designed to comfort and encourage Machiavelli: 'We have taken special
pleasure in this new magistracy, and we pray to God that the election [of the
Nove] will be such as to provide a solid foundation, because we believe that this
city has in recent times accomplished nothing more honourable and more
conducive to its security than this, provided it is well used, in which good men
must apply all their zeal and not let themselves be diverted by those who, with
other purposes, do not have at heart the welfare of this city as much as they
should in its new-found liberty, which is a divine and not a human gift provided
it is not corrupted by malice or ignorance: you, who have so great a part in this,
must not desist in anything, unless you wish to provoke the ire of God and men
[*et voi che ci havete tanta parte, non mancate in alcuna cosa, nisi velitis habere Deum et
homines iratos*]' (M 1093a; G 267–8). It may have been some comfort for
Machiavelli to learn that the cardinal, and, we may assume, his brother,
supported the *Ordinanza* in such high-minded terms. But Francesco Soderini
was also telling him to persist in a project that had many enemies – and which
had the name of Niccolò Machiavelli written all over it.

In June 1507, with the controversy over the militia still swirling around
Machiavelli, came the episode of his contested appointment as ambassador to
the imperial court. Piero Soderini selected Machiavelli for the mission but had
to yield to pressure from the *ottimati* for the election of one of their own; in
what was probably a compromise choice, Francesco Vettori became the
republic's envoy to Maximilian. The history of this diplomatic mission – in
which Machiavelli did ultimately play a role when Soderini had him join Vettori
with supplementary instructions in December – has been analysed by
Devonshire Jones.[5] What interests us here is Machiavelli's reaction to the
disappointment of losing the prestigious appointment that, in Soderini's
original intention, would have been his. We know something of this reaction
from a remarkable letter written to Machiavelli by Filippo Casavecchia on 30
July 1507. They had been friends and colleagues for many years: Casavecchia is
mentioned in letters to Machiavelli as early as 1500,[6] and in 1507 he was serving
as military commissioner in Fivizzano. And their friendship would continue, as
still other letters from Casavecchia over the next few years, and the
correspondence *post res perditas* between Machiavelli and Vettori, attest. The
letter of 30 July 1507 was evidently a response to something Machiavelli had
written to Casavecchia on the subject of friendship, and – it seems – betrayal, in

[5] Rosemary Devonshire Jones, *Francesco Vettori, Florentine Citizen and Medici Servant* (London, 1972), pp. 10–33.
[6] M 1020b, 1024b; G 91, 100. For a brief sketch of Casavecchia's life and his association with Machiavelli, see Paolo Malanima, 'Filippo Casavecchia' in *Dizionario biografico degli italiani*, XXI, pp. 269–70.

the immediate aftermath of Machiavelli's removal from the diplomatic post that he had coveted. "'If I grieved, I now grieve again'", Casavecchia began, slightly modifying a verse from Dante (*Inferno*, XXVI, 19):

whereas I thought that men of your quality ought to be the crutches and support of my life and should resolve my doubts, now you come at me with things in which you might as well be asking which came first, the heavenly sphere or astrology, or which is denser, water or the terrestrial globe, or which are more perfect, triangular figures or round circles.

Clearly, Machiavelli had posed a question that Casavecchia judged anywhere from difficult to impossible. That Machiavelli's query had concerned friendship and its role in politics emerges from the next few lines of Casavecchia's letter: 'Don't you know that there have been only very few friendships that in the course of time do not become their opposite? (*Hor non sapete voi che poche poche amicitie sono state quelle che in prociesso di tempo non diventino il suo contrario?*)' Machiavelli must have lamented the loss of his appointment in terms of betrayed friendship and loyalty. Whomever he had in mind (it was probably Soderini), Machiavelli was apparently reacting to a decision governed by genuine differences of policy – many *ottimati* favoured formal negotiations with the emperor as a way of diminishing the republic's dependence on France – in terms of a transgression of personal trust. Casavecchia's consolatory letter thus began by reminding Machiavelli that, like all things subject to the 'process of time', friendships change and become their opposite. Children, he argued, enjoy changing friendships just as they do the colours of their clothes. Lack of compassion, poverty, envy and indignation among grown men all have the effect over time ('con lungezza di tempo') of turning friends into the worst of enemies. After asserting all this in a series of rhetorical questions governed by the opening 'Don't you know that . . .?', Casavecchia connected the precariousness of friendship to the adversities of politics with another rhetorical question: 'And don't you know that Rome's power and greatness were undone an infinite number of times because of friendships?' He offered a series of examples of broken friendships with enormous political consequences: Collatinus and Sextus Tarquinius, Marius and Sulla, Caesar and Pompey, Antony, Octavian, and Lepidus. And he could fill pages with similar examples from the Hebrews, Greeks, and Latins.

But what need is there to search for ancient examples, when, in our own modern times, and with our own eyes, we have seen our fatherland again and again in the greatest ruin and trouble on account of similar cases?

He cited the example of Dietisalvi Neroni and Piero di Cosimo de' Medici, and that of Giuliano de' Medici and Francesco Pazzi: neither friendship was able to prevent disastrous consequences (in the anti-Medicean conspiracies of, respectively, 1466 and 1478).

Thus one can justifiably say that for the most part the ruin of cities is caused and generated by natural and everyday friendships which, with time and especially in powerful men, give rise to such and similar results for the reasons already explained. And therefore, dearest friends – [Casavecchia was now addressing both Machiavelli and unnamed others – but who?] – I exhort and urge you, indeed I beg you to conduct yourselves with moderation and civility with each other, first because I believe friendships are more likely to last if you do, and also in order to avoid the suspicions and jealousies that habitually arise in such cities. (M 1095b–1096b; G 272–75)

This was all some kind of a joke, but one with a serious purpose and, as we shall see, a warning for Machiavelli. The pompous and pretentious dissertation on friendship and the political ruin of cities reads like a sermon by Savonarola, complete with scholastic language, historical examples, and moral exhortation.[7] Casavecchia was trying to make Machiavelli laugh in a moment in which the latter was more inclined to feel sorry for himself. The letter's last paragraph confesses the humour and links it to the humiliation Machiavelli believed he had suffered in being denied the mission to Maximilian. 'But lest this letter of mine become the singing of a silly tale [*cantafavola*], I'll put a stop to my sermon [*sermone*] and remind you of just one thing, and that is to have patience concerning your German triumph' – Casavecchia was evidently being ironic – 'and that those who boast of having denied you [the German triumph] do not and will not have the prize in Asia.' Machiavelli had, in other words, lost one, but future contests would turn out differently. Casavecchia was in effect telling Machiavelli to put things in perspective, not to exaggerate or overly dramatise a political disappointment into accusations of disloyalty or betrayal. The humorous purpose of the sermon on friendship may have been to mimic Machiavelli's own laments and to show him what he sounded like when he became overly moralistic and temporarily lost his political savvy. Casavecchia added a postscript in which the depth of his warning became clearer. 'I ask you not to mind giving my greetings to the magnificent Gonfalonier when you go up there; but this word [of greeting] would have to be on the end of a musket for you to get up there and reluctantly do it.' Although the precise sense of this sentence is not clear, it suggests that Machiavelli's anger was indeed focussed on Soderini. And, given this dangerous and misplaced anger against the one person whose protection and support Machiavelli could not do without, Casavecchia made an ominous prediction: 'But of one thing I am certain: that one day you will plunge yourself into oblivion [*ma io sono chiaro d'una cosa: che voi metterete un dì in oblivione voi medesmo*], and let this be enough.'[8]

Casavecchia's warning was in essence that Machiavelli was not accepting the

---

[7] Mario Martelli briefly discusses Casavecchia's letters to Machiavelli in 'I "Ghiribizzi" a Giovan Battista Soderini', *Rinascimento*, second series, 9 (1969), 159–62. See also Giulio Ferroni, 'Le "cose vane" nelle *Lettere* di Machiavelli', *La Rassegna della letteratura italiana*, 76 (1972), 221–3.

[8] Jean-Jacques Marchand's comment on Casavecchia's letter points to a similar interpretation; see his *Niccolò Machiavelli: I primi scritti politici (1499–1512)* (Padua, 1975), p. 159, n. 5.

vicissitudes and occasional setbacks of politics with enough dexterity and self-protective sang-froid. More specifically, he was cautioning him not to lash out – or to grumble too loudly – against his own superiors: and here there is a certain similarity between what Casavecchia was saying and what others, including Biagio Buonaccorsi, had tried to tell him some years earlier. Another of Machiavelli's colleagues and friends, Alessandro Nasi, also wrote on 30 July with a similar message, addressing him in terms that were more wish than, for the moment, fact: 'Machiavel gentile e non sciagurato, che ne sei guarito interamente' – roughly, 'My gracious and not so unfortunate Machiavelli, now fully recovered from it [i.e. the humiliation]' – ' . . . I'm happy that you've got the matter of the imperial appointment out of your system and that you're now completely well again; and I think it's for the best, especially for you, that you should be here in Florence rather than in Germany . . .' And toward the end of Nasi's letter a familiar theme: 'And if in the midst of all this you wrote now and again, it wouldn't be a mortal sin' (M 1097a; G 275–6). The picture of Machiavelli that begins to emerge is that of an intense man who demanded as much of his friends as he did of the republic he served, who was stubborn and quick to criticise but reluctant to forgive, and who sometimes failed to take into account the ordinary, natural weaknesses and shortcomings of others. This is what his chancery colleague Agostino Vespucci had been trying to tell him as early as October 1502 when he wrote that he wouldn't want Machiavelli to

neglect anything that might make it impossible for you to continue to hold this office in the future. And if, my dear Niccolò, some people are now muttering under their breath [about you], soon enough these grumblings must come out into the open. You know the minds of men; you know their deceits and affectations, their jealousies and hatreds; you know therefore on what sort of people one depends entirely in times like these. (M 1034a; G 122)

The whole sense of this is that Machiavelli, whatever he *knew* of the 'simulationes ac dissimulationes, simultates et odia' of men, did not always prudently *act* on the basis of that knowledge. And on the level of personal relations, Biagio Buonaccorsi was saying something similar in October 1506 when he admonished Machiavelli: 'But you always want to excuse yourself, either on the grounds of carelessness [*trascurataggine*] or because you're so busy; this just won't do with friends, because they want to be acknowledged as such.' It was in this same letter that Biagio, no doubt in an effort to reinforce the point that Machiavelli's way of dealing with friends often got him into trouble, reported Alamanno Salviati's cutting description of Machiavelli as 'cotesto ribaldo' (M 1087a; G 253).

If 1507 was a year of disappointment for Machiavelli, 1509 was his moment of triumph. The militia was an accomplished fact, despite all the controversy of the previous years. On 20 February Buonaccorsi told him not to worry about some recent and ineffectual murmurs of opposition, but in the same letter he urged him to write to Niccolò Capponi, one of the military commissioners, 'who grumbles and complains that you have never written to him' (M 1105a; G 301). The very next day Biagio wrote again to say that Capponi's irritation was having repercussions in Palazzo Vecchio: 'il che non è punto piaciuto allo ufitio'. Biagio then offered some advice: 'Yet powerful men always have to be in the right, and one must show deference toward them [*pure e più potenti sempre hanno ad haver ragione et a lloro si ha ad havere respecto*].' In words that on the surface expressed confidence in Machiavelli's prudence and tact *vis-à-vis* 'e più potenti', Biagio was in fact reiterating an old worry about the secretary: 'You, of course, are accustomed to being patient and to knowing how to conduct yourself in delicate situations of this sort, even though this one is not of great importance, since you have to be away [from the city and the palace]: and if one or two letters will make him [Capponi] happy, that's not very much trouble.' But the matter had come to the attention of Soderini himself, and Biagio reported that he had spoken 'at length about this yesterday evening' with the Gonfalonier, who asked Biagio to write to Machiavelli and urge him, for his – Soderini's – sake, to be patient. As we have already seen, and as was evidently still the case in 1509, many Florentines felt the kind of resentment toward Machiavelli that Niccolò Capponi made known, directly or indirectly, to Soderini. Much of the rest of Biagio's letter of 21 February was yet another attempt to make Machiavelli aware of this and to exhort him to make the kinds of gestures and to demonstrate the 'respect' that the magistrates, and especially the *ottimati* among them, expected of a chancery official. Since Machiavelli's reluctance to do these things occasionally made life difficult for Soderini, it seems likely that Biagio was actually conveying advice from the Gonfalonier himself.

One thing I want to remind you of is that, when you write [official dispatches], report every little detail that happens there as in Pisa, because such details give great satisfaction and pleasure to the *brigata* [of the chancery, presumably] and these are the things that will carry you to the heights [*che ri porteranno in cielo*] . . . This evening, all your letters, beginning with this latest one, will be read before the [council of the] 80 and the [Otto di] Pratica, and this will be so from now on; so send us some of those letters that you are accustomed [to write] . . . Also, write every now and then to the Nove [of the *Ordinanza*], because everyone wants to be pampered and esteemed [*perché ogni uno vuole essere dondolato et stimato*], and a man in your position just has to do this; and four good words with a couple of dispatches will be sufficient, and it will seem to them that they have been properly considered: do it, please [*et quattro buone parole con due advisi satisfaranno, et parrà sia tenuto conto di loro: fatelo, ve ne prego*]. (M 1105b–1106a; G 302–3)

One can hardly miss the sense of condescension with which Machiavelli – and Buonaccorsi too – regarded the officeholders and magistrates that they served and, to some degree at least, had to please. Machiavelli, in particular, must have considered them tiresome and presumptuous amateurs whose demands for respectful attention only got in the way of the serious work he had to do. But, unlike Buonaccorsi and the other members of the chancery, Machiavelli evidently made little attempt to hide this attitude; if anything, he made it dangerously apparent even to people whose favour and protection he might some day need. The source of the specific complaint that prompted Biagio's letters of 20 and 21 February 1509 is especially revealing in this regard, for Niccolò Capponi was brother-in-law to Francesco Vettori. Even before Vettori's marriage to Maddalena Capponi, family ties and friendship had linked him to the future Gonfalonier of the last republic.[9] It was, of course, to Vettori that Machiavelli turned in 1513 in search of patronage and help, and the point is quite simply that Vettori's willingness to do something for Machiavelli could not have been enhanced by old resentments and grievances toward the 'quondam segretario' on the part of men, like Niccolò Capponi, who remained close to Vettori. We do not know how seriously Machiavelli offended Capponi in 1509; but that he even risked offending people who ought to have been on his side – for Capponi was among the *ottimati* supporters of the Soderini regime – leaves little to wonder at in contemplating the antagonism toward Machiavelli of the regime's critics and enemies. Machiavelli hurt himself by giving the impression that he regarded with some contempt the very government and political leaders for whom he worked. He took offence at the criticism and complaints about him that reached the Palazzo Vecchio, interpreting them as a failure to recognise his personal worth and the magnitude of his efforts. Piero Soderini, who understood the secretary, warned him – as Casavecchia did in 1507 – not to see matters in such terms. Writing on 22 February 1509, immediately after Buonaccorsi's two letters, the Gonfalonier told Machiavelli that

we have received two of yours, to which we respond briefly, reminding you that it's only natural in this world to receive great ingratitude for great and good accomplishments, but not from everyone. Continue doing well as you have done till now, and soon our Lord God, and later various people, will help you. (M 1106b; G 304)

Machiavelli must have complained to Soderini about the 'ingratitude' of those who opposed or criticised him, and Soderini – like Buonaccorsi, Casavecchia, Agostino Vespucci, and how many others? – was trying to tell him that opposition, criticism, contention, and disagreement were 'only natural in this world [*il naturale di questo mondo*]', especially the world of republican politics.

In June of 1509 Machiavelli's friends wrote to congratulate him for the triumph over Pisa. His militia had contributed decisively to the victory, and he was one of the co-signers of the formal act of submission that returned the port city to Florentine rule after fifteen years. Vespucci enthusiastically declared him to be 'non minima portio rei' and both flattered and chided him by saying:

---

[9] Devonshire Jones, *Vettori*, pp. 2–7.

If I didn't think that you would take excessive pride in it, I would dare to say that you conducted such a good operation with your battalions that, not by delaying but by hastening matters, you have restored the *rem florentinam* to its former condition. (M 1107b; G 306–7)

Vespucci was playing on Ennius' comment on Quintus Fabius Maximus the Temporiser, who had 'restored the republic to us by delaying'. In comparing Machiavelli to one of the legendary saviours of the Roman republic, Vespucci was acknowledging the exalted terms in which he feared Machiavelli might have been tempted to see his own success; but in simultaneously withholding the comparison ('Nisi crederem te nimis superbire, oserei dire che . . .'), he was again warning Machiavelli that it was not in his interest to let his part in the victory go to his head or to advertise too loudly his sense of vindication *vis-à-vis* his critics and opponents. Little more than a week later, on 17 June, Casavecchia wrote a similar message of congratulation and caution. 'Truly one can say that the reason for this [victory] is your person and the great part [you had in it] . . .' The words of warning came later:

Niccolò, if ever one was wise, this is the time to be so. Your philosophy, I think, will never appeal to crazy people [*a' pazzi*], and the wise people are not enough to suffice: you know what I mean, even if I'm not saying it very well. Every day I discover in you the greatest prophet that the Hebrews or any other nation ever had. Niccolò, Niccolò, verily I tell you that I cannot say what I would like to say. Therefore, be happy for that good friendship we have had together, and do not let it seem burdensome to come and stay with me for four days. (M 1108b; G 308–9)

He tried to entice Machiavelli with visions of plentiful trout and good wine; two weeks later he repeated the invitation, joking that 'if you come, I don't think you'll lose your job because of it [*quando vegniate, non credo però perdiate lo stato*]' (M 1109a; G 310). The 'philosophy' to which Casavecchia referred on 17 June may be Machiavelli's theories about the militia, or, perhaps, more generally, his often critical stance toward the republic's leadership and policies. The image of Machiavelli as 'el maggiore profeta che avessino mai li Ebrei o altra generatione' is of course in one sense a compliment; but no one had to remind Machiavelli of the precarious position of prophets, of how they often isolated themselves and, despite their wisdom, lost honour in their country – and especially not when the memory of Savonarola's martyrdom was so fresh. Casavecchia's warning to Machiavelli was not to expect, even in this moment of vindication, that his critics would vanish or that his 'philosophy' would gain general acceptance: hence, not to press his momentary advantage with further polemical expressions of impatience with the republic's political leadership. This, he insisted, was a good time for a vacation, for a little dilution of the intensity that sometimes made the chancery prophet hard to take. Apparently Machiavelli did not accept the invitation, for at the end of July Casavecchia sent him a gift of some trout with a request for news of what was happening in the Venetian territories in the aftermath of Agnadello. Again he cautioned Machiavelli to respect conventions:

because here I get a confusing picture of these matters, I wish all the more to understand the truth of them, but not a *discorso* of the sort that your most recent letter engages in (since I almost judge myself unworthy) – rather of the sort that is appropriate to a completely uninformed person of the plebeian order, and in which you hold to the customary way [of discussing such things].

Through all the joking about his unworthiness and ignorance, Casavecchia was telling Machiavelli, as Buonaccorsi and others had tried repeatedly to do, to write the kind of letters and dispatches that people expected: 'restandovene ad l'usato' (M 1109b; G 314).

But that is precisely what was always difficult for Machiavelli: to do the conventional, ordinary thing that his position required and that his superiors expected of him. Sometimes he could even joke about it himself. In November 1509 he was in Verona waiting for the imperial court; for a few days he had little to do except wait, and on the 29th he wrote to Luigi Guicciardini in Mantua:

I'm marooned here like you, because here no one knows anything about anything; and yet, in order to seem alive, I go on fantasising tirades that I write to the Dieci . . . [*Io sono qui in isola secha come voi, perché qui si sa nulla di nulla; et pure, per parere vivo, vo ghiribizando intemerate che io scrivo a' Dieci . . .*] (M 1111a; G 319)

These lines are particularly illuminating because of the ambivalence and contradiction that they display. In a rare interlude of inactivity, in which he had nothing to write to his government, Machiavelli here reveals how much he depended on that temporarily absent activity for his sense of himself. Having no news to report, 'perché qui si sa nulla di nulla', he daydreamed about letters he would have liked to write to the Dieci. So much did he identify with his work and its everyday responsibilities that even the imaginary *ghiribizzi* born of idleness exhibit direct continuity with that activity. Writing letters and reports to his government was, in short, as much a matter of inner need ('per parere vivo') as official obligation. That was one side of Machiavelli. The other side emerges from the kind of letters he imagined himself writing – if only he could: *intemerate* – tirades, diatribes, harangues – full of accusations and criticisms aimed at his own political superiors. Outwardly he may have tried to conform and to mask his private feelings, like a good secretary and soldier; but it must have been clear, not merely to Luigi Guicciardini, Piero Soderini, Biagio Buonaccorsi, Filippo Casavecchia and Agnolo Tucci, but to everyone who knew anything of the impatient and sometimes excessively independent secretary, that underneath his formal compliance with the conventions of the chancery he harboured a multitude of negative and often scathing judgements about the political leaders, institutions, and policies that he served.[10] How can we not connect the general awareness of this attitude with Machiavelli's unpopularity – and with his dismissal in November 1512?

This ambivalence – dependence and detachment, one might even say devotion and rejection – remained at the heart of everything Machiavelli ever wrote about the Florentine republic. He could scarcely imagine himself apart from it, but he could never accept it as it was. What made Machiavelli controversial was not, once again, any partisan attachment to a faction. It was rather this tendency to stand back from the whole system and to find fault with its imperfections, slowness, and confusion, to express his irritation and impatience with politicians who, in his view, were blind to the best interests of the republic, and to judge their actions and policies by exacting, not to say impossible, standards, that made people dislike him. He could not restrain himself even when he needed to persuade his own government to cooperate with the militia project. In *La cagione dell'ordinanza*, a memorandum (probably of 1506) to the Signoria in which he described and justified the preliminary organisation he had already given to the *contado* militia and then urged its extension into the city, Machiavelli wrote lines that illustrate perhaps better than any others the lack of restraint that must have seemed gratuitous even to those who agreed with him:

Everyone knows that anyone who speaks of empire, kingdom, principate, [or] republic – anyone who speaks of men who command, beginning at the top and going all the way down to the leader of a gang – speaks of justice and arms. You, as regards justice, have very little, and, of arms, none at all [*Voi, della iustitia, ne havete non molta, et dell'armi, non punto*]. (M 37b–38a)

It was probably not the best way to secure the co-operation of his friends and win over his critics. But it was certainly not a partisan criticism; indeed, it implicated everyone, indiscriminately, in a collective failure from which – or at least such was the implication – only Machiavelli's truth could save the republic. That attitude, and the conflict at its core, spelled trouble for Machiavelli and left him isolated (in another 'isola secha') in 1512–13; but it also opened up horizons of theory and history that would have been inaccessible either to a conventional chancery secretary who knew *and* accepted the limitations of his position, or to a political partisan who knew *and* accepted the inherent limitations and imperfections of republicanism.

[10] For an evaluation of the substance and purpose of this polemic as it emerges in Machiavelli's own writings before 1513, see Marchand, *I primi scritti*, esp. pp. 327–30; also Gennaro Sasso, *Niccolò Machiavelli: Storia del suo pensiero politico* (Bologna, 1980), part I, pp. 13–289.

PART II

Machiavelli and republican ideas

6

◁ ═══ ▷

Machiavelli's *Discorsi* and the pre-humanist origins of republican ideas

QUENTIN SKINNER

I

By the end of the twelfth century, a distinctive system of republican government had come to be well established in most of the major cities of the *Regnum Italicum*. The cities were generally controlled by chief magistrates known as *podestà*, so called because they were vested with supreme power or *potestas* over the citizens under their charge. A *podestà* normally held office for a period of six months or at most a year, and conducted his administration by means of a series of executive councils. All the members of such councils, including the *podestà* himself, enjoyed a status no higher than that of public servants of the commune that elected them.[1] The system thus represented a complete repudiation of the familiar Medieval principles of lordship and hereditary rule.[2]

Scholars have generally agreed, however, that the cities initially failed to develop anything in the nature of a corresponding civic ideology. They altogether lacked the means to conceptualise and legitimate their elective and self-governing arrangements. This development had to await the recovery and dissemination of Aristotle's moral and political theory in the latter part of the thirteenth century. Aristotle's *Politics* in particular 'provided a unique key to the new world of urban politics', whereas 'no such guide had existed before the rediscovery' of his texts.[3] It was thus 'the politics of the polis' that came to be 'cardinal to the constitutional theory of Italian cities'.[4]

Some scholars have gone even further, claiming that we cannot speak even at this juncture of a distinctive ideology of self-governing republicanism. Hans Baron in particular has insisted that such an ideology was formulated for the

---

[1] For an excellent outline of the system see D. Waley, *The Italian City-Republics*, 3rd edn (London, 1988), esp. ch. 3, pp. 32–68. See also E. Artifoni, 'I podestà professionali e la fondazione retorica della politica communale', *Quaderni storici*, 63 (1986), pp. 687–719, at pp. 688–93.

[2] On the contrast between traditional views of government as lordship and the emergence of a different view in thirteenth-century Italy see J. Catto, 'Ideas and experience in the political thought of Aquinas', *Past and Present*, 71 (1976), 3–21.

[3] See N. Rubinstein, 'Political theories in the Renaissance' in *The Renaissance: Essays in Interpretation*, A. Chastel, ed. (London, 1982), pp. 153–200, at p. 153.

[4] See J.G.A. Pocock, *The Machiavellian Moment* (Princeton, NJ, 1975), p. 74.

first time in Florence at the start of the fifteenth century.[5] Only then did the humanists begin to argue that the values of political liberty and participative citizenship can only be sustained under elective systems of republican rule. Only at that point, therefore, can we begin to speak of what Baron has called 'the new philosophy of political engagement'.[6] Florence, in this interpretation, was 'unique among the cities of Medieval Europe in giving rise to such a developed set of ideas appropriate to urban life'.[7]

There can be no doubt that the revival of Aristotelianism and the rise of Florentine humanism were both of vital importance in the evolution of republican thought.[8] But it is misleading to suggest that it was only with the emergence of these intellectual movements that an ideology of self-governing republicanism began to be formulated. The articulation of such an ideology can in fact be traced to a period scarcely later than the creation of the communes themselves.[9] Although the writers of this pre-humanist era had no access to Greek philosophy, they were able to draw on a number of Roman moralists and historians who had written with scarcely less eloquence about the ideals of freedom and citizenship. By basing themselves on these authorities – and in particular on Sallust and Cicero – they were able to construct a full-scale defence of the special virtues of republican rule.

To Cicero they were especially indebted for his analysis of the civic virtues in the *De Officiis*.[10] But they owed an even deeper debt to Sallust's histories, and in particular to the opening of the *Bellum Catilinae* with its explanation of the rise and fall of republican Rome. The importance of Sallust's histories for the evolution of republican thought has not been greatly emphasised.[11] But he

---

[5] On this allegedly 'new outlook' and 'new ideology' see H. Baron, *The Crisis of the Early Italian Renaissance* (Princeton, NJ, 1966), esp. pp. 29, 49, 121. For examples of other scholars endorsing similar claims see the references in Q. Skinner, *The Foundations of Modern Political Thought*, vol. I: *The Renaissance* (Cambridge, 1978), pp. 27, 79 and notes.

[6] See Baron, *Crisis*, p. 459 and cf. R. Witt, 'The rebirth of the concept of republican liberty in Italy' in *Renaissance Studies in Honor of Hans Baron*, A. Molho and J. Tedeschi, eds. (Florence, 1971), pp. 173–99, esp. at p. 175.

[7] G. Holmes, 'The emergence of an urban ideology at Florence', *Transactions of the Royal Historical Society*, 23 (1973), 113. Cf. also pp. 111, 112.

[8] On the former theme see W. Ullmann, *Medieval Foundations of Renaissance Humanism* (London, 1977) and the valuable series of essays collected in C. Davis, *Dante's Italy and Other Essays* (Philadelphia, 1984). On the latter see the classic accounts in Baron, *Crisis* and Pocock, *The Machiavellian Moment*. For an attempt to survey both strands of thought see Skinner, *The Foundations*, esp. Vol. I, pp. 49–112.

[9] I have already tried to establish this point in my 'Ambrogio Lorenzetti: the artist as political philosopher', *Proceedings of the British Academy*, 72 (1986), 1–56, esp. at 3–31. I partly draw on that account in what follows, although I am here concerned with a different set of issues.

[10] For a valuable recent examination of medieval uses of Cicero see C. J. Nederman, 'Nature, sin and the origins of society: the Ciceronian tradition in medieval political thought', *Journal of the History of Ideas*, 49 (1988), 3–26. For Cicero as a source of ideas specifically about the virtues see R. Tuve, 'Notes on the virtues and vices', *Journal of the Warburg and Courtauld Institutes*, 26 (1963), 264–303 and Q. Skinner, 'Ambrogio Lorenzetti', esp. 25–30.

[11] This is partly because modern scholars have tended, somewhat anachronistically, to exclude Sallust from the ranks of 'political' writers. This applies even to Nederman's discussion: see, for example, Nederman, 'Nature, sin and the origins of society', 6. But for two excellent accounts of

exercised an overwhelming influence on pre-humanist debates about city government, an influence that can still be discerned in a number of much later and more sophisticated humanist treatises. When Machiavelli remarks in the *Discorsi* that 'everyone has read Sallust's account of the Catilinarian conspiracy', it seems that he may not have been altogether wide of the mark.[12]

My first concern in what follows will accordingly be to excavate this lowest and least investigated stratum in the history of Renaissance republicanism. I shall then turn to consider the relationship between this pre-humanist literature and the classic restatement of the republican case to be found in Machiavelli's *Discorsi*. My eventual aim will be to indicate the remarkable extent to which Machiavelli continued to present his defence of republican values in traditional terms.

II

To recover the outlook of the earliest spokesmen for the communes, we need to concentrate on two closely related bodies of literature. First we need to consider the numerous treatises on the *Ars dictaminis* issued by the *Dictatores* or teachers of rhetoric associated with the law-schools of Medieval Italy.[13] These treatises generally comprised a set of model speeches and letters, often preceded by a theoretical discussion of the rhetorical arts.[14] The value of these sources derives from the fact that a large number of the speeches and letters they contain were specifically designed for use on public occasions by such officials as ambassadors and city magistrates. As a result, they commonly include a great deal of information about the values and attitudes informing the conduct of city government in the pre-Renaissance period.[15]

A number of these writings survive from as early as the start of the twelfth century. Hugh of Bologna's *Rationes dictandi*, for instance, appears to have been

the use of Sallust by medieval writers see B. Smalley, 'Sallust in the Middle Ages' in *Classical Influences on European Culture AD 500–1500*, R.R. Bolgar, ed. (Cambridge, 1971), pp. 165–75, and (for a discussion centering specifically on Italy) N. Rubinstein, 'Some ideas on municipal progress and decline in the Italy of the Communes' in *Fritz Saxl, 1890–1948: A Volume of Memorial Essays*, D.J. Gordon, ed. (London, 1957), pp. 165–83. Smalley stresses the danger of anachronism at pp. 174–5.

[12] N. Machiavelli, *Il principe e Discorsi*, ed. S. Bertelli (Milan, 1960), III. 6, p. 409. 'Ciascuno ha letto la congiura di Catilina da Sallustio'. For other references to Sallust in the *Discorsi* see I.46, p. 236 and II.8, p. 297.

[13] On these writers the classic study remains P.O. Kristeller, 'Humanism and scholasticism in the Italian Renaissance' in *Renaissance Thought and its Sources*, M. Mooney, ed. (New York, 1979), pp. 85–105. But for a different approach see the admirably documented discussion in R. Witt, 'Medieval "Ars dictaminis" and the beginnings of humanism: a new construction of the problem', *Renaissance Quarterly*, 35 (1982), 1–35. For an excellent recent survey, citing many of the writers I discuss, see also Artifoni, 'I podestà professionali'.

[14] See J.J. Murphy, *Rhetoric in the Middle Ages* (Berkeley, CA, 1974), esp. 218–20 on Hugh of Bologna's early distinction between the introductory theoretical treatise (the *Ars*) and the ensuing model examples (the *dictamina*).

[15] A point excellently brought out in H. Wieruszowski, '*Ars dictaminis* in the time of Dante' in *Politics and Culture in Medieval Spain and Italy* (Rome, 1971), pp. 589–627.

produced around the year 1120.[16] For the most part, however, the earliest surviving examples date from the opening decades of the next century, by which time the genre had become well established, not to say highly repetitious in content.[17] Among the more important examples from this era are Raniero da Perugia's *Ars notaria* of *c.* 1215,[18] Thomas of Capua's *Ars dictandi* of *c.* 1230,[19] Boncompagno da Signa's *Rhetorica novissima* of 1235,[20] and above all, Guido Faba's numerous writings of the same period,[21] including his *Dictamina rhetorica* of 1226–8,[22] his *Epistole* of 1239–41[23] and his *Parlamenti ed Epistole* of 1242–3.[24] Finally, by the end of the thirteenth century a number of similar treatises began to appear in the *volgare*.[25] Matteo de' Libri's vernacular *Arringhe* dates from *c.* 1275,[26] Giovanni da Vignano's *Flore de parlare* from *c.* 1290,[27] Filippo Ceffi's *Dicerie* from *c.* 1330.[28]

The other body of writings we need to consider are the treatises on city government designed specifically for the guidance of *podestà* and other magistrates. This genre was originally an offshoot of the *Ars dictaminis*, with

[16] See Murphy, *Rhetoric in the Middle Ages* and for an edition see Hugh of Bologna, *Rationes dictandi* in *Briefsteller und Formelbücher des Elften bis Vierzehnten Jahrhunderts*, L. Rockinger, ed., 2 vols. (Munich, 1863), I, pp. 53–94.

[17] For a survey of the literature of this period see Murphy, *Rhetoric in the Middle Ages*, pp. 194–268.

[18] E. Monaci, 'Sulle formole volgari dell' *Ars notaria* di Raniero di Perugia' in *Rendiconti della Reale Accademia dei Lincei*, 14 (1905), 268–81, discusses Raniero's *Dictamina* and republishes a number of fragments. For the suggested date see G. Bertoni, *Il duecento* (Milan, 1947), p. 253.

[19] For an edition, and for the suggested date, see Thomas of Capua, *Ars dictandi*, ed. E. Heller (Heidelberg, 1929).

[20] For an edition see Boncompagno da Signa, *Rhetorica novissima*, ed. A. Gaudenzi, in *Bibliotheca Juridica Medii Aevi*, vol. II (Bologna, 1892), pp. 247–97. For the suggested date see A. Gaudenzi, 'Sulla cronologia delle opere dei dettatori Bolognesi', *Bullettino dell' istituto storico italiano*, 14 (1895), pp. 85–174, at p. 112.

[21] For a full list of Faba's rhetorical writings see V. Pini, 'La *Summa de vitiis et virtutibus* di Guido Faba', *Quadrivium*, 1 (1956), pp. 41–152, at pp. 42–3 and notes.

[22] The edition I use is G. Faba, *Dictamina Rhetorica*, ed. A. Gaudenzi in *Il propugnatore*, 1892–3, reprinted in *Medium Aevum*, G. Vecchi ed. (Bologna, 1971). For the date of the *Dictamina Rhetorica* see Gaudenzi, 'Sulla cronologia', p. 133.

[23] The edition I use is G. Faba, *Epistole*, ed. A. Gaudenzi in *Il propugnatore*, 1892–93, reprinted in *Medium Aevum*, G. Vecchi ed. (Bologna, 1971). For the date of the *Epistole* see Gaudenzi, 'Sulla cronologia', p. 145.

[24] The edition I use is G. Faba, *Parlamenti ed Epistole* in A. Gaudenzi, *I suoni, le forme e le parole dell' odierno dialetto della città di Bologna* (Turin, 1889), pp. 127–60. For the date of the *Parlamenti* see Gaudenzi 'Sulla cronologia', p. 148.

[25] Note, however, that Faba had pioneered the production of vernacular *Dictamina* a generation earlier. See A. Castellani, 'Le formule volgari di Guido Faba', *Studi di filologia italiana*, 13 (1955), 5–78.

[26] The edition I use is Matteo de' Libri, *Arringhe*, ed. E. Vincenti (Milan, 1974), pp. 3–227. For the date of the *Arringhe* see P.O. Kristeller, 'Matteo de' Libri, Bolognese notary of the thirteenth century, and his *Artes Dictaminis*' in *Miscellanea Giovanni Galbiati, ii (Fontes Ambrosiani 26)* (Milan, 1951), pp. 283–320, at p. 285n.

[27] The edition I use is Giovanni da Vignano, *Flore de parlare*, ed. E. Vincenti in Matteo de' Libri, *Arringhe* (Milan, 1974), pp. 229–325. For the date of the *Flore* see C. Frati, '"Flore de parlare" o "Somma d'arengare" attribuita a Ser Giovanni Fiorentino da Vignano', *Giornale storico della letteratura italiana*, 61 (1913), pp. 1–31 and 228–65, at p. 265.

[28] The edition I use is F. Ceffi, *Dicerie*, ed. G. Giannardi in *Studi di filologia italiana*, 6 (1942), pp. 27–63. For the date of the *Dicerie* see S. Giannardi, 'Le "Dicerie" di Filippo Ceffi', *Studi di filologia italiana*, 6 (1942), pp. 5–63, at pp. 5, 19.

most of the early treatises still containing model letters and speeches in addition to general advice on how to manage city affairs.[29] The earliest surviving work of this description is the anonymous *Oculus pastoralis*, which has usually been dated to the early 1220s.[30] This was shortly followed by Orfino da Lodi's *De sapientia potestatis*, an advice book composed in leonine verse during the 1240s.[31] The next such work – the fullest and most important from this pre-humanist period – was Giovanni da Viterbo's *Liber de regimine civitatum*, which was probably completed in 1253.[32] This was in turn followed – and to some degree plagiarised – by Brunetto Latini in his *Livres dou Trésor* of 1266, a widely used encyclopedia which concludes with a section entitled 'On the government of cities'.[33]

These writers are all fully committed to the view that the best form of constitution for a *commune* or *civitas* must be of an elective as opposed to a monarchical character. If a city is to have any hope of attaining its highest goals, it is indispensable that its administration should remain in the hands of officials whose conduct can in turn be regulated by established customs and laws. To understand how this conclusion was reached, we accordingly need to begin by asking what these writers had in mind when they spoke about the goals or ends of communities, and in particular about the highest goal to which a city can aspire.

The goal they emphasise above all is that of attaining greatness – greatness of standing, greatness of power, greatness of wealth. This preoccupation is in part expressed in a distinctive literature devoted to celebrating the *magnalia* or signs of greatness in cities. The most famous contribution to this genre, Leonardo Bruni's *Laudatio Florentinae Urbis*, is of course a much later work, composed in 1403–4 in the highest humanist style.[34] But there are several examples dating

---

[29] For this connection between rhetoric and politics – between the rhetor and the rector – see Artifoni, 'I podestà professionali'.

[30] The edition I use is D. Franceschi, 'Oculus pastoralis' in *Memorie dell'accademia delle scienze di Torino*, 11 (1966), 3–70. For the suggested date of 1222 see Franceschi, 'Oculus pastoralis', p. 3. But A. Sorbelli, 'I teorici del reggimento communale', *Bullettino dell' istituto storico italiano per il medio evo*, 59 (1944), pp. 31–136, at p. 74, suggests 1242.

[31] The edition I use is Orfino da Lodi, *De regimine et sapientia potestatis*, ed. A. Ceruti in *Miscellanea di storia italiana*, 7 (1869), 33–94. For the suggested date see Sorbelli, 'I teorici', 61.

[32] The edition I use is Giovanni da Viterbo, *Liber de regimine civitatum*, ed. C. Salvemini in *Bibliotheca juridica medii aevi*, vol. III, (Bologna, 1901), pp. 215–80. For the suggested date see G. Folena, '"Parlamenti" podestarili di Giovanni da Viterbo', *Lingua Nostra*, 20 (1959), pp. 97–105, at p. 97. But F. Hertter, *Die Podestaliteratur italiens im 12. und 13. Jahrhundert* (Leipzig, 1910), pp. 52–3 suggests 1228, while Sorbelli, 'I teorici', pp. 94–6, suggests 1263.

[33] The edition I use is B. Latini, *Li Livres dou Trésor*, ed. F. Carmody (Berkeley, CA, 1948). On the date and sources of the *Trésor* see Sorbelli, 'I teorici', 99–104 and F. Carmody, 'Introduction' to Brunetto Latini, *Li Livres dou Trésor* (Berkeley, CA, 1948), pp. xiii–xx, xxii–xxxii.

[34] For an edition see Hans Baron, *From Petrarch to Leonardi Bruni* (Chicago, 1968), pp. 217–63. The classic analysis is given in Baron, *Crisis*, pp. 191–224. But Baron, as often, marks too sharp a break with pre-humanist discussions, especially when he speaks of 'a new ideal of "greatness"' in the *Laudatio*. See Baron, *Crisis*, pp. xvii, 202–4. For a contrasting appraisal see J.E. Seigel, '"Civic humanism" or Ciceronian rhetoric? The culture of Petrarch and Bruni', *Past and Present*, 34 (1966), 3–48.

from the period when the ideology of the city-republics was first being formulated. One of the earliest is the anonymous poem in praise of the city of Lodi, *De laude Civitatis Laudae*, probably written in the 1250s;[35] perhaps the best-known is Bonvesin della Riva's panegyric on Milan, *De magnalibus Mediolani*, which was completed in 1288.[36]

The same preoccupation with glory and greatness suffuses the pre-humanist treatises on city government. The main inspiration for their claim that these are the highest ends of civic life derives of course from the Roman historians and moralists, with the most influential statements of the belief being due to Sallust. Not only do they draw on his account in the *Bellum Catilinae* of how the Roman republic grew to greatness – how the *respublica crevit*.[37] They also like to quote the passage from the *Bellum Iugurthinum* in which the king of Numidia congratulates Jugurtha on the honour and glory brought by his deeds, while adjuring him at the same time to remember how small communities succeed in rising to greatness – how *parvae res crescunt*.[38]

All the pre-humanist writers speak in similar terms. The *Oculus pastoralis*, which opens with a set of model speeches designed for incoming *podestà*, particularly advises them to promise that their rule will conduce 'to increase and glory and honour', and will thereby ensure 'that the city grows to greatness'.[39] The model speeches included in Giovanni da Viterbo's *Liber de regimine civitatum* similarly emphasise the value of 'increase', as well as the importance of ensuring that cities are able to grow and flourish.[40] By the end of the thirteenth century, we find the same ideas beginning to be expressed in the vernacular. Matteo de' Libri advises both ambassadors and *podestà* to promise that they will ensure increase and growth,[41] while Giovanni da Vignano's model speech for outgoing *podestà* bids them express the hope that the city they have been administering 'will at all times grow and increase', above all in prosperity.[42]

At the same time, the vernacular writers of this period begin to invoke a new concept to describe their vision of the proper ends of civic life. They begin to

---

[35] The edition I use is G. Waitz, 'De Laude civitatis Laudae' in *Monumenta Germaniae Historica* vol. 22 (Hanover, 1872), pp. 372–3. For the suggested date see J.K. Hyde, 'Medieval descriptions of cities', *Bulletin of the John Rylands Library*, 48 (1965), pp. 308–40, at p. 340.

[36] The edition I use (which includes a translation into Italian) is Bonvesin della Riva, *De Magnalibus Mediolani*, tr. G. Pontiggia, ed. M. Corti (Milan, 1974). For a later celebration of Milan (dated *c.* 1316 in Hyde, 'Medieval descriptions of cities', p. 340) see Benzo d'Alessandria, *De Mediolano Civitate*, ed. L.A. Ferrai in *Bullettino dell' istituto storico italiano*, 9 (1890), 15–36.

[37] Sallust, *Bellum Catilinae*, tr. J.C. Rolfe (London, 1921), x.1, p. 16.

[38] Sallust, *Bellum Jugurthinum*, tr. J.C. Rolfe (London, 1921), x.6, p. 148.

[39] See Franceschi 'Oculus pastoralis, p. 25 on conducing 'ad incrementum et gloriam et honorem' and p. 27 on the hope that 'excrescit civitas'.

[40] See Viterbo, *Liber de regimine civitatum*, p. 231, col. 2 on the importance of ensuring that 'civitates crescunt'. Cf. also p. 232, col. 1 on the value of 'incrementum' and 'maximum incrementum'.

[41] See Libri, *Arringhe*, p. 10 on the duty to bring 'acresimento de ben en meglo' and p. 70 on the duty to assure 'bon stato, gradeça et acresemento'.

[42] See Vignano *Flore de parlare*, p. 286 for the wish 'che questa terra sempre acresca'.

speak of *grandezza*, using a term evidently coined to supply the lack, in classical Latin, of an expression at once denoting grandeur and magnitude. We already find Guido Faba speaking in this fashion in his *Parlamenti ed Epistole* of the early 1240s. In his model speech for the use of newly elected *podestà*, Faba advises them to promise 'to do whatever may be necessary for the maintenance of the standing and the *grandeça* of the commune, and for the increase of the honour and glory of those friendly to it'.[43] Shortly afterwards the same terminology recurs in the vernacular passages of Giovanni da Viterbo's *Liber de regimine civitatum*. An incoming *podestà*, he advises, must vow to uphold 'the honour and *grandecça* and welfare' of the city given into his charge.[44] By the next generation, we find the same terminology in standard use among the writers of vernacular *Dictamina*. Matteo de' Libri suggests that city magistrates should promise at the time of their election to uphold 'the good standing, repose and *grandeça*' of the city';[45] outgoing magistrates should proclaim that they have in fact upheld its '*grandeça*, honour, good standing and repose'.[46] Giovanni da Vignano echoes the same sentiments in virtually the same phraseology, continually urging ambassadors and magistrates alike to speak of their city's 'exaltation, *grandeça* and honour'[47] of its 'good standing, *grandeça* and repose'[48] and at the same time of 'the honour, *grandeça*, unity and repose' of all its citizens.[49]

Given this emphasis on *grandezza*, it is not surprising that these writers are especially concerned to establish what policies need to be pursued if this goal is to be achieved. Initially they simply tend to reiterate the familiar Augustinian assumption that no community can hope to flourish unless it lives in perfect peace. The *Oculus*, for example, contains a model speech for chief magistrates to deliver in the face of warring factions, warning them that 'only through quiet and tranquillity and peace can a city grow great'.[50] Latini similarly lays it down in his chapter on the virtue of concord that 'peace brings very great good, while war lays it waste'.[51] The same argument was subsequently reiterated by numerous writers of vernacular *Dictamina*. Matteo de' Libri strongly associates the rule of those who enable their communities 'to live in total tranquillity' with

---

[43] See Faba *Parlamenti ed Epistole*, p. 156 on the need 'de fare quelle cose . . . che pertegnano ad statum et a grandeça di questo communo, et ad adacresamento de gloria e d'onore de tuti quilli c'ameno questa citade'. Cf. the very similar formula at p. 143.

[44] See Viterbo, *Liber de regimine civitatum*, p. 234, col. 2 on the need to act 'ad honore et grandecça, et utilitate de questu communu'. Cf. also p. 231, col. 1 on the need to promote 'granneça'.

[45] Libri, *Arringhe*, p. 105: 'buono stato, riposo et grandeçça.'

[46] *Ibid.*, p. 99: 'grandeça, honori, bon stato e bon reposo'. For further references to the ideal of *grandezza* in Libri, see pp. 12, 28, 53, 69–70, 93, 110, 112, 114.

[47] Vignano, *Flore de parlare*, p. 237: 'exaltamento, grandeça et honore'.

[48] *Ibid.*, p. 289: 'bom stato, grandeça e reponso'.

[49] *Ibid.*, p. 251: 'honore, grandeça e unità e reposo'. For similar formulae see pp. 237, 239, 245, 251, 286–7.

[50] Franceschi, 'Oculus pastoralis', p. 27: 'Per quietam autem tranquilitatem et pacem ipsius excrescit civitas.' Cf. also pp. 53, 59.

[51] Latini, *Li Livres dou Trésor*, p. 292: 'pais fait maint bien et guerre le gaste'.

the attainment of 'honour and good standing'.[52] Filippo Ceffi writes even more emphatically, offering repeated assurances that if a city 'can manage to maintain itself in a good and peaceable state', this will always conduce 'to your honour and your *grandezza*'.[53]

Soon after the start of the fourteenth century, however, a number of writers began to voice a certain anxiety about such unqualified celebrations of peace.[54] Sallust was again their main authority at this point. As he had emphasised at the start of the *Bellum Catilinae*, it was during the period when Rome had been forced to wage continual wars against savage neighbouring peoples, and subsequently against the invading Carthaginians, that the republic had originally grown to greatness. By contrast, it was when this period was followed by an era of peace and plenty that the Roman civic spirit had begun to decline. The fruits of peace proved to be avarice and self-interest, and with the resulting loss of civic virtue the free and self-governing republic eventually collapsed.[55]

With traditional systems of communal government everywhere falling prey to the rise of *Signori* in the early fourteenth century,[56] a number of Italian historical and political writers began to express similar doubts. Albertino Mussato, for example, prefaces his history of the collapse of civic liberty in his native Padua with an explanation taken almost word-for-word from Sallust's account.[57] The same theme was later to assume an even greater prominence in *quattrocento* humanist histories designed to celebrate the virtues of republican freedom.[58] The fear that long periods of peace may lead to enervation and decadence is forcefully expressed, for example, at several points in Poggio's *Historiae Florentini Populi*. A love of peace, he implies, may sometimes pose a threat to liberty.[59] If freedom and self-government are to be upheld against the encroachments of tyranny, it may sometimes be necessary to fight for liberty instead of insisting on peace at any price.

There is one point, however, on which all these writers are agreed. Even if it

---

[52] See Libri, *Arringhe*, p. 79 for the connection between being able 'permanere in gran tranquillitate' and the capacity 'aquistar honor et bon stato'. Cf. also pp. 99, 114, 147.

[53] See Ceffi *Dicerie*, p. 27 for the claim that, if your city 'possa mantenersi in buono e pacifico stato', this will conduce 'a vostro onore e grandezza'. For other formulae to the same effect see pp. 36, 47, 61.

[54] For a survey contrasting the 'orientations' of peace and liberty in this period see N. Valeri, *La libertà e la pace: orientamenti politici del rinascimento italiano* (Turin, 1942).

[55] Sallust, *Bellum Catilinae*, VI–XIII, pp. 11–23.

[56] For a classic survey of this transition see F. Ercole, *Dal commune al principato* (Florence, 1929).

[57] This is pointed out in Rubinstein, 'some ideas on municipal progress', p. 172 and note.

[58] See the discussion of Poggio's republicanism in J. Oppel 'Peace vs. liberty in the Quattrocento: Poggio, Guarino, and the Scipio–Caesar controversy', *Journal of Medieval and Renaissance Studies*, 4 (1974), 221–65.

[59] See the discussion, modelled on Sallust, at the start of Book V of Poggio's *Historiae* in Poggio Bracciolini, 'Historiae Florentini Populi' in *Opera Omnia*, ed. R. Fubini, 4 vols. (Turin, 1966), II, pp. 81–493, at p. 299 and cf. the account in Oppel, 'Peace vs. liberty', pp. 223–4.

may sometimes be necessary to wage war on others in the name of liberty and *grandezza*, the preservation of peace within one's own city must never be jeopardised. The avoidance of internal divisions and discord is regarded by everyone as an indispensable condition of civic greatness.[60]

Once again, it is Sallust who is most often quoted to this effect. The passage invariably cited is the speech from the *Bellum Jugurthinum* in which the king of Numantia addresses Jugurtha and his other two heirs. 'I bequeath to all three of you', he is made to say, 'a kingdom that that will prove strong if you conduct yourself well, but weak if you behave badly. For it is by way of concord that small communities rise to greatness; it is as a result of discord that even the greatest communities fall into collapse.'[61]

The negative aspect of this admonition was taken up by all the pre-humanist writers on city government. 'It is due to the fact that all cities nowadays are divided within themselves', Giovanni da Viterbo insists, 'that the good effect of government is no longer felt.'[62] Latini makes the same point in the course of advising magistrates on what to do if they find themselves in charge of a city 'at war with itself'. 'You must point out how concord brings greatness to cities and enriches their citizens, while war destroys them; and you must recall how Rome and other great cities ruined themselves by internal strife.'[63] Matteo de' Libri offers precisely the same advice in a model speech designed for captains of city militias to declaim in order to stiffen the resolve of ruling magistrates to deal with internal faction-fights. 'Think of Florence and Siena, and of how they have destroyed themselves by internal war; think of Rimini, and of many other places throughout this country, and of how internal hatred has ruined them.'[64]

More optimistically, many of these writers also take up the positive aspect of Sallust's argument. 'Cities that are ruled and maintained in a state of peace', Giovanni da Viterbo declares, 'are able to grow, to become great, and to receive the greatest possible increase.'[65] Latini underlines the same point, referring his

---

[60] On civic discord as a prime enemy of peace see Skinner, 'Ambrogio Lorenzetti', pp. 8–9 and 33.

[61] Sallust, *Bellum Catilinae*, x.7, p. 148: 'Equidem ego vobis regnum trado firmum, si boni eritis, sin mali, imbecillum. Nam concordia parvae res crescunt, discordia maxumae dilabuntur.' The last sentence was apparently proverbial: it is quoted as such in Seneca, *Epistulae Morales*, vol. 3, tr. R. Gummere (London, 1925), Epistola xcIV, sec. 46, p. 40. It is strongly echoed by a number of pre-humanist writers – for example by Orfino da Lodi (see Lodi, *De regimine*, p. 57) and by the author of *De Laude Civitatis Laudae* (see Waitz, 'De Laude civitatis Laudae', p. 372.)

[62] Viterbo, *Liber de regimine civitatum*, p. 221, cols. 1–2: 'Nam cum civitates omnes hodie sunt divise . . . cesset bonus effectus regiminis.'

[63] Latini, *Li Livres dou Trésor*, p. 404: 'die comment concorde essauce les viles et enrichist les borgois, et guerre les destruit; et ramentevoir Romme et les autres bonnes viles ki por la guerre dedans sont decheues et mal alees'.

[64] Libri, *Arringhe*, p. 147: 'Pensative de Florencia, de Sena, commo son gite per la guerra dentru . . . Pensative de Rimino, comm' è conço per l'odio dentro, e de multe terre de quella contrata.' Cf. also p. 193.

[65] Viterbo, *Liber de regimine civitatum*, p. 231, col. 2: 'civitates reguntur et tenentur pacifice, crescunt, ditantur et maximum recipiunt incrementum'.

readers directly to Sallust for the judgement that, just as discord destroys the greatest undertakings, so 'small things, through concord, are able to grow great'.[66] Likewise Matteo de' Libri, in a model speech designed for *Capitani* to deliver if civic discord impends, advises them to remind the parties involved that 'concord and unity cause everything to advance and grow great'.[67]

One of the problems that most preoccupies these writers is accordingly that of understanding how civic concord can best be preserved. The authority to whom they generally turn at this juncture is Cicero, for whom the ideal of a *concordia ordinum* had been of such overriding importance. Cicero had laid it down in a highly influential passage in Book I of the *De officiis* that the surest way 'to introduce sedition and discord into a city is to look after the interests of only one part of the citizens, while neglecting the rest'.[68] It follows that the key to preserving civic concord must be to give precedence to the ideal of the common good over any selfish or factional interests. Cicero had summarised this conclusion in the form of two basic precepts for the guidance of magistrates, both of which he claimed to have taken from Plato. 'First, they must look after the welfare of every citizen to such a degree that, in everything they do, they make this their highest priority, without any consideration for their own advantage. Secondly, they must look after the welfare of the whole body politic, never allowing themselves to care only for one part of the citizens while betraying the rest.'[69]

Among the writers I am considering, both these suggestions about the avoidance of discord were widely taken up. In the *Oculus pastoralis*, the model speech of the incoming *podestà* ends with the assurance that he will act 'to promote the welfare of the whole community', thereby guaranteeing it 'honour, exaltation and benefit, and a happy state'.[70] Giovanni da Viterbo quotes the entire passage from Cicero's *De officiis* in which the connections between the avoidance of discord and the promotion of the common good are explained.[71] Latini also quotes Cicero's precepts,[72] and subsequently adds in his chapter 'Of Concord' that, if this virtuous condition is to be attained, 'we must follow nature and place the common good above all other values'.[73]

---

[66] Latini, *Li Livres dou Trésor*, p. 292: 'Salustes dist, par concorde croissent les petites choses et par discorde se destruisent les grandismes.' For earlier allusions to Sallust's formulation see above, n. 61.

[67] Libri, *Arringhe*, p. 18: 'la concordia et l'unitate acrese et avança tuti bene'.

[68] Cicero, *De officiis*, tr. W. Miller (London, 1913), 1.25.85, p. 86: 'Qui autem parti civium consulunt, partem neglegunt, rem perniciosissimam in civitatem inducunt, seditionem atque discordiam.'

[69] *Ibid.*, 1.25.85, p. 86: 'unum, ut utilitatem civium sic tueantur, ut, quaecumque agunt, ad eam referant obliti commodorum suorum, alterum, ut totum corpus rei publicae curent, ne, dum partem aliquam tuentur, reliquas deserant'.

[70] See Franceschi, 'Oculus pastoralis', p. 26 on the need to act 'pro utilitate communitatis istius' in order to bring it 'ad honorem, exaltationem et comodum ac felicem statum'.

[71] See Viterbo, *Liber de regimine civitatum*, p. 268, col. 2.

[72] See Latini, *Li Livres dou Trésor*, p. 267.

[73] *Ibid.*, p. 291: 'devons nous ensivre nature et metre avant tout le commun profit'. For further references in Latini to the ideal of the common good, see his concluding chapter, esp. pp. 408, 415, 417. Cf. also the references to the 'bene comune' in Ceffi, *Dicerie*, pp. 46, 57.

This still left the question of how to ensure in practice that the common good is followed, and thus that no member of the community is ever neglected or unfairly subordinated to anyone else. Here again the writers I am considering remain in complete agreement with their Roman authorities. This can only be brought about, they all declare, if our magistrates uphold the dictates of justice in all their public acts. The ideal of justice they define, in accordance with the principles of Roman law, as a matter of giving to each his due, *ius suum cuique*. But to ensure that everyone receives his due, they argue, is the same as ensuring that no one's interests are excluded or unfairly subjected to those of anyone else. The ideal of justice is thus seen as the bedrock: to act justly is the one and only means to promote the common good, without which there can be no hope of preserving concord and hence of attaining greatness.

Once again, Sallust provides one of the main inspirations for this argument. As he had put it with characteristic succinctness in the *Bellum Catilinae*, it was 'by acting with justice as well as with industry that the Roman republic grew to greatness'.[74] But the writers I am considering are even more indebted at this point to a similar passage from the start of Cicero's *De officiis*. Introducing the topic of justice, Cicero had begun by declaring that it constitutes the primary means 'by which the community of men and, as it were, their common unity, is preserved'.[75]

These sentiments are often transcribed almost *verbatim* by the pre-humanist writers on city government. Giovanni da Viterbo begins his treatise by laying it down that the prime duty of chief magistrates is 'to render to each person his due, in order that the city may be governed in justice and equity'.[76] The importance of this principle, as one of his model speeches later explains, stems from the fact that 'when cities are ruled by these bonds of justice, they grow to greatness, become enriched and receive the greatest possible increase.'[77] Latini likewise argues at the start of his chapter 'On the government of cities' that 'justice ought to be so well established in the heart of every *signor* that he assigns to everyone his right'.[78] The reason, he similarly explains, is that 'a city which is governed according to right and truth, such that everyone has what he ought to have, will certainly grow and multiply, both in people and in wealth, and will endure for ever in a good state of peace, to its honour and that of its friends'.[79]

---

[74] Sallust, *Bellum Catilinae*, x.1, p. 16: 'labore atque iustitia res publica crevit'.

[75] Cicero, *De officiis*, 1.7.20, p. 20: 'qua societas hominum inter ipsos et vitae quasi communitatis continetur'. Cf. also the claim in Cicero, *De inventione*, tr. H. Hubbell (London, 1949), II.53.160, p. 328 to the effect that it is *iustitia* which serves to maintain the *communes utilitates*.

[76] Viterbo, *Liber de regimine civitatum*, p. 220, col. 1: 'ius suum cuilibet reddatur, et regatur civitas in iustitia et equitate'.

[77] *Ibid.*, p. 231, col. 2: 'Per haec enim frena [iustitia et equalitas] civitates reguntur . . . crescunt, ditantur et maximum recipiunt incrementum.' Cf. also p. 234, cols. 1 and 2.

[78] Latini, *Li Livres dou Trésor*, p. 392: 'Justice doit estre si establement fermee dedens le cuer au signor, k'il doinst a chascun son droit.'

[79] *Ibid.*, p. 403: 'La cités ki est governee selonc droit et selonc verité, si ke chascuns ait ce k'il doit avoir . . . certes, ele croist et mouteplie des gens et d'avoir et dure tousjours en bone pais a l'onour de lui et de ses amis.'

By the time we come to the writers of vernacular *Dictamina* at the end of the century, we find these connections between justice, the common good, and the attainment of greatness being presented almost as a litany. 'He who loves justice', as Matteo de' Libri proclaims 'loves a constant and perpetual will to give to each his right; and he who loves to give to each his right loves tranquillity and repose, by means of which countries rise to the highest *grandeça*.'[80] Giovanni da Vignano writes in virtually identical terms, thereby furnishing yet a further summary of the ideology I have been anatomising. Justice forms the basis of good government; to act justly is to give to each his due; to give to each his due is the key to maintaining civic concord; and 'it is by means of all these things', Giovanni concludes, 'that countries are able to rise to *grandeça*'.[81]

With this injunction to love justice and treat it as the foundation of civic greatness,[82] we reach the heart of the ideology articulated by the early *Dictatores*. But there still remained one question of the highest practical importance. Under what system of government have we the best hope of ensuring that our leading magistrates do in fact obey the dictates of justice, such that all these other benefits flow from their rule?

It is at this point that the *Dictatores* respond with their celebration of the system of government most familiar to them: the system based on ruling councils chaired by elected magistrates. If justice is to be upheld and civic greatness attained, they all agree, government by hereditary princes or *Signori* must at all costs be avoided; some form of elective and self-governing system must always be maintained.

Once again, the authorities most often invoked in support of this basic political commitment are the apologists of the Roman republic in its final phase. The vehement anti-Caesarism of Cicero's *De officiis* naturally made it a key text.[83] But the most frequently quoted argument against hereditary rule was yet again taken from Sallust's *Bellum Catilinae*. The danger with kingship, Sallust had declared, is that 'to kings, good men are objects of even greater suspicion than the wicked.'[84] The reason is that 'to kings, the good qualities of others are invariably seen as a threat'.[85] This explains why 'it was only when the city of Rome managed to become liberated from its kings that it was able, in such a short space of time, to rise to such greatness.'[86] Only when everyone is allowed

---

[80] Libri, *Arringhe*, p. 34: 'quel k'ama iustitia ama constante e perpetua voluntate de dare soa raxone a çascuno; e ki ama soa raxone a çascuno, ama tranquilitate e reposo, per le qual cose le terre montano in grand grandeça'. Cf. also pp. 130, 160–2.

[81] Vignano, *Flore de parlare*, p. 296: 'per le qua' cose fare le terre montano in grandeça'.

[82] For the significance among these writers of the specific injunction 'Diligite iustitiam' see Skinner, 'Ambrogio Lorenzetti', pp. 14–17.

[83] For Cicero's denunciation of Julius Caesar as a tyrant see *De officiis*, II.7. 23, p. 190.

[84] Sallust, *Bellum Catilinae*, VII.3, p. 12: 'Nam regibus boni quam mali suspectiores sunt.'

[85] *Ibid.*, VII.3, p. 12: 'semperque eis [viz. regibus] aliena virtus formidulosa est'.

[86] *Ibid.*, VII.3, p. 12: 'Sed civitas . . . adepta libertate quantum brevi creverit.'

to contend for honour, without fear of exciting envy or enmity from their rulers, can the greatest heights of civic glory be scaled.

Among the pre-humanist writers, it is Latini who reiterates this argument with the strongest emphasis. His chapter 'Of signories' opens with the briskest possible statement of the case. 'There are three types of government, one being rule by kings, the second rule by leading men, the third rule by communes themselves. And of these, the third is far better than the rest.'[87] At the start of his chapter 'On the government of cities' he proceeds to give his grounds for this conclusion. Where kings and princes enjoy ultimate control, as in France and most other countries, they consider only their own interests, 'selling offices and assigning them to those who pay most for them, with little consideration for the good or benefit of the townsfolk'.[88] But where the citizens themselves retain control, as in Italy, 'they are able to elect, as *podestà* or *signore*, those who will act most profitably for the common good of the city and all their subjects'.[89]

The pre-humanist writers assign no distinctive name to the form of government they most admire. They remain content to describe it simply as one of the types of *regimen* or *reggimento* by which a *civitas* or *commune* can lawfully be ruled.[90] Where they are any more specific, they merely add that the *regimen* in question can be described as one in which power remains in the hands of the commune itself.[91] Save for one or two remarks in Giovanni da Viterbo,[92] and later in Albertino Mussato,[93] there are no signs of the later disposition to use the term *res publica* to distinguish such elective forms of government from hereditary monarchies. Still less is there any hint of the suggestion canvassed by Cicero at one point in the *De officiis* to the effect that such regimes are the only forms of *res publicae* truly worthy of the name.[94]

There is one point, however, at which a number of these theorists make use of a concept that was later to become central to – indeed definitive of – the political vocabulary of Renaissance republicanism. As we have seen, they treat it as a distinctive virtue of elective systems that they guarantee the equality of all

---

[87] Latini, *Li Livres dou Trésor*, p. 211: 'Seignouries sont de iii manieres, l'une est des rois, la seconde est des bons, la tierce est des communes, laquele est la trés millour entre ces autres.'

[88] See *ibid.*, p. 392 for the accusation that, in France and other kingdoms, rulers 'vendent les provostés et les baillent a ciaus ki plus l'achatent (poi gardent sa bonté ne le proufit des borgois)'.

[89] *Ibid.*, p. 392: 'en Ytaile . . . li communité des viles eslisent lor poesté et lor signour tel comme il quident qu'il soit plus proufitable au commun preu de la vile et de tous lor subtés'.

[90] See, for example, Faba, *Dictamina Rhetorica*, p. 54; Viterbo, *Liber de regimine civitatum*, p. 222, col. 1; Ceffi, *Dicerie*, p. 45.   [91] See, for example, Latini, *Li Livres dou Trésor*, pp. 211, 392.

[92] See Viterbo, *Liber de regimine civitatum*, p. 255, col. 2, p. 262, col. 1 and p. 272, col. 1 for the use of the term *res publica* to describe self-governing cities.

[93] A. Mussato *De Gestis Italicorum Post Mortem Henrici VII Caesaris Historia*, ed. L. Muratori in *Rerum Italicarum Scriptores*, (1727), vol. 10, cols. 569–768, at col. 722: 'Formam publicam tenendam in civitate, ne figura reipublicae adeo usque deleta sit, quin faciem effigiemque habere censeatur.'

[94] See Cicero, *De officiis*, 11.8.29. This passage, implying that Rome was only a true *res publica* under its traditional constitution, is, I think, crucial to understanding the process by which the term *res publica* eventually ceased to be used to refer to any type of body politic, and instead came to be used specifically to describe elective systems of government such as Cicero had in mind.

citizens before the law. No one's interests are excluded, no one is unfairly subordinated to anyone else. But this, they point out, is in effect to advance a thesis about political liberty. It is to say that only under elective regimes are individuals able to live a free way of life, unconstrained by any unjust dependence or servitude. As a result – following a usage already established by Cicero[95] – they begin to describe such regimes as 'free governments', commending them as the only means of ensuring that every citizen is permitted to live 'in a free state'.[96]

We already encounter an intimation of this development at the start of Giovanni da Viterbo's *Liber de regimine civitatum*, where he argues that the term *civitas* itself derives from the phrase *civium libertas*.[97] A further hint occurs in Bonvesin della Riva's panegyric on Milan, whose chapter in praise of the city's traditional form of communal government is entitled 'The commendation of Milan by reason of its liberty'.[98] A generation later, the contrast with the servitude to be expected under hereditary *Signori* is strongly drawn by Albertino Mussato in recounting the fall of the Paduan commune. Mussato repeatedly equates the attempt by his fellow-citizens to uphold their *res publica* against the challenge of the Della Scala with the attempt 'to fight in defence of the liberty of our native land'.[99]

It is in Filippo Ceffi's *Dicerie*, however, that the upholding of liberty is most emphatically connected with elective forms of government. In his model speech for citizens to use when receiving a new *podestà*, Ceffi characterises such magistrates as the preservers of liberty.[100] In a later speech designed for a similar occasion, he advises citizens to remind the incoming *podestà* of their expectation 'that they will be able to live both in safety and in a state of liberty' under his rule.[101] Most striking of all is his model speech designed for citizens to use in the event of having to capitulate to a *signore*. Here Ceffi explicitly equates such a change of government with the forfeiture of liberty. What he advises the leaders of a commune to say in such a predicament is that 'due to the harshness of war, we find ourselves obliged to hand over our liberty and our system of justice, which have been in our possession for many years'.[102]

---

[95] See, for example, his distinction between living under tyranny and living 'in libera civitate' in Cicero, *De officiis*, II.7.23–4, p. 190. Cf. also II.22.78–9, p. 254 on the liberty of citizens.

[96] It is thus an exaggeration to maintain, as for example Witt has done, that 'a republican concept of *libertas*' only re-emerges in 'the early years of the Quattrocento'. See Witt, 'Rebirth', p. 175. But cf. *ibid.*, pp. 186–8 for an interesting discussion of some earlier accounts.

[97] Viterbo, *Liber de regimine civitatum*, p. 218, col. 2: 'Civitas autem dicitur civium libertas.' Cf. also the connection between liberty and self-government noted in *ibid.*, p. 271, col. 1.

[98] Riva, *De Magnalibus Mediolani*, p. 166: 'De commendatione Mediolani ratione libertatis.'

[99] See, for example, Mussato, *De Gestis Italicorum*, p. 658: 'pro patria [*sic*] libertate decertant'.

[100] Ceffi, *Dicerie*, p. 32. Cf. also p. 35.

[101] *Ibid.*, p. 41: 'che noi possiamo iscampare e vivere liberamente sotto la vostra segnoria'. Cf. also p. 44.

[102] *Ibid.*, p. 61: 'per asprezza di guerra, siano condotti a donare nostra libertade e giustizia, la quale abbiamo posseduta per molti anni'. As Rubinstein has shown, the assumption that the preservation of liberty requires the maintenance of a self-governing republic became a

III

I now turn to Machiavelli's discussion of republican liberty in the *Discorsi*. Recent commentators have generally placed their main emphasis on the originality of Machiavelli's account and the extent to which it diverges from received beliefs. As a result, the many continuities between his arguments and those of the earliest protagonists of republicanism have not perhaps been adequately recognised. My first aim in what follows will be to show that, even when advancing his most consciously novel claims, Machiavelli remains in close intellectual contact with the assumptions of the writers I have so far been examining, and above all with their Roman authorities.

One of the features of Machiavelli's analysis that most astonished his contemporaries was his defence of the 'tumults' that disfigured the political life of early republican Rome.[103] According to Machiavelli, it was actually 'due to the disunion between the Plebs and the Senate', and the turmoil to which this gave rise, that Rome 'managed to become a perfect republic'.[104] The resolution of this paradox is proffered in Book I, chapter 4. Those who condemn Rome's tumults, Machiavelli declares, 'are failing to recognise that there are two contrasting outlooks in every republic, that of the leading men and that of the ordinary citizens, and that all the laws made in favour of liberty are born of the disunity between them'.[105] Such critics, he suggests, 'thus appear to be complaining about the very things that were the primary cause of Rome's maintaining her freedom'.[106] Rome's critics are 'concentrating on the clamour and outcry that arose from her tumults' when they ought to be reflecting instead 'on the splendid consequences to which they gave rise'.[107] These splendid consequences, as Machiavelli's chapter-heading explains, were that 'the disunion between the plebs and the senate in Rome enabled that republic to become at once free and great'.[108]

commonplace of political rhetoric in Florence in the later fourteenth century. See the important discussion in N. Rubinstein, 'Florence and the despots: some aspects of Florentine diplomacy in the fourteenth century', *Transactions of the Royal Historical Society*, ser. 5, (1952), pp. 21–45. It appears, however, that what was generally being claimed in such arguments was that the preservation of liberty *requires* political independence and republican self-government, not that the term 'liberty' somehow *means* 'political independence' or 'republican self-government' as Rubinstein suggests at pp. 29–30.

103 On contemporary reactions to Machiavelli's argument see, for example, Skinner, *The Foundations*, I, pp. 181–2.

104 Machiavelli, *Il principe e Discorsi*, I.2, p. 135: it was 'per la disunione della Plebe e del Senato' that Rome 'feca una republica perfetta'.

105 *Ibid.*, I.4, p. 137: 'non considerino, come e' sono in ogni republica due umori diversi, quello del popolo et quello de' grandi; e come tutte le leggi che si fanno in favore della libertà, nascono dalla disunione loro'.

106 *Ibid.*, I.4, p. 137: 'coloro che dannono i tumulti intra i Nobili e la Plebe mi pare che biasimino quelle cose che furono prima causa del tenere libera Roma'.

107 *Ibid.*, I.4, p. 137: 'che considerino più a romori ed alle grida che di tali tumulti nascevano, che a buoni effetti che quelli partorivano'.

108 *Ibid.*, I.4, p. 136: 'Che la disunione della Plebe e del Senato romano fece libera e potente quella republica.'

This analysis has been interpreted as Machiavelli's way of voicing dissent from the widespread admiration among his contemporaries for the proverbial serenity of Venice.[109] As we have seen, however, the assumption that internal discord is invariably fatal to civic greatness had been central to the whole development of Italian republicanism. Everyone had treated the preservation of concord, the avoidance of internal strife, as indispensable to upholding the common good and thereby attaining greatness. By insisting that tumults represent a prime *cause* of freedom and greatness, Machiavelli is placing a question-mark against this entire tradition of thought. What he is repudiating is nothing less than the Ciceronian vision of the *concordia ordinum*, a vision hitherto endorsed by the defenders of self-governing republics in an almost uncritical way.

There is a further point at which Machiavelli appears to be offering a critical commentary on traditional republican thought. This is in his formulation of the doctrine that political actions should be judged not by their intrinsic rightness but by their effects. The notorious passage in which he puts forward this doctrine occurs in his discussion of Romulus' founding of Rome in Book 1, chapter 9. 'No discerning person', he maintains, 'will ever criticise anyone for taking any action, however extreme, which is undertaken with the aim of organising a kingdom or constituting a republic. For it is right that, although the fact of the extreme action may accuse him, its effect should excuse him. It is those who use violence to destroy things, not to reconstitute them, who alone deserve blame.'[110]

This way of expressing the point again suggests a criticism of conventional pieties. As we have seen, it had generally been assumed that the common good can only be secured if rulers behave with complete justice, ensuring that everyone receives his due and that no one is unfairly subordinated to anyone else. Machiavelli's strongly contrasting conclusion derives from a recognition of the fact that this is unduly optimistic, since the two ideals are potentially incompatible. When you act to promote the common good, you always run the risk 'that this will sometimes turn out to the disadvantage of one or another private individual'.[111] It follows that, if the promotion of the common good is genuinely your goal, you must be prepared to abandon the ideal of justice. This is the hard lesson that Romulus is praised for having learned so well. He realised that 'when the effect is good, as it was in his case, this will always serve to excuse

---

[109] For example in Pocock, *The Machiavellian Moment*, p. 186. Cf. also pp. 196–9.

[110] Machiavelli, *Il principe e Discorsi*, 1.9, pp. 153–4: 'né mai uno ingegno savio riprenderà alcuno di alcune azione straordinaria, che per ordinare un regno o constituire una republica usasse. Conviene bene che, accusandolo il fatto, lo effetto lo scusi . . . perché colui che è violento per guastare, non quello che è per racconciare, si debbe riprendere.'

[111] *Ibid.*, 11.2, p. 280: 'quantunque e torni in danno di questo o di quello privato'.

whatever was done'.[112] By contrast, this is the principle that Piero Soderini, the leader of the Florentine republic during Machiavelli's own lifetime, is severely criticised for having failed to grasp. Soderini never appreciated that 'one must at no point allow an evil to continue out of regard for a good when the good can easily be overwhelmed by the evil'. As a result he refused to do evil in order that good might come of it; and as a result of that decision he brought ruin on the republic as well as himself.[113]

I turn finally to consider the positive resemblances between the arguments of the *Discorsi* and the earliest traditions of Italian republicanism. The continuities are much more fundamental than has usually been recognised. For all the novelty of his analysis, Machiavelli remains content to fit his ideas into a traditional framework, a framework based on linking together the concepts of liberty, the common good and civic greatness in a largely familiar way.

First of all, Machiavelli fully endorses the long-standing view that the highest ends to which any city can aspire are those of civic glory and greatness. He initially announces this commitment in the opening chapter of Book I. First he turns to consider those cities which were originally founded by their own citizens 'without having any particular prince to direct them'.[114] Among these, he observes, both Athens and Venice can be numbered, 'both of which managed to rise from these small beginnings to the *grandezza* they now enjoy'.[115] Next he considers the contrasting case of cities originally founded by princes. 'Due to the fact such cities do not have free beginnings', he argues, 'it very seldom happens that they are able to rise to greatness.[116] Not only does Machiavelli announce the theme of *grandezza* at the outset; he also hints at a link between *grandezza* and *libertà*, thereby introducing what later proves to be one of his major arguments.

Turning next to the case of ancient Rome, Machiavelli repeatedly makes it clear that for him the basic question is how the early republic managed to rise to such unparalleled heights of greatness. The question recurs throughout Book I, in the course of which Machiavelli discusses the Roman republican constitution. He constantly asks himself what features of the constitution enabled the republic 'to attain Roman *grandezza*',[117] 'to come to its ultimate *grandezza*,'[118] 'to arrive at that *grandezza* which it acquired'.[119] The same topic recurs even more

---

[112] *Ibid.*, 1.9, pp. 153–4: 'quando sia buono [viz., lo effetto] come quello di Romolo, sempre lo scuserà'.

[113] *Ibid.*, III.3, p. 387: 'non si debbe mai lasciare scorrere un male rispetto ad uno bene, quando quel bene facilmente possa essere da quel male oppressato'.

[114] *Ibid.*, 1.1, p. 126: 'sanza altro principe particulare che gli ordinasse'.

[115] *Ibid.*, 1.1, p. 126: 'talché ogni piccolo principio li poté fare venire a quella grandezza nella quale sono'.

[116] *Ibid.* 1.1, p. 126: 'E per non avere queste cittadi la loro origine libera, rade volte occorre che le facciano progressi grandi.'   [117] *Ibid.*, 1.6, p. 146: 'pervenire alla romana grandezza'.

[118] *Ibid.*, 1.20, p. 185: 'venire a quella sua ultima grandezza'.

[119] *Ibid.*, 1.6, p. 143: 'venire a quella grandezza dove ei pervenne'.

prominently in Book II, the main concern of which is to analyse Rome's military policies. Here Machiavelli primarily devotes himself to examining the techniques of warfare that enabled the Romans 'to attain *grandezza*'[120] or, more imposingly, 'to help themselves on the way towards supreme *grandezza*'.[121] Finally, the same theme is no less pervasive in Book III, the principal aim of which is 'to show how much the actions of individual men contributed to making Rome great, and brought about in that city so many good effects'.[122]

Machiavelli also endorses the traditional belief in the importance of the common good. He agrees that, unless each citizen behaves with *virtù*, and in consequence places the good of his community above all private ambitions and factional allegiances, the goal of civic *grandezza* can never be attained. He states this assumption most firmly in Book II, chapter 2 – the crucial passage in which he spells out the special virtues of republican government. 'It is not the pursuit of individual good', he declares at that point, 'but rather the pursuit of the common good that brings greatness to cities.'[123] It is because of their clear recognition of this fact, Book I repeatedly affirms, that the highest praise must be accorded to those who have founded constitutions. Romulus, for example, is said to have understood the importance of the common good so well that even his fratricide can be excused, since this too 'was something that was done for the common good and not out of personal ambition'.[124] The same perception is said to have guided the leading citizens of Rome whose achievements are outlined in Book III. Fabius, Manlius, Camillus and many others are particularly singled out for helping Rome along the pathway to greatness by acting 'entirely in favour of the public', placing 'the public welfare' and 'the public benefit' above all other values.[125]

This analysis is corroborated by Machiavelli's account of corruption. To be a corrupt citizen is to place one's own ambitions or the advantages of a party above the common good. It is Machiavelli's contention that to act in this way is invariably fatal to the cause of civic freedom and greatness. As he explains early in Book I, it is always private or factional forces 'that ruin a free way of life'.[126] The claim is underlined in the discussion of the Decemviri later in Book I. 'It is when the people cannot agree to make a law in favour of liberty, but instead form parties that turn to support some particular leader, that tyranny at once

---

[120] See *ibid.*, II.13, p. 312, speaking of 'i modi necessari a venire a grandezza'.

[121] *Ibid.* II.6, p. 294: 'per facilitarsi la via a venire a una suprema grandezza'.

[122] *Ibid.* III.1, pp. 383–4: 'dimostrare a qualunque quanto le azioni degli uomini particulari facessono grande Roma e causassino in quella città molti buoni effetti'.

[123] *Ibid.*, II.2, p. 280: 'non il bene particulare ma il bene comune è quello che fa grandi le città'.

[124] *Ibid.*, I.9, p. 154: 'quello che fece fusse per il bene comune e non per ambizione propria'.

[125] See *ibid.*, III.23, p. 452 on Manlius acting 'tutto . . . in favore del publico'; III.30, p. 467 on Camillus acting 'ad utile publico'; III.47, p. 502 on Fabius acting 'per beneficio publico'.

[126] *Ibid.*, I.7, p. 147: 'forze private . . . che sono quelle che rovinano il vivere libero'.

rises up.'[127] Finally, Machiavelli draws the same moral from his account of the fall of the Roman republic in Book III. 'Sulla and Marius managed to find troops willing to follow them in actions contrary to the common good, and it was by these means that Caesar was then able to place his country in subjection.'[128]

Machiavelli's constitutional proposals are also largely dependent on traditional arguments. He presents them most clearly – both in a negative and a positive form – in the programmatic passage at the start of Book II. His negative thesis states that the common good is scarcely ever promoted under princely or monarchical rule. The explanation he offers is precisely the one that the earliest protagonists of republican government had taken from Sallust: kings are always liable to be suspicious of just those men of eminent talent who are most capable of serving their country well. In expressing this doubt, moreover, Machiavelli writes in a manner strikingly reminiscent of Sallust's own account. Even under the rule of a *virtuoso* tyrant, he declares, 'no benefit to the body politic can possibly result'. For 'no one exercising a tyranny can ever confer honours on any citizens under his rule who are truly good and capable, since he will never wish to have cause to fear them'.[129] This means that 'it is usually the case, whenever there is a princely form of rule, that the prince's behaviour is harmful to the city, while the behaviour of the city is harmful to the prince'.[130]

Machiavelli's positive thesis states that the only way to ensure the promotion of the common good must therefore be to maintain a republican form of government. The inference is resoundingly drawn in the same crucial passage at the start of Book II. 'There can be no doubt that it is only in republics that this ideal of the common good is properly considered. For it is only in republics that everything which needs to be done to attain this objective is followed out.'[131]

The vocabulary Machiavelli employs at this point would not of course have been familiar to the pre-humanist writers on city government. Following their Roman authorities, they had generally used the terms *res publica* and *repubblica* to denote the broad idea of the body politic, and thus to speak of any lawfully constituted regime. Nevertheless, the claim Machiavelli uses the term *repubblica* to express is one that all of them would have endorsed. As we have seen, they had all taken it for granted that, if the common good is to be upheld, it is

[127] *Ibid.*, I.40, p. 227: 'E quando e' non convengano a fare una legge in favore della libertà, ma gettasi qualcuna delle parti a favorire uno, allora è che subito la tirannide surge.'
[128] *Ibid.*, III.25, p. 456: 'Silla e Mario peterono trovare soldati che contro al bene publico gli seguitassono; per questo Cesare potette occupare la patria.'
[129] See *ibid.*, II.2, p. 280, claiming that even under 'uno tiranno virtuoso', 'non ne risulterebbe alcuna utilità a quella republica . . . perché e' non può onorare nessuno di quegli cittadini che siano valenti e buoni che egli tiranneggia, non volendo avere ad avere sospetto di loro.'
[130] *Ibid.*, II.2, p. 280: 'quando vi è uno principe, dove il piú delle volte quello che fa per lui offende la città, e quello che fa per la città offende lui'.
[131] *Ibid.*, II.2, p. 280: 'E sanza dubbio questo bene comune non è osservato se non nelle republiche: perché tutto quello che fa a proposito suo si esequisce.'

indispensable to maintain an elective system of government as opposed to any form of princely or monarchical rule.

Finally, Machiavelli proceeds to draw from this line of reasoning the inference that the earliest apologists of the communes had already drawn. He insists that it is only under such elective constitutions that the goal of civic greatness can ever be achieved. He presents this final conclusion in two stages, and at each point he again invokes and develops a number of traditional arguments.

He begins by connecting the capacity to achieve civic greatness with the enjoyment of 'a free way of life'. The key statement of the case again appears at the start of Book II. 'It is easy to understand how an affection for living a free way of life springs up in peoples. For one sees by experience that cities have never increased either in power or in wealth unless they have been established in liberty.'[132] This point is then underlined – as in a number of pre-humanist writings on city government – by means of a strong allusion to Sallust's argument in the *Bellum Catilinae*. As we have seen, Sallust had observed that 'it was only when the city of Rome managed to become liberated from its kings that it was able, in such a short space of time, to rise to such greatness'. Machiavelli expresses the same sentiment in a remarkably similar style. 'Above all it is most marvellous to consider the greatness to which Rome rose after she had liberated herself from her kings.'[133]

Having connected liberty with greatness, Machiavelli completes his argument by adding that it is only possible to live 'in a free state' under a self-governing republic. It is true that he is not completely consistent in drawing the corollary that servitude will prove inevitable under monarchical forms of government.[134] But in general he makes a sharp distinction between the freedom of republics and the slavery imposed not merely by tyrants[135] but even

---

[132] *Ibid.*, II.2, p. 280: 'E facil cosa è conoscere donde nasca ne' popoli questa affezione del vivere libero: perché si vede per esperianza le cittadi non avere mai ampliato né di dominio né di ricchezza se non mentre sono state in libertà.'

[133] *Ibid.* II.2, p. 280: 'Ma sopra tutto maravigliosissimae è a considerare a quanta grandezza venne Roma poiché la si liberò da' suoi Re.'

[134] He remarks at the outset that he will concentrate on those cities which 'have been far removed from all external servitude, and have at once been able to govern themselves by their own will'. See *ibid.*, I.2, p. 129, speaking of cities 'lontano da ogni servitú esterna, ma si sono subito governate per loro arbitrio'. At that point he assumes that such self-governing arrangements can take the form 'either of republics or of principalities'. See I.2, p. 129: 'governate . . . o come republiche o come principato'. In the course of his subsequent analysis, moreover, he reverts at several points to the suggestion that monarchical regimes may sometimes be compatible with liberty, and thus with the maintenance of what he calls a genuinely 'civil' or 'political' way of life. See, for example, 1.25, p. 193 and III.1, p. 380.

[135] Freedom and tyranny are of course consistently contrasted. For general statements see *ibid.*, III.7, p. 412 and III.8, p. 416. For the case of Athens see I.2, pp. 133–4. For the case of the later Tarquins in Rome see 1.17, pp. 177 and III.2, p. 384.

by the best kings and princes.[136] He first insists on the contrast at the beginning of Book I. Describing the early history of Rome, he concedes that 'Romulus and the other kings enacted many good laws of a kind compatible with a free way of life.' 'Nevertheless', he goes on, 'their aim was to establish a kingdom and not a republic, with the consequence that, when the city became free, it still lacked many things that needed to be established in favour of liberty.'[137] The implication that one can only hope to live in genuine liberty under a republic is later spelled out at a considerable number of points. The moment, for example, when the Romans first 'elected two consuls in place of their king' is described as 'the beginning of their free way of life'.[138] Likewise, the period when the various peoples of Italy 'were all of them free' is described as a time 'when one never hears tell of there being any kings'.[139]

The essence of Machiavelli's republicanism can thus be summarised in the form of two connected propositions: first, that no city can ever attain greatness unless it upholds a free way of life; secondly, that no city can ever uphold a free way of life unless it maintains a republican constitution. With this statement of the case, Machiavelli not only presents a wholehearted defence of traditional republican values; he also presents that defence in a wholeheartedly traditional way.[140]

---

[136] For the fullest statement of the argument that it is only possible to live in freedom under a self-governing regime and that such regimes are to be contrasted with principalities, see *ibid.*, I. 16, pp. 173–5.

[137] *Ibid.* I.2, p. 134: 'Perché Romolo e tutti gli altri Re fecero molte e buone leggi, conformi ancora al vivere libero; ma perché il fine loro fu fondare un regno e non una republica, quando quella città rimase libera vi mancavano molte cose che era necessario ordinare in favore della libertà.'

[138] See *ibid.*, I.25, p. 192 for the claim that it was when the Romans 'in cambio d'uno re creati duoi consoli' that they established 'loro vivere libero'.

[139] See *ibid.* II.2, p. 279 for the claim that the time when the people of Italy 'erano tutti popoli liberi' was a time when 'né si ragiona mai che vu fusse alcuno re'. The same chapter goes on (p. 283) to explain the loss of a love of liberty in modern Italy in terms of the fact that there are fewer republics than in ancient times.

[140] I have revised this paper extensively in the light of the comments I received at the Conference in Florence for which it was written. For providing me with criticisms at that time I am especially grateful to Steven Lukes, Nicolai Rubinstein, Judith Shklar and Maurizio Viroli. For further help with the revised version I am greatly indebted to John Dunn and Susan James.

7

Machiavelli and the republican idea of politics

MAURIZIO VIROLI

If there is a single point on which scholars have reached a wide consensus, it is that Machiavelli created a new theory or a new science of politics. Be it his sin or his greatest contribution to modern culture, what seems to be beyond dispute is that Machiavelli rejected the republican idea of politics and provided us with a new account of what politics is all about. Against the classical view that politics is the art of establishing and preserving a good community, Machiavelli, it has been argued, emphasised that the goal of politics is the pursuit of power and that the 'political man' cannot be the 'good man of the ancients'. While several scholars have stressed that the originality of Machiavelli lies in the redefinition of the aim of politics,[1] others have emphasised his contribution to a new methodology of political enquiry.[2]

This agreement among contemporary scholars, could easily be corroborated by the opinions of the political writers of the sixteenth and the seventeenth centuries who called Machiavelli the corruptor of the true (Aristotelian) idea of politics and pointed to him as the thinker who transformed the most noble of humane arts into the art of tyrannical rule. For instance, Innocent Gentillet wrote that Machiavelli invented 'des Maximes tous meschantes, et basty sur icelles non une science politique mais tyrannique'.[3]

I would like to thank Quentin Skinner, Judith Shklar, George Kateb, Gisela Bock and Istvan Hont for their comments and editorial help on earlier drafts of this essay.

[1] See, for instance, B. Croce, *Elementi di politica* (Bari, 1925). Against Croce Isaiah Berlin claimed that it is more appropriate to speak of conflict between two moralities, instead of discovery of the autonomy of politics (I. Berlin, 'The originality of Machiavelli' in *Studies on Machiavelli*, Myron P. Gilmore, ed. (Florence, 1972), pp. 147–206; see also Friedrich Meinecke, *Die Idee der Staatsräson in der neueren Geschichte* (Munich and Berlin, 1929), 3rd edn, pp. 36–7; J.H. Hexter, *The Vision of Politics on the Eve of the Reformation* (New York, 1973), p. 228; G. Ritter, *Die Dämonie der Macht* (Munich, 1948) 6th edn, p. 14.

[2] Ernst Cassirer wrote: 'What Galileo gave in his *Dialogues*, and what Machiavelli gave in his *Prince* were really "new sciences" . . . Just as Galileo's Dynamics became the foundation of our modern science of nature, so Machiavelli paved a new way to political science.' E. Cassirer, *The Myth of the State* (New Haven, 1946), p. 130; See also G. Prezzolini, *Machiavelli anticristo* (Roma, 1954), p. 18. On the same line, A. Renaudet wrote that the distinctive contribution of Machiavelli was the creation of 'une méthode strictement positive' for the study of political science. A. Renaudet, *Machiavel* (Paris, 1955), pp. 117; for a comprehensive account see V. Sellin, 'Politik' in *Geschichtlichen Grundbegriffe* (Stuttgart, 1978), vol. IV, p. 790; the interpretation of Machiavelli as the innovator of the science of politics who radically rejected the classical tradition is also stressed by Sheldon Wolin, *Politics and Vision* (Boston and Toronto, 1961), pp. 201–37.

[3] I Gentillet, *Discours sur les moyens de bien gouverner et maintenir en bonne paix un royaume ou autre principauté* (1576), A. d'Andrea and P.D. Stewart, eds. (Florence, 1974), p. 20. In *Le Livre de l'institution du Prince* (1548), Guillaume Budé contrasted 'le régime politique et l'honnesteté morale' with the vices that often follow from power and superiority.

However, one political writer in early modern Europe turned the predominant view of Machiavelli upside down and claimed that the great accomplishment of the Florentine secretary was his recovery of the republican ideal as opposed to politics as the art of tyranny. I am referring to James Harrington, who made this point forcefully in the 'Preliminaries' of *Oceana*, issued in 1656. The premise of his argument, which deserves lengthy consideration, is the distinction between 'ancient' and 'modern' prudence. 'Ancient prudence' was revealed to mankind by God himself and was followed by the Greeks and the Romans. The government which was instituted according to ancient prudence was the government *de jure*, that is 'the civil society instituted and preserved upon the common right and interest'. Modern prudence, on the contrary, 'is the art whereby one man or a few men, subject a city or a nation and rule it according to his or their private interests'. Since in the government *de facto* laws are made to protect the interests of one man, or of the few, it may be said that this is government by men and not by laws. Having clarified the distinction between ancient and modern prudence, Harrington writes:

The former kind is that which Machiavelli (whose books are neglected) is the only politician that hath gone about to retrieve and that Leviathan (who would have his book imposed upon the universities) goes about to destroy.[4]

The interpretative dilemma seems clear: what did Machiavelli do with the concept of politics? Did he dismantle or recover the republican view of politics as the art of instituting and preserving the good political community?

What also seems clear is that the question goes beyond the field of Machiavelli studies. Implicitly or explicitly, we are all using the supposedly Machiavellian understanding of politics as games of power, convenience and self-interest which are to be discussed in the language of an empirical science. If we discovered that Machiavelli had actually told us a completely different story, that politics pertains only to the preservation of a community of men grounded upon justice and the common good, we might be tempted to reconsider our mental habits concerning politics. An accurate historical understanding of Machiavelli's language could produce an interesting theoretical account, one which would, as is often the case, have its own moral.

To reach a satisfactory understanding of what Machiavelli meant by the word *politico* (and its correlatives and synonyms) and how he transformed its classical

---

[4] J. Harrington, *The Commonwealth of Oceana* in J.G.A. Pocock, ed., *The Political Works of James Harrington* (Cambridge, 1977), p. 161. Hannah Arendt wrote that Machiavelli is the only post-classical political theorist who made an extraordinary effort 'to restore politics to its old dignity'. Arendt's view, however, is totally at odds with Harrington's interpretation since she identifies the recovery of the classical idea of politics in the passages of *The Prince* and the *Discourses* where Machiavelli describes the rise of private men to princedom or to a public position. See *The Human Condition* (Chicago, 1958), p. 35; for a useful account of the English interpretations of Machiavelli, see Felix Raab, *The English Face of Machiavelli* (London, 1964).

meaning, the most advisable strategy is to start by describing the conventional ways of speaking about politics in the literature of his time. Having identified what it actually meant to speak of politics, we may hope to understand whether, or to what extent, Machiavelli endorsed, rejected or reworked the predominant conventions.

THE CLASSICAL IDEA OF POLITICS REDISCOVERED: POLITICS AND *CIVITAS*

In the political language of early modern Europe, the word *politicus* and its correlatives were used to refer exclusively to the *civitas*, which was understood as a community of men gathered together to live in justice under the rule of the same laws. Justice and laws moderate men's passions and allow them not only to live in security but also to enjoy the good life and to share concord and friendship. This concept of politics, which came into circulation as early as the thirteenth century, was related to the various dimensions of the existence of the *civitas*, the masterpiece of ancient legal and political wisdom which reappeared as a historical possibility at the end of the Middle Ages.

On the other hand, the writers who referred to princely or monarchical government used the qualification *politicus* to denote moderation or restraint of the power of the king in the name of equity or through the existing bodies of customary laws or collegial bodies intended to prevent arbitrary decisions. Even when applied to monarchical rule, the word *politicus* retained some flavour of the vocabulary of the city: the empire of law, justice, moderation and collegiality in the exercise of supreme authority.

In the chapter of the *Policraticus* (1159) designed to explain that the prince, although 'legis nexibus absolutus', is 'legis tamen servus et aequitatis', John of Salisbury stresses that the law is a gift of God and those who want to live politically ('in politice rei') must live under the rule of the law.[5]

According to Ptolemy of Lucca, the 'dominium politicum', as opposed to the 'dominium despoticum', has to be moderate ('oportet esse suave') and the rulers ('rector politicus') must judge the people only according to the laws.[6] In the 'principatus politicus', examples of which can be found in the Roman Republic and in the Italian city-states of his time, rulers are elected and rule according to virtue. Contrary to practices under 'principatum regni', in the 'principatus politicum' rulers are bound by the laws of the city and cannot overstep them.

---

[5] John of Salisbury, *Policraticus*, eds. A.M. Webb and C.I. Clemens (London, 1909), Bk IV, ch. 2, vol. I, p. 237.

[6] Ptolemy of Lucca, *De regimine principum ad regem Cypri*, in S. Thomae Aquinatis, *Opuscula Philosophica*, ed. P. Fr. Raymundi Spiazzi O.P. (Turin, 1954), Bk II, ch. 8.

Once again the word *politicus* is associated with the features of the city: moderation, elective rulers, the rule of law, justice.[7]

Most of the vocabulary of politics was borrowed from the works of Aristotle. Through translations and commentaries a vocabulary became available in which politics was associated only with the city, the good community where men can live a life of virtue. From the works of Aristotle scholars derived a set of conventions which became an essential component of early modern political language.

Politics, to summarise the most conventional themes, is the most excellent of humane arts because it leads men to attain the highest good, the good of the community.[8] Above all politics provides justice ('est autem politicum bonum quod iustum'). But justice alone is not the sole purpose of the institution of the city. The city is qualitatively different from a political alliance or a commercial partnership. Its aim is to create a good life for and to encourage virtuous behaviour in its citizens ('bonarum ergo actionum ponendum esse politicam communionem, sed non ipsius convivere').[9] The city is grounded upon friendship – defined as the desire to do and share things in common – and solidarity, not upon the mere exchange of commodities or reciprocal protection. Where there is envy and contempt, no political community can exist. *Political* rule is qualitatively different from domestic, monarchical and, above all, despotic rule. Political rule pertains to a community of free and equal individuals ('politica autem liberorum et aequalium principatus') and its distinctive features are elective magistracies and the consequent interchangeability of rulers and ruled ('in politicis quidem igitur principatibus plurimis transmutatur principans et subiectum').[10] The city has its order, the constitution, which states the rules for appointing magistrates and for exercising supreme authority. What is totally alien to the vocabulary of politics is tyranny, the arbitrary rule that contradicts the very essence of the *politia* ('omnium minime politia haec est').[11]

The concept of politics that came into circulation in the thirteenth century had no negative connotations whatsoever. On the contrary, politics was regarded as the 'architectural science', whose aim was to design the shape of the city and arrange the place and the functions of the other arts.

For Aquinas as well, politics was 'principalissima' among humane sciences,

[7] See *De regimine principum*, Bk IV, ch. 1. Both the derivation of the *civitas* from *polis* and the collegiality inherent in the concept of *civitas* are well stated in this passage: 'si autem per multos, veluti per consules, dictatorum et tribunos . . . talem regimen politiam appellant, a quod est pluralitas, sive civitas, quia hoc regimen proprie ad civitates pertinet'.

[8] 'Quoniam autem in omnibus quidem scientiis et artibus bonum finis, maximum itaque et maxime in principalissima omnium haec autem est politica potentia', *Aristoteles politicorum libri octo*, tr., Guilelmi de Moerbeka, ed., F. Susemihl (Leipzig, 1872), Bk III, 12. 1.

[9] *Ibid.* (Susemihl), Bk III, 9. 14.   [10] *Ibid.* (Susemihl), Bk I, 12. 2.

[11] *Ibid.* (Susemihl), Bk VI, 1. 7.

although second to theology, which considers the ultimate goal of the whole universe. Whereas the discussion of the ultimate goal of the universe is the prerogative of theology, politics is entitled to speak about the highest goal in earthly life, that is the city ('ad politicam pertinere considerationem ultimi finis humanae vitae').[12] While all communities and arts existing in the city have specific interests ('aliquod particulare et praesens commodum'), politics bears the responsibility for a lifetime 'interest' ('quod est utile per totam vitam').[13] Because its aim is precisely to order the city and the prerogatives of all its arts and communities, politics fully deserves the qualification of 'prudentia architectonica'.[14]

Leonardo Bruni's translations of Aristotle signal another important step towards the identification of the vocabulary of politics with the vocabulary of the *civitas*. For Bruni, the group of moral disciplines that the Greeks called *politica* must be rendered by 'precepta circa rempublicam'. The time has come, he stresses in the prologue to his translation of Aristotle's (pseudo) books on economics, to use our own vocabulary instead of the alien Greek words ('nos nostris vocabulis uti magis decet que alienis'). The goal of politics is to shape the order and the life of the city. What, in Moerbecke's words, pertained to 'politici intellectus et theoria' becomes, in Bruni's vocabulary, a matter of 'civilis intelligentia et speculationis'.[15] While Moerbecke kept the Greek word *politia* to denote the constitution of the city, Bruni refers to it with the Latin word *respublica* and defines it as 'istitutio civitatis circa magistratus honoresque publicas quemadmodum debet impartiri et in quo potestas dominandi summa debeat consistere et quis sit finis cuiusque societatis'.[16] In this shift from *politia*-rooted words to *civitas*-rooted words, the image of the city is expressed in a vocabulary that becomes predominant in Renaissance humanist political literature. The *civitas* is much more than a source of protection and a supplier of material needs, it is the humane community where the citizens have in common laws, magistracies, and religious and public ceremonies. In a true city the relationships between citizens are relationships of friendship and solidarity. When envy and animosity take the place of friendship, the city becomes just a crowd of strangers and enemies.[17] A well-ordered city is a self-governing community in which the populace has a place in public life ('quiescere autem plebem non principantem nullum signum est bene constitute civitatis')[18] and the citizens alternate in public offices ('in civilibus principatibus plerumque commutatur qui preestet is qui subest').[19] Only in such a good city can men enjoy happiness and a truly humane life. The art that teaches what a *civitas* is and how it is to be preserved, deserves the highest rank among humane disciplines:

[12] Sancti Thomae Aquinaris, *In decem libros Ethicorum Aristotelis ad Nichomachum expositio*, ed., R. Spiazzi (Turin, 1964), Bk I, lectio II, 31.   [13] *Ibid.*, Bk VIII, lectio IV, 1669.   [14] *Ibid.*
[15] *Aristotelis politicorum libri octo* (Paris, 1506), Bk VII, 2.   [16] *Ibid.* (Bruni), Bk IV, 1.
[17] *Ibid.* (Bruni), Bk III, 6.   [18] *Ibid.* (Bruni), Bk II, 8.   [19] *Ibid.* (Bruni), Bk I, 8.

nulla profecto convenientior disciplina homini esse potest quam quid sit civitas et quid respublica intelligere et per que conservetur intereatque civilis societas, non ignorare.[20]

Bruni does not provide a word to replace the Greek *politia*, but resorts instead to paraphrases which focus on the city and its preservation as the object and the aim of the art of politics ('de civitatibus eorumque gubernationae conservationemque traduntur'.[21]

Bruni's translation represented an important contribution to the acquisition of the concept of politics as the art of the city. Long before Bruni's translation was published, however, politics had already received its noble rank. In *Li livres dou trésor* (1266), Brunetto Latini listed politics (*la politique*) as the highest among the humane sciences and the most noble activity of man. The aim of politics is to rule a city according to reason and justice ('ele nous ensegne governer les etranges gens d'un regne et d'une vile, un peuple et une comune en tens de pes et de guere, selonc raison et selonc justice').[22] In his accounts of politics as the architectural science, Latini explicitly mentioned Aristotle's *Nicomachean Ethics*. However, his conceptualisation of the city as a people gathered together to live in the same place under the same laws was borrowed from Cicero: 'por ce dist Tuilles ke cités est un assamblemens de gens a abiter un lieu et vivre a une loi'.[23] Another reference to Cicero concerns the relationship between rhetoric, the art of persuading, and politics, the art of ruling a city. Ruling a city requires the ability to speak in a way that befits a community of free and equal citizens. Without language there can be no justice, no friendship, no humane community ('car se parleure ne fust cités ne seroit, ne nus establissemens de justice ne de humaine compaignie').[24] Through language men can express not only pain or pleasure, as animals can, but they can also argue about what is just and unjust and can enjoy conversation with their fellow-men. The proper place for men to express themselves through speech and conversation is the political community, which must be seen as the natural place for men living a truly humane life.[25]

---

[20] *Leonardo Aretini in libros politicorum Aristotelis de greco in latini traducto prologus*, in *ibid*.

[21] *Ibid. Prologus*.

[22] B. Latini, *Li Livres dou Trésor*, ed. F.J. Carmody (Berkeley and Los Angeles, 1948), Bk I, 4, 5. Brunetto Latini, wrote Giovanni Villani, taught the Florentines how to rule the republic according to politics ('fu cominciatore e maestro in digrossare i Fiorentini, e farli scorti di bene parlare, e in sapere guidare e reggere la nostra repubblica secondo la politica', *Cronica* (Florence, 1845), Bk VIII, ch. 10). [23] B. Latini, *Li Livres dou Trésor*, Bk III, 73, 3.

[24] *Ibid.*, Bk III, ch. 1, 9–13.

[25] The eulogy of rhetoric as an indispensable foundation of the good political community was a current theme in humanistic literature. Language – wrote, for instance, Poliziano – 'una res et dispersi congregavit et dissidentes inter se conciliavit et legibus moribusque, omnique denique humano cultu civilique coniunxit. Quo propter etiam deinceps in omnibus bene constitutis beneque moratis civitatibus una omnium semper eloquentia effloruit summumque est fastigium consecuta' in E. Garin, ed., *Filosofi italiani del Quattrocento* (Florence, 1942), p. 412; see also J. Seigel, *Rhetoric and Philosophy in Renaissance Humanism* (Princeton, 1968).

This eulogy of the *civitas* can also be found in the late thirteenth century in writers, like Egidius Romanus, who advocated the superiority of hereditary principality over republican rule. The political community is the natural destiny of man ('communitatem politicam sive civitatem esse aliquid secundum naturam').[26] To live 'politically' means to live under laws and good institutions ('vivere politicum secundum aliquas leges et secundum aliquas laudabiles ordinationes').[27] He who refuses to live in a political community either lowers himself to the level of a brute beast, or ambitiously seeks to be, like God, above laws and justice.

The image of the *civitas* as the natural destiny of man was echoed also in the works of Baldus de Ubaldis, who was, along with Bartolus, the father of the modern legal concept of *civitas*. 'Politicus', he wrote, is the appropriate qualification for a people living in a *civitas*: 'iste populus quandoque muris cingitur, et incolit civitatem; et idem proprie dicitur politicus a polis quod est *civitas*'.[28] The basic feature of the *civitas* is the rule of law and justice and the word *politicus* refers to a *respublica* ruled in justice: 'ad rempublicam, ut respublica salubriter regatur; et hoc pertinet ad politicam'.[29]

By the beginning of the fourteenth century, as Nicolai Rubinstein correctly points out, 'the word *politicus* and its Latin and Italian equivalents *civilis* and *civile*, had been squarely pre-empted for the republican regime'.[30] However, in the political literature of the fourteenth and fifteenth centuries, politics is still discussed above all as the discipline of the *civitas*. One may even notice – not surprisingly, since the main feature of the *civitas* is the rule of the law – that the language of politics borrows substantially from the language of civil jurisprudence and the art of politics is often made coincident with the art of legislation. In his famous treatise, *De Tyranno*, for instance, Coluccio Salutati contrasted the *principatus politicus*, where authority is 'legibus restricta', with the

---

[26] Egidio Colonna (Aegidius Romanus), *De regimine principum*, reprint from the edition of Rome (*apud* Bartholomeum Zannettum), 1607 (Scientia Verlag, Aalen, 1967), Bk III, Part I, ch. 4.

[27] *Ibid.*, Bk III, 2.

[28] Baldus of Ubaldis, *Commentaria super prima et secunda parte Digesti veteris* (Lyons, 1498), J.I. Rubr. (fol. 4r). On Baldus' theory of citizenship see Joseph P. Canning, 'A fourteenth-century contribution to the theory of citizenship: political man and the problem of created citizenship in the thought of Baldus de Ubaldis' in *Authority and Power: Studies on Medieval Law and Government presented to Walter Ullmann on his Seventieth Birthday*, eds. P.A. Linehan, and B. Tierney, (Cambridge, 1980), pp. 197–212; *idem, The political thought of Baldus de Ubaldis* (Cambridge, 1987), esp. pp. 93–206.

[29] Baldus of Ubaldis, *In primam Digesti veteris partem commentaria* (Venice, 1616), I.I. Rubr. n. 20. For justice as the essential quality of the *civitas*, see Baldus of Ubaldis, *Praelectiones in Quatuor Institutionum Libros* (Venice, 1599), I.3 (De iustitia et iure): 'iustitia prout est virtus politica, dicta a polis, quod est civitas . . . Et ponitur in diffinitione constans et perpetua, ad denotandum quod ita est impossibile civitas sine iustitia regi, quae est virtus politica, sicut est impossibile montes de uno loco ad alium transferri.'

[30] N. Rubinstein, 'The history of the word "politic" in early-modern Europe' in *The Languages of Political Theory in Early-Modern Europe*, ed. A. Pagden (Cambridge, 1987), p. 45.

regimen dispoticum, which belongs to the sphere of economics ('secundum finis rationem ad iconomicam spectat').[31]

The term *scientia civilis* is never used to denote the pursuit of power or the enlargement of the *stato* of the prince. As Salutati stresses in the *De nobilitate legum et medicinae*, the manifesto of the humanist celebration of politics, the *scientia civilis* concerns only the *civitas*, the community of men 'legum conglutinati vinculis'.[32] The true purpose of politics is the ordering of the laws designed to promote the common good and ensure the enjoyment of 'politica felicitas'. The laws are the substance of politics ('robustissima et maxima politice pars sunt').[33] From salutati's text it is clear that to speak of politics as the exercise of power against law and justice would be a barbarism. Through politics and laws, men's passions and customs submit to rule ('ratio et mensura')[34] so that living under the guidance of reason, men may truly be men. Since politics bears the responsibility for the health of the soul – the noblest part of man – it deserves the highest rank among humane sciences.

In the words of the great jurist Ulpianus, the *civilis sapientia*, which teaches men to make good laws and to preserve the city, fully deserves to be considered the true philosophy ('vera philosophia').[35] The point that without civil science (*civilis disciplina*) there can be no justice, no equity in punishing crimes or rewarding good deeds, in sum, no civil life, was almost a commonplace in humanist literature.[36] Without *ius civile* neither private nor public matters can be rightly administered ('nec rem privatam ullam nec publicam absque iure civili recte administrari ullo modo posse').[37] However, when the *civitas* is ruled according to the principles of *civilis disciplina*, it can rightly be said that the city belongs to the citizens, that they share much in common and that it is a great thing for them to belong to the city:

Sanctissimum primo ac dulcissimum patriae nomen. habet enim haec ad eam rem non parvas necessitudines. magnum est enim ex eadem esse civitate, praesertim ubi libere

---

[31] Coluccio Salutati, *De tyranno*, in *Abhandlungen zur Mittlern und Neuren Geschichte*, Alfred von Martin, ed. (Berlin and Leipzig, 1913), p. viii.

[32] Coluccio Salutati, *De nobilitate legum et medicinae*, ed. E. Garin (Florence, 1947), ch. 10.

[33] *Ibid.* ch. 17.

[34] *Ibid.*, ch. 9. See also ch. 20 where Salutati stresses the identity of politics and laws: 'idem esse politicam atque leges'.

[35] 'Oratio domini Andreae magistri Hugonis de Senis quam recitavit in principio studii Florentiae' in K. Müllner, *Reden und Briefe italienischer Humanisten* (Munich, 1970) (reprint of the Vienna edition, 1899), pp. 113–14.

[36] See, for instance, Lapo de Castiglionchio, 'Oratio Bononiae habita in suo legendi initio ad scolares et alios tunc ibi praesentes' in *ibid.* p. 131. On the assimilation of the *homo politicus* to the civil scientist see Donald R. Kelley, '*Jurisconsultus perfectus*: the lawyer as a Renaissance man', unpublished paper; see also his 'Vera Philosophia: the philosophical significance of Renaissance jurisprudence', *The Journal of the History of Philosophy*, 14 (1976), 267–79.

[37] Lapo de Castiglionchio, 'Lapus Casteliunculus Roberto Strozzae s.p.d.' in Müllner, *Reden und briefe*, p. 259.

vivitur. multa sunt civibus inter se communia, iura leges, forum, senatus, honores magistratusque omnes, communis etiam hostis, communis spes commune periculum.[38]

In the language of the humanists politics is properly speaking a philosophy of the city. Its goal is to shape public institutions and nothing can be as noble as to deal with problems that affect the concrete lives of many individuals. As Guicciardini wrote in the Proemio to his *Dialogo del reggimento di Firenze:*

É tanto bello, tanto onorevole e magnifico pensiero el considerare circa e' governi publichi, da' quali depende el bene essere, la salute, la vita degli uomini e tutte le azione egregie che si fanno in questo mondo inferiore, che ancore che non s'avessi speranza alcuna che quello che si pensa o si disegna potessi mai succedere, non si può dire se non che meriti di essere laudato chi applica l'animo e consuma ancora qualche parte del tempo nella contemplazione di sì onesta e sì degna materia.[39]

The *civilis disciplina* goes beyond the formal design of the constitution and the body of civil laws, for it must also be capable of shaping the citizens' passions and inclinations. Only *civilis disciplina* can manage to instil in citizens habits of friendship and civic virtue that can guarantee a lasting concord among different orders of citizens. Francesco Patrizi wrote that like a choir, where harmony is produced through different voices, a well-ordered city creates a concord out of diversity.[40] But if we want to achieve concord and see feelings of friendship flourishing among the citizens, we must follow the basic precepts of Roman civil science and institute justice and equality before the law: 'Aequalitas inter cives concordiam parit, sine qua infirma nec stabilis omnino civilis societas esse cernitur.'[41]

Political treatises of the Quattrocento stressed that no true *vivere politico* can ever be achieved without civic equality and concord. Matteo Palmieri, in his *Vita civile*, eloquently made the point in the most classical Ciceronian terms:

Le divisioni civili sono quelle che sempre hanno disfatto et per l'avenire disfaranno ogni repubblica. Niuna cosa è tanto cagione delle discordie et sedizioni civili quanto gl'ingiusti governi. Piglino exemplo coloro che posseggono la dolce libertà . . . ministrino debitamente il dovere a ciascuno privato et in pubblico accio ne segua l'unito amore della cittadinesca concordia, le quali cose, secondo gli approvatissimi philosophi, sono la vera forteza et principali stabilimenti del politico vivere.[42]

The same unequivocal Ciceronian themes were reiterated by Alamanno Rinuccini in a public *oratio* delivered in 1493, five years before Machiavelli's

---

[38] *Ibid.*, p. 250. The passage is clearly borrowed from Cicero: 'Civibus multa inter se sunt communia, forum, fana, porticus, viae, leges, jura, judicia, suffragia, consuetudines: praeterea et familiaritates multaeque cum multis res rationesque contractae', *De Divinatione*, 2, 1.

[39] F. Guicciardini, *Dialogo del reggimento di Firenze* in *Opere*, ed. Emanuella Lugnai Scarano (Turin, 1974), p. 299.

[40] Francesco Patrizi, *De institutione reipublicae libri IX*, Editio postuma (Paris, 1534), Bk v, 2.

[41] *Ibid.*, Bk I, ch. 6.

[42] Matteo Palmieri, *Vita civile*, ed. G. Belloni (Florence, 1982), pp. 136–7.

appointment to the chancery of the Florentine republic. As long as cities and empires were justly ruled, they increased in glory and reputation. Besides, the people does not ask for anything but justice and if justice is provided to all, the city enjoys peace and concord. Cicero, concluded Rinuccini, was perfectly right in ranking justice as the queen of virtues. Both ancient history and modern experience prove that justice and good laws are the necessary foundations for the liberty of the city and for the preservation of the 'humano vivere et maxime politico et civile'.[43]

At the outset of early modern history, the experience of Italian city-republics provided the most favourable ground for the classical idea of politics to enjoy renewed popularity. In the late Middle Ages the *civitas* reappeared as a historical and political reality and its reappearance was accompanied by the rediscovery of the art of the *civitas*, the republican art of politics. This rebirth was no doubt the highest moment of glory for politics in modern times. What made the art of politics so praiseworthy was its object, the good community where men live in justice under the same laws. In the linguistic conventions of the period, the vocabulary of politics is never divorced from that of *civitas* and its distinctive qualities; the rule of law, justice, liberty, self-government, concord and virtue. Politics, shall we say, circulated only within the confines of the city; outside the city or against civil life politics had no place.

MACHIAVELLI'S *VIVERE POLITICO*

Machiavelli began his intellectual career when the age of city-republics and the great days of the *civilis disciplina* were almost over. However, if we consider how Machiavelli used the words *politico* and *civile*, we must conclude that he did not reject their conventional meanings. For him the word *politico* is always linked with the familiar vocabulary of the *civitas* and never used against it. The only sense in which Machiavelli introduces an important amendment to the conventional vocabulary of politics concerns the assessment of the value of concord versus the necessary enlargement of the social basis of the city. As we shall see, Machiavelli's innovation amounts to a problematic account of the dilemmas of republican politics, not a dismissal of this idea of politics.

As we have seen, the literature available to Machiavelli conventionally employed the word *politico* in order to contrast authority restrained by laws with the authority 'legibus soluta', that is tyrannical rule. In *Discorsi* I, 25, Machiavelli fully endorses the current linguistic convention.

He who wishes to abolish or proposes abolishing an ancient form of

---

[43] Alamanno Rinuccini, *Lettere ed orazioni*, ed. V. Giustiniani (Florence, 1953), p. 202. See also p. 191: 'Tacerommi di dire lessersi per quello medesimo giorno corroborate et vivificate le vostre sacrosante et inviolabili leggi, nella cui observantia consiste 1 fondamento d' ogni buono et polytico viver.'

constitution in a city ('un antico vivere') in favour of a new and free form ('uno vivere nuovo e libero'), writes Machiavelli, must retain 'as much as possible of what is old, and that, if changes are made in the number, authority and period of office of the magistrates, they should retain the traditional names'. He concludes:

E questo (. . .) debbe osservare colui che vuole ordinare uno vivere politico, o per via di repubblica o di regno; ma quello che vuole fare una potestà assoluta, la quale dagli autori è chiamata tirannide, debbe rinnovare ogni cosa.[44]

To have supreme authority *legibus restricta* is the best guarantee for the city being ruled justly and in moderation. The rule of law is as recommended for princely rule as for popular government. History provides infinite examples of princes *legibus soluti* who were inconstant, ungrateful or imprudent; a prince who can do what he pleases, writes Machiavelli, 'è pazzo'. A populace unrestrained by laws can easily be undisciplined and infuriated ('sciolta ed infuriata'). However, while an undisciplined populace can be restrained by the words of a good man, in the case of a bad prince, there can be no remedy but the sword ('nè vi è altro rimedio che il ferro').[45]

In a *vivere civile*, and even more in a republic, no exceptions to the laws or privileges are to be tolerated. Even those who are guilty of the worst crimes against the city are to be punished according to the laws. Appius Claudius was a cruel tyrant who despised the people and the laws of Rome; however, to deny him the right to appeal to the people was, comments Machiavelli, 'scarely in accordance with civic customs' ('fu cosa poco civile').[46]

In order to preserve a true *vivere civile* it is not enough to have the rule of law in the formal sense. The content of laws and institutions must also embody the common interest of the city, and not factional interests. If the institutions (*ordini*) and the laws of the city are designed to sustain the interests of a faction, we have instead of the 'vero vivere libero e civile', and the rule of law, the rule of factions ('con le sètte più che con le leggi si vuole mantenere').[47]

Along with the rule of law, Machiavelli's use of the word *politico* reiterates another distinctive feature of the republican vocabulary of politics, namely the concept of civic equality. As he writes in *Discorsi*, Bk 1, ch. 55:

Quelle repubbliche dove si è mantenuto il vivere politico ed incorrotto non sopportono che alcuno loro cittadino nè sia nè viva a uso di gentiluomo: anzi mantengono intra loro

---

[44] N. Machiavelli, *Discorsi sopra la prima deca di Tito Livio* (Milan, 1960), Bk 1, ch. 25. 'This, as I have said, should be observed by one who proposes to set up a political regime, whether by way of a republic or by way of a monarchy. But he who proposes to set up a despotism, or what writers call a "tyranny", must renovate everything, as will be said in the next chapter.' All quotations in English are from *The Discourses of Niccolò Machiavelli*, tr. Leslie J. Walker (New Haven, 1950).

[45] *Ibid.*, Bk 1, ch. 58.   [46] *Ibid.*, Bk 1, ch. 45.

[47] N. Machiavelli, *Istorie fiorentine*, in Bk III, ch. 5, pp. 419–20.

una pari equalità ed a quelli signori e gentiluomini che sono in quella provincia sono inimicissimi.[48]

In connecting *politico* with civic equality, Machiavelli followed a convention of the republican political language of his time and restored a principle that Cicero and Livy recommended as the necessary foundation of the *respublica*. In the republican vocabulary civic equality meant above all the equality of the citizens before the law. In the *De Officiis*, Cicero had described the *aequum ius*, the latin equivalent of civic equality, as the principle that must dictate relations between citizens in such a way that everyone must deal with his fellow-citizens on the basis of equality ('aequo et pari iure')[49] with neither arrogance nor obsequiousness. In Livy, the *aequum ius* becomes a criterion for the interpretation of social conflicts in the early Roman Republic. The conflicts around the *aequum ius* originated from the opposing passions of those who disliked being forced to obey the laws like all ordinary citizens and those who wanted the laws to be universally applied and did not tolerate someone being above the laws. The classic example is that episode of the young aristocrats under the monarchy of Tarquinius the Proud, who enjoyed unrestrained licence and could not stand the civic equality ('aequato iure omnium')[50] imposed by the republic. The liberty of all, they complained, is our servitude. Under the rule of the law there is no more room for licence and privilege. While the monarch is susceptible to private favours and distinguishes between friends and enemies, the law is deaf ('lex rem surdam, inexorabilem esse') and for those who transgress there is neither indulgence nor exception. The rich and powerful tend always to be unhappy with civic equality and try to set themselves above the laws.[51] If the *vivere politico* is to flourish, the concern of good rulers must then be the preservation of civic equality.

Along with civic equality, the republican writers and their humanist disciples also insisted on another no less important dimension of equality: the *aequa libertas*, that is equal access to the highest offices on the basis of virtue. In his history, Livy presented most of the quarrels between the Plebs and the Senate as

---

[48] Machiavelli, *Discorsi*, Bk I, ch. 55; in the Leslie J. Walker translation the passage is rendered as follows: 'The second reason why in these German towns political life survives uncorrupted, is that they do not permit any of their citizens to live after the fashion of the gentry. On the contrary, they maintain there in perfect equality, and to lords and gentry residing in that province are extremely hostile.' *The Discourses of Niccolò Machiavelli*. In the *Discursus florentinarum rerum post mortem iunioris Laurentii Medices*, Machiavelli contrasts the great power of the Medici family with the possibility of having a 'civiltà' in Florence: 'E' Medici che governavano allora, per essere nutriti et allevati con li loro cittadini, si governavano con tanta familiarità, che la faceva loro grazia: ora, sono tanto divenuti grandi, che passando ogni civiltà, non vi può esser quella domestichezza e, per conseguente, quella grazia' in *Arte della guerra e scritti politici minori*, ed. S. Bertelli (Milan, 1951), p. 265; see also pp. 267–8 concerning the impossibility of instituting a republican government where there is marked social inequality.

[49] Cicero, *De Officiis*, Bk I, ch. 34, 124.   [50] Livy, *Ab urbe condita*, Bk II, ch. 3.

[51] Machiavelli, *Discorsi*, Bk I, ch. 2.

conflicts concerning access to the magistracies. The political moral that Livy always tried to convey to the reader was that the highest offices are to be open to the most virtuous citizens regardless of their social position or their birth. Unless *aequa libertas* is properly maintained, the city cannot achieve liberty and greatness. A good example of conflict concerning the *aequa libertas* can be found in Bk IV, where Livy considers the claims of the plebeians for the restoration of mixed marriages and the right to appoint a plebeian consul. The prevention of mixed marriages and the prohibition of electing a plebeian consul. The prevention of mixed marriages and the prohibition of electing a plebeian consul, says the plebs' spokesman, makes us feel in exile within our own city and actually divides the city in two ('duasque ex una civitate faciatis').[52] We only want it to be recognised that we too are citizens even if we do not possess as many riches as others do. If you accept our claims and allow virtuous citizens to be appointed consul even if they are plebeian, as equal liberty prescribes, there will again be one single city.[53]

The current thought in the works of the humanists was that the stability and prosperity of the city requires that the best citizens, those who distinguish themselves by their virtue occupy the highest ranks. Machiavelli repeats the conventional theme: good political order requires that the wisest and most honoured citizens sit in the highest magistracies. He stresses this point in the *Discursus florentinarum rerum*, a text intended to propose constitutional reform for Florence. Having explained that the major institutions of the city, the Signoria and the Collegi, should be reformed so that the wisest and most honoured citizens might be appointed to them, Machiavelli argues that if the reform is not carried out the best citizens, who personify the majesty of the state, will be confined to a purely private status or to the less important public institutions. Such a situation contradicts all principles of political order:

Non è possibile dare questa maestà a' primi gradi dello stato di Firenze, mantenendo la Signoria e i Collegi nel termine che sono stati per lo addietro: perché, non potendo sedere in quelli, rispetto al modo che si creano, uomini gravi e di reputazione se non di rado, conviene questa maestà dello stato, o collocarla più basso, et in luoghi transversali, o volgerla agli uomini privati: il che è contro ad ogni ordine politico.[54]

Machiavelli's message is unequivocal: if a *vivere politico* is to be preserved, the highest magistracies must be open to the best citizens. The example to be followed is once again that of the Roman republic, in which civic virtue was rewarded and poverty did not block access to the highest magistracies.[55] The good city has its hierarchies and the *vivere politico* has nothing to fear from the higher rank or nobility of some citizens. The question is how rank and

---

[52] Livy, *Ab urbe condita*, Bk IV, ch. 4.   [53] *Ibid.*, Bk IV, ch. 5.
[54] Machiavelli, *Discursus florentinarum rerum*, p. 269.
[55] See for instance *Discorsi*, Bk III, 25: 'per la povertà non ti era impedita la via a qualunque grado ed a qualunque onore, e come e' si andava a trovare la virtú in qualunque casa l'abitasse'.

reputation are achieved. For reputation to be obtained through 'private means' ('facendo beneficio a questo o a quello privato, col prestargli denari maritargli le figliole e facendogli simili privati favori i quali si fanno gli uomini partigiani')[56] is fatal to the *vivere politco*. On the contrary, reputation obtained through 'public means', such as wise advice or good deeds, produces the greatest benefit for civil life and must be recognised as the most legitimate source of access to the magistracies.

As we have seen, in the ideological context of the time, the word *politicus* was used to denote not only the political constitution of the city in the strict sense, but to denote also the concrete collective life of the city, the customs, the habits and the passions of the citizens. The *vivere politico* demands that citizens be willing to give priority to the interests of the city over their own particular interests. In other words, the *vivere politico* requires habits of civic virtue both in magistrates and ordinary citizens. In a corrupt city, where citizens give priority to their particular interests, no *vivere politico* can exist.

Whether derived from Aristotelian or Roman sources, the contrast between corruption and *political* life was commonplace in the humanists' works. In this respect, Machiavelli follows the current conventions of the vocabulary of politics. After having reported the episode of Manlio Capitolino, who failed in his ambitious designs because the city was still virtuous, he concludes:

> Dove sono da considerare due cose: l'una, che per altri modi si ha a cercare gloria in una città corrotta che in una che ancora viva politicamente; l'altra (che è quasi quel medesimo che la prima), che gli uomini nel procedere loro e tanto più nelle azioni grandi debbono considerare i tempi ed accomodarsi a quelli.[57]

Rome was said to still live 'politically' since both the customs and the habits of the citizens were shaped by civic virtue. For Machiavelli, like his republican teachers, politics is not just to do with the formal structure of the constitution; a primary aim of politics is to shape, to educate the passions of the citizens. In full agreement with the classical view, Machiavelli too uses the word *politico* to denote, in a sense that may be unfamiliar to us, the practical life of a community.

Salutati had argued that politics wants the citizen to be good ('vult politica civem bonum');[58] Machiavelli repeated this same concept: a city that wants to live politically demands good citizens. In this respect, politics has an important ally in religion. A republic where citizens hold strong religious beliefs is held in great respect, is good and united ('buona e unita').[59] On the contrary, in

---

[56] *Ibid.*, Bk III, ch. 28.

[57] *Discorsi*, Bk III, ch. 8; 'There are two things here which should be borne in mind. One is that, in order to obtain glory, a man must use different methods in a city that is corrupt from what he would use in one in which political life is still vigorous. The other, which is almost the same as the first, is that in the way they behave, and especially where deeds of moment are concerned, men should take account of the times, and act accordingly.'

[58] Salutati, *De nobilitate legum et medicinae*, ch. 20.   [59] *Discorsi*, Bk I, ch. 2.

pointing out the corruption of Rome under the emperors, Machiavelli mentions 'the Capitol demolished by its own citizens, ancient temples lying desolate, religious rites grown corrupt, adultery rampant throughout the city'.[60] And with reference to Florence at the times of the fights between the Albizzi and the Ricci he stresses that there was no friendship or unity among the citizens and that this was also due to the fact that both religion and the fear of God had disappeared ('e perché in tutti la religione e il timore di Dio è spento, il giuramento e la fede data tanto basta quanto l'utile').[61] For Machiavelli, religion is one of the most reliable foundations for the greatness of the city. Religion, when properly used, can instil in the people the courage and willingness to fight with the utmost determination against the enemies of the city. But religion also helps in creating good citizens and good customs. As he himself explains:

E vedesi, chi considera bene le istorie romane, quanto serviva la religione a comandare gli eserciti, ad animire la Plebe, a mantenere gli uomini buoni, a fare vergognare i rei.[62]

In Machiavelli's vocabulary politics is still concerned with real life, with the *ethos* of the city and an essential component of this concern was religion.[63] His considerations concerning the political usefulness of religion were certainly, and explicitly, utilitarian. In stressing the *ethos* and religion as substantial components of the *vivere politico*, Machiavelli was making a major point; he was once again drawing the attention of his contemporaries to one of the precepts of the ancient *prudentia civilis*.

We have seen that along with the emphasis upon civic virtue, another recurrent convention of the vocabulary of politics was the recommendation to preserve concord as one of the necessary foundations of the *vivere politico*. In this respect Machiavelli parts company with the humanist and the Ciceronian tradition. The point has been convincingly discussed by Quentin Skinner[64] and here I confine myself to showing that the revision of the traditional advice implied, simultaneously, a reformulation of the classical image of the *vivere politico*. While the classical advice stated that in order to enjoy the *vivere politico* we must devote our best cares to preserving peace and concord, Machiavelli

---

[60] *Discorsi*, Bk I, ch. 10.   [61] *Istorie fiorentine*, Bk III, ch. 5.

[62] *Discorsi*, Bk I, ch. 11; but see also chs. 12–15. The importance of religion for military achievements is stressed with particular emphasis in the *Arte della guerra*: 'Valeva assai, nel tenere disposti gli soldati antichi, la religione e il giuramento che si dava loro quando si conducevano a militare; perchè in ogni loro errore si minacciavano non solamente di quelli mali che potessono temere dagli uomini, ma di quegli che da Dio potessono aspettare', in *Arte della guerra e scritti politici minori*, p. 441.

[63] In the *Legation* from 3 October 1506, Machiavelli reports the speech of an orator of Bologna to the pope who along with the *vivere politico* stressed the religiosity of the city: 'mostrorno in ultimo el politico vivere di quella città, e con quanta religione e osservanzia di legge'. N. Machiavelli, *Legazioni e commissarie*, ed. S. Bertelli (Milan, 1964), vol. II, p. 1007.

[64] Q. Skinner, *The Foundations of Modern Political Thought*, 2 vols. (Cambridge, 1978), vol. I, pp. 113–15.

stressed that we must learn to preserve the *vivere politico* by dealing with social conflicts.

Machiavelli discusses this question at length in the famous sixth chapter of Bk I of the *Discorsi*, where he addressed the question 'whether in Rome such a form of government could have been set up as would have removed hostility between the populace and the senate'. In his typical style of reasoning, Machiavelli contrasts two possible answers exemplified in the Roman model on the one hand and in the Venetian or Spartan model on the other. Rome had a large population and employed it in war, and consequently though Rome acquired a great empire, there were also endless opportunities for rebellion amongst the plebs. Venice did not employ its populace in war and Sparta kept its populace small and did not admit foreigners into its city. Both republics maintained peace but they were not in a position to expand. When they tried to enlarge their territories both of them failed and collapsed. Considering the question on rational grounds, the best solution would be closer to the Venetian or the Spartan model, rather than the Roman one. Reason would certainly recommend that one shapes the constitution of the city so that it is well-organised for defence, in order to discourage those who are eager to subjugate it. At the same time, so as not to arouse fear of subjugation in its neighbours, the city has to state that it will not expand. If this balance could be maintained, comments Machiavelli, the city would enjoy both the true *vivere politico* and true concord: 'E sanza dubbio credo che potendosi tenere la cosa bilanciata in questo modo, che e'sarebbe il vero vivere politico e la vera quiete d'una città.'[65] But if such a city is led by necessity to expand, it would be unprepared for the task and would collapse in failure. Even in the happy event that the city never needs to expand, idleness will either emasculate it or provide a breeding-ground for factions. In this case, too, the result would be the loss of liberty. The conclusion of Machiavelli's line of reasoning is well-known: 'credo ch'e' sia necessario seguire l'ordine romano, e non quello dell' altre repubbliche'. The constitution of a city must be designed in a way that allows the inhabitants to increase in number and gives the populace, who bear the burden of war, their place in institutional life. The squabbles and conflicts that a Roman-like constitution is likely to produce should be considered inevitable inconveniences if the city is to remain free and able, if need be, to expand.

One could argue that in recommending the Roman model, Machiavelli was actually sacrificing the substance of the *vivere politico* in the pursuit of greatness. He was perfectly aware that the pursuit of greatness is in the long run fatal to the liberty of the city. The history of Rome itself provided the most convincing example. Having expanded over an immense territory, Rome was forced to

---

[65] *Discorsi*, Bk I, ch. 6; 'Nor have I the least doubt that, if this balance could be maintained, there would be genuine political life and real tranquillity in such a city.'

keep its armies far away for long periods and to prolong military commands accordingly. This turned out to be one of the causes of the loss of liberty.[66] Along with the prolongation of terms in office and military commands, the other major cause of the collapse of Roman liberty was the extreme virulence of the conflicts between the plebs and the senate over the Agrarian Laws. Rome had always been a tumultuous republic. But the proposal of the Agrarian Laws pushed the hostility far beyond the bounds of the civil life ('e si accese per questo tanto odio intra la Plebe ed il Senato che si venne nelle armi ed al sangue, fuori d'ogni modo e costume civile').[67] Rome's liberty would have survived longer, Machiavelli commented, if the city had been kept more tranquil and had proceeded more slowly in its conquests. We read in *Dell'asino d'oro* that the ambition to expand has always destroyed states, and the great wonder is that although everyone agrees on this no one does anything about it: 'Questo appetito gli stati distrugge: e tanto è più mirabil che ciascuno conosce questo error, nessun lo fugge.'[68]

Having said this, the logical conclusion would be a strong recommendation to avoid designing a constitution with a view to expansion and to institute the 'vero vivere politico e la vera quiete della città'. But as we have seen, this is not Machiavelli's advice and thus one might wonder whether he was not in fact abandoning the classical concept of the *vivere politico* or, at least, was arguing in favour of risking the collapse of the *vivere politico* in the pursuit of greatness.

In politics there is no such thing as a perfect solution. Any course of action involves risks and the best solution to any problem opens up new questions at a different level.[69] Machiavelli was arguing not that we should give priority to the pursuit of greatness over the preservation of the *vivere politico* but that we must be able to fight, if necessary, to defend our *vivere politico*. Expansion and war (although the first does not necessarily imply the second),[70] can have no priority over the liberty and the good order of the city. The point that Machiavelli stresses again and again is that a city must be in a position to fight to protect its

---

[66] *Discorsi*, Bk III, 24.   [67] *Discorsi*, Bk I, ch. 37.

[68] N. Machiavelli, *Dell' asino d'oro*, 46–7, in N. Machiavelli, *Il teatro e gli scritti letterari*, ed. F. Gaeta (Milan, 1965), p. 287.   [69] *Discorsi*, Bk I, ch. 6.

[70] Territorial expansion can be achieved without war through leagues or federations of cities following the example of the ancient Tuscans. Of three possible methods of expansion adopted by republics, the Roman way – forming alliances in which you reserve leadership, and thus the whole authority for yourself – is for Machiavelli the most praiseworthy. The worst method of expansion is to make other states subjects instead of allies, as Sparta and Athens (and Florence) did. However, as the Roman model may be too difficult to apply, the recommended policy (and Machiavelli explicitly referred to Florence) would be to follow the example of the ancient Tuscans. Even if they did not acquire an empire like that of Rome they deserve the greatest glory since they acquired enough power to live securely and enjoy good customs: 'Perchè se quelli non poterono . . . fare uno Imperio simile a quel di Roma, poterono acquistare in Italia quella potenza che quel modo del procedere concesse loro. Il che fu per un gran tempo sicuro, con somma gloria d'imperio e d'arme, e massime laude di costumi e di religione' *Discorsi*, Bk II, ch. 4. See also *Discorsi*, Bk II, 19 and the letter to Vettori of 25 August 1513, in *Lettere*, ed. F. Gaeta (Milan, 1981), p. 294.

liberty and that both citizens and rulers must go to war in order to have peace but should not disturb peace in order to have war. To protect its liberty a city must love peace and know how to make war: 'amare la pace e saper fare la guerra'.[71] If the cost of having a city capable of fighting and, if necessary, expanding, is civil conflict, then the city must be prepared to deal with it. In recommending the tumultuous but powerful Roman republic over the peaceful but weak republics of Venice and Sparta, Machiavelli was not dismissing the republican ideal of politics as the art of establishing a free and virtuous city. He was simply pointing out to his contemporaries that politics must face the additional task of handling civic discord as a fact of life in the city. Machiavelli did not change the goal of politics, which remains for him the *vivere politico*; he tried however to argue that the *vivere politico* was not necessarily compatible with civic concord. Machiavelli's message is that the aim of politics is the same, but that we must be aware of the challenges of necessity and know that the task is of the utmost difficulty.

In Machiavelli's language, politics is still the art of the city. But the city must be established and preserved in an insecure world where liberty can be sustained only through virtue and conflict. Politics must order all the other arts which are cultivated in the city with an eye to the common good.[72] Only republican politics can succeed in building a city where virtue is honoured and rewarded, poverty is not despised, military valour is esteemed and the citizens love each other and are attached to the public rather than the private good. Whoever achieves such a city creates the conditions under which men can be happier than in a corrupt city. The classical celebration of the city reappears in Machiavelli's words in the most eloquent tones: 'la quale cosa chi ordina, pianta arbori sotto l'ombra de'quali si dimora più felice e più lieto che sotto questa.'[73]

If politics is the art of the city, we have already found an answer to the puzzle of *The Prince*. As has been emphasised by a few scholars, Machiavelli never uses the word *politico* or its equivalent in *The Prince*.[74] For a book that has been celebrated and attacked as the keystone of the new science of politics, this is somewhat surprising. But if the reconstruction I have suggested thus far is correct, the absence of any *politico*-rooted word in *The Prince* should be not surprising at all. The vocabulary of politics is appropriate within a discourse on the city, but since *The Prince* is not a discourse on the city there is no reason for Machiavelli to use its vocabulary. To do this would be to speak improperly. At

---

[71] N. Machiavelli, *Dell'arte della guerra*, p. 342.   [72] *Ibid.*, p. 325, 'Proemio'.

[73] *Ibid.*, pp. 332–3.

[74] The point has been forcefully made by Dolf Sternberger, *Machiavellis 'Principe' und der Begriff des Politischen*. In *The Prince*, wrote Sternberger, 'die Wörter "Politik", "politisch", und "Politiker" kommen in dem ganzen Buche *De Principatibus* oder *Il Principe* nicht ein einziges Mal vor', *Machiavellis 'Principe' und der Begriff des politischen* (Wiesbaden, 1974), p. 35. See also John H. Whitfield, *Discourses on Machiavelli* (Cambridge, 1969), pp. 163–79 and N. Rubinstein, 'The history of the word "politicus",' pp. 53–4.

the very beginning of *The Prince*, Machiavelli states as clearly as possible that the subject matter of his treatise is the principalities and how they can be ruled and preserved:

lascierò indietro el ragionare delle republiche, perché altra volta ne ragionai a lungo. Volterommi solo al principato, et andrò tessendo li orditi soprascritti, e disputerò come questi principati si possino governare e mantenere.[75]

Princely rule, be it hereditary or newly founded, cannot in any sense be equated with the *civitas*,[76] and the art of preserving princely rule does not coincide with the art of instituting or preserving a *vivere politico*. The reason Machiavelli did not use the word *politico* or its equivalent in *The Prince* was simply because he was not writing about politics as he understood the term.

Machiavelli avoided using the word *politico* in matters regarding the status of a prince, or a ruling group, or in matters related to territoriality. He confined his use of the word to the sphere of the city. In doing so he contributed to the preservation of the conventional meaning of politics as the art of the city. At the same time, as we have seen, he introduced a major change in the classical vocabulary in that he stressed that we must abandon our hope of having a 'vero vivere politico', that is a free and tranquil city, and we must face the difficult task of preserving the *vivere politico* in a tumultuous city. Machiavelli while keeping politics within its traditional sphere, tried at the same time to make his readers fully aware of the challenging task which lies before the true political man who wants to institute and preserve the good city.

THE *POLITICUS VIR*

Machiavelli believed himself to be competent and trained in a particular art or skill, namely the 'arte dello stato'.[77] For Machiavelli the art of the state was his true calling, the only art he felt himself inclined and attracted to.[78] His friends

---

[75] N. Machiavelli, *Il Principe*, in *Il Principe e i Discorsi*, ed. S. Bertelli (Milan, 1960), pp. 15–16; in the letter to Vettori from 10 December 1513, Machiavelli stresses that the topic of *The Prince* is 'che cosa è principato, di quale spetie sono, come e' si acquistono, come e' si mantengono, perché e'si perdono', *Lettere*, p. 304.

[76] To apply the vocabulary the *civitas*, the princely rule has to display specific qualifications as is the case of the 'principatibus civilis' discussed in ch. IX, 'De principatu civili': 'Ma, venendo all'altra parte, quando uno privato cittadino, non per scelleratezza o altra intollerabile violenzia, ma con il favore delli altri sua cittadini diventa principe della sua patria, il quale si può chiamare principato civile . . .', *Il Principe e i Discorsi*, p. 45.

[77] Niccolò Machiavelli to Francesco Vettori, Florence, 10 December 1513, in Machiavelli, *Lettere*, p. 305.

[78] 'Pure, se io vi potessi parlare, non potre' fare che io non vi empiessi il capo di castellucci, perché la fortuna ha fatto che, non sapendo ragionare nè dell'arte della seta, nè dell'arte della lana, nè de' guadagni nè delle perdite, e' mi conviene ragionare dello stato, et mi bisogna o botarmi di stare cheto, o ragionare di questo', Niccolò Machiavelli to Francesco Vettori, Florence, 9 April 1513, in *ibid.*, pp. 239–40.

too considered him a person who possessed an outstanding talent for the 'arte dello stato'. Asking Machiavelli's opinion concerning the best policy for the pope to adopt towards the new alliance between the French king and Venice, Francesco Vettori stresses that even though Machiavelli had been out of public office for two years, he had certainly not forgotten the art ('ancora che siano due anni passati vi levasti di bottegha, non credo habbiate dimenticato l'arte').[79]

The 'arte dello stato' is an important component of the art of the city. The skill of foreseeing dangers before it is too late to adopt countermeasures, and the ability to understand the actual intentions of one's neighbours, two of the most basic elements of the art of the state, are of primary importance for the preservation of the city.[80] But the 'arte dello stato' can also be employed to destroy a city and to deprive it of liberty. In *The Prince*, where he displays his knowledge of the 'arte dello stato',[81] Machiavelli explains at length what should be done to subjugate a *civitas* accustomed to live in liberty.[82]

When he speaks of the 'arte dello stato', Machiavelli uses the word *stato* in the sense of the 'status' (the pre-eminent rank) of a prince, or a king, or the territory over which he is ruling. In his response to the cardinal of Rouen, Machiavelli argued that if the Italians had not mastered the art of war, the French were ignorant of the art of the state.[83] Machiavelli meant that the French did not know the basic rules to be followed in order to preserve their dominion over a foreign province such as Italy ('per tenere uno stato in una provincia disforme').[84] The questions on which Machiavelli was requested to give advice as an authority on the 'arte dello stato' were conflicts among states over matters of territorial expansion.[85] When he claims to know the 'arte dello stato', Machiavelli is clearly referring to the talent for preserving, and, if possible, improving one's status.[86] But the 'arte dello stato' is not the same as the art of

---

[79] Francesco Vettori to Niccolò Machiavelli, Rome, 3 December 1514, in *ibid.*, p. 349.

[80] An interesting reference to the skill of the state as the capacity to discuss and decide upon public matters with mature understanding, can be found in Guicciardini, *Discorso di Logrogno*, in F. Guicciardini, *Opere*, p. 276.

[81] 'Et per questa cosa [*Il principe*], quando la fussi letta, si vedrebbe che quindici anni che io sono stato a studio all'arte dello stato, non gli ho nè dormiti nè giuocati'; letter to Vettori on 10 December 1513, in *Lettere*, p. 305.

[82] *Il Principe*, ch. v ('Quomodo administrandae sunt civitates vel principatus, qui antequam occuparentur, suis legibus vivebant').

[83] '. . . perchè dicendomi el cardinale di Roano che li Italiani non si intendevano della guerra, io li resposi che ch'e' Franzesi non si intendevano dello stato', *ibid.*, ch. III.   [84] *Ibid.*, ch. III.

[85] See, for instance, the letter to Vettori of 29 April 1513, in *Lettere*, pp. 250–8.

[86] See, for instance, the letter to Vettori of 10 December 1513, where Machiavelli stresses that the Medici would greatly benefit from his experience and competence in the 'arte dello stato', *ibid.*, p. 305. In another letter to Vettori, of 10 December 1514, having been requested by his friend to display his knowledge of the 'arte dello stato' Machiavelli begins by making clear that what is at stake is the possibility of the pope preserving the status of the Vatican State 'volendo mantenere la Chiesa nella riputazione che l'ha trovata', p. 351.

the city because the *stato* is not the equivalent of the *civitas* or the *vivere politico*.[87] The whole point can be better discussed if we turn our attention from the goal or object of politics to the agency of politics, the political man. In order to understand Machiavelli's position towards the classical conventions of the political man, we shall try to reconstruct the images of the political man which circulated in the intellectual context of the fifteenth and sixteenth centuries. Having done so, we will be in a better position to answer the question of who, for Machiavelli, is the true political man.

Along with the celebration of civil discipline, the political writers of the thirteenth to fourteenth centuries placed an equal emphasis on the glorification of the political man, the *politicus vir* or the *rector civitatis*, who succeeds in establishing and preserving the *civitas*. The glorification of the political man was a basic Ciceronian theme. Besides the *De Officiis*, the most frequently quoted text was the *Somnium Scipionis*, the actual source of the medieval and humanist tradition of the political virtues ('virtutes politicae').[88] The text, reissued and made popular by Macrobius, contained an eloquent celebration of the *rectores civitates* where pagan values are assimilated into the Christian language. In a well-known passage of the *Somnium*, Cicero argues that for all the great men who devoted themselves to the good of their *patria* there is a place in the heavens where they enjoy perennial *beatitudo*. Macrobius' explanation for this passage is that God loves the *civitas* above all else and thus Cicero is perfectly right in saying that the good *rector civitatis* will immediately return to the heavens whence all men came. By ordering the laws and ensuring justice, political men lead their fellows to live a life of virtue which is in turn the pathway to true happiness. The true *politici*, concludes Macrobius, fully deserve the perennial enjoyment of *beatitudo*.

As stressed by Brunetto Latini in his commentary on Aristotle's *Ethics*, the

---

[87] The meaning of the word *stato* has been the subject of a vast scholarly literature. In contrast with the views of F. Ercole, *La politica di Machiavelli* (Rome, 1926), pp. 123–42, Fredi Chiappelli pointed out that in *Il Principe*, Machiavelli's genuine political treatise, the word *stato* denotes, with a few exceptions, the political organisation of a people over a territory independent from the particular form of their government or regime – that is, the modern abstract notion of the state (*Studi sul linguaggio di Machiavelli* (Florence, 1952), pp. 59–68). An opposite view is suggested by J.H. Hexter, who stressed that *Il Principe* does not contain the conception of the state as an abstract political body which transcends the individuals who compose or rule it ('"Il Principe" and "lo stato"', *Studies in the Renaissance*, 4 (1957) pp. 113–38). My opinion is that what we mean by the word *stato* is expressed by Machiavelli in the phrases *vivere comune* and *vivere insieme*, rather than in the word *stato*. Nevertheless, even if the word *stato* were the equivalent of the modern concept of 'the state', it could not still be equated with the concept of the *vivere politico*. The *vivere politico* is a specific form of political organisation which precludes tyranny and despotic rule. In contrast, any form of political organisation is a state, as we can clearly see from *Il Principe*, ch. IV where Machiavelli speaks of 'lo stato del Turco', a despotic state, along with 'lo stato di Francia', a moderate kingdom, or (ch. V) 'gli stati che (. . .) sono consueti a vivere con le loro legge e in libertà', that is the republics.

[88] See J.P. Canning, *The Political Thought of Baldus de Ubaldis*, pp. 160–1.

good ruler of the city deserves great merit for making the citizens good and keen to perform virtuous deeds. He succeeds in doing so to the extent that he preserves the rule of law over men.[89]

To be a good *politicus* and thus entitled to perennial glory, the *rector civitatis* must be a good and virtuous man who rules the city, in the words of John of Viterbo, 'in iustitia et equitate'.[90] The *rector civitatis* must be wise, and must love justice, he must not be crafty ('sapiens et iustitie amator, non callidus'). No action can be right if it contradicts justice and there are no circumstances under which justice can be dismissed. As John of Viterbo quotes from Cicero: 'nullum enim tempus est quod justitia vacare debeat'.[91] The classical republican sources also provided all the other virtues which qualify one as a good political man. He has to love the truth ('veritatis amator') and to possess a good mind; to display magnanimity but not be pompous or vainglorious; he must not be greedy or obstinate; he must be capable of checking his passions, and be constant and moderate; he must be eloquent but not loquacious.

The works of Aristotle also provided important elements for the re-definition and the acquisition of the classical concept of political man in the early modern languages. Given the specific features of the people and the place, the true political man, like the good legislator, knows the best constitution to be introduced in a city. The creation of the political constitution is the masterpiece of the political man. However, it is a no less praiseworthy or difficult task to restore an already existing city than it is to found a new one. Both tasks can be managed only by the true political man, in the Moerbecke translation, the 'vere politicum',[92] the 'vere civilem hominem' in the Bruni edition.[93]

The true political man cannot impose injustice or rule in a despotic way. To wonder whether it is permissible for a political man to be unjust is plainly absurd ('existimare civile disciplinam esse dominari . . . hoc autem absur-dum').[94] The virtues that are required of the political man are in general the same ones that ordinary citizens must have, if they are to have a good city. But, the political man must possess an outstanding degree of prudence and be able to foresee dangers, 'in principio fit malum cognoscere sit non cuiuscunque, sed politici vir';[95] 'tamquam malum ab initio exoriens cognoscere non cuius sit sed civilis viri'.[96]

In the language of the humanists, the Platonic *politikòs* also assumed the

---

[89] 'Lo buono et nobile reggitore della città fa buoni e nobili cittadini che osservano la lege, e fanno l'opera ch'ella comanda . . .', *Il tesoro di M. Brunetto Latino Fiorentino, precettore del Divino poeta Dante, nel quale si tratta di tutte le cose che a mortali appartengono* (Venice, 1533), p. 125. See also A. Sorbelli, 'I teorici del reggimento comunale', *Bullettino dell'istituto storico italiano per il medio evo*, 59 (1944), pp. 31–136.

[90] John of Viterbo, *Liber de regimine civitatum*, ed. G. Salvemini in *Bibliotheca juridica medii aevi*, 3 vols. (Bologna, 1901), III, p. 220.   [91] *Ibid.*

[92] *Aristoteles politicorum libri octo* (tr. Moerbecke), VI, 1.   [93] *Ibid.* (tr. Bruni), Bk IV, 1.

[94] *Ibid.* Bk VII, 2.   [95] *Ibid.* (tr. Moerbecke), Bk VIII, 8.   [96] *Ibid.* (tr. Bruni), Bk VIII, 8.

features of the *civilis vir*. In his *Epitome* to the *Statesman*, Marsilio Ficino reiterated the classical idea that the rule of a single man is most conducive to peace and reproduces in the humane city the rule of God over the universe ('in unum esse imperium omnium conferendum ut humana gubernatio divinae quam simillima sit, siquidem, et Deus unus mundi totius est rector').[97] The good king, however, like the good shepherd or the good captain of a ship, must take care of those who are under his rule and not pursue his own interest. The true king is therefore a citizen among citizens whose excellence is grounded upon his justice and prudence:

Eiusmodi vero gubernatorem atque curatorem saepius civilem vocat virum quam regem significans adeo humanum ac fieri possit, mitem esse debere, ut inter cives videatur esse concivis, prudentia, iustitia, cura potius quam alio quonvis excessu superior.[98]

Though he embodies most features of the Greek *politikòs*, the *civilis vir* of the humanists was a distinctly Roman legacy and his qualifications were the full possession of all the virtues and service to the republic. As Francesco Patrizi eloquently stated: 'Civilem virum si quis paucis verbis determinare volet, dicet eum virum bonum et Reipublicae utilem.'[99]

Like the sailor, whose duty it is to lead the ship to a safe harbour, the *civilis vir* must lead the republic to the destination and goal for which it has been instituted, namely the liberty and good life of its citizens. To fulfil his duty, the political man must be temperate, constant, prudent and just. He must possess all these virtues to qualify as a *bonus vir* and be able to succeed in the task of ruling the *respublica*. The four virtues are like four sisters and none of them can be perfect without the assistance of the others. Fortitude (*fortitudo*) without prudence turns into temerity, prudence without justice becomes craftiness (*calliditas*) or malice (*malitia*); temperance without fortitude is slothfulness, justice without temperance becomes cruelty. If the ruler displays the proper combination of virtues, the city can avoid sedition and discord and last forever ('rempublicam diuturnum, atque immortale animal').[100]

Thanks to these virtues, the *civilis vir* is able to be a true 'rector and moderator', preserving order and peace in the city. The *civilis vir* must be a moderator in the sense of being able to restrain men's passions through sanctions and persuasion and, above all, by defining the appropriate place for each component of the city and shaping a harmonious system. Moderation, wrote Cicero in the *De Officiis*, consists in the ability, in acting and speaking, to place each thing in its proper place ('loco suo collocare'). The city is composed of different groups with different and conflicting inclinations and passions. The

[97] Marsilio Ficino, *In librum Platonis de regno, vel civilem. Epitome* in Marsilii Ficini, *Opera* (Turin, 1959) (reprint of the Basle edition, 1576), vol. II, p. 1295.   [98] *Ibid.*
[99] Francesco Patrizi, *De institutione reipublicae libri IX*, Bk v, ch. 2 (Paris, 1585).   [100] *Ibid.*

masterpiece of *civilis ratio* is precisely to moderate this variegated and conflictual system through the definition of every component's appropriate place.

The Ciceronian doctrine of moderation became a recurrent theme in humanist literature on politics. For instance, Leonardo Bruni, in the conclusion to his *Laudatio Florentinae Urbis*, summarised the excellence of that city as the moderation of its institutional arrangements which gave each component with its appropriate place.

Quem admodum enim in cordis convenientia est, ad quam, cum intense fuerint, una ex diversis tonis fit armonia . . . eodem modo hec prudentissima civitas ita omnes sui partes moderata est . . . Nichil est in eam preposterum, nichil inconveniens, nichil absurdum, nichil vagum; suum queque locum tenent, non modo certum sed etiam congruentem: distinta officia, distincti magistratus, distincta iudicia, distincti ordines.[101]

In the intellectual context of the late fifteenth and early sixteenth century, the conventional image of the political man was clearly defined: a good man (*bonus vir, uomo buono*) who never abandons the path of virtue and is devoted to the common good of the city. He is *rector* and *moderator*; he keeps the republic on its course and finds an appropriate place for each component of the city. If the city is corrupt, the task of the political man is even harder, he must reform the constitution and the laws of the city in order to restore political life. His skill consists above all in his capacity to speak, persuade and deliberate with prudence. But when the city has to be reformed, the political man must also be capable, like a good architect, of shaping new political institutions. No humane achievement can surpass the preservation or the reform of the city, the highest good on earth, and for this the political man is entitled to perennial glory.

When Machiavelli began his intellectual career he could draw on this image of the political man which the humanists derived from classical republican sources. In order to arrive at a satisfactory understanding of Machiavelli's position regarding the classical concept of politics, I shall now discuss how he confronted the conventional idea of the *civilis vir*.

THE *UOMO BUONO* AND THE ART OF MODERATION

At the outset of the *Discorsi*, Machiavelli presents his heroes: the founders of republics and kingdoms as opposed to those who imposed tyrannies; Scipio versus Caesar, Agesilaus, Timoleon, Dion of Syracuse versus Nabis of Sparta and Dionysius; the princes of republics and the emperors who ruled under the laws versus Caligula, Nero and Vitellius. He places in opposition the good princes ('principi buoni'), or simply the good ('i buoni'), against wretched and corrupt tyrants.[102] And in the *Proemio* of Bk II, he writes that a city in which the

---

[101] Leonardo Bruni, *Laudatio Florentinae Urbis* in H. Baron, *From Petrarch to Leonardo Bruni. Studies in Humanistic and Political Literature* (Chicago), 1968, p. 259. [102] *Discorsi*, Bk I, ch. 10.

vivere politico has been instituted by an excellent man lasts and flourishes thanks to his virtue.[103]

Only the excellent men who institute a *vivere politico* in a city or preserve or reform a city deserve true glory. Nothing is as beloved by God, writes Machiavelli in the *Discursus florentinarum rerum*, as the deeds of those who did good for their country and reformed kingdoms or republics by laws:

Io credo che il maggiore onore che possono avere gli uomini sia quello che voluntariamente è loro dato dalla loro patria: credo che il maggiore bene che si faccia, e il più grato a Dio, sia quello che si fa alla sua patria. Oltre di questo, non è esaltato alcuno uomo tanto in alcuna sua azione, quanto sono quelli che hanno con leggi e con istituti reformato le repubbliche e i regni: questi sono, dopo que gli che sono stati Iddii, i primi laudati.[104]

Both the founders of republics and kingdoms and the good political men who preserved the order of the city were above all *moderatores* and *rectores*. The great legislators of antiquity displayed their outstanding talents in the design of political constitutions where all components of the city had their proper place. Lycurgus, who assigned the kings, the aristocracy and the populace to their rightful places ('ordinò in modo le sue leggi in Sparta che dando le parti sue ai Re, agli Ottimati e al Popolo') and 'introduced a form of government which lasted for more than eight hundred years to his very great credit and to the tranquillity of the city'.[105] Solon, on the contrary, in establishing a place for the populace alone and neglecting to assign places for the other components of the city, failed to create a truly moderate constitution. As a consequence, forty years later, the Athenian democracy fell under the domination of the tyrant Pisistratus. The best example of moderate constitution, however, was the Roman republic. But the Roman republic achieved a perfectly moderate constitution only when the plebs obtained their place in the institutional life of the city through the Tribunes, along with the nobility, represented by the Senate and the consuls. It was precisely in virtue of this moderation that the Roman republic qualified as the 'perfect republic' ('perfetta repubblica').

Any city that intends to preserve its liberty must have its moderator. In the *Discursus florentinarum rerum*, Machiavelli's basic recommendation to Cardinal Giulio de' Medici was to reform the constitution of Florence in such a way that all three types of men living in the city had their place:

Coloro che ordinano una repubblica debbono dare luogo a tre diverse qualità di uomini, che sono in tutte le città; cioè primi, mezzani e ultimi.[106]

If he fails to do so, the city will never rid itself of the disorders that produced its decline. Whether it is because the populace was not represented ('il popolo non

---

[103] *Discorsi*, Bk II, 'Proemio'.   [104] *Discursus florentinarum rerum post mortem*, p. 275.
[105] *Discorsi*, Bk I, ch. 2.   [106] *Discursus florentinarum rerum post mortem*, p. 268.

vi aveva dentro la parte sua'),[107] or because the populace wanted to expel the nobility from the government of the city,[108] the outcome was a constant oscillation between tyranny and licence, two equally condemnable extremes which jeopardise the liberty of the city.[109] The only chance the badly ordered city has to recover is the coming of a 'wise, good and powerful citizen' ('un savio, buono e potente cittadino'), who introduces institutional reforms and laws which can moderate the appetites of the nobility and the populace ('da il quale si ordininino leggi per le quali questi umori de'nobili e de' popolani si quietino o in modo si ristringhino che male operare non possino')[110] and thus restore liberty.

The good man who wants to rescue his city from corruption or preserve its good political order must be able not only to shape laws and institutions, but also to speak and to persuade. He must be not only a good architect but also a good orator capable of persuading the soldiers, of lightening their fears, firing them with courage, increasing their determination, reproaching them, filling them with hopes, and doing everything to either extinguish or excite human passions. As representative of the city he has to be capable of finding the right wording in dealing with foreign rulers, addressing the people in the Great Council and discussing it with the senators or his councillors.

The city is a universe of passions for it is inhabited by real human beings who love, hate, fear, hope, have ambitions and desires, who want to be recognised, esteemed and rewarded. Some of them seek domination; many others seek security for themselves and their relatives. The art of politics concerns the unstable universe of human passions, and the living *ethos* of a community.[111] For the purpose of restraining and educating human passions so that a free and ordered city can be established through them, those who possess the *civilis disciplina* must be able to use both the instrument of the laws and the tools of language. Such good, wise and powerful men, who are 'good and prudent', 'good and merciful' and who populate so many pages of the *Istorie*, the *Discorsi*, the *Arte della guerra*, and the *Prince*, if we read also the 'Exhortatio', exhibit all the features of the republican civil man, the good man who reforms the institutions and laws of the city to the greatest benefit of all citizens.

Machiavelli never rejects the conventional image of the political man as a good man who benefits the *vivere politico*. His hero is, as he was for the republican writers of Rome and for their humanist disciples, the good man, not the emperors or the princes, even if they were great conquerors and military commanders: Caesar and Pompey attained fame (*fama*), but not glory. To attain glory it is not enough to be a great captain; one must also be a good man who

[107] *Ibid.*, p. 262.   [108] *Istorie Fiorentine*, Bk III, ch. 1.   [109] *Ibid.*, Bk IV, ch. 1.   [110] *Ibid.*
[111] S. Wolin, on the contrary, stresses that Machiavelli is one of the forerunners and founders of 'the great tradition of interests politics', *Politics and Vision*, p. 236.

devotes his talents to preserving the liberty of the republic and not to destroying it, as Caesar and Pompey did. Lasting though their fame may be, it can never parallel the glory of Scipio and Marcellus:

e dico che Pompeo e Cesare, e quasi tutti quegli capitani che furono a Roma dopo l'ultima guerra cartaginese, acquistarono fama come valenti uomini, non come buoni; e quegli che erano vivuti avanti a loro, acquistarono gloria come valenti e buoni.[112]

If, as I think we must, we take seriously the many times Machiavelli mentions the good man (*uomo buono*), we can more easily grasp the meaning of those passages in *The Prince* which have always been quoted to prove that Machiavelli rejected the republican idea of politics.

A man who wants to be good under all circumstances, Machiavelli writes in the famous fifteenth chapter of *The Prince*, will certainly come to ruin among the many who are not good. Therefore 'è necessario a uno principe, volendosi mantenere, imparare a poter essere non buono, et usarlo e non usare secondo la necessità'.[113] What Machiavelli seems to accomplish in writing that the prince must learn to be 'non buono' is to make explicit the dilemmas inherent in the conventional account of the political man as a good man which his contemporaries failed to acknowledge. In so doing they failed to be ideologically prepared to tackle successfully the concrete problems of pursuing the goal of civil philosophy.

The need to learn how not to be good is not relevant only to the prince who is concerned with the preservation of his *stato*. The political leaders of republics might also easily find themselves forced to break promises, be unjust, and deceive. The inability of Pier Soderini to drop his natural patience and humility brought him to ruin and with him the ruin of the Florentine republic.[114] According to Machiavelli, the principle of never breaking a covenant or promise was a form of weakness, not, as humanist orthodoxy proclaimed, a virtue of the ideology of *Florentina libertas*.[115]

Far from being a problem only for the new prince, the need to use extraordinary means also arises for the civil man who pursues the goal of the restoration of political life (*vivere politico*) in a corrupt city. Reforming a defective institution which has proved to be incapable of checking corruption can be done either all at once or little by little. Both ways, explains Machiavelli,

---

[112] *Arte della Guerra*, p. 337; 'I say, then, that Caesar and Pompey, and almost all the Roman generals who lived after the Second Punic War, acquired their reputation as skillful men, not as good citizens; but those who lived before that time won glory by being both civic-minded and skillful' (tr. Neal Wood, Milan, 1961, p. 17); see also Victor A. Santi, '"Fama" e "laude" distinte da "gloria" in Machiavelli', *Forum Italicum*, 12 (1978), 206–15.   [113] *Il Principe*, p. 65.
[114] *Discorsi*, Bk III, ch. 9.
[115] For instance, wrote Leonardo Bruni, 'Quod cum a principio vidisset, et ita iustum esse censuisset ob nullam utilitatis speciem adduci unquam potuit ut pacta, conventa, federa, iusiurandum, promissa violaret', *Laudatio Florentinae urbis* in H. Baron, *From Petrarch to Leonardo Bruni*, p. 253.

are very unlikely to succeed. Even in the happy event that some prudent man sees that the old institutions will soon be inadequate and will bring about the corruption of the city, he will not be able to persuade his fellow citizens of the need for reform, because men who are accustomed to a certain way of life are unwilling to change it on the grounds of pure conjecture. As regards immediate reform, anyone planning to carry this out must resort to extraordinary means, such as force and arms, in order to become prince of the city and have the absolute power necessary to succeed in the restoration of political life. Machiavelli clearly states in the *Discorsi* the dilemma of a politics aiming at the restoration of the corrupt city:

E perchè il riordinare una città al vivere politico presuppone uno uomo buono, e il diventare per violenza principe di una repubblica presuppone uno uomo cattivo; per questo si troverrà che radissime volte accaggia che uno buono, per vie cattive, ancora che il fine suo fusse buono, voglia diventare principe; e che uno reo, divenuto principe voglia operare bene, e che gli caggia mai nello animo usare quella autorità bene che gli ha male acquistata.'[116]

The good man must become bad (*cattivo*) in order to achieve what classical republican writers have always considered the worthiest goal for a truly good man to pursue. Having revealed how difficult the task of republican politics is, Machiavelli did not suggest dismissing it as a worthy goal. On the contrary, he recommended the restoration of liberty and a political constitution in a corrupt city as the most glorious aim to which a man can possibly commit himself. If a man is truly eager to acquire eternal glory, he should ask God to allow him to live in a corrupt city in order to have the chance to reform it.[117]

In writing the *Discorsi*, Machiavelli's purpose was to excite in the young the desire to emulate ancient virtue and follow the precepts of republican politics – the art of the good city. This was the last resort of a good man prevented by the evil circumstances of his time from carrying out the principles of a true politics:

Perchè gli è offizio di uomo buono, quel bene che per la malignità de' tempi e della fortuna tu non hai potuto operare, insegnarlo ad altri, acciocché sendone molti capaci, alcuno di quelli più amato dal Cielo possa operarlo.[118]

Here, he was speaking about himself and making explicit the goal he was trying to achieve. This was the message he wanted to convey to future

[116] *Discorsi*, Bk I, ch. 18; 'But, to reconstitute political life in a state presupposes a good man, whereas to have recourse to violence in order to make oneself prince in a republic supposes a bad man. Hence very rarely will there be found a good man ready to use bad methods in order to make himself prince, though with a good end in view, nor yet a bad man who, having become a prince, is ready to do the right thing and to whose mind it will occur to use well that authority which he had acquired by bad means.' [117] *Ibid.*, Bk I, ch. 10.
[118] *Ibid.*, Bk II, 'Proemio'; 'For it is the duty of a good man to point out to others what is well done, even though the malignity of the times or of fortune has not permitted you to do it for yourself, to the end that, of the many who have the capacity, some one, more beloved of heaven, may be able to do it.'

generations: if you want eternal glory, you must devote yourself to the establishment and the preservation of the *vivere politico* following the example of the heroes of republican politics. However, he was not in a position to promise, as Macrobius and Palmieri did, that after their death they would go directly to heaven and enjoy eternal happiness. He knew they were more likely to go to hell. Future generations who wanted to devote themselves to the noble goal of politics must know that *Scipio's Dream* was only a dream.

Though he admired the princes and the captains who knew how to use the 'arte dello stato', Machiavelli never presented any of them as true heroes of politics.[119] He repeatedly flirted with the masters of state craft, but his deepest love was for those who possessed the art of instituting a political life. No other goal is as truly worthy of a good man, even if it requires him to do evil.

Machiavelli did not reject the republican concept of politics and the political man. Rather he reworked the vocabulary of civil philosophy to make it useful in a new political context. The age of the city-republics witnessed the renewed fortunes of the art of the city; in the new era, the age of princes, the art of the state was about to replace the language of politics as the art of the city, and the statesman to supplant the political man. The possibility of seeing the good and free city taking the place of princely government depended upon the appearance on stage of a truly political man capable also of using the art of the state, if necessary. Machiavelli's purpose was to educate such a great political man. He believed that only then would a free city once again come into existence.

---

[119] See, for instance, his letter to Vettori from 31 January 1515: 'Duke Valentino, whose works I should always imitate if I were a new prince, realizing this necessity, made Messer Rimirro President in Romagna; that decision made those people united, fearful of his authority, fond of his power, and trustful in it; and all the love they felt for him, which was great considering his newness, resulted from this decision', *The Letters of Machiavelli*, ed. A. Gilbert (New York, 1961), p. 186.

8

◁ ═══════════════════════════════════ ▷

The theory and practice of warfare in Machiavelli's republic

MICHAEL MALLETT

'E principali fondamenti che abbino tutti li stati, così nuovi, come vecchi e misti, sono le buone leggi e le buone armi. E perchè non può essere buone leggi dove non sono buone armi, e dove sono buone armi conviene sieno buone leggi, io lascerò indrieto el ragionare delle leggi e parlerò delle armi.'[1] By starting with so well-known a quotation, for which I apologise, I want to emphasise two initial points. Machiavelli's reputation as a writer on military matters is not dependent on the *Arte della Guerra* or even on the collection of shorter pieces on war; it lies at the heart of his whole thinking and depends on *Il Principe* and the *Discorsi* as much as on the more specific works. One has, in fact, to draw a distinction between his practical ideas, both on past warfare, which fill the *Storie Fiorentine*, and on future possibilities, as in the *Arte della Guerra*, and the conceptual ideas on the role of war in politics and state-building which are much more widely diffused throughout his writing.[2]

Federico Chabod when he wrote of Machiavelli that 'he who was in his political thought a man of the Renaissance, became a man of the thirteenth century when he turned to military matters' was thinking essentially of the practical side, as was Piero Pieri when he concentrated on Machiavelli as an organiser of militia and a proponent of a new infantry.[3] It is these practical aspects which have aroused, in fact, the greatest dissent and even derision, from the famous anecdote of Machiavelli's vain attempts to drill the Black Bands of Giovanni de' Medici to the current vogue for reassessing his exaggerated

---

[1] N. Machiavelli, *Il Principe*, ch. XII.
[2] For the most influential general discussions of Machiavelli's military ideas, see M. Hobohm, *Machiavellis Renaissance der Kriegskunst* (Berlin, 1913); F.L. Taylor, *The Art of War in Italy, 1494–1529* (Westport, CT, 1973) (first published Cambridge, 1921), pp. 167–78; F. Chabod, 'Del "Principe" di Niccolò Machiavelli' in *Scritti su Machiavelli* (Turin, 1964), pp. 74–9 (first published in 1925; English translation in *Machiavelli and the Renaissance*, London, 1958, pp. 85–93); P. Pieri, *Guerra e politica negli scrittori italiani* (Milan, 1955); F. Gilbert, 'Machiavelli and the renaissance of the art of war' in *Makers of Modern Strategy*, E.M. Earle, ed. (Princeton, 1952), pp. 3–25; S. Anglo, *Machiavelli: A Dissection* (London, 1971), pp. 116–42.
[3] Chabod, *Machiavelli and the Renaissance*, p. 103n; N. Machiavelli, *Dell'arte della guerra*, ed. P. Pieri (Rome, 1937), Introduction; P. Pieri, *Il Rinascimento e la crisi militare italiana* (Turin, 1952), pp. 436–8, 525–35.

denunciations of the *condottieri*.[4] It is very easy to point out in the *Arte della Guerra* both the undue reliance on inappropriate classical examples and indeed the misuse of ill-understood classical examples. It is well known that the treatise, while immediately popular, actually had little impact on the development of specialist thinking about war.[5] Machiavelli was never present at a serious battle nor had he been on campaign with a large army.

However, the conceptual ideas about war cannot be dismissed so lightly. Good laws and good arms, the concern to recreate the links between the civilian and military spheres, to draw the military world and war back into the heart of political and civic life, to use military training to encourage civic virtue and patriotism; these were all messages that Machiavelli conveyed more clearly, more coherently than any of his contemporaries. States had to be strong to survive; strength meant good military institutions and resolute decision-making; these depended on both princes and peoples. The great fault of the *condottieri* was that their presence had emasculated the citizens and for this they had to be made objects of ridicule themselves. States, whether princedoms or republics, must depend on their own arms – *le armi proprie*; this is the conceptual framework of Machiavelli's approach to the military problems of Florence. In *Il Principe* there is no discussion of whether this should be the private army of the prince, a warrior class of the citizenry, a select militia, or a mass levy. The practical solution for Florence emerges as a select, partly trained militia raised in haste for a particular purpose, and because of the relative failure of this solution Machiavelli's reputation as a military theorist suffers yet again. My purpose in this essay is to re-examine this particular problem of *armi proprie* and how it came about that Machiavelli's practical solution to it was so unsatisfactory.

The theoretical background to a militia revival is well known and I do not wish to review the humanist literature which precedes Machiavelli on this subject.[6] The dilemma which faced the humanists from Petrarch to Patrizi in their concern to free Italian states from their dependence on unreliable mercenaries for their own defence, was a threefold one. First, the belief that the true republic should live at peace and eschew war altogether was still influential. Secondly, the concern about mercenaries clashed with a widespread admiration for effective military achievement and glory which the *condottieri* were not

---

[4] M. Bandello, *Le Novelle*, I, nov. 43. The issue of Machiavelli's exaggerations and the 'bloodless battles' is discussed in the works cited above; but see also W. Block, *Die Condottieri: Studien über die sogenannten ublütigen Schlachten*, Historische Studien, 110 (Berlin, 1913); H. Delbruck, *Geschichte Geschichte der Kriegskunst*, IV (Berlin, 1920), p. 21; P. Pieri, *Il Rinascimento, passim*; M.E. Mallett, *Mercenaries and their Masters; Warfare in Renaissance Italy* (London, 1974), pp. 195–9 (Italian edition, *Signori e Mercenari* (Bologna, 1984)).

[5] See P. Pieri's edition cited above; N. Machiavelli, *L'Arte della Guerra e scritti politici minori*, ed. S. Bertelli (Milan, 1961), pp. 309–20.

[6] For the most complete account of this debate in English, see C.C. Bayley, *War and Society in Renaissance Florence* (Toronto, 1961), particularly pp. 178–240.

entirely incapable of stimulating. Thirdly, if mercenaries were to be rejected, the ill-organised and internally divided states would be faced with the practical problem of finding a viable alternative. Hence to limit the search for the origins of Machiavelli's ideas to this particular theoretical debate is not very fruitful.

In fact, solutions to the dilemma were gradually emerging in the fifteenth century. Most Italian states were moving towards an increased control over their military resources by creating institutions for the permanent employment of troops and accepting the financial implications of this. Whether the troops concerned were *lanze spezzate*, i.e. veteran men-at-arms employed directly by the state and commanded by permanent commanders appointed by the state, or a *famiglia ducale*, or some other form of permanent princely bodyguard, or *condottieri* with fiefs and long contracts settled within the frontiers of the state, most of them were no longer the temporarily hired mercenaries which the humanists derided. The 'mercenary period' – in the true sense of the word – of Italian history was really over early in the fifteenth century; Florence was the exception to this.[7] To understand Machiavelli's preoccupation with war, with defence of the state, with *armi proprie*, one has to look closely at the military problems of Florence in the fifteenth century.

The creation of permanent military establishments in the fifteenth century meant the gradual provision of new institutions and methods of control; it meant the emergence of effective recruiting and supervisory mechanisms, of billeting and provisioning procedures which diminished the possibility of tensions between permanent troops and the local populations, of skilled bureaucrats and administrators who specialised in military affairs, and above all of fiscal resources which enabled the troops to be properly paid. Florence was very slow to develop these mechanisms and was, for most of the century, considered the weakest of the major Italian powers. It was reluctant to spend money on defence in peacetime, partly because of an anxiety to keep taxes down and not drain capital out of the economy, partly because the repayment of accumulated war debts consumed a high proportion of available revenue. There was no continuity of control of military affairs at the highest level; the maintenance of small standing forces in peacetime was the responsibility of the Ufficiali della Condotta, a relatively lowly committee which carried little prestige and which was firmly based in Florence itself. In peacetime the Ufficiali employed few agents, troops were not inspected and were rarely paid. In war a powerful Dieci di Guerra was elected and a whole process of rapid mobilisation had to be thrown into gear. In the circumstances it was inevitable that Florence should seek to raise troops quickly by going for large contracts with a small number of available *condottieri*, and that the terms negotiated under pressure would be more unfavourable to the employer than usual. Those who were

---

[7] Mallett, *Mercenaries, passim.*

prepared to serve Florence in this piecemeal way were either discontented with their existing employers, or genuinely faithless and unscrupulous, or unemployed and probably almost unemployable. They would know that as soon as the war was over their contracts would end, and they would guess that at that moment their pay would be thousands of florins in arrears. These were not conditions calculated to produce faithful, effective service.[8] Florence, uniquely among Italian states, offered free billets to its troops for their short contracts without creating a realistic system of compensating the unfortunate country householders who had to bear the burden. Milan and Venice both had a system of making all troops pay rent for their billets, and a special tax – the *tassa dei cavalli* – was raised from all the country areas to provide additional pay to enable the troops to bear this charge. The system worked much better and enabled long-term billeting to be imposed without unduly exacerbating relations between soldiers and countryfolk.[9] This is a typical example of the poor military institutions which Machiavelli denounced but which were in fact peculiarly Florentine. Florence had few men experienced in presiding over the essentially spasmodic army organisation; the work was done in wartime by temporary commissaries and seconded chancellors. It is interesting that two Florentines who did have such experience in the second half of the fifteenth century, Orfeo da Ricavo and Sforza Bettini, acquired it and utilised it largely in the service of other Italian states.[10]

One area of defence on which Florence was willing to spend money was on fortifications. Perhaps this was seen as a safer investment and certainly the running costs were much lower; it was also true that the terrain of Tuscany was very appropriate fortification country. But more significant, as an explanation of Florentine enthusiasm and as a topic for discussion by Machiavelli, was the dual role of fortifications. They could defend the state against both external and internal enemies. The citadel placed athwart the walls of a subject city served both to dominate and control the city, and to strengthen its outer defences against attack from outside. A key factor in Florentine territorial expansion was the building of such citadels, but this dual function of fortifications led both to ambiguities in Machiavelli's treatment of the problem and to his eventual rejection of fortifications as a suitable defence for a republic. In *Il Principe* he accepts that a well-fortified city can be very secure, but still suggests that it is

---

[8] M.E. Mallett, 'Preparations for war in Florence and Venice in the late fifteenth century' in *Florence and Venice: Comparisons and Relations*, 1 (Florence, 1979), pp. 149–64; *idem*, 'The military organisation of Florence and Venice in the fifteenth century', in *16 Settimana di studio dell'Istituto Francesco Datini: Gli aspetti economici della guerra in Europa* (Prato, 1984), forthcoming.

[9] M.E. Mallett and J.R. Hale, *The Military Organisation of a Renaissance State: Venice c. 1400–1617* (Cambridge, 1984), pp. 128–36; for discussion of Florentine and Milanese practices, see Lorenzo de' Medici, *Lettere*, v, ed. Michael Mallett (Florence, 1990), nn. 491, 494.

[10] For information on these men, see Lorenzo de' Medici, *Lettere*, I–VI, Florence, 1976–90, *ad indices*.

better for the prince to rely upon the loyalty and goodwill of his subjects. In the *Discorsi* it is the potentially repressive role of fortresses which concerns him, and at the same time we get the argument that strong walls tend to weaken the resolve and capacity of the citizens to defend themselves. This was a classical and a humanistic debate which gains new prominence in Machiavelli in the light of Florence's predilection for fortress-building.[11]

All this, then, is the military background to Machiavelli's preoccupation with war. This is not the moment either to expand the picture by comparisons of the Florentine situation with that of other Italian states, nor to speculate further about the reasons for the backwardness of Florence in military developments. But for Machiavelli the image of a militarily weak Florence, regarded in Italy as the gullible paymaster of other people's troops, must have been a peculiarly potent one. The events of the last years of the century only highlighted the problems: the new fortifications at Sarzana and Sarzanella were tamely surrendered to the French in 1494, while the citadels of Pisa did nothing to stop the Pisan revolt; neither *condottieri* nor French auxiliaries were able to recover Pisa; in 1501 Florence was helpless to resist as Cesare Borgia marched arrogantly through Tuscany. It is not hard to understand Machiavelli's passion nor his tendency to exaggerate in his search for solutions to these problems.

There is one final point that needs to be made which is a part of this background, although not specifically a military one. The republic about which Machiavelli was writing was no longer a city-state in the true sense of the word. The expansion of Florence in the late fourteenth and early fifteenth centuries had created a whole new area of interest, administration, potential exploitation and defence, which Florentines had gradually to assimilate. Machiavelli's political thinking is full of half-conscious adjustments to the fact of the state beyond the walls of Florence, even though much of the language is still that of traditional city-state republicanism. It is particularly true that the preoccupation with force, both to create empire and to defend empire, can only be understood in the light of these changed circumstances.

However, to return to our original problem, the provision for the defence of the state through *armi proprie*; the solutions being developed by the other Italian states did not satisfy Machiavelli because, while they provided an increasingly disciplined and, in a certain sense, increasingly effective, military, they did not provide for the universal strengthening of the morale and collective virtue of the citizenry which Machiavelli was seeking. This could only come from some form of conscription, an arming of a substantial body of the subjects of the state, in fact a militia or even a permanent national army.

---

[11] J.R. Hale, 'To fortify or not to fortify? Machiavelli's contribution to a Renaissance debate' in *Essays in honour of John Humphreys Whitfield*, H.C. Davis *et al.*, eds. (London, 1975), pp. 99–119 and republished in J.R. Hale, *Renaissance War Studies* (London, 1983), pp. 189–210. For Machiavelli's discussions, see *Il Principe*, chs. x and xx, *I Discorsi*, II, 24.

For much of the fifteenth century militias had tended to play a very limited role in Italian warfare. The increasing specialism and skill of the professional cavalry and infantry companies had left little room for untrained and hastily armed levies. Defence of hearth and home was still a situation in which able-bodied numbers could assist, but beyond that a militia contingent could not be expected to move far from its home area nor endure the rigours of a long campaign. As pioneers and *guastatori*, however, militia levies had played an increasing role. Fifteenth-century warfare was filled with field fortifications and engineering works of all types despite Machiavelli's assertions to the contrary; huge armies of peasants were levied to dig miles of defensive ditches, to create gun emplacements, fortified camps and roads across marshes. Such activity was perhaps more common in Lombardy than in Tuscany, but nevertheless every Florentine army was accompanied by local levies for these purposes.[12]

However, in the second half of the fifteenth century the example of the French *francs-archers*, a select and partly trained militia created by Charles VII in the 1440s, was being noted and imitated in Italy. The Venetians in 1477 put into action a plan for the raising of 15–20,000 select militia from the Veneto to be trained by professional infantry constables and used to stem the periodic Turkish incursions into Friuli. They were known as the *provisionati di San Marco* and were exempt from taxes and paid for their periods of training and service. Such schemes were reactivated periodically over the next thirty years both in the Veneto and in some of the princely states. Particular emphasis was placed on training handgun men in the villages, and creating stockpiles of appropriate arms.[13]

However, all these ventures were seen as essentially supplementary to the professional troops. As Machiavelli himself noted with bitterness, when the French army went to war in earnest the *francs-archers* were left behind and Swiss mercenaries were hired in their place.[14] Militia made up a relatively small proportion of the Venetian army at Agnadello in 1509 and large numbers of professional infantry had to be hired for that campaign to stiffen the militia.

So, discussion of and experiments with selected and reasonably intensively trained infantry militias were very much in the air at the end of the fifteenth century. These were practical solutions to the sudden expansion of infantry forces of the day and the cost of maintaining professional troops, both in terms of pay and loss of labour to the economy. They did not represent the final absorption of classical ideas, nor were they peculiarly republican solutions. No one, least of all Cesare Borgia, relied on even these new militias to provide the main defence of the state. The army which Borgia used to break out of the

---

[12] Bayley, *War and Society*, pp. 219–40; Mallett, *Mercenaries*, pp. 182–4 and 226–7.

[13] For the *francs-archers*, see A. Spont, 'La milice des francs-archers', *Revue des Questions Historiques*, 61 (1897); for the Venetian militias, Mallett and Hale, *The Military Organisation of a Renaissence State*, pp. 78–80. [14] Machiavelli, *Il Principe*, ch. XIII.

Romagna in January 1503 after he had disposed of his *condottieri*, to the evident glee of Machiavelli, was composed of hardened men-at-arms in the personal service of the Duke, and professional Spanish and Romagnol infantry. The latter were, of course, his own subjects but he was fortunate in having one of the main recruiting grounds for professional infantry, the Val di Lamone, in his state and he took full advantage of this.[15]

But let us return finally to Machiavelli who saw all these things but had the immediate problem in 1505 and 1506 of reducing Pisa. The Ordinanza which he finally persuaded the Signoria to create in 1506 was perhaps the beginning of a great experiment, a new way of arming the republic, but it was more importantly an attempt to solve the specific problem of Pisa. This it succeeded in doing by attrition, but the defects of the new organisation were obvious. There was a reluctance to pay the militiamen even for their periods of service; they were recruited solely from the *contado* on the grounds that Florentines would be unlikely to agree to serve, and anyway arming the citizens of the city might be dangerous; they were armed *alla Svizzera*, which was already outdated, and not with guns in any numbers; captains were rotated to avoid any prominent man gaining a following; they were commanded by a foreigner, first the notorious Don Michelotto and then Jacopo Savelli. All this militated against the force qualifying seriously as an incipient national army.[16] The way forward towards a greater reliance by states on their own arms did not lie along the path of part-time militias.

Machiavelli's militia was not a revived thirteenth-century militia nor, of course, was the state which it had to defend still a thirteenth-century city-state. However, it was founded on certain anachronistic assumptions; the debate which surrounded it and the restraints built in by Florentine prejudice against arming subjects and Florentine fears of creating a weapon in the hands of factional and individual interest, helped to cripple it. Perhaps the conclusion we can draw is that Machiavelli's basic concepts were mistaken. Good laws needed to precede good arms in the sense that he intended them; the ideal military solutions would only emerge in a settled state with just and equitable institutions, a state which might expect to attract the sort of patriotism which Machiavelli was seeking.

However, a final point of a more positive nature can be made. The growth of permanent military forces was accompanied by, and indeed necessitated, an extension of the tentacles of government. Concern for recruiting, billeting, provisioning, training and disciplining of troops inevitably meant bureaucrats, inspectors, paymasters and marshals going out into the countryside. The militia

[15] J. Larner, 'Cesare Borgia, Machiavelli, and the Romagnol militia', *Studi Romagnoli*, 17 (1966).
[16] *Arte della Guerra*, ed. Bertelli, pp. 79–89; Bayley, *War and Society*, pp. 240–67; C. Dionisotti, 'Machiavelli, Cesare Borgia e Don Michelotto', *Rivista storica italiana*, 79 (1967).

debate and the experiment itself must have brought some of these effects to Florence. Florentines were steadily becoming aware of the implications of the wider state in many ways other than just buying estates in it, and the militia 'movement' must have strengthened this tendency. It proposed substituting for the essentially sedentary Ufficiali della Condotta the Nove della Ordinanza e della Milizia, the role of which had inevitably to be played out outside the city; it would have led to a substantial extension of the power and interests of the state. But that is a different Machiavellian theme for another occasion.

9

◁ ═══════════════════════════════════════ ▷

Civil discord in Machiavelli's *Istorie Fiorentine*

GISELA BOCK

I

In the prologue to the *History of Florence* (*Istorie Fiorentine*), which Machiavelli wrote between 1520 and 1525 and which comprises the period between the decline of the Roman republic and the end of the Quattrocento, the author explains the 'ordini e modi' which he followed in writing this history. While praising the 'two excellent historians' Leonardo Bruni and Poggio Bracciolini for their 'description of the wars waged by the Florentines against foreign princes and peoples', he also criticises them for having neglected what he considered the specific and crucial element in the history of his city: 'civil discord and internal strifes and their consequences' or, as he writes a little later, 'the hatreds and divisions in the city'. The *Istorie Fiorentine* does not only deal, as did the *Prince*, with 'the actions of the great men', but with actions that seemed 'insignificant' and 'unworthy' to be described in detail and to become part of historical memory.[1] This vision of Florentine history seemed so crucial to Machiavelli as even to cause him to alter his original project. Initially, he intended to start with the year 1434 when Cosimo il Vecchio returned from exile to Florence and established his regime, and this was probably due to fact that it was a Medici – Cardinal Giulio and future Pope Clement VII – who had conferred this task upon him. It was precisely his interest in understanding civil discord that made him go back to the origins of the city.[2] Again in the prologue, he summarises the content of the *Istorie Fiorentine* and his historiographical perspective:

If any republic ever had notable divisions, those of Florence were most notable: for most of the other republics of which we have some notice have been content with one division

[1] Machiavelli, *Istorie Fiorentine* (from now on quoted as *IF*), 'Proemio', p. 632; *Il Principe*, 'Dedica', p. 257. Machiavelli's writings are quoted from *Tutte le Opere*, ed. M. Martelli (Florence, 1971). For comments on the *IF*, see the edition by V. Fiorini (1894), repr. Florence, 1978. The translations of Machiavelli are mainly based on *The History of Florence*, ed. M.P. Gilmore (New York, 1970) and on *The Discourses*, ed. M. Walker (London, 1950). The other translations are mine, and I would like to thank Ian Fraser for translating the first version. For Machiavelli's critique and use of Leonardo Bruni's and Poggio Bracciolini's histories of Florence see A.M. Cabrini, *Per una valutazione delle 'Istorie Fiorentine' del Machiavelli. Note sulle fonti del Secondo Libro* (Florence, 1985).

[2] *IF*, pp. 632–3; R. Ridolfi, *Vita di Niccolò Machiavelli*, 7th edn (Florence, 1978), pp. 284–90, 305–42.

through which, as things went, they may sometimes have prospered, sometimes ruined their city; but Florence, not content with one, made many of them. In Rome, as everybody knows, after the kings had been driven away, the discord between the nobles and the plebs emerged, and this division continued until the ruin of the republic. Similarly in Athens and in all the other republics which flourished at that time. But in Florence, first the nobles were divided among themselves, then there was division between the nobles and the *popolo*, and finally between the *popolo* and the plebs; and it often happened that one of those parties, having gained the upper hand, split in two. From these divisions there came as many deaths, as many exiles, as many destructions of families, as ever arose in any city whose history is known to us.

Machiavelli presents here a gloomy picture of the history of Florence, a city of which, a century earlier, Bruni had written not merely a glorifying history but even a *Laudatio*, and Bruni and many others had compared it to the Roman and the Athenian republics.[3] Machiavelli too hints at this comparison in the prologue, referring specifically to the 'disunity between the nobles and the plebs' in the Roman republic. A few years earlier, he had studied this phenomenon in his *Discorsi sopra la prima deca di Tito Livio*, and also in the prologue to the *Discorsi* he had underlined the centrality of the 'civic disputes which arise between citizens'. The fundamental affirmation of the *Discorsi* in this context has been analysed in depth, namely that – in the words of the heading to Book I, chapter 4 – 'Discord between the Plebs and the Senate of Rome made this Republic both Free and Powerful'. In the subsequent chapters, Machiavelli dwelt at length and in detail on these divisions and his positive assessment of them, demonstrating the intrinsic conflictuality of the political universe, describing civil discord not as a disruptive element, but as the leaven and cement of a free republic, and presenting the common good as the result of compromises and balances between the nobles and the plebs.[4]

Later, however, in the *Istorie Fiorentine*, Machiavelli seems to have abandoned this positive evaluation of civil conflict. The variegated vocabulary he uses in this connection would not seem to leave any doubt as to the negativity of the phenomenon: *discordia (civile), divisione, odio, inimicizie, disunione, disordine, disparere, parti, sètte* and, occasionally, *fazioni* and *contenzioni*. On the other side,

[3] Leonardo Bruni, *Laudatio Florentinae Urbis*, ed. H. Baron in *From Petrarch to Leonardo Bruni* (Chicago, 1968), pp. 217–63; H. Baron, *The Crisis of the Early Italian Renaissance*, 2nd edn (2 vols., Princeton, NJ, 1966) esp. pp. 54–80; N. Rubinstein, 'Machiavelli e le origini di Firenze', *Rivista storica italiana*, 79 (1967), 952–9; R. Fubini, 'Osservazioni sugli "Historiarum Florentini populi libri XII" di Leonardo Bruni' in *Studi di storia medievale e moderna per E. Sestan*, (Florence, 1980), vol. I pp. 403–48; A. Moulakis, 'Leonardo Bruni's constitution of Florence', *Rinascimento*, 26 (1986), pp. 141–90.

[4] *Discorsi*, I, 'Proemio', p. 76; *Discorsi*, I/4–6, pp. 82–7; G. Sasso, 'Machiavelli e i detrattori antichi e nuovi di Roma. Per l'interpretazione di Discorsi I, 4' in *Atti dell' Accademia Nazionale dei Lincei. Memorie, Classe di scienze morali, storiche e filologiche*, ser. VIII, vol. XXII, fasc. 3, pp. 319–418; G. Sasso, *Niccolò Machiavelli* (Bologna, 1980), pp. 446–78, 487; G. Cadoni, 'Machiavelli teorico dei conflitti sociali', *Storia e politica*, 17 (1978), pp. 197–220; G. Procacci, 'Machiavelli rivoluzionario' in N. Machiavelli, *Opere scelte*, ed. G.F. Berardi (Rome, 1969), pp. xv–xxxv.

to the vision of a well-ordered city he applies a vocabulary that includes such terms as *unione, amicizia, quiete, pace, stabilità, amore* or *amore della patria.* Already in the prologue, the author underlines that the historical study of the 'causes of hatred and divisions in the city' might be a useful lesson to those citizens who govern the republic on how to attain 'unity'.

While the assessment of civil conflict in the *Discorsi* had broken with a tradition of political thought that had always condemned discord as both cause and effect of bad government and corruption,[5] its evaluation in the *Istorie Fiorentine* instead seems to seize on and reaffirm that tradition. Describing, deploring and criticising the divisions had also been an integral part of Fiorentine historiographical tradition, from Giovanni Villani, Marchionne di Coppo Stefani, Piero Minerbetti and Giovanni Cavalcanti to Piero Parenti, Bartolomeo Cerretani and Francesco Guicciardini.[6] Moreover, the topic was part of the political language in the Florentine government. In particularly critical moments, 'pratiche super unione' (deliberations about unity) were promoted, and there was discussion both of discord and of the need for, and ways of reaching, concord, the common good, love, and unity. On several occasions laws were brought in against political groupings, whether public or secret, more or less organised: what we today would call 'parties' and in Florence at those times were called *intelligenzie, compagnie, parti* or *sètte.*[7]

Against this background, I wish to present some aspects of Machiavelli's thinking on civil discord. Even though this issue has played an important part in general and specific works on Machiavelli, few authors have examined it in a systematic way and for its own sake, and they usually focus only on the above-mentioned passages in the *Discorsi.* This chapter will contribute to these studies from the perspective of the *Istorie Fiorentine* and therefore of Machiavelli's latest stage of life. It may help to illustrate the nature of his republicanism since his thought on social and political conflict was at its centre.

It may also contribute to answer some open questions about Machiavelli's political and historical thinking. Firstly, is there a contradiction or not between the positive view of conflict in the *Discorsi* and the negative one in the *Istorie Fiorentine?* Has the author of the latter resigned and given himself up to the

[5] Q. Skinner, *The Foundations of Modern Political Thought* (2 vols., Cambridge, 1978), vol. I, esp. pp. 181–2, 235.

[6] See e.g. G.A. Brucker, *Florentine Politics and Society 1343–1378* (Princeton, 1962), pp. 131–2; D.J. Wilcox, *The Development of Florentine Humanist Historiography in the 15th Century* (Cambridge, MA, 1969), pp. 73–81; N.C. Struever, *The Language of History in the Renaissance* (Princeton, NJ, 1970), pp. 115–43; N. Rubinstein, 'Politics and constitution in Florence at the end of the 15th century' in *Italian Renaissance Studies*, E.F. Jacob, ed. (London, 1960), pp. 148–83, p. 170; M. Phillips, 'Machiavelli, Guicciardini, and the tradition of vernacular historiography in Florence', *American Historical Review*, 84 (1979), p. 102; L. Green, *Chronicle into History. An Essay on the Interpretation of History in Florentine Fourteenth-century Chronicles* (Cambridge, 1972), pp. 39–43, 95–102, 106–7.

[7] Rubinstein, 'Politics and constitution in Florence', p. 168 and 'Machiavelli e le origini di Firenze', pp. 957–8.

utopia of a quiet, united, homogeneous and stable order, of social peace, to the myth of the Venetian republic with its actual or alleged absence of internal conflicts, which he had vehemently questioned in the *Discorsi*? And has the author of the *Istorie Fiorentine* abandoned his penetrating and disturbing, unscrupulous and 'machiavellian' analysis of the functioning and relationships of power, the issue, not so much of a 'demony of power',[8] but of the dynamics of power? In other words: Has nothing remained of the *Principe* and the *Discorsi* in the *Istorie Fiorentine*?

Secondly, various modern scholars have seen Machiavelli's positive judgement of discord and parties, especially in the *Discorsi*, as an important precursor of the positive evaluation or legitimacy of modern political parties.[9] This view, however, is controversial; it may be questioned on the grounds that the conflicting parties in Florentine history might not really have been forerunners of modern parties or that Machiavelli's thought may be seen in a different light. As to the latter question it was, for instance, Rousseau who saw it in a different way. In the *Contrat social* he condemned the 'sociétés partielles', an embryonic form of modern parties,[10] as being contrary to the 'volonté générale', and he cited in confirmation of his opinion none other than Machiavelli with a passage from the *Istorie Fiorentine* on 'divisions'.[11] Indeed, the commentator on the *Contrat social* in the Pléiade edition criticises Rousseau for having misunderstood Machiavelli and assumes that Machiavelli would have given a positive verdict on such 'sociétés partielles'.[12] What do the *Istorie Fiorentine*, as a document of Machiavelli's political thought, contribute to the solution of this problem?

Thirdly, as we have seen, Machiavelli mentions some of the subjects of civil conflict: the *nobili*, the *popolo* and the *plebe*. He deals with an issue which even centuries later continued to divide the major historians of Florence, such as Gaetano Salvemini and Nicola Ottokar: namely, whether the discord among sections of the commune is to be seen as a conflict among groups that we today would call 'classes', or else as a conflict among families, clans, client groups or

---

[8] G. Ritter, *Die Dämonie der Macht* (Munich, 1948; 1st edn 1940); see also F. Meinecke, *Die deutsche Katastrophe* (Wiesbaden, 1946), pp. 79–86 ('Der Massenmachiavellismus'); E. Faul, *Der moderne Machiavellismus* (Cologne, 1961).

[9] E. Faul, 'Verfemung, Duldung und Anerkennung des Parteiwesens', *Politische Vierteljahresschrift*, 5 (1964), pp. 68–9; S. Bertelli, 'Embrioni di partiti politici alle soglie dell'età moderna' in *Per Federico Chabod (1901–1960). Atti del seminario internazionale*, S. Bertelli, ed., vol. I: *Lo stato e il potere nel Rinascimento*, Annali della Facoltà di Scienze Politiche (Perugia, 1980–1), pp. 17–35; G. Silvano, '*Vivere civile*' e '*Governo misto*' a Firenze nel primo Cinquecento (Bologna, 1985), pp. 170–3; Rubinstein, 'Politics and constitution in Florence', pp. 166–83.

[10] R. von Albertini, 'Parteiorganisation und Parteibegriff in Frankreich 1785–1940', *Historische Zeitschrift*, 193 (1961), p. 534.

[11] J.-J. Rousseau, *Contrat social* in *Oeuvres complètes* (Paris, 1964), vol. III, ed. R. Derathé, p. 372 ('Il importe donc pour avoir bien l'énoncé de la volonté générale qu'il n'y ait pas de société partielle dans l'Etat'), with note referring to *IF*, VII/1. [12] *Ibid.*, p. 1458, note 4.

patronage systems.[13] What answer do the *Istorie Fiorentine*, as a document of historical thought and interpretation, provide?

An attempt to extract from a historiographical work which reconstructs and interprets the past – and this is the primary character of the *Istorie Fiorentine* – the political views of its author, meets particular methodological problems. The more an author uses the description of the past merely to express and corroborate his own political opinions and values, the more he tends to project the present upon the past (with the risk of anachronism) and theory onto history (risking an ahistorical procedure). Conversely, reading the *Istorie Fiorentine* solely to pick out Machiavelli's political opinion – and this has often been done – presupposes that he was a poor historian, incapable or unwilling to let himself be guided by the sources more than by his own preconceived opinions and political partiality. This is indeed a common opinion of Machiavelli as a historian, and he is said to have violated history which to him was no more than 'ancilla scientiae politicae'.[14] Other historians, however, have praised him as a true historian and the *Istorie Fiorentine* as a watershed in the history of historiography precisely because he did not follow the earlier Florentine chronicles – his main sources – in simply lining up more or less important and heterogeneous events in chronological order, but instead selected and structured sources and events in view of the essential causes and forces in Florentine history, and because he presented them in a perspective of 'impartiality'.[15] This discord among historians on how to evaluate *Machiavelli*

---

[13] G. Salvemini, *Magnati e popolani in Firenze dal 1280 al 1295* (Florence, 1899); N. Ottokar, *Il Commune di Firenze alla fine del Dugento* (Florence, 1926; repr. 1962); for the use of the term 'class' in this context see the sensitive remarks by Cadoni, 'Machiavelli teorico', p. 198, note 4. Faul in 'Verfemung', sees the rise of 'parties' as closely linked to class struggle. For more recent statements of the above-mentioned historical problem see, e.g., N. Rubinstein, 'Oligarchy and democracy in 15th century Florence' in *Florence and Venice: Comparisons and Relations* (Florence, 1980), vol. I, pp. 99–115; L. Martines, ed. *Violence and Civil Disorder in Italian Cities, 1200–1500* (Berkeley, CA, 1972); D. Kent, *The Rise of the Medici. Faction in Florence 1426–1434* (Oxford, 1978); J.N. Stephens, *The Fall of the Florentine Republic, 1512–1530* (Oxford, 1983); H.C. Butters, *Governors and Government in Early Sixteenth-century Florence, 1502–1519* (Oxford, 1985).

[14] E. Fueter, *Geschichte der modernen Historiographie* (Munich and Berlin, 1911 (*Storia della storiografia moderna* (Milan and Naples, 1970)), p. 66 (Italian translation, p. 86); similar and negative judgements on *Machiavelli storico*, particularly when measured against today's historical writing, may be found in R. Romano, *La storiografia italiana oggi* (Rome, 1978), p. 22; E.W. Cochrane, *Historians and Historiography in the Italian Renaissance* (Chicago, 1981), pp. 265–70; Felix Gilbert, 'Machiavelli's *Istorie Fiorentine*' in M.P. Gilmore, ed. *Studies on Machiavelli* (Florence, 1972), p. 99; F. Gilbert, *Machiavelli and Guicciardini, Politics and History in Sixteenth-century Florence* (Princeton, NJ, 1965). For a critical review of this interpretation, see A. Garosci, *Le Istorie Fiorentine del Machiavelli* (Turin, 1973), p. 190.

[15] This was Gervinus' view, and he compared Machiavelli with Thucydides in this respect (G. Gervinus, *Geschichte der florentinischen Historiographie* (Frankfurt, 1871; 1st edn 1833)). Other authors who see the *IF* in a more positive light and Machiavelli as an outstanding historian, are, e.g. F. Gaeta, 'Introduction' to N. Machiavelli, *Istorie Fiorentine* (Milan, 1962), pp. 45–62 and 'Machiavelli storico' in R. Aron *et al., Machiavelli nel 5 centenario della nascita* (Bologna, 1973), pp. 139–51; Garosci, *Le Istorie Fiorentine del Machiavelli*; G.M. Anselmi, *Ricerche sul Machiavelli storico* (Pisa, 1979); Carlo Dionisotti, 'Machiavelli storico' in C. Dionisotti, *Machiavellerie* (Turin, 1980),

storico and how to relate him to *Machiavelli politico* is still alive and has brought to the fore important new investigations. Since the early nineteenth century when it was discovered that Machiavelli had used Cavalcanti as a major source, many other sources have been identified.[16] Such studies confirm that Machiavelli's political views are implicit in his historical account (as political views may be implicit in other historical narratives), but that they can be gathered only from painstaking comparison with his sources; no passage of the *Istorie Fiorentine* may be used to demonstrate the author's implicit or explicit political view without examining if and how it was taken over from one of the sources or if it was Machiavelli's original contribution. This is not the place, however, to pursue that procedure.

The 'impartiality' which Gervinus referred to, means that Machiavelli – as other early modern Italian historians – presents events and activities from the different and sometimes opposing perspectives of their protagonists and he by no means always and explicitly tells us how he himself evaluates them. This is most obvious in the fictive speeches of individuals and groups which present – following and renewing a historiographic tradition which lasted from Thucydides to the seventeenth century – what the author interprets to be their causes and motives and the inner logic of events.[17] Such speeches from the *Istorie Fiorentine* have often been singled out in order to demonstrate the political views of its author; yet this procedure does not always take sufficient account of their historiographical function. To use them for the reconstruction of Machiavelli's political thinking requires not taking them out of, but placing

pp. 365–409; N. Rubinstein, 'Machiavelli storico', *Annali della Scuola Normale di Pisa, Classe di lettere e filosofia*, ser. 3, 17/3, pp. 695–733. For the state of contemporary historiography against which Machiavelli needs to be evaluated, see also H. Baron, 'Das Erwachen des historischen Denkens im Humanismus des Quattrocento', *Historische Zeitschrift*, 147 (1932), 5–20; E. Garin, 'La storia nel pensiero del Rinascimento' in E. Garin, *Medioevo e Rinascimento* (Bari, 1964), pp. 179–95; A. Buck, *Das Geschichtsdenken der Renaissance* (Krefeld, 1957); M.P. Gilmore, 'The Renaissance conception of the lessons of history' in his *Humanists and Jurists* (Cambridge, MA), pp. 1–37. F. Gilbert, 'The Renaissance interest in history' in *Art, Science and History in the Renaissance*, Ch. Singleton, ed. (Baltimore, 1967), pp. 373–87; M.B. Becker, 'Towards a Renaissance historiography in Florence' in *Renaissance. Studies in Honor of Hans Baron*, A. Molho and John A. Tedeschi, eds. (Florence, 1971), pp. 141–71; D. Hay, *Annalists and Historians: Western Historiography from the Eighth to the Eighteenth Centuries* (London, 1977); M. Phillips, *Francesco Guicciardini: The Historian's Craft* (Toronto, 1977); R. Black, 'The new laws of history', *Renaissance Studies*, 1 (1987), 126–56.

16 See e.g. B. Richardson, 'Notes on Machiavelli's sources and his treatment of the rhetorical tradition', *Italian Studies*, 26 (1971), 24–48; Anselmi, *Ricerche sul Machiavelli storico*, pp. 115–59; Cabrini, *Per una valutazione delle 'Istorie Fiorentine'*; Rab Hatfield, 'A source for Machiavelli's account of the regime of Piero de' Medici' in Gilmore, ed. *Studies on Machiavelli*, pp. 319–33.

17 Struever, *The Language of History in the Renaissance*, esp. pp. 72–3, 125–43; Anselmi, *Ricerche sul Machiavelli storico*, pp. 182–6; R. Aguirre, 'Machiavelli's use of fictive speeches in the Istorie Fiorentine,' unpublished PhD Dissertation, University of Oregon, 1978; G. Bock, 'Machiavelli als Geschichtsschreiber', *Quellen und Forschungen aus italienischen Archiven und Bibliotheken*, 66 (1986), 178–84.

them in the context both of the historical narrative and the entire sequence of the speeches.

An example concerning the subject of civil discord is the speech of Gualtieri di Brienne, Duke of Athens and governor of Florence in the 1340s, presented by Machiavelli as a tyrant who destroyed the civil liberties with demagogy and violence and justified his tyranny pointing out that 'those cities alone are in slavery that are disunited, while the united are free'.[18] This phrase has been described as 'la plus profonde et la plus essentielle des vérités' in Machiavelli's eyes, indicating that his concept of liberty meant to 'écraser tout germe de dissension civile'.[19] Yet, this interpretation does not take into account that the Duke's sentence was a response to the no less important preceding speech of a group of republican-minded citizens ('who loved their country and liberty') who, protesting against the Duke's tyranny, stressed and threatened that 'the only lasting government is one based on the people's will'.[20] On the level of the author's personal opinion, it has been plausibly argued that the citizens' speech corresponds more closely to Machiavelli's own view than the Duke's who merely instrumentalises the traditional language of liberty for the sake of tyranny.[21] On the level of historiographical presentation we are dealing with an antilogy, a set of two opposing speeches which present contrasting viewpoints and leave the judgement, at least in part, to the reader; here it is of course not without significance that the tyrant is able to apply the language of liberty to his own ends. On the level of Machiavelli's political thinking, the two speeches may be seen to express precisely his complex treatment and ambivalent evaluation of civil discord which is the subject of this chapter and which should not be reduced to one of these opposing opinions.

The *Istorie Fiorentine* includes some passages which express his political thinking not only implicitly but also explicitly, without direct recourse to sources and fiction, namely – besides the prologue – the first chapters of the eight books which introduce their main subjects and sometimes summarise the previous one; three of them, the introductions to Books III, IV and VII, deal with civil discord, and the following considerations are mainly based on them. However, despite their more theoretical style, they cannot be separated from the historical narrative. Their character as a summary and interpretation of the historical account – and not simply as a preconceived political theory – has

---

[18] *IF*, II/35, p. 683.

[19] M. Marietti, 'Machiavel historiographe des Médicis' in *Les Ecrivains et le pouvoir en Italie à l'époque de la Renaissance*, ed. A. Rochan, vol. II, no. 3, 2nd series (Paris, 1974), p. 147.

[20] *IF*, II/34, p. 682 ('quello dominio è solo durabile che è voluntario'). Both speeches are not in the source (Villani); see Machiavelli, *Istorie Fiorentine*, ed. V. Fiorini (1894/1978), p. 237–8, 240.

[21] By Fiorini, p. 240 (see previous note). Moreover, the Duke has only an indirect speech, the citizens a direct one. See also Garosci, *Le Istorie Fiorentine del Machiavelli*, pp. 210–12.

recently been confirmed by the fact that the introductions to the books I–VI were written after the narrative of these books.[22] Dealing with them therefore means tracing Machiavelli's political thinking within his historical thinking as well as tracing his historical thinking within his political thinking.

II

The introduction to Book III, praised by Federico Chabod as a marvellous analysis of the Italian cities' evolution and problems,[23] is located chronologi-in the second half of the fourteenth century, and summarises the previous book while alluding to the following one. 'Those serious, though natural enmities, which occur between the common people and the nobility' are caused by the 'desire of the latter to command and the former not to obey'; these two contrasting attitudes are the *umori* and their diversity, and they are the cause of 'all the evils that arise in cities'. This assertion, of an anthropological character, is to be met with frequently in Machiavelli's works: according to him, there are various *umori* or *sorte* or *qualità* of men – sometimes two (*nobili* and *popolo*), sometimes three (*nobili, popolo* and *plebe*) – and the enmities among them are natural, i.e. exist in every city, are inevitable and ineliminable, comprehensible and perhaps even legitimate.[24] On this anthropological ground, the author continues with a comparison between the Roman and Florentine republics. He begins with one parallel: the 'diversity of humours' that kept Rome disunited likewise kept Florence divided. However, as elsewhere in Machiavelli's writings, the same causes may have different effects, and the evil may have positive effects, though still remaining evil.[25] The effects of the evil of the enmities were positive in Rome and negative in Florence: here the parallelism between the two republics becomes transformed into a polemical contrast, polemical with respect to the humanist tradition which glorified Florence by equating it with the glorious Roman republic. According to Machiavelli, Romans and Florentines handled their discordances in quite different ways: 'The early quarrels between the nobles and the people in Rome were settled by discussions, those in Florence by fighting. In Rome, they ended with laws, in Florence with the exile and death of many citizens. In Rome they increased military *virtù*, in Florence they destroyed it altogether.' Three different effects,

---

[22] E. Levi, 'Due nuovi frammenti degli abbozzi autografi delle Istorie Fiorentine del Machiavelli', *Bibliofilia*, 69 (1967), 309–23. [23] F. Chabod, *Scitti su Machiavelli* (Turin, 1964), pp. 72–3.

[24] *IF*, III/1, pp. 690–1; see also *IF*, II/12, p. 666; II/34, p. 681; II/36, p. 684; II/42, p. 689; *Principe*, IX, p. 271; *Discorsi*, I/5, p. 83; *Discursus* p. 27. For the *umori* see also Sasso, *Niccolò Machiavelli*, pp. 446–7, 460–5.

[25] *IF*, III/1, pp. 690–1; see also *Principe*, VIII, pp. 270–1. Guicciardini strongly criticised this view: 'Non fu adunche la disunione tra la plebe e el senato che facessi Roma libera e potente . . . Laudare le disunione è come laudare in uno infermo la infermità, per la bontà del remedio che gli è stato applicato' (*Considerazioni sui Discorsi del Machiavelli*, in: *Opere*, (Turin, 1970) vol. I, pp. 615–16). See Skinner, *The Foundations*, vol. I, pp. 181–2.

then, to which there follows a fourth that is striking because it breaks the simplistic counterpoint between a glorious Rome and a wretched Florence: 'In Rome they changed the state of equality among the citizens to a state of very great inequality, in Florence they led from inequality to a remarkable state of equality.'[26]

At a stroke, Machiavelli has reversed the terms of comparison between Rome and Florence, since the concept of equality has clearly positive associations in his thinking, as it does in the Florentine republican tradition. In the *Discorsi*, he had stated that equality is a precondition for a true republic, and while he maintains this assertion in the *Discursus florentinarum rerum post mortem iunioris Laurentii Medices*, written around 1520, here he also proposes an 'equality' within the constitution: the restitution of the Consiglio Maggiore which had been abolished in 1512, and the broadening of the social basis of government so that each of the 'humours' would have 'la parte sua' in government.[27] Machiavelli's 'equality' is not economic or social, but legal and political, meaning equality before the law and equal access to office; in the terms of the *Discorsi*, it is not 'equalità di sustanze' or 'della roba', but 'equalità di grado' or 'de' onori'.[28] In Book II of the *Istorie Fiorentine*, he had described the struggles between people and nobles in Florence for and against this kind of equality, the abolition of the privileges of the old feudal nobility, and he had defined equality more specifically as abolition of their juridical and military power. But he had also described how not only were these privileges abolished, but it was sought to exclude the aristocracy entirely from government, from office, from the city, and when an excluded nobleman aspired to an office, he even had to be recognised as a *popolano*; conversely, to be declared noble meant to lose access to office.[29]

Machiavelli strongly criticises this practice in the introduction to Book III, placing this criticism right after his praise of equality. He does so again through

---

[26] *IF*, III/1, p. 690: 'Quelle [nimicizie] di Roma da una ugualità di cittadini in una disaguaglianza grandissima quella città condussono, quelle di Firenze da una disaguaglianza ad una mirabile ugualità l'hanno ridutta.'

[27] *Discorsi*, I/55, pp. 136–9; *Discursus*, pp. 25–9; for the Consiglio Maggiore see N. Rubinstein, 'I primi anni del Consiglio Maggiore di Firenze', *Archivio storico italiano*, 112 (1954), 151–94; 'Politics and constitution in Florence'; 'Florentine constitutionalism'; 'Oligarchy and democracy'; for the ideal of 'equality' see Skinner, *The Foundations*, vol. I, pp. 166, 170, 236–8, 259; Rubinstein, 'Florentine constitutionalism' and 'Machiavelli e le origini di Firenze', p. 958; Cadoni, 'Machiavelli teorico', p. 199; Carlo Dionisotti, 'Machiavelli letterato' in Dionisotti, *Machiavellerie*, p. 213; Sasso, *Niccolò Machiavelli*, pp. 471–4, 490–1, 521–6. For the *Discursus* see esp. G. Guidi, 'Niccolò Machiavelli e i progetti di riforme costituzionali a Firenze nel 1522', *Il Pensiero Politico*, 2 (1969), 580–90 and 'La teoria delle "tre ambizioni" nel pensiero politico del primo '500', *Il Pensiero Politico*, 5(1972), 241–59; R. von Albertini, *Das florentinische Staatsbewusstsein im Übergang von der Republik zum Prinzipat* (Berne, 1955),|pp. 46, 84–5; Sasso, *Niccolò Machiavelli*, pp. 524–6, 610–15; Silvano, *Vivere civile*, pp. 91–109.

[28] *Discorsi*, I/6, p. 85; I/37, pp. 118–20; Sasso, *Niccolò Machiavelli*, pp. 484–5.

[29] *IF*, II/11–14, pp. 665–7; II/42, pp. 689–90; III/2–4, pp. 691–2; III/19, pp. 706–7.

the comparison between Rome and Florence, again reversing it in the sense of Roman positiveness and Florentine negativeness. He explains how a natural and universal fact like the 'diversity of humours' could possibly produce such diverse effects in different cities. The 'parties' to the fight had had 'diverse aims' and 'diverse desires' in the two cities, and he goes on with a new list of contrasts: 'The people of Rome wanted to enjoy the chief honours with the nobles, the people of Florence fought to have the government to themselves without the participation of the nobility'; the Roman people's 'desire was more reasonable', whereas that of the Florentine people 'was unjust and abusive'. Therefore, the Roman nobility conceded the people's request 'without resorting to violence', whereas in Florence 'the nobility prepared to defend themselves more efficiently', and this 'led to bloodshed and exile'. The laws and reforms introduced in Rome after these conflicts were for the 'common good', but in Florence 'in favour of the victor'. In Rome the accession of men of the people to government caused them to become similar to the nobility and to assume the latter's *virtù*, including the military commitment; in Florence it produced the opposite effect, so that the nobles, in order to be readmitted to government, had to become like men of the people and – an argument that recalls the *Principe* – 'not only to be like the *popolani* in their behaviour, in their opinions, and in their style of living, but they had to be seen to be so'.[30] Thus, Florence 'became more and more humble and base'.

At this climax of condemnation of the conflicts in Florence there follows a second abrupt turn, again reversing the comparison between the two cities. Machiavelli continues: 'And whereas Rome, when its *virtù* had turned into pride, was reduced to such a state that she could not be held together without a prince, Florence has reached a stage where she could easily be reformed by a wise lawgiver and given any form of government.'[31] It is clear, and undisputed among scholars, that the last sentence refers not only to the preceding Book II, but also and mainly to the *Discursus* just mentioned, written at the same period, and is to be read as a call for the introduction of a republican order in accordance with Machiavelli's proposal, addressed to Giulio de' Medici who commissioned both the *Istorie Fiorentine* and the *Discursus* and who was then informal leader of the government of Florence.[32]

Less clear, however, is the meaning of the reversal of the comparison between Rome and Florence. Machiavelli seems to fall into open contradiction

---

[30] *IF*, III/1, pp. 690–1; see *Principe*, XVIII, p. 284.

[31] *IF*, III/1, p. 691; the same idea is expressed in a speech by republican-minded citizens in *IF*, III/5, p. 694: 'la Italia tutta e questa città è condotta in tanta ugualità che per lei medesima si può reggere . . . E questa nostra republica massimamente si può . . . non solamente mantenere unità, ma di buoni costumi e civili modi riformare, pure che Vostre Signorie si disponghino a volerlo fare.'

[32] Rubinstein, 'Machiavelli e le origini di Firenze', p. 958; Marietti, 'Machiavelli historiographe', p. 109.

by ultimately maintaining that the civil and better kind of discord led to the decline of the Roman republic, the rise of Caesar, and was therefore harmful to Rome, whereas the uncivil and dangerous kind of discord in Florence was beneficial to a republican order. Or has he perhaps started to revise his earlier vision, considering it an idealisation of a much cruder and crueller history of the Roman republic on one side, and an exaggeration of Florentine corruption on the other? Vittorio Fiorini, author of the important, and only, detailed commentary on the *Istorie Fiorentine*, published in 1894, could not explain this contradiction otherwise than by asserting that 'in reality no logical connection need be sought between what was said previously and the two new observations: instead, the latter must be regarded as an appendix without any connection with the rest'. In other words: as an addition without significance, better not to have been written.[33] This explanation is hardly convincing, particularly in view of the usual acuteness of Machiavelli's language and reflection and especially when it comes to contradiction, irony or provocation. Yet, an alternative explanation may be found by coming back to the *Discorsi sopra la prima deca di Tito Livio*, Book 1, chapter 37, where we find a similar contradiction.

This chapter deals not with the merits and glory of the Roman republic, but with its failures and ultimate fall. Machiavelli identifies the cause of the decline precisely in what he earlier saw as the cause of its freedom and power, namely the discord between nobles and people, when it came to the point of exasperation. In order to explain this, he places a general consideration ahead of the historical argument, again of an anthropological kind. Men fight each other because of need, and if there is no need, they do so because of ambition; this is because nature has created them in such a way that 'though all things are objects of desire, not all things are attainable; so that desire always exceeds the power of attainment, with the result that men are ill content with what they possess and their present state brings them little satisfaction'. Therefore, the Roman plebs was not satisfied with its political influence through the tribunes, and it wished to share not only the 'onori', but also 'le sustanze', 'la roba', property and wealth. This happened in the struggles around the agrarian law at the time of the Gracchi, which set a limit to land ownership and provided for conquered lands to be divided up among the plebs, and this 'caused the destruction of the republic'. The cause was not only, or not so much, the shift from the political to the economic struggle – Machiavelli in fact writes that the Gracchi's intentions were more praiseworthy than their prudence – as the methods of this struggle, namely violence 'in which neither moderation nor respect for civic customs was shown', a shift from 'civil discord' to 'civil war'. In the course of these events,

---

[33] Fiorini, in Machiavelli, *Istorie Fiorentine*, p. 271. To my knowledge, no alternative explanations have been proposed, but Sasso, *Niccolò Machiavelli*, p. 508, note 69, has suggested the link between *IF*, III/1 and *Discorsi*, 1/37.

Machiavelli underlines several factors: the power of the nobility which has increased through the republic's expansion and was now used against the plebs, the use not of political and constitutional but of private means, the emergence of individual leaders (*capi*) on both sides – Sulla for the nobility, Marius for the plebs – and the final victory of Caesar who took sides, against Pompey, for the plebs and thus became 'Rome's first tyrant, after which that city never again recovered its liberties.'[34]

Machiavelli himself seems not to have been entirely satisfied with his introductory and anthropological explanation of this account which named civil discord as cause both of Roman liberty and its destruction. Therefore he added an epilogue in which he himself stresses the contradiction to Book 1, chapter 4, which 'seems to be incompatible with this conclusion'. But nevertheless he insists: 'I am not on this account inclined to change my opinion.'[35] He insists because according to him the historical circumstances have changed, and he indicates three of them. Firstly (and as if he wished to balance the introduction where he had attributed the fault to the ambition of the plebs), the ambition of the nobility is so great that, in order to avoid the ruin of the city, it needs to be checked; if the plebs had not done so, servitude would have come even earlier. Secondly, he again emphasises the link between violence and the struggle for wealth: men care more for property than for honours and therefore 'when it came to property' ('come si venne alla roba') which the Roman nobility obstinately defended, the plebs had recourse to violence. Thirdly, he argues that the Gracchi pursued the wrong policy by urging the conflict and thus accelerating the evil they intended to combat, instead of temporising it. For this issue, he refers to an earlier chapter where he discussed a parallel in the history of Florence: Cosimo il Vecchio would not have become 'principe della republica' without the exasperated opposition of those who, realising that his increasing reputation posed a threat to the republic, sought to remove this danger by removing Cosimo and thereby – by sending him into exile, hence committing an injury and reinforcing his 'party' – helped him to come to power.[36] As to the contradiction which Machiavelli

---

[34] *Discorsi*, 1/37, p. 120; the anthropological consideration: 'Perché la natura ha creati gli uomini in modo che possono desiderare ogni cosa, e non possono conseguire ogni cosa . . .' (p. 119). See also Sasso, *Niccolò Machiavelli*, pp. 487–94, 530–4.

[35] *Discorsi*, 1/37, p. 120 ('E benché noi mostrassimo altrove, come le inimicizie di Roma intra il Senato e la Plebe mantenessero libera Roma, per nascerne, da quelle, leggi in favore della libertà; e per questo paia disforme a tale conclusione il fine di questa legge agraria; dico come, per questo, io non mi rimuovo da tale opinione'). Compared to Guicciardini's critique of the contradiction (see note 25 above), Machiavelli seems to stress it.

[36] *Discorsi*, 1/37, p. 120 ('come di sopra largamente si discorse, non si fa altro che accelerare quel male, a che quel disordine ti conduce: ma, temporeggiandolo, o il male viene più tardo, o per se medesimo col tempo, avanti che venga al fine suo, si spegne'); see *Discorsi*, 1/33, p. 115; *IF*, IV/27, pp. 731–3 (Niccolò da Uzano advises not to use force and exile against Cosimo il Vecchio).

reflects upon, he seems to say that it is to be sought not in his thinking but in the historical events and the course of history itself.

This parallel in the *Discorsi* shows that the similar contradiction in the *Istorie Fiorentine* is not a mistake or superfluous, but deliberate and decisive. In both works, Machiavelli's political and historical interest prohibits him from merely glorifying the Roman republic and simply presenting it as a model to be imitated;[37] he also insists on its deficiencies which are not to be followed. Moreover, the reference at the beginning of Book III of the *Istorie Fiorentine* to its decline seems to have a specific and important function. It is no accident that the comparison between Rome and Florence is worked out exclusively in these pages.[38] Why did Machiavelli use it specifically to introduce this book? The reason seems evident: it is in Book III that he presents, following the struggles between *popolo* and *nobili* and the ultimate fall of the nobility in Book II, the struggles between *plebe* and *popolo*, and this process also marks the passage from the struggle for honours and office to that for property and wealth and to violence. It is the story of the revolt of the Ciompi, the Florentine woolworkers, that shook the city for three months in 1378. The contradiction in the introduction refers to the contradictory course of Florentine history.

Machiavelli gives the Ciompi revolt more space than any other event taking the same length of time. He describes it as a culminating moment of the communal divisions, attributing to it a deep and lasting significance for the city's history.[39] Its salient points may be read almost as a counterpoint to his presentation of the struggles around the agrarian law in the *Discorsi* – the passage from political to economic struggle, from civil discord to civil war, the recourse to private means, the emergence of individual leaders on both sides, the brief victory of *plebs* and *popolo minuto* and the slow rise to power of those of the *popolo grasso* who took their part – members of the Medici family – outside the traditional republican institutions.

But nonetheless, Machiavelli's historical account of the Ciompi revolt is not simply modelled upon Roman similarities, but follows its own dynamics, with an attitude similar to that with which he had once approached ancient authors: 'Tucto mi transferisco in loro.'[40] Most historians before him – including his sources – and most historians following him up until the nineteenth century saw the cause of the revolt, and of discord in general, either in instigation by the devil or in punishment for the sins of the citizens, or else in inscrutable fate or

---

[37] Sasso, *Niccolò Machiavelli*, pp. 487–91, 530–4.

[38] Some brief references to ancient history appear in the prologue (see above), in IV/1, p. 715; V/4, pp. 740–1.

[39] *IF*, III/18, p. 706: 'Dalla quale (i.e. divisione tra i popolani nobili e i minori artefici) perché seguirono in varii tempi di poi effetti gravissimi, e molte volte se ne arà a fare menzione, chiamereno l'una di queste parte popolare e l'altra plebea.' See also IV/2 and IV/3, p. 716; *IF*, IV/9–10, pp. 720–1; IV/28, p. 734.   [40] Letter of 10 December 1513, p. 1160.

individual immoral behaviour, or else in manipulation of the people by some nobleman, or – in the case of the Ciompi – in the reprehensible claims of men incapable of exercising public office.[41] Machiavelli was perhaps the first historian to see the causes not in moral terms, but in political ones, and above all in the material conditions and rational interests of the Ciompi themselves. He thus arrived at a conclusion that has not been surpassed by modern historiography.

According to him, there existed 'the *popolo minuto's* hatred of the rich citizens and the leaders of the guilds, since they did not feel remunerated for their labours as they believed they rightly deserved'. This aspiration for higher wages was pursued up to a certain point within the framework of the constitutional order of the *arti*, guilds or corporations. Since the *popolo minuto* and the *plebe* were not organised in 'Guilds of their own', but were included in, and subordinated to, the guilds dominated by their employers, 'they did not feel that the justice was done to them to which they were entitled'.[42] Initially they sought to attain their goal by setting up new corporations that would allow access to the magistracies and to justice for the plebs too, but then had recourse to violence. This shift of political method is introduced, in Machiavelli's account, by the speech of an anonymous Ciompo to the crowd for which the author did not have – as in the case of other speeches – a model in one of his sources. It is a famous piece in Machiavelli's prose and interpretation, and some, among them Karl Marx, have regarded it as inspired by Catiline's speech in Sallust. Yet, the Ciompo's speech is part of a public and popular rebellion in the context of civil discord, not of a secret and aristocratic conspiracy like Catiline's, and in its focus on political relations of power and violence it reminds one much more of Machiavelli's *Principe*.[43]

---

[41] Eugenio Garin, 'Echi del Tumulto dei Ciompi nella cultura del Rinascimento' in *Il Tumulto dei Ciompi. Un momento di storia Fiorentina ed europea* (Florence, 1981), pp. 59–93; Ernesto Sestan, 'Echi sul Tumulto dei Ciompi nella cronistica e nella storiografia' in *ibid.* pp. 125–60; L. Green, *Chronicle into History*, pp. 90–102; D.J. Wilcox, *Development*, pp. 51–3, 149–51.

[42] *IF*, III/12, p. 700. See also V. Hunecke, 'Il Tumulto dei Ciompi – 600 Jahre danach', *Quellen und Forschungen aus italienischen Archiven und Bibliotheken*, 58 (1978), 360–410 and 'The conference on the Tumulto dei Ciompi held in Florence, 16–19 September 1979', *Journal of Italian History*, 2 (1979), 281–92; J.M. Najemy, '*Arti* and *Ordini* in Machiavelli's *Istorie Fiorentine*' in *Essays presented to Myron P. Gilmore*, ed. by S. Bertelli and G. Ramakus, vol I, Florence, 1978, pp. 161–91; *idem* '"Audiant omnes artes"; corporate origins of the Ciompi revolution' in *Il Tumulto dei Ciompi*, pp. 59–93. A. Bonadeo, *Corruption, Conflict, and Power in the Works and Times of Niccolò Machiavelli* (Berkeley, CA, 1973), does not include the Ciompi revolt in the chapter on civil conflict.

[43] *IF*, III/13, pp. 700–2. For Marx's comparison see N. Badaloni, 'Natura e società in Machiavelli', *Studi Storici*, 10 (1969), 675–708, p. 700; Ragionieri, 'Biografie di Marx e di Engels', *Critica marxista*, 5 (1969), 146; it was criticised by O. Tommasini, *La vita e gli scritti di Niccolò Machiavelli*, vol. II (Rome, 1911), p. 524. For Machiavelli's own presentation of Catilina, who represents not civil discord, but the *coup d'état*, see *Discorsi*, I/10, p. 92; III/6, pp. 209–10; von Hentig, *Studien zur Psychologie des Staatsstreichs und der Staatsgründung* (Berlin, 1924); for the difference between both see, e.g. *IF*, VIII/1, pp. 817–18.

The Ciompo sets out with an analysis of such relations: to be sure, 'to take up arms, burn and rob citizens' houses' is an evil, but a necessary evil, since there is no other way to avoid the punishment for the evils already committed than by 'redoubling evils'. Wealth should be taken away from the rich because on one hand it has been acquired by deceit and violence, and on the other hand 'faithful servants always stay servants, and good men remain always poor; nor do any ever emerge from servitude but the disloyal and bold, nor from poverty save the rapacious and fraudulent'. At the centre of the speech is an argument in favour of an equality that is not only political but also economic: 'Be not deceived about that antiquity of blood by which they exalt themselves above us. For all men had one common origin, are all equally ancient, and nature made them all alike. Strip us naked and you will see that we are all the same. Dress us in their clothes and them in ours; we shall surely look noble and they ignoble. For it is only poverty and wealth that make us unequal.'

In the context of the entire Book III – its introduction, the historical narrative and the three major speeches – Machiavelli seems to judge the revolt in the following terms. The passage from the struggle for equality of honours to that for equality of wealth is not necessarily illegitimate, and is in any case comprehensible and rational in terms of human nature; but it also brought about the move from constitutional to violent means that the author condemns.[44] Yet, he condemns them not as sin and, as in the epilogue of *Discorsi* I, 37, he attributes them not to human nature, but to historical development and change ('Do not impute the old disorders to human nature, but to the times, and since times may change, you may hope for better fortune for our city, if better institutions are created').[45] He condemns them because they ruin the republic, and it is no accident that the speech of the Ciompo is the only one among the major three of this book which does not refer to the 'patria'.

Two further motives of his judgement are important for the subject of civil discord. The rebels did not only want to take part in government and wealth, but to exclude their enemies from it; according to the Ciompo, 'now is the time not only to free yourselves of them but to become so superior to them that they may have more to rue and fear you than you them'. In Machiavelli's eyes they attempted, and for a while succeeded, to become 'principe dello stato'; in the *Istorie Fiorentine* this term frequently refers to groups, not to individuals.[46] Secondly, the revolt was not only an expression of discord and divisions, but the rebels also systematically pursued a policy of division, including alliance

---

[44] The three major speeches of Book III summarise these motives: *IF*, III/5, pp. 692–5; III/11, pp. 699–700; III/13, pp. 700–2. The author also gives explicit judgements on their content: 'Queste parole, perché erano vere . . .' (p. 700); 'queste persuasioni accesono forte . . . al male' (p. 702).

[45] *IF*, III/5, pp. 694–5.

[46] *IF*, III/13, pp. 701–2; III/21, p. 709; III/22, p. 709 ('tutta la parte che era principe'). In II/26, p. 675, Lucca is described as 'principe di se stessa'.

with some patricians, among them Salvestro de' Medici.[47] It is here that Machiavelli saw the origins of the Medici's rise to power – he was the first one to do so – because the restoration of the rule of the oligarchy after 1382 brought about a *stato* which was 'no less harsh to its citizens nor less oppressive in its early stages than the regime of the plebs'.[48] In 1434 Cosimo il Vecchio could base himself on those who were no longer satisfied with it.

This is the subject of Book IV, and its introduction deals again with discord and division. There are cities which, even though being formally republics, are not 'well-ordered'. Their frequent changes of 'governi e stati' are not, 'as many believe', between liberty and servitude, but between servitude and licence, the former being the rule of the nobility and the latter that of the *popolani*; in both cases, liberty is but a name, since neither the laws nor the magistrates are respected, and in both cases it is only through individual leaders that a minimum of stability is maintained ('both of them must be upheld by the *virtù* and fortune of a man, who can fail through death or become useless because of political trouble'). Obviously, this refers to Florence and to the conflicts described in the previous and subsequent books. Machiavelli then dwells, as already twice before, on the possibility, though uncertain and rare, that a 'wise, good and powerful citizen' may appear who establishes laws and a constitution which check the opposing 'humours' of the nobles and the people, so as to prevent them from doing harm, and which simultaneously guarantee stability and continuity, so as to render the original legislator superfluous.[49] This vision has a double function. On one side, it announces Giovanni Bicci's and Cosimo de' Medici's future roles, on the other side it was again addressed to Giulio de' Medici who had commissioned the *Istorie Fiorentine* and who was called upon, in Machiavelli's contemporaneous *Discursus*, to establish precisely such a republican order that could later do without a Medici leader; in fact, in the early 1520s it seemed that the Medici family would become extinct after Giulio's death.[50]

The introduction to Book VII deals with discord from a new perspective. Machiavelli develops here a concept which he had not yet touched upon in the earlier introductions: the *sètte* (sects, factions), namely the divisions not between the horizontal, class-like *umori* but between vertical groups such as families (*case*), clans, client groups, patronage systems. It is against these groups and their conflicts, much more than against discord between classes, that he unleashes all his wrath. It is a deception and a hope, he writes, to assume that a republic may exist in perfect unity of purpose. But he distinguishes between

---

[47] *IF*, III/13, p. 701; III/18, p. 706; IV/2, p. 716.   [48] *IF*, III/21, p. 709.

[49] *IF*, IV/1, pp. 715–16; see also *IF*, III/1, p. 691; III/5, pp. 614–15; IV/10, pp. 720–1.

[50] See *IF*, IV/3, pp. 716–17; IV/14, 16, pp. 722–4; IV/26, p. 731; *Discursus*, p. 30; *Minuta di provvisione per la Riforma dello Stato di Firenze l'anno 1522*, p. 23.

two types of divisions, and this is the passage that Rousseau was later to cite in support of his condemnation of 'sociétés partielles':

Some divisions harm republics, and others benefit them. The ones that harm are those accompanied by *sètte* and partisans, those that benefit are carried on without *sètte* and partisans. So since the founder of a republic cannot make provisions against civil discord, at least he should take care that there are not *sètte*.[51]

The *sètte* are different from the *umori* which Machiavelli had described in the introduction to Book III; the latter are natural, unavoidable and may even lead, if checked and handled in a civilised way, to equality and the common good, the former are merely struggles for power, are avoidable and hence should be avoided. There are two different ways of arriving at political power: either through 'vie publiche', within the constitutional institutions, or through 'modi privati', outside or against such institutions, by securing – through wealth, generosity or protection – 'partisans' that support the benefactor and his sect for their own benefit and not for the common good. To the earlier condemnation of the rise to power through violent means, Machiavelli adds that of power reached through private wealth, and it is obvious that this verdict also refers to Cosimo de' Medici's policy. Machiavelli sees in the history of Florence not only negative forms of conflict – the introduction to Book III has shown this – but ultimately the negative ones predominated; hence his overall judgement:

The enmities in Florence were always through *sètte* and therefore always harmful. The winning side only remained united for as long as the opposing sect was alive. As soon as the defeated side was broken, the reigning faction was no longer restrained by fear or internal discipline, and it split up again.

Again, the reference to the 'founder of a republic' in this introduction seems to be addressed to Giulio de' Medici; in similar words, Machiavelli asked him in the *Discursus* to provide that 'the powerful men cannot form *sètte*, which are the ruin of a state'.[52]

Whereas in the sequence of the general introductions to the eight books the term *sètte* appears only in that to Book VII, in the historical narrative it had appeared much earlier. In Book I, covering the history of the peninsula since the barbarian invasions until 1434, it referred to religious sects; in Book II, which deals with the origins of Florence until the plague of 1348, it appears very rarely and the prevailing term for the communal divisions is *parte* – for the Guelph and Ghibelline factions as well as for the different social strata. In Book III, *sètte* are very much in the foreground, referring to powerful, rival families and to the revival of the old divisions between the Guelphs and the Ghibellines ('la nuova

---

[51] *IF*, VII/1, pp. 792–3; see note 11 above.
[52] *IF*, VII/1–2, pp. 792–4; VII/6, pp. 796–7; IV/26–7, pp. 731–3; *Discursus*, p. 24.

setta di guelfi'). On the eve of the Ciompi revolt we find the first great accusation against the *sètte*, 'le famiglie fatali', in the speech of an anonymous citizen who asked the Signoria for a reform that would wipe out 'those institutions which promote the *sètte*' and would thus lead to a 'truly free and civil life'. In Book IV, the term is almost never used – except for Giovanni Bicci being described as an ardent opponent of *sètte* in general – and the competing families and oligarchic groups are usually called *parte* (the Medici, Albizzi, the Parte Guelfa). In Books V and VI, which deal with the relations between Florence and the other Italian states, *sètte* are the armies of the *condottieri* which Machiavelli had so often criticised.[53] Book VII – preceded by the introductory consideration on *sètte* – does not use the term, and instead we find *divisione, parte, civili discordie, fazioni, contenzioni civili*; the same holds for Book VIII.

From this use of the term *sètte* – its more theoretical definition in the introduction to Book VII as well as in the historical account – it is clear that Machiavelli sees them in entirely negative terms, but that he tries to separate them from the legitimate and 'natural' groups which he had theorised about in the introduction to Book III. It seems then that Rousseau did not really misunderstand Machiavelli when he cited his distinction between two kinds of divisions in the *Contrat social*; Rousseau also distinguished between two kinds of 'différences' of interest among the citizens: one which does not exclude, and even leads to, the 'volonté générale' or 'common interest', in contrast to that which is organised in 'associations partielles' in such a way that they take the place of, and win over, the 'volonté générale'. Obviously, the latter correspond to Machiavelli's 'sètte'. As to Machiavelli's thinking as an anticipation of the legitimacy of modern parties, on the linguistic level he uses *parte* both for the legitimate *umori* and the illegitimate *sètte*, but he clearly condemns lobby-like groups based on the securing of *partigiani* and *amici*. On the political level he pleads – in the *Discorsi* and the *Istorie Fiorentine* – for the abolition of vertical contrapositions and for the acceptance and tolerance of horizontal divisions, based on social differences, not on clans.[54]

Machiavelli's attempt to sort out and separate the two different kinds of discord – carefully distinguished in the introductions to Books III, IV and VII – is counterbalanced, or perhaps jeopardised, by their dynamic overlap and interaction in the historical events which he narrates. He finds mainly two such dynamics. The groups of both kinds remain united as long as they are

---

[53] *IF*, I/5, p. 637; III/3, pp. 691–2; III/5, pp. 692–5 ('famiglie fatali'); *IF*, IV/11, p. 721; V/2, p. 739 ('sette di armi'); VI/23, p. 780.

[54] Hence, concerning the *sètte* which Machiavelli sees embodied most clearly in the *Parte Guelfa*, his attitude is by no means an 'entschiedenste Abkehr von der mittelalterlichen Tradition' (Faul, 'Verfemung', pp. 67–8); but it is true for his opinion on the *umori*. See also Bertelli, 'Embrioni di partiti politici', pp. 34–5. For the concept of 'tolerance' see *Discorsi*, I/6, pp. 86–7: 'Credo ch'e' sia necessario . . . quelle inimicizie che intra il popolo ed il senato nascessino, tollerarle, pigliandole per uno inconveniente necessario a pervenire alla romana grandezza.'

suppressed, and they divide themselves once they are in power. Secondly, the *sètte* usually use, in their own conflicts and for their own ends, one of the social classes and their conflicts, and vice versa. In Book II, the division between Guelphs and Ghibellines is a conflict between families and simultaneously instrumentalises and represents the conflict between nobles and the people. In Book III, Machiavelli summarises the interaction:

On the side of the Guelph party were all the families of the old nobility and the greater part of the most powerful *popolani*, with Messer Lapo (di Castiglionchio), Piero (degli Albizzi) and Carlo (Strozzi) as leaders. On the other side were all the lesser *popolani*, the leaders being the Eight of the War Council, Messer Giorgio Scali, and Tommaso Strozzi, with whom the Ricci, Alberti and the Medici went along. The rest of the multitude, as almost always happens, sided with the party of the malcontents.[55]

The divisions and alliances between classes or parts thereof, and families or parts thereof, cause him to summarise a similar situation in Book IV in the words of Niccolò da Uzano, when he advised the anti-medicean *parte* in 1433 not to kill Cosimo: 'You have christened our party the nobles' party and the opposition the plebeian party', but this does not correspond to reality, because

many families, even many households, are divided; people side with them against us out of envy for brothers or kinsmen. I will remind you of some of the most important cases, and you can think of the others for yourself. Of Maso degli Albizzi's sons, Luca has gone over to their party out of envy for Rinaldo; in the Guicciardini household, of the sons of Luigi, Piero opposes Giovanni and favours our enemies; Tommaso and Niccolò Soderini oppose us openly because of the hatred they bear their uncle, Francesco. Hence, taking into consideration the character of both parties, I do not know why our party should deserve to be called noble any more than theirs does.[56]

On the other hand, the rise of the 'parte de' Medici' is seen both as a result of its rivalry with the anti-Medicean part of the oligarchy and of its alliance with the lower classes who resented the oligarchical rule. Both *Istorie Fiorentine* and *Discursus* leave no doubt as to Machiavelli's belief, and criticism of the fact, that Cosimo gradually undermined the republic and transformed it into a *principato*. At first, the Medici were able to use civil discord in their favour ('civil discord always increased Cosimo's power in Florence'); later, after the 1460s, 'lo stato de' Medici' succeeded in extinguishing open and public conflict and Cosimo was no longer of 'equal authority' but became the 'only authority' in the city. He became 'principe nella sua patria', and 'lo stato di Cosimo' tended 'more toward a principate than a republic'.[57] But both texts also leave no doubt that

[55] *IF*, III/8, p. 696. For another example of such interaction of *umori* and *sètte* see *IF*, II/12, p. 666.
[56] *IF*, IV/27, p. 732. For this speech, Machiavelli had a source in Cavalcanti, but he completely rewrote it: Cavalcanti *Istorie Fiorentine*, ed. G. Di Pino (Milan, 1944), pp. 143–4. See also the references in note 39 above.
[57] *IF*, VII/5, pp. 795–6; VIII/1, p. 817; *Discursus*, p. 24–5. See also J.M. Najemy, 'Machiavelli and the Medici: the lessons of Florentine history', *Renaissance Quarterly*, 35 (1982), 551–76.

Machiavelli was equally critical of the *parte* of Cosimo's opponents, because they aspired to precisely the same end – the term *principe* is often used in respect to them – and he saw their oligarchical hegemony as equally harmful to the republic.[58] Machiavelli's view of the overlap between the *sètte* and more acceptable kinds of civil discord, and of the predominance of the *sètte* in Florentine history may well be due, as has been suggested, to his insight 'that the real cause of the irruption of *sètte* on to the political stage was the impossibility of mediating the heightened conflict between *popolo* and *grandi*'.[59]

This historical development – or rather Machiavelli's study of it – may be the reason why he presented his theoretical reflections about the *sètte* only in the seventh introductory chapter and not in the earlier ones or in the prologue, even though this concept proved so central to his overall judgement on the harms and benefits of civil discord to the republic, particularly in his later years (the *Discorsi* had dealt with *sètte* in quite a different way).[60] In fact, during the fifteenth century the open conflict between nobility and people had moved to the back of the political stage, and it revived when the Consiglio Maggiore was introduced in 1494.[61] Machiavelli's own political experience had been shaped by this revival, even though it was only *post res perditas* that he pronounced on, and took sides in, these tensions.[62] This experience may have shaped his insight not only into Florentine politics, but also into Florentine history. When, after having written the narrative of Books I–VI of the *Istorie Fiorentine*, he wrote the introductions to these six books and then took up the seventh, the debate on the Florentine constitution and its reform, in which he actively participated, had recently reached a culminating point. His *Discursus*, which included historical sections, and the *Istorie Fiorentine*, which included theoretical sections, were not only an expression of the more 'democratic' reform tendencies, but also an attempt to reflect both theoretically and historically on the problems of and obstacles to such a reform, particularly among the

---

[58] *IF*, III/9, p. 697; III/18, p. 706; III/21, p. 709; III/22, p. 709; IV/27, pp. 732–4; VII/12, p. 801; *Discursus*, pp. 24–6. The anti-medicean faction pursued, according to Machiavelli, a policy which ran counter to the Medicis' financial generosity but was equally harmful to the republic: the imposition of taxes ('gravezze'), particularly on the lower classes, for the purpose of war. The Medici are presented as supporters of a more benevolent taxation (*IF*, IV/4–10, pp. 717–21; IV/14–15, pp. 722–4; VII/17, pp. 829). In *IF*, IV/14, Machiavelli argues very similarly as in *Discorsi*, I/37 in terms of human nature and of equality (see note 34 above): 'Ma come accade che mai gli uomini non si sodisfanno, e avuto una cosa, non vi si contentando dentro, ne desiderano un'altra, il popolo, non contento alla ugualità della gravezza che dalla legge nasceva, domandava che si riandassero i tempi passati, e che si vedesse quello che i potenti, secondo il catasto, avevano pagato meno . . .' (p. 723). Machiavelli seems to underline, in important sections, 'le sustanze' which were so crucial to *Discorsi*, I/37 and to the Ciompi revolt.

[59] Cadoni, 'Machiavelli teorico', p. 220.   [60] *Discorsi*, II/5, p. 154; III/1, p. 195.

[61] Rubinstein, 'I primi anni' and 'Oligarchy and Democracy', pp. 107–10, his contribution to this volume and his comments at the 1987 conference; see also Samuel Cohn, 'The character of protest in mid-Quattrocento' in *Il Tumulto dei Ciompi*, pp. 199–219, esp. pp. 218–19.

[62] See Robert Black's chapter 4 in this volume; Ridolfi, *Vita*, p. 213.

'Florentines who are unable to keep liberty and cannot put up with servitude'.[63] He used current terms of the Florentine tradition of political language and transformed them into categories and typologies, attempting – theoretically – to control civil discords by naming them and – politically – by tolerating and institutionalising them within the constitutional framework.[64]

There are differences, then, in Machiavelli's judgement on civil discord between the *Discorsi* and the *Istorie Fiorentine*, but not contradictions, and the choice is not between a Machiavelli who analysed and favoured the *principato* and unscrupulous politics, and a resigned Machiavelli who believed in a harmonious, unified and pacified republic. Precisely because he was a convinced republican – in respect to the city-state[65] – he perceived and analysed the fact that in republics there are contrasting interests, harsh conflicts, power relations, tyranny and amorality. But it is only in the republican order that the discords among the various human *umori* can and must be expressed; on the other hand, it is these very discords that continually threaten it. They are both the life and the death of the republic.

[63] *IF*, ii/36, p. 684; similarly in *IF*, iii/5, p. 694. For the debate on the Florentine constitution, which lasted until the suppression of the conspiracy of 1522, see esp. von Albertini *Das florentinische Staatsbewusstsein*; Guidi, 'La teoria delle "tre ambizioni"'; Silvano, '*Vivere civile*'. Machiavelli's insistence on the *sètte* in the introduction to Book vii might suggest the possibility that he wrote it after 1522; I am grateful to Nicolai Rubinstein for drawing my attention to this possibility. For the problem of the chronology of Machiavelli's writing the first books of the *IF*, see Ridolfi, *Vita*, esp. pp. 315–320, 328, 566; Levi, 'Due nuovi frammenti'; Felix Gilbert, 'Machiavelli's *Istorie Fiorentine*: an essay in interpretation' in Gilmore, ed. *Studies on Machiavelli*, pp. 73–99; Carlo Dionisotti, 'Machiavelli storico' in Dionisotti, *Machiavellerie*, pp. 365–409.

[64] I am grateful to John Najemy who underlined, at the 1987 conference, the importance of Machiavelli's efforts at, and faith in, controlling political processes by naming and categorising them.

[65] In the *IF*, Machiavelli does not – or at least not in any explicit way – ground his favourable judgement on the discord of the *umori* on the view that they constitute the dynamic force for expansion and empire, as he did in the *Discorsi* (see *Discorsi*, 1/4 and, e.g., note 54 above). Therefore, the argument of the *IF* seems not to contribute to the question as to whether Machiavelli's positive view of civil discord was secondary to that of expansion or vice versa. But it suggests that at least for the late Machiavelli, civil discord was more crucial than expansion and empire.

PART III

Machiavelli and the republican heritage

10

The Machiavellian moment and the Dutch Revolt: the rise of Neostoicism and Dutch republicanism

MARTIN VAN GELDEREN

In the first half of the sixteenth century, when their republic was starting to collapse, Florentine political theorists confronted the problem of the instability of their republic. As trained humanists, standing in the tradition of fifteenth-century Florentine political thought, they conceptualised the fight for the stability of the republic in terms of a fight between *virtù* and *fortuna*, thus giving rise to a distinct republican political language. According to Pocock's analysis the republican language of the Machiavellian moment, with Machiavelli as one of the leading authors, has been of tremendous importance in the development of modern political thought in that it shaped an Atlantic republican tradition up to the American revolution.[1]

In the second half of the sixteenth century the Low Countries were also faced with a collapse of their *res publicae*, during what is now called the Dutch Revolt. The decades of resistance to the government of Philip II, of his abjuration by the States-General in 1581, and of the haphazard foundation of the Dutch Republic have produced an impressive body of political literature. This article is a first attempt to study the relationship between the political thought of the Dutch Revolt (1555–90) and the 'Machiavellian moment'. Its aim is briefly to reconstruct the development of Neostoic and republican patterns of ideas during the Revolt and to indicate their relation to the political language of the Machiavellian moment.[2]

---

[1] J.G.A. Pocock, *The Machiavellian Moment. Florentine Political Thought and the Atlantic Republican Tradition* (Princeton, 1974).

[2] In two articles Pocock himself has studied the relation between the Machiavellian moment, the Atlantic republican tradition and Dutch seventeenth- and eighteenth-century political thought. See J.G.A. Pocock, 'The problem of political thought in the eighteenth century: patriotism and politeness (with comments of E.O.G. Haitsma Mulier and E.H. Kossmann)', *Theoretische Geschiedenis*, vol. 9, no. 1 (April 1982), pp. 3–37; and J.G.A. Pocock, 'Spinoza and Harrington: An exercise in comparison', *Bijdragen en Mededelingen betreffende de Geschiedenis der Nederlanden*, vol. 102, no. 3 (1987), p. 435–49. Recent reactions to his interpretations are found in: E.H. Kossmann, 'Dutch Republicanism' in E.H. Kossmann, *Politieke theorie en geschiedenis; verspreide opstellen en voordrachten* (Amsterdam, 1987), pp. 211–34 and E.O.G. Haitsma Mulier, 'The language of seventeenth-century republicanism in the United Provinces: Dutch or European?' in *The Languages of Political Theory in Early-modern Europe*, ed. Anthony Pagden, (Cambridge, 1987), pp. 179–95.

NEOSTOICISM

In 1589 Justus Lipsius, 'professor historiarum et iuris' at the recently founded University of Leiden published his *Politicorum sive civile doctrinae libri sex*, his *Sixe bookes of politickes or civil doctrine* as the 1594 English translation was titled.[3] With his *Politics* Lipsius wanted to instruct people, and princes in particular, in government how they, employing the precepts of the classic authors, should 'set forward in the way of civil life [*vita civilis*], and finish thy journey without wandering'[4] and without being carried away by the whims of fortune.

Completely in line with the humanist fashions of his time Lipsius argued that to attain a *vita civilis*, 'that which we leade in the societie of men, one with another, to mutuall commoditie and profit, and common use of all',[5] man had to be guided by prudence and virtue.

In the Lipsian analysis government was crucial in attaining the *vita civilis*. Quoting Seneca and Livy, Lipsius described government as 'the chaine by which the commonwealth is linked together . . . the vitall spirit, which so many millions of men do breath'.[6] Government is the 'rod of Circes, which tameth both men, and beasts, that are touched therewith, whereby each one is brought in awe and due obedience, where before they were all fierce and unruly'.[7] Lipsius left no doubt that among the possible forms of government princely rule was to be preferred. The principality, which he defined as 'the governement of one, imposed according to custome, and lawes, undertaken, & executed for the good of the subiects',[8] was not only the most 'ancient kind of commanding', and 'most agreeable to nature', it was also consonant with reason.[9]

As Lipsius' definition explicitly stated, the prince ruled for the benefit of his subjects. The ultimate purpose of the principality was to serve the *bonum publicum*. Quoting Cicero, Lipsius argued that 'a governour of a state, ought to propose, and set before him, the happie life of his citisens: that the same may be strengthened in wealth, aboundaunt in riches, renowned and magnificant in glorie, honest and venerable thorow vertue'.[10] To accomplish his task, and thus to achieve greatness, a prince needed prudence in his actions and virtue in his life, as Lipsius put it. Above all a virtuous prince needed the sun of justice, 'the foundation of eternall fame and renowne'[11] and the moon of clemency, 'a vertue

---

[3] In 1590 a Dutch translation was published. Its title was *Politica . . . Dat is: vande regeeringhe van landen ende steden in ses boecken begrepen. Waer inne een yeghelijck vorst, oft andere inde regeeringhe ghestelt zijnde, claerlijck mach sien, hoe dat hij die ghemeene sake behoorlijck sal moghen bedienen* ('Politics . . . That is: of the government of countries and cities comprehended in six books. Wherein each prince, or other set in government, can see clearly how he should properly serve the commonwealth')..

[4] Justus Lipsius (1594), *Sixe bookes of politickes or civile doctrine, written in Latine by Iustus Lipsius: which doe especially concerne Principalitie* (London; reprinted in the series 'The English experience', no. 287, Amsterdam/New York, 1970), p. 1.   [5] *Ibid.*   [6] *Ibid.*, pp. 16–17.

[7] *Ibid.*, p. 17.   [8] *Ibid.*, p. 19.   [9] *Cf.* Lipsius, *Sixe bookes*, p. 18.   [10] *Ibid.*, p. 23.

[11] *Ibid.*, p. 28, where Lipsius is quoting Cicero's *De Officiis*.

of the mind, which with judgment, enclineth from punishment, or revenge, to lenitie'.[12] Justice had to be complemented by loyalty [*fides*], and, since the prince 'is but a man, though he rule over men', clemency needed the company of 'modestie'.

In the first book of his politics Lipsius had already argued that virtue was to be accompanied by prudence, especially because 'al vertue consisteth in election and meanes to bring things to passe, which we cannot purchase without prudence: therefore without it vertue is not obtained'.[13] In the third book of the *Politics* Lipsius argued that a prince was first of all in need of what he called 'forraine prudence'. As it was impossible for the prince to acquire perfect knowledge, he needed good counsel. More specifically the prince needed two sorts of assistants: 'counsellers', who assisted 'with their opinion and speach', and 'ministers', like 'governors, presidents, officers of the Exchequer, Iudges', who assisted 'with action, and handy worke'. Lipsius described in detail what sort of counsellors and ministers a prince needed, and how their work should be organised.

In discussing the 'proper prudence' of the prince himself, Lipsius argued that the prince needed both civil and military prudence. In his analysis of civil prudence Lipsius put forward his controversial claims concerning heresy. As Lipsius was of opinion that 'one religion is the author of unitie; and from a confused religion there always groweth dissention',[14] he judged it a matter of civil prudence to persecute and punish public heresy.[15]

Another controversial aspect of Lipsius' analysis of civil prudence was his plea for a 'mixed prudence'. Lipsius argued that occasionally it was necessary to intermingle prudence with a 'fewe drops of deceipt'. In a rhetorical vein he asked whether 'the Prince may not sometimes having to deale with a foxe, play the foxe, especially if the good and publike profit, which are always conioyned to the benefit, and profit of the Prince, doe require it?'[16] The ultimate criterion for Lipsius here was 'the good of the common wealth', that is, he judged it

---

[12] *Ibid.*, p. 31. [13] *Ibid.*, p. 11. [14] *Ibid.*, p. 62.

[15] In the Lipsian analysis those who 'erre in private' were not to be persecuted: 'No Prince can rule the mindes in like sort as he may the tongs of men. God is the king of mens minds' (p. 65). It was a matter of temperance to deal with this sort of heresy by way of teaching and instruction. His plea for the persecution of public heresy brought Lipsius into conflict with Coornhert, who furiously attacked Lipsius in the 'Proces van ketterdoden en dwang der conscientien', accusing him of being a papist and a Machiavellian. According to De Nave it was primarily because of this conflict that Lipsius decided to leave Leiden in 1591. Eventually he returned to Louvain. See Francine de Nave, 'De polemiek tussen Justus Lipsius en Dirck Volckertsz. Coornhert (1590): Hoofdoorzaak van Lipsius' vertrek uit Leiden (1591)', *De Gulden Passer*, 48 (1970), pp. 1–39. For a more balanced view see M.E.H.N. Mout, 'In het schip: Justus Lipsius en de Nederlandse Opstand tot 1591' in *Bestuurders en geleerden*, S. Groenveld, M.E.H.N. Mout and I. Schoffer, eds. (Amsterdam/Dieren, 1985), pp. 55–64, who makes it clear that Lipsius also left Leyden because he did not agree with political developments in the United Provinces.

[16] Lipsius, *Sixe bookes*, p. 113.

prudent for the prince to employ 'light' and 'middle' deceipt – and Lipsius took great pains to explain these concepts – if the *bonum publicum* was at stake.

Next to civil prudence Lipsius stressed the importance of military prudence. In the fifth book of the *Politics* he developed a detailed blue-print for a disciplined, virtuous standing army. The soldiers for this army should be 'elected', as Lipsius put it, out of the proper subjects. Strangers not only were 'treacherous' and 'rebellious', they also lacked the affection for prince and country which was 'ingrafted' in the subjects by nature.

Lipsius' analysis of how, and on basis of what criteria, these soldiers had to be elected from the subjects, offered one of the few instances in the *Politics* where the citizens are brought to the fore. The citizen, in fact, was the missing character in the *Politics*. However, Lipsius had discussed the role of the citizen in political life in another book, his famous *De Constantia*, published in 1584.

The *Two bookes of constancie*, the title of the English translation published in 1594, were intended to offer a word of comfort *in publicis malis*. *De Constantia* was, in the words of Oestreich, 'a work of moral philosophy with a humanist foundation, a prescription for the behaviour of the individual in the state, society and politics'.[17] It urged the reader to endure the times of troubles with constancy, which was defined as the 'sincere and immovable strength of the mind that is neither elated nor downcast by outward or fortuitous circum-stances'.[18] Strength in this context referred to what Lipsius called 'a firmness implanted in the heart, not by any delusion or opinion, but by judgment and right reason'.[19] Guided by reason one should patiently endure the whims of fortune and fate without lamenting. As Lipsius stressed, such an attitude did not amount to defeatism. It was the result of calculation on the scale of reason, that taught one to act and to acquiesce at the proper moment.

De Constantia warned against a too strong affection for the fatherland. It reminded the reader that the Patria had been founded by the ancestors out of private interests, because they realised it would contribute to their own welfare. It was proper for the citizen to love and defend his country, even to die for it. However, he should not lament it. For ultimately only heaven was man's one and true fatherland. The earthly fatherland was submitted to the laws of growth and decline. And Providence could not be resisted. Thus, as Oestreich put it, 'there is only one duty which the civis must always perform: in the fortunes and misfortunes of political life he must retain his constancy, follow reason and curb his natural instincts'.[20]

These ideas were reflected in the final book of the *Politics*, that dealt with civil war. According to Lipsius nothing was more 'miserable' and 'dishonorable' than civil war, 'the verie sea of calamities', and he urged princes to prevent it. In

---

[17] Gerhard Oestreich, *Neostoicism and the Early Modern State* (Cambridge, 1982), p. 13.
[18] J. Lipsius, *Twee boecken van de Stantvasticheyt* (Leiden, 1584), p. 21. See Oestreich, *Neostoicism*, p. 19. [19] *Ibid.* [20] *Ibid.*, p. 29.

this context the citizens were warned never to cause a civil war, or to participate in it, not even in the case of tyranny: 'Let them endure things present, in hope of amendment'.[21]

Lipsius was the first Dutch political thinker to acknowledge openly Machiavelli's value as political analyst[22] and it is tempting to put his *Politics* next to Machiavelli's. For both the essence of the art of politics was to establish how virtue could conquer fortune in order to realise a *vivere civile*. Both Machiavelli's and Lipsius' accounts squarely stood within the humanist tradition of the study of politics. As trained humanists both employed the language and the 'organising categories' of this tradition. Thus their analyses of princely rule were embedded in the humanist mirror-for-princes tradition. The prince was presented as the *vir virtutis*, who with virtuous and prudent acts had to fight capricious fortune in order to achieve glory and greatness. The qualities the prince needed to do so were scrupulously outlined and both Machiavelli and Lipsius presented thorough humanist analyses of classical virtues like clemency, modesty and prudence.

However, at the same time, at crucial points both Machiavelli and Lipsius discarded the humanist mirror-for-princes tradition. First of all, and here Lipsius was surely following the Machiavellian lead,[23] both argued that the traditionally overarching virtues of justice and honesty should be hurt if the common good was at stake. Secondly, Machiavelli and Lipsius had a much keener eye for the realities of power politics than their humanist predecessors. Thus they stressed the importance of a strong and disciplined army, Machiavelli arguing for a disciplined civic militia, and Lipsius arguing for a disciplined standing army which was largely chosen from the subjects themselves.

However, although Machiavelli and Lipsius worked out of the same political language, and performed a number of strikingly similar innovations with regard to the humanist mirror-for-princes tradition, there are essential differences between their political theories. Lipsius was by no means the 'philosopher of [republican] liberty' Machiavelli had been.[24] On the contrary, Lipsius' *Politics* contained no conception of liberty whatsoever. As Oestreich especially has shown, Lipsius was one of the leading protagonists in the rise of Neostoicism. In its essence, according to Oestreich, the Neostoic doctrine

---

[21] Lipsius, *Six bookes*, p. 202.
[22] Others did so in private. For example, Aggaeus of Albada, another important political thinker of the Dutch Revolt, who in a letter written in 1571 to Hector of Aytta recommended Machiavelli's historical work. *Cf.* K. van Berkel, 'Aggaeus de Albada en de crisis in de Opstand (1579–1587)', *Bijdragen en mededelingen betreffende de Geschiedenis der Nederlanden (BMGN)*, 96 (1981), no. 1, p. 5. For the reception of Machiavelli's work in the Dutch republic I refer to Haitsma Mulier (chapter 12 in the present volume) who also discusses Lipsius.
[23] See also Francine de Nave, 'Peilingen naar de oorspronkelijkheid van Justus Lipsius politiek denken', *Tijdschrift voor rechtsgeschiedenis*, 38 (1970), p. 474.
[24] The term is Quentin Skinner's. See Quentin Skinner, *Machiavelli* (Oxford, 1981), ch. 3, pp. 48ff.

'demanded self-discipline and the extension of the duties of the ruler and the moral education of the army, the officials, and indeed of the whole people, to a life of work, frugality, dutifulness and obedience'.[25] As such, Oestreich argued, Neostoicism, and Lipsius in particular, provided the philosophical and moral foundation for the modern state: 'For the Lipsian view of man and the world, carried over into the realm of politics, entails rationalization of the state and its apparatus of government, autocratic rule by the prince, the imposition of discipline on his subjects, and strong military defence.'[26] Oestreich even claimed that Lipsius' Neostoic ideology offered the first blueprint for 'the qualities and duties of a modern bureaucracy'.[27]

Unlike modern bureaucracies, however, the 'counsellers' and 'ministers' from the third book of the *Politics* do not seem to represent a relatively autonomous apparatus of government, a rationalised power structure which would exist independently of those in charge of government. They were still very much the personal advisers of the prince, appointed by him to enhance his prudence. The Lipsian governmental apparatus still seems to be the patrimony of the prince, and in this sense it is premature to present Lipsius as the philosopher of the modern state.

This does not alter the fact that the Neostoic plea for princely rule differed widely from the Machiavellian republic. Whereas Machiavelli accepted the inevitability of opposing groups of citizens, and pleaded for a balanced republican structure of government that created room for fruitful and active participation in government by all groups,[28] Lipsius simply abhorred any sign of civic discord. The crux of his argument was that a *vivere civile* could only be attained by means of unified, virtuous princely rule. In his analysis civic virtue amounted to a patient fulfilment of tasks in obedience to the prince.[29] In short, while Machiavelli was 'the philosopher of liberty', Lipsius was 'the philosopher of constancy and obedience'.

REPUBLICANISM

Neostoicism was a typical offspring of Renaissance humanism. Quentin Skinner has emphasised that the 'vocabulary of Renaissance moral and political thought' as a whole was to an important extent derived from 'Roman Stoic sources'.[30] However, according to Oestreich, as a coherent moral and political philosophy Neostoicism was especially developed in the Netherlands, and Oestreich did

---

[25] Oestreich, *Neostoicism*, p. 7.   [26] *Ibid.*, p. 30.   [27] *Ibid.*, p. 45.

[28] See Gisela Bock (ch. 9 in the present volume) for an analysis of Machiavelli's thoughts concerning civic discord.   [29] *Cf.* Oestreich, *Neostoicism*, p. 35.

[30] Quentin Skinner, *The Foundations of Modern Political Thought*, vol. 1: *The Renaissance* (Cambridge, 1978), p. xiv.

not hesitate to speak in terms of the 'Netherlands movement'.[31] According to Oestreich, as a political philosophy Neostoicism was particularly practical in character. Neostoic theorists sought to give answers to the pressing political problems of the day. Thus, Lipsius' blueprint for a disciplined standing army was adapted and applied – with great success – by Maurice of Nassau in the war against Spain. At the same time, Lipsius was rather elusive with regard to other pressing and very actual political problems. Lipsius neither explicitly commented upon the rightfulness of the resistance against Philip II and the abjuration of the Spanish king by the States-General, nor did he explicitly discuss what sort of government the Dutch provinces needed in the 1580s and afterwards. The provincial States and the States-General, so prominent in actual Dutch politics, did not enter the Lipsian analysis of politics at all.[32] In this sense Lipsius' *Politics*, probably deliberately, stood somewhat aloof from the mainstream of political debate in the Netherlands. In this debate conceptions of liberty were of crucial importance.[33] From the very beginning of the protests against the policy of Philip II's government, its religious policy of persecuting Protestant heretics in particular, the defence of the liberty of the fatherland had been a leading theme in political literature. In his *Defence of the Count of Hoorne* Jacques of Wesembeeke, former pensionary of Antwerp, stressed how, traditionally, liberty had been cherished in the Netherlands. It was argued that the prosperity of the Dutch provinces was built upon their liberty. In the words of another political treatise of the 1560s, 'Merchandise', 'Manufacture' and 'Negotiations' were the sisters of 'Liberté', who herself was presented as the daughter of the Netherlands.[34]

However, as Wesembeeke and other authors pointed out in detail, the policy of the central government was destroying both liberty and prosperity. This would lead 'to the complete ruination of the whole country, which was standing solely on its liberty and freedom (and the trade, merchandise and the multitude of goods and persons, which through this had come by themselves)'.[35] It became a commonplace to state that the principal aim of the resistance was 'none other than to defend the liberty of the fatherland, to free oneself of

---

[31] *Cf.* Oestreich, *Neostoicism*, Part I, *passim*. In the light of Montaigne's work, for example, Oestreich's claim seems a little too enthusiastic.

[32] In itself Lipsius' silence here was probably highly significant for his views. As Mout has made clear Lipsius, who was in touch with the leading politicians of his day, in his more private contacts favoured a more centralised princely rule for the Netherlands. He considered the States' government of the 1580s a catastrophe. See Mout, 'In het schip', *passim*.

[33] The following is a highly condensed abstract of the reconstruction of the political thought of the Dutch Revolt as undertaken in my PhD thesis 'The political thought of the Dutch Revolt (1555–1590)', European University Institute, Florence, 1988, of which a revised version will be published by Cambridge University Press.

[34] *Complainte de la désole Terre du Pais Bas* (1568), p. 3.

[35] J. of Wesembeeke, *De beschriivinge van den geschiedenissen in der Religien saken toeghedragen in den Nederlanden* (1567), p. 39.

servitude, to reform all the abuses and orders, which, under the shadow of religion and the authority of His Majesty held the States and the whole country in check, in sum to redress everything which is against liberty, under whatever title it may have been introduced, be it religion, the authority of His Majesty or whatever else'.[36] As this quotation from the *Discours contenant le vray entendement de la Pacification de Gand*, published in 1579, revealed, there was in this conception a strong connection between the liberty of the fatherland and the personal liberty of its inhabitants. The basic argument was that if the liberty of the country was lost, its inhabitants would become 'the worst slaves in the world'.[37]

In the political treatises that sought to justify the resistance against the government of Philip II, the evildoers such as Granvelle and Alva were accused of violating the privileges, liberties and franchises of the Dutch provinces. These privileges were presented as the very embodiment of liberty. For example, in 1574 a *True warning* against Philip's governor Requesens argued that the 'ancestors deserve high praise for having maintained those laudable customs and laws. We should all set ourselves to have them maintained from now on, if we want to be free, and not slaves; if we want to be governed with justice and not overtaken by violence and tyranny'.[38]

The privileges were the fundamental laws of the country and the oath, by which Philip II in accordance with the traditions of the Burgundian Netherlands had sworn to uphold and protect the privileges, became presented as the sealing of a formal contract between the overlord and his subjects, on whose terms he had been accepted. The oath was, as the States of Holland and Zeeland argued in 1573, the 'sole and right foundation on which both the power and authority of the prince and the loyalty and obedience of the subjects is grounded'.[39] The terms of the contract between prince and people were stipulated in the privileges.

Special reference was usually made to the Joyous Entry of Brabant, the main privilege of Brabant which from 1356 was confirmed by every Duke of the province on the occasion of his inauguration and which arranged the distribution of powers in Brabant to a considerable extent. An important aspect of the Joyous Entry was that it contained a clause of disobedience which granted the subjects the right to disobey a prince who violated the privilege until he had mended his ways.

Jacques of Wesembeeke was among the first to point out that the privileges ordained the prince to seek the approval and consent of the States in matters of

---

[36] *Discours contenant le vray entendement de la Pacification de Gand* (1579), p. 23. See also p. 95.

[37] Wesembeeke, *De beschriivinge*, p. 38.

[38] *Waerachtighe waerschowinge teghens de absolute gratie ende generael pardon by Don Loys de Requesens* (Dordt, 1574).

[39] *Sendbrief in forme van supplicatie aen die Conincklicke Maiesteyt van Spaengien* (Delft, 1573), p. Aiij.

great importance, especially when 'the welfare and tranquillity of the country', its 'freedom' and the 'salvation, bodies and goods' of its inhabitants were at stake.[40] This idea was turned into a basic principle of the Dutch political order. A *Defence and True Declaration*, published in 1571, asserted boldly that 'princes have in all ages from tyme to tyme bene subiect to the power of the generall Parliamentes, have bene elected by them, and confirmed of them, without whose assent and authority they never would decree anything and it is manifestly provided and established by the privileges of Brabant and customes of Flaunders, that they never have authoritie to do it hereafter'.[41] It was the States, who, as the States of Holland and Zeeland put it in 1573, 'in the name of the towns and the whole community'[42] accepted a prince and it was their principal task to guard the country's liberty. As the States of Holland and Zeeland urged the States-General in 1573: 'You are the States of the country; which is to say, the upholders and protectors of its liberty and of its privileges; it is your bounden duty by God and all people to defend and to maintain them.'[43]

The prince had to rely completely on the States, 'the chiefe and principall heads of the people representing the body of the multitude'.[44] He was but 'a servant and professor of the country's rights, laws and regulations',[45] appointed to administer justice in accordance with the privileges.

In this vision the States were not only the guardians of liberty, they also formed the main decision-making bodies in the Dutch political order.

A few years later some tracts made the ideological move of representing the States as the leading sovereign power in the Dutch political order. In 1579 a *Brief Discourse* reiterated the view that 'the States have always had so much authority and respect that the dukes and princes have not been able to make any alterations in the matter of sovereignty or been able to levy duties or other taxes, to have new money minted, or to make peace or war without the express consent of the States. This and many other rights and prerogatives are clear from their privileges, the laws and constitutions of the country'.[46] In short, so the *Brief Discourse* argued, the States had 'reserved to themselves the power to decide on all matters concerning sovereignty'.[47]

In 1587, amidst the grave political crisis concerning the position of the

---

[40] J. of Wesembeeke, *Bewijs van den ontschult van Philip van Montmorency, graaf van Hoorne* (1568), p. 151.

[41] *A Defence and True Declaration of the things lately done in the lowe countrey whereby may easily be seen to whom all the beginning and cause of the late troubles and calamities is to be imposed* (London, 1572), p. E7. The *Defence and True Declaration* was a translation of the *Libellus Supplex Imperatoriae*, published in 1570.

[42] *Copie eens sendtbriefs der Ridderschap, Edelen ende Steden van Holland* (Dordrecht, 1573), p. Aiij.

[43] *Copie eens sendtbriefs*, p. Aiij.

[44] *Certeine letters wherein is set forth a Discourse* (1576), p. 62. The original Dutch version of this booklet was published in 1574.

[45] *Vertoog ende openinghe om een goede, salighe ende generale vrede te maken in dese Nederlanden* (1576), p. A5.

[46] *Brief discours sur la negotiation de la paix* (1579), p. B.   [47] *Ibid.*, p. Bij.

governor general, the Earl of Leicester, the States of Holland explicitly addressed the issue of sovereignty. In his famous *Short Exposition*, the pensionary of Gouda, François Vranck, unequivocally asserted that the authority of States was 'the foundation on which the common state of the country rests, which cannot be offended without ruining the common good [*ghemeene saecke*]'[48] and he concluded 'that the sovereignty of the country is with the States in all matters'.[49]

Vranck explicitly stressed the importance of the towns. He pointed out that the authority of the States did not simply spring from the people who happened to participate in it. They only formed the States 'in virtue of the commission of their principals',[50] the nobles and the towns, whom they represented. Nobles and towns were the two orders, the two estates of the province and Vranck depicted the towns of Holland as highly independent political entities, governed 'absolutely' by the city magistrates without the interference of the prince.

According to Vranck this form of government had a long and flourishing history in the provinces of Holland, Zeeland and West-Vrieslandt. The Counts of Holland and Zeeland, he argued, had never taken major political decisions without the advice and consent of the States. The Counts simply had no power in their own right. They were completely dependent on the States, whose special task it was to maintain the rights, freedoms and privileges of the country. Vranck asserted that, due to the 'unity, love and understanding' between Counts and States, this form of government had brought Holland and Zeeland honour, prosperity and 800 years of freedom from foreign oppression. However historically wrong this assertion might have been, it was by no means exceptional. In his *Necessary considerations on a treaty with the Spaniard*, Willem Verheyden warned his fellow countrymen to mistrust the appeasing attitude of Philip II's government and of his governor Parma in particular, who, according to Verheyden, merely applied the teachings of Machiavelli's *Prince*.[51] Verheyden urged his fellow countrymen to uphold the 'exceptional freedom which we have inherited from our ancestors'.[52] Concord was to be retained and measures were to be taken to protect 'a freedom which, I say, for a period of 1,500 years, has never been burdened with slavery by foreign nations'.[53]

---

[48] *Corte verthoninghe van het recht byden Ridderschap van Hollandt ende Westvrieslant van allen ouden tijden in den voorschreven Lande gebruyckt, tot behoudenisse vande vryheden, gherechticheden, Privilegien ende Loffelicke ghebruycken vanden selven Lande* (Rotterdam, 1587), p. Biiij.

[49] *Ibid.* [50] *Ibid.*, p. Bij.

[51] W. Verheyden, *Nootelijcke consideratien die alle goede liefhebbers des Vaderlandts behooren rijpelijck te overweghen opten voorgeslaghen Tractate van Peys met den Spaengiaerden* (1587), fol. B.

[52] *Ibid.* fol. B3.

[53] *Ibid.* fol. C3. In the French version of this pamphlet Verheyden said that this liberty had existed 'depuis le temps de Iule Caesar'. *Cf. Considérations necessaires sur un traicté avec l'espagnol* (1587), fol. C3.

It became a political dogma, and an important part of what has been called the Batavian myth[54] to argue that the liberty of the United Provinces, and of Holland in particular, had been raised by the Batavians, the classic and direct ancestors of the Dutch, and that it had been maintained vigorously ever since. The highlight in this respect was doubtless Grotius' *Treatise of the antiquity of the Batavian now Hollandish Republic'*. Grotius set out to prove that the supervision of the Batavian and Hollandish common good had always resided with the States: 'This power of the States has been the foundation of the republic, the resort of equal justice, the bridle of princely highness.'[55] As such the States had been respected and obeyed by military commanders, kings and counts. They had protected the holy and unbreakable privileges and they had carried Holland's liberty through heavy tempests. Grotius took great pains to show the antiquity of the free Hollandish republic and of its form of government, which was aristocratic in character. The republic had always been governed by the 'Ottimati' [*treffelixten*], representing the two *ordines* of Holland, in the States.[56] Grotius argued that 'for more than 1,700 years the Batavians, now called Hollanders, have used the same government, of which the highest power had been and still is with the States'.[57] The States had always sought to preserve liberty, deeply cherished by the Batavians. Already during the time of the Roman empire they had been respected as 'authors of liberty',[58] as a free, self-governing people willing to do their utmost to retain their freedom.

In truly humanist fashion Grotius' treatise on the republic of Holland, which was published in 1610, in many ways epitomised a pattern of ideas that presented the Dutch political order as built upon liberty, privileges and sovereign States. This pattern of ideas had been developed step by step from the 1560s onwards in a large body of political treatises that first sought to justify the resistance to Philip II and later tried to answer the pressing questions concerning the political course the United Provinces were to take.

In a certain sense, though it was certainly not a watertight, consistent theory,

---

[54] For the history of the Batavian myth see I. Schöffer, 'The Batavian myth during the sixteenth and seventeenth centuries' in *Britain and the Netherlands*, vol. v: *Some Political Mythologies*, J.S. Bromley, E.H. Kossmann, eds. (The Hague, 1975), pp. 78–101. Schöffer points out that the idea of Batavian freedom had come up at the end of the fifteenth century. The Batavian myth gained momentum through sixteenth-century humanism, largely due to the rediscovery of Tacitus' *Germania*. In the 1580s a number of studies focussing on the history of the Batavians were published. Thus, during the Revolt this became a fashionable topic. For example, in Latin Leiden, whose university soon became famous because of its Tacitus studies, was baptised 'Lugdunum Batavorum'.

[55] H. Grotius, *Tractaet vande Oudtheyt vande Batavische nu Hollandsghe Republique* (The Hague, 1610), p. ij.   [56] *Ibid.*, p. 2.

[57] *Ibid.*, pp. 46–47. Grotius explained that in the republic there had also been an element of princely rule. However, the Batavian military commanders, the counts of Holland and the present governors had always been the minor power.

[58] *Ibid.*, p. 19. According to Grotius the Batavians were later called Frisians because this word was so close to the word 'freedom'. See p. 22.

this pattern of ideas represented a 'philosophy of liberty'. From the very beginning liberty was presented as the political value *par excellence*, the 'daughter of the Netherlands', the source of prosperity and justice. The resistance to Philip II was essentially presented as the defence of this very liberty, which was threatened by the lust for power and the tyrannical ambitions of Philip II's government. In fact the political order itself was argued to be deliberately created by the ancestors in order to safeguard liberty. It tried to achieve this goal by means of what can be called a constitutional framework consisting of a set of fundamental laws, the privileges, and institutions, the States. The privileges were the guarantees of liberty. To become lord of the country, a prince had to take a solemn oath to uphold the privileges. They bridled the prince and they contained the terms on which the prince had been accepted, some would say elected, by the States on behalf of the people. The States were representative institutions which owed their authority to their constituent principals, in the case of Holland the nobles and especially the towns. They had been created to check and bridle the prince and to take the important political decisions. Moreover, as sovereign powers it was their prime task to protect the privileges. They were the principal guardians of liberty.

However, in this conception of the Dutch political order, the States were not the only ones to guard liberty. The Hollandish States themselves argued that the protection of the 'freedom, trade and welfare', of the country ought 'to be observed with diligence by each one in accordance with his profession and possibilities'.[59] As some treatises outlined, there was a civic duty to protect liberty. This view was in particular articulated in *Political Education*, a treatise published in 1582. With frequent references to Cicero, *Political Education* pointed out that it was the principal duty of a good patriot to serve the fatherland and to fight for liberty. It was argued that 'for the sake of liberty, and in order to maintain it, one should consider nothing too arduous, and that one should be prepared to die rather than submit to slavery'.[60]

At this point it is tempting to try and draw parallels between the philosophy of liberty as developed during the Dutch Revolt and the Machiavellian republican philosophy of liberty. Machiavelli too cherished liberty as a political value *par excellence*, representing it as the key to greatness.

Machiavelli pointed out that a community could only be free if it was able to govern itself. Liberty entailed self-government. Machiavelli stressed that self-government was a precondition for the personal liberty of the members of a community. They could only hope to escape from political servitude and to have the freedom to pursue their own goals, if the community of which they were members could govern itself in accordance with its own will. As there was

---

[59] *Sendtbrieven byde Ridderschappe, Edelen ende steden van Holland, Representeerende den Staten vanden selven Lande, laetsgheschreven ende ghesonden aenden Byrghermeesteren . . . van Amsterdam* (Delft, 1577).
[60] *Politicq Onderwijs* (Mechelen, 1582), p. B.

no guarantee that the benefit of a ruling prince coincided with the benefit of the community as a whole, Machiavelli concluded that a republican form of government was preferable. As Skinner has pointed out, 'this conclusion – that personal liberty can only be fully assured within a self-governing form of republican community – represents the heart and nerve of all classical republican theories of citizenship'.[61] Addressing the question that marked the Machiavellian moment, how to preserve the free and self-governing republic through time, Machiavelli stressed the vital importance of *virtù*. The republic was what Pocock has called a 'structure of virtue', which meant that 'it was a structure in which every citizen's ability to place the common good before his own was the precondition of every other's, so that every man's virtue saved every other's from that corruption part of whose time-dimension was *fortuna*'.[62]

Machiavelli's answer was a complex one. A crucial part of his argument was that fundamental laws should be devised which more or less forced the individual citizens to place the common good above their private interests. Thus a mixed constitution was needed that merged the three pure Aristotelian forms of government into a 'mixed government', 'one in which the instabilities of the pure forms are corrected while their strengths are combined'.[63] Machiavelli also stressed the importance of vigilance. He pleaded in favour of a strong military defence, based on a virtuous civic militia, and he actually went so far as to conclude that 'the pursuit of dominion abroad' is 'a precondition of liberty at home'.[64]

At certain points the pattern of ideas concerning liberty, as developed during the Dutch Revolt parallels the Machiavellian philosophy of liberty. Both conceived of liberty first of all in terms of self-governance; both recognised that the preservation of the liberty of the commonwealth is a precondition of personal liberty; both argued that to preserve the liberty of the commonwealth one ought to devise proper laws, set up proper institutions and have virtuous citizens and virtuous political leaders; both favoured a 'mixed' form of government.[65]

Next to these parallels crucial differences are to be discerned. First of all, though both philosophies of liberty argued that the freedom of the community

[61] Quentin Skinner, 'The idea of negative liberty: philosophical and historical perspectives' in *Philosophy in History*, eds. Richard Rorty, J.B. Schneewind, Quentin Skinner (Cambridge, 1984), pp. 207–8.
[62] Pocock, *The Machiavellian Moment*, p. 184. See also Skinner, *Machiavelli*, especially pp. 53–7.
[63] *Ibid.*, p. 65.   [64] *Ibid.*, p. 73.
[65] As I have argued elsewhere, if it is the essence and defining characteristic of the republican philosophy of liberty that, unless a commonwealth is maintained in a state of freedom, its inhabitants will lose their personal liberty, and that to preserve the liberty of the commonwealth good laws, proper institutions and civic virtue are required, the philosophy of liberty as developed during the Dutch Revolt with regard to the Dutch political order is principally republican in character.

as a whole was a precondition of the personal liberty of its members, they had strongly diverging ideas concerning personal liberty. For Machiavelli the essence of personal liberty was that men were free 'to marry as they chose; to bring up their families without having fear for their honour or their own welfare; and to be in a position "freely to possess their own property"'.[66] The Dutch ideas also conceived of personal liberty as the free enjoyment of 'body and goods'. However, at the heart of the ideas on personal liberty, as developed during the Dutch Revolt, was the idea that freedom of conscience was the essence of personal liberty. As an anonymous author put it in 1579: 'Everyone knows that the liberty of humans lies above all in the soul, which is our principal part, and because of which we are called humans. The liberty of the soul is the freedom of conscience, which consists in a person being allowed to take up and keep the religion his conscience guides him to, with no one having the right or the power to prohibit or hinder him in this.[67]

The exact meaning and scope of freedom of conscience was a matter of debate among the Dutch revolutionaries. Expressing what can be called the minimal position in the debates on freedom of conscience, the 1579 Union of Utrecht, one of the 'constitutional' documents of the new republic, guaranteed freedom of religion and ordained that no one was to be questioned or persecuted because of his religion. Others, and the leading protagonist here was doubtless Coornhert, argued that freedom of conscience implied freedom of expression and freedom of public worship, thus giving rise to fierce dispute. This dispute reflected a fundamental turn in the conceptions of personal liberty, which, deeply influenced by the Reformatory developments, took place in the course of the sixteenth century. What was at stake now was the freedom of individuals, as far as religion was concerned, to believe what they wanted and to speak freely about their beliefs. Such a conception of freedom was simply alien to the Florentine conceptions at the Machiavellian moment.

A second crucial difference between the Dutch and the Machiavellian views on liberty was that, unlike Machiavelli's, the Dutch republican view of the political order as built on the trinity of liberty, privileges and States was not developed out of the republican language of the Machiavellian moment. Though there were frequent references to the classic authors of republican theory, the political thinkers of the Dutch Revolt did not conceive of the fight for the preservation of the old freedom and the old political order – for that is how they represented the resistance and abjuration – in terms of a fight between *virtù* and *fortuna*. Florentine political thought does not seem to have exerted a positive appeal on the theorists of the Dutch Revolt. Unlike Venice, praised by numerous theorists, Florence had suffered the fate the Dutch were trying to avoid. Machiavelli, in general, was presented as the author of *The Prince*, as 'the compass of the Italian princes' like Farnese, in 1587 Philip II's governor in the reconquered southern Netherlands, teaching them to lie and cheat, and to discard justice.[68] In fact it was not unusual to present the alleged Philip II's Machiavellianism as the root cause of the Dutch troubles.

CONCLUSION

At first sight the relation between the political thought of the Dutch Revolt and the republican theory of the Machiavellian moment is intriguing and in a certain way ironic.

On the one hand, Neostoicism was developed out of the same classic tradition as Florentine republican theory. To an important extent Neostoicism and republican theory had the same epistemological foundation. Neostoicism employed the same 'language' and used the same conceptual scheme and identical organising categories as republican theory. However, in arguing that the *vita civilis* could only be attained in a political order that was marked by unified, virtuous princely rule, Neostoicism plainly refuted republicanism.

On the other hand, the Dutch Revolt witnessed the rise of a republican conception of the Dutch political order as built upon liberty, privileges and sovereign States. Though this conception contained a distinct pattern of republican ideas, it was not developed out of the same political language as the republican theory of the Machiavellian moment. It did not employ the conceptual schemes and the organising categories of Florentine republican theory. It did not conceive the fight over the *res publica* in terms of *virtù* and *fortuna*.

The republican theory of the Machiavellian moment itself does not seem to have been an important source of inspiration for the political authors of the Dutch Revolt. However, the republicanism of the Machiavellian moment and the republicanism of the Dutch revolt may have had a number of important sources of inspiration in common. Of course it is extremely difficult to retrace the origins of sixteenth-century Dutch republicanism, but this does not mean that nothing is to be said on this matter.

First of all it is important to point out that the Dutch printing presses, Plantijn's office in Antwerp being the most spectacular example, in impressive numbers published editions of classic works. The classics were also translated into the vernacular. For example, Coornhert, one of the leading philosophers during the Dutch Revolt, translated amongst other works Boethius' *De*

---

[68] Willem Verheyden, *Nootelijcke consideratien*, fol. B. In the French version Verheyden put it this way: 'Nicolas Machiavelli, l'oreillier, le guide & miroir des Italiens, n'apprend il point un Prince à se tourner selon les ventz, disant, qu'il faut qu'il apparoisse humain, loyal & pitoiable, & qu'il soit le contraire, advenant le besoing? c'est à dire inhumain, desloyal & cruel; & qu'il n'est tenu d'estre tousiours garny de vertu, moyennant qu'il ait apparance de l'estre?' Verheyden, *Considérations nécessaires*, fol. B.

consolatione philosophia, Homer's *Odyssey* anc Cicero's *De officiis*. The political thinkers of the Dutch Revolt frequently referred to classic authors amongst whom Cicero and Sallust seemed to be the favourites. Thus, it can be argued that the republicanism of the Revolt may have been partly the result of the appropriation of the classics in the Netherlands, which implies that it was partly an offspring of Dutch humanism.

Secondly, there is a remarkable similarity between the Dutch republican conceptions of liberty and what Skinner has called 'the scholastic defence of liberty', as developed in the course of the fourteenth century with Marsiglio of Padua and Bartolus of Sassoferrato as leading authors.[69] As Skinner has argued, Marsiglio and Bartolus conceived of liberty in republican terms as political independence and self-government. They saw civil discord as the main danger to liberty. Marsiglio and Bartolus argued that to ensure that sectional interests were set aside and that citizens equated their own good with the good of the community as a whole, an efficient and complex constitutional framework was needed. Its leading principle was that the people (conceived of as a *universitas*, not as a mere sum of individuals) were and remained the sovereign authority in a body politic. If the people conceded authority to a 'ruling part', it was essential to ensure that the 'ruling part' was kept firmly under control. To achieve this goal the scholastic theorists of liberty favoured a number of constitutional arrangements: the ruler was to be elected, he was only allowed a minimal discretion in administering the law (which was his basic task) and a complex network of checks amongst the magistrates and ruling councils was to be devised.

Later this analysis was reiterated and elaborated by authors like Mario Salomonio, whose treatise on the sovereignty of the Roman patriciate was completed in 1514 and published in 1544.

Essentially the 'scholastic defence of liberty' was built on constitutional devices, and in this respect theorists of the Dutch Revolt may have followed its lead. Authors like Marsiglio, Bartolus and Salomonio were probably well known in the Netherlands, especially amongst those who had studied law. A fine example here is Aggaeus of Albada's annotated publication of the acts of the 1579 Cologne peace negotiations, which appeared in 1581. Albada, spokesman for the States-General during the negotiations, not only referred to Bartolus, he also based his argument concerning popular sovereignty to a considerable extent on Salomonio's work, which he quoted at length.[70]

In Pocock's analysis Bartolus' and Marsiglio's work are presented as typical of the 'language of law', the other dominant political language of early modern

---

[69] See Quentin Skinner, *The Foundations*, pp. 53–66.
[70] Aggaeus of Albada, *Acten vanden Vredehandel geschiet te Colen* (Leiden, 1581), pp. 101, 105, 161–2. For another example see the treatise *Politicq Onderwijs*, whose author supported his argument with especial reference to Cicero and Bartolus.

Europe, which, at least according to Pocock, differed widely from the republican language. While the 'republican vocabulary . . . articulated the positive conception of liberty', contending 'that homo, the animale politicum, was so constituted that his nature was completed only in a vita activa practiced in a vivere civile',[71] the 'juristic presentation of liberty' was basically 'negative': 'it distinguished between libertas and imperium, freedom and authority, individuality and sovereignty, private and public'.[72] Neglecting the republican aspects of the scholastic conception of liberty, Pocock has argued that in the juristic vocabulary the essence of citizenship was the possession of rights, whereas in the republican vocabulary the essence of citizenship was participation.

It seems possible – and tempting – to conclude that the conception of Dutch political order as built upon liberty, privileges and sovereign States has its place in the history of the political 'language of law'. However, if this conclusion has some validity, one should add that the use of the 'language of the law' by the political authors of the Dutch Revolt was by no means incompatible with the articulation of republican ideas.

Surely, for the theorists of the Dutch Revolt, as in scholastic theory, the defence of liberty was essentially based on a constitutional framework of fundamental laws, the privileges, and a system of checks, with the States in a leading role. Moreover, the theorists of the Dutch Revolt did indeed stress the importance of rights and they also developed a theory of sovereignty, based on the sovereign position of the States, that ultimately coincided with popular sovereignty.

At the same time, as the reconstruction of the development of republican ideas during the Revolt has shown, the vision of the Dutch political order as built upon liberty, privileges and sovereign States, contained a conception of republican self-government. The appeal to the privileges during the Revolt was not merely an appeal to constitutional rights which were being violated. Of course privileges, like the Joyous Entry and the Grand Privilege of 1477, were by no means constitutions in the modern sense of the term. At most privileges, as they accumulated, began to function as 'implicit constitutions'.[73] Privileges were acquired, and often extorted, by cities, guilds, clergy, nobility, etc. from late medieval dukes, counts and other lords. Above all privileges dealt with the problems of the day, and reflected the power relations between the parties involved. Their application was never a simple legal matter, but depended primarily on fluctuations in power relations.

[71] J.G.A. Pocock, 'Virtues, rights and manners. A model for historians of political thought' in J.G.A. Pocock, *Virtue, Commerce and Industry* (Cambridge, 1985), pp. 40–1.   [72] *Ibid.*, p. 40.
[73] W.P. Blockmans, 'La signification "constitutionelle" des privilèges de Marie de Bourgogne (1477)' in: *1477. Le privilège général et les privilèges régionaux de Marie de Bourgogne pour les Pays-Bas* in the series Ancien Pays et Assemblées d'États, vol. LXXX (Kortijk-Heule, 1985), p. 507.

At the same time privileges had important ideological dimensions. The Joyous Entry and the Grand Privilege were extorted at moments when the central government lacked the power to resist the demands of the provinces. Limiting the authority of the central government, they reflected the political views of the provinces and of the cities in particular, often playing a leading role. During the fourteenth and fifteenth centuries the Burgundian Netherlands showed a continuous growth of civic consciousness on the part of the great cities.[74] As Blockmans has stressed,[75] the great cities and those of Brabant and Flanders in particular, consistently sought to create a political order marked by a weak but efficient central government and dominated by cities which wanted to act as self-governing city-republics. Privileges were one of the means to achieve this goal. Thus, the privileges of 1477 can be said to express 'a conception of a federative state, dominated by the great cities'.[76]

In other words, privileges were not just about rights, they were also about participation. When the theorists of the Dutch Revolt appealed to the privileges they were not merely demanding the protection of rights, they were also demanding participation in the decision-making process, especially for the states, whose 'principals' as the 'Short Exposition' called it in 1587, were of course the cities. In short, if the political authors of the Dutch Revolt were employing the 'language of law', for them this language was perfectly suited to express republican claims.[77]

In doing so they articulated republican attitudes that had a long and powerful tradition in the Burgundian Netherlands. The 'great tradition of revolt' as Blockmans has called it, was undoubtedly a major source of inspiration for the political thought and the political praxis of the Dutch Revolt. Thus, when, during the 1570s radical Reformed Protestants tried to impose a new political order on Flanders and Brabant, they were following the traditional model of 'the city-state system, based on the supremacy of the major cities each in their quarter, as they had shaped it during the recurrent revolutionary periods of the 14th and 15th centuries'.[78]

Perhaps for contemporaries such conclusions might have come as no big surprise. In fact, as early as 1566, that is amidst the time of troubles, the Florentine Lodovico Guicciardini, who spent most of his life in Antwerp,

---

[74] For fourteenth-century Brabant this has been shown in P. Avonds, *Brabant tijdens de regering van Hertog Jan III (1312–1356); De grote politieke krisissen*, (Brussels, 1984).

[75] See W.P. Blockmans, 'Alternatives to monarchical centralization: the great tradition of Revolt in Flanders and Brabant' in *Republiken und Republikanismus im Europa der frühen Neuzeit*, H.G. Koenigsberger, ed. (Munich, 1988), pp. 145–154.

[76] Blockmans, 'La signification', p. 516. Thus the great cities favoured co-operation. They were not seeking to destroy central government completely but were attempting to turn it into an efficient part of a federative structure.

[77] As it was, of course, as Skinner has shown, for Marsiglio and Bartolus. See Skinner, *The Foundations*, pp. 53–66.

[78] Blockmans, 'Alternatives', p. 154.

described this city in his famous *Descrittione di tutti i Paesi Bassi* as a perfect Polybian republic, comparable to the republic of Lacedaemon:

Antwerp has as her lord and prince the Duke of Brabant, Margrave of the Holy Empire, but with all the many great privileges it has accumulated from antiquity on, she governs and rules herself almost in the way of a free city and republic. Indeed, in my view complete scrutiny shows it to be a way of governing little different from the form which Polybius, the excellent philosopher and historian, outlined for a true and happy republic; for he wanted her to be a mixture of three types of states, Monarchy, Aristocracy and Democracy, in which the prince has his empire, the 'ottimati' their authority, and the people the power and weaponry.[79]

[79] Lodovico Guicciardini, *Descrittione di tutti i Paesi Bassi* (Antwerp, 1566), p. 132. Lodovico was a nephew of Francesco Guicciardini.

11

◁ ══ ▷

Milton's republicanism and the tyranny of heaven

BLAIR WORDEN

What was republicanism in seventeenth-century England? The term was rarely owned to, and was more commonly one of abuse. Yet there was a movement which needs a word. I mean by republicanism the movement of intellectual protest which opposed the rise of the Renaissance and Baroque monarchies of early modern Europe, and which, in articulating that opposition, drew extensively on the political writings and the political practices of classical antiquity. This was the republicanism whose vocabulary Niccolò Machiavelli had done more than any other writer of the Renaissance to shape. By 1600 Italian republicanism had lost its vitality, although remnants of it survived in Venice, whose constitution was admired elsewhere in Europe as a modern equivalent to that of republican Rome. In the seventeenth century it was in England that Machiavelli's ideas were most substantially developed and adapted, and that republicanism came once more to life; and out of seventeenth-century English republicanism there were to emerge in the next century not only a theme of English political and historical reflection – of the writings of the Bolingbroke circle and of Gibbon and of early parliamentary radicals – but a stimulus to the Enlightenment in Scotland, on the Continent, and in America.[1]

Before the civil wars of the 1640s, republicanism never appeared publicly in didactic or unambiguous form. Few people in Elizabethan or early Stuart England seem to have supposed that the rules of the ancient constitution could be fundamentally changed. The habits of deference, the fear of rebellion, the external threats – those deterrents strengthened the hold of the ancient constitution and confined alternative constitutional theory to abstract specu-lation and to imaginative literature. In Sir Philip Sidney's *Arcadia* (*c.* 1580), it is only the 'discoursing sort of men' who, on the demise of Basilius, an event clearly intended to foreshadow the death of Queen Elizabeth, want 'the state altered and governed no more by a prince', and argue for the introduction of Spartan or Athenian models. Elsewhere Sidney, while advising his brother Robert to study the 'good laws and customs' of Venice, warned him that 'we

---

[1] I describe seventeenth-century English republicanism, more fully than in the present essay, in a chapter of the forthcoming *Cambridge History of Political Thought 1450–1750*, ed. J.H. Burns. The reader who seeks documentary support for statements about republicanism in the earlier part of the present essay is referred to that chapter.

can hardly proportion [them] to ourselves, because they are of a quite contrary government'.[2] Sidney knew his Machiavelli, and the next generation of intellectuals knew their Machiavelli better still. Yet the Florentine's appeal was not an unambiguously republican one. Together with the revulsion engendered by Renaissance courts – by their corrupting techniques of power, by their luxurious ostentation, by their lascivious manners – there could be found, often in the same writers, the fascination with statecraft which made Machiavelli's *The Prince* as influential as his *Discourses*, the black Tacitus a rival to the red Tacitus.

No such tension disturbs the certainties of John Milton, who cites *The Discourses* but not *The Prince*, who is repelled by 'tyrannous aphorisms' and 'reason of state',[3] and to whom Tacitus is simply the 'greatest possible enemy to tyrants'.[4] Milton's pamphlets belong, after all, to a later generation. It took a political revolution to create outward and partisan republicanism in England. In 1649 revolution came. The regicide was not the fruit of republican theory. Most of its organisers were concerned to remove a particular king, not kingship. They cut off King Charles' head and wondered what to do next. In that quandary they saw no practicable alternative to the abolition of monarchy. It was not the victory of the regicides but their failures which encouraged republican speculation. The impermanence of the successive improvised regimes of the Interregnum suggested the need to look more deeply into the principles on which a durable alternative to Stuart rule might be built. Nourished by constitutional failure at home, republicanism throve too on military and naval success abroad. The exploits of the Commonwealth in its wars with Ireland, Scotland and Holland, exploits which contrasted so markedly with England's feeble diplomatic role under the kingly rule of the previous half century, earned awed comparisons with the feats of republican Greece and Rome.

The 1650s are the first and most fertile of the three stages of seventeenth-century English republicanism: the decade of the *Oceana* of James Harrington, the most original republican theorist of the century; of the republican editorials written for the government newspaper *Mercurius Politicus* by Marchamont Nedham; and of the influence of Algernon Sidney and of Henry Nevile in the Rump Parliament which Milton served. The principal works of Sidney and Nevile – the former's *Discourses concerning Government* and the latter's *Plato Redivivus* and his translation of Machiavelli's works – were, however, written later in the century. Their composition belonged to the second stage, the crisis

[2] *The Countess of Pembroke's Arcadia*, ed. Jean Robertson (Oxford, 1973), pp. 320–1; *The Works of Sir Philip Sidney*, ed. Albert Feuillerat (4 vols., Cambridge, 1912–26), iii. 127.

[3] *Complete Prose Works of John Milton*, ed. D.M. Wolfe *et al.* (8 vols., New Haven, 1953–82), i. 573, ii. 375. Parenthetical references to Milton's prose works in my text refer to this edition. When quoting Milton in translation, however, I refer to *The Works of John Milton*, ed. F.A. Patterson *et al.*, (18 vols., Columbia, 1931–4) hereafter cited as *Columbia Milton*, where the original is reproduced on facing pages.   [4] *Columbia Milton*, vii, 317–19.

of 1673–83 provoked by the threats of absolutism and of a popish succession. The last stage came in the 1690s, when fears of mercenary parliaments and of standing armies occasioned the tracts and the editions of Robert Molesworth, Walter Moyle, John Trenchard and Milton's biographer John Toland. The development and variation of republican theory across those three generations are less imposing than the continuity, even the repetition of a body of ideas which the work of Zera Fink, Caroline Robbins, Felix Raab and John Pocock has brightly illuminated.

What was Milton's place among the republican writers of the 1650s? We should not think of them as a closed circle. Seventeenth-century republicans were often distinguished – none of them more clearly than Milton – by a proud independence of mind and spirit which inhibited sustained co-operation. Even so, we know Milton to have been a 'great crony' and 'particular friend' of Marchamont Nedham, his fellow advocate of classical liberty and fellow apologist for the regimes of the 1650s.[5] Nedham was a close associate of Milton's friend and fellow civil servant Andrew Marvell, himself an 'intimate friend' of James Harrington, to whom Milton may have been close by 1648.[6] Whatever the extent or the limits of Milton's relations with those men, no one articulated more eloquently than he the republican understanding of the contrast between healthy and unhealthy government: in 'a free common-wealth', he wrote in early 1660,

they who are greatest are perpetual servants and drudges to the public at their own cost and charges . . . are not elevated above their brethren, live soberly in their families, walk the streets as other men, may be spoken to freely, familiarly, friendly, without adoration. Whereas a king must be adored like a demigod, with a dissolute and haughty court about him, of vast expense and luxury, masks and revels, to the debaushing [debauching] of our prime gentry . . . and all this . . . to pageant himelf up and down in progress among the perpetual bowings and cringings of an abject people. (*Complete Prose Works*, vii. 425–6)

Yet behind that rhetoric we would search in vain for a systematic republican theory. That would not in itself be grounds for excluding Milton from the canon of republicanism, which was never a self-contained or self-sufficient programme, and which made its greatest political and imaginative impact in a diluted rather than a concentrated form – as, in Pocock's words, 'a language rather than a programme'. Even so, there may seem to be grounds for questioning whether Milton can helpfully be called a republican at all. Certainly

---

[5] *The Early Lives of Milton*, ed. Helen Darbishire (London, 1932), pp. 44, 74.

[6] B. Worden, 'Andrew Marvell, Oliver Cromwell, and the Horatian Ode' in *Politics of Discourse*, K. Sharpe and S. Zwicker, eds. (Berkeley and Los Angeles, 1987), pp. 147–80. A poem by 'J. Harington' appears on the same page as Milton's in the volume for Henry Lawes in 1648 (*ibid.*, n. 38). Of course, 'J. Harington' may not be our James Harrington – who did, however, have sufficient poetic inclinations to make and publish translations of Virgil. Equally the presence of two authors on a single page does not prove friendship between them – but it may be an indication of it, as in the case of Marvell and Nedham in 1649: *ibid.*, pp. 159ff.

he supported the regicide, which, he claimed, 'the Greeks and Romans' would have accounted 'a glorious and heroic deed' (iii. 212, vii. 420). Yet that commitment sets him apart from most of the other writers whom we think of as classical republicans; for while Milton exulted in the claims which 'justice and victory' and divine providence had bestowed on the Cromwellian army (iii. 194), other republicans condemned the king's execution as a violent coup, with no roots in political consent or civic virtue. Milton was almost alone among the republicans again in his willingness to support and serve the semi-monarchical protectorate of Oliver Cromwell, a regime bitterly condemned by most of the others as a usurpation. Only after the protectorate had fallen did Milton voice, briefly, an unambiguous hostility to kingship – even to 'the fond conceit of something like a Duke of Venice' (vii. 447). Earlier he had repeatedly explained that his target was not kings but tyrants. 'If I inveigh against tyrants', he asked in 1654, 'what is that to kings? . . . As much as a good man differs from a bad, so much do I maintain that a king differs from a tyrant.'[7] In any case, how high did political thought lie among Milton's scholarly and ethical priorities? 'Piety and justice', he proclaimed in 1641, 'are our foundresses; they stoop not, neither change colour for aristocracy, democracy or monarchy' (i. 605–6). Was it not Harrington's insistence on republican forms that caused Milton's breach with him in 1659–60? Did Milton not, like Cromwell, regard political forms as expendable, mere means to the higher ends of godly reformation and liberty of conscience?

Yet those objections may derive not so much from a distance between Milton's thought and that of his republican contemporaries as from a misrepresentation of the nature of seventeenth-century republicanism. Milton was far from alone among the republicans in distinguishing between kingship and tyranny. 'Nothing is farther from my intention', declared Algernon Sidney, 'than to speak irreverently of kings'. Republicans after all knew from Aristotle and Polybius that a healthy and durable state is one in which there are mixed or balanced the three principles of government – the one, the few and the many – and their corresponding political forms. They were normally prepared to concede the validity of 'mixed', 'limited', 'regulated' monarchy, which they acknowledged to be legal so long as it was rooted in consent, and which they contrasted with the evils of 'absolute monarchy' and of hereditary monarchy; Milton, in distinguishing between the 'Turkish tyranny' of the Stuarts and the 'regulated monarchy' which Stuart rule had perverted (iii. 453), is in the republican mainstream. We should not, however, be too readily impressed by such distinctions. The hearts of republican writers were less ready than their heads to grant a constitutional role to 'single persons'. In practice the republicans, Milton among them, forgot the distinction between kingship and

---

[7] *Columbia Milton*, viii. 25.

tyranny more often than they made it. In theory they, and he, subscribed to the ideal of the Aristotelian king, the personification of justice and reason; but though Milton like his colleagues revered Aristotelian rulers when he found them – a Marcus Aurelius, an Agricola, an Alfred – he found very few of them, and concurred with Algernon Sidney's view that in seventeenth-century England virtuous kingship was the remotest of possibilities, and no more relevant to the solution of England's difficulties than the Spartan and Athenian models which in the *Arcadia* of Algernon's great uncle had been 'a matter more in imagination than practice'. Milton resembles Algernon Sidney again in acknowledging the theoretical right, awarded by the Aristotelian and Ciceronian principle of distributive justice, of a supremely meritorious man to rule. Indeed in 1654 he justified the rule of Cromwell in precisely those terms (*Columbia Milton* viii. 223). Elsewhere, however, Milton (again like Sidney) invokes the principle not as a practical aspiration but to emphasise its impracticality, or to offer a reproachful contrast with contemporary rulers and practices (*Complete Prose Works*, iii. 204–5, 460, 486, iv. 366, 427, vii. 377).

Republicanism may be but one of many strands in the mind and imagination of a proudly solitary writer, but it may also be a larger one than Milton's critics have understood. It may be prominent even at moments when his thought can seem to us at its most individual. If politics were for him always subordinate to larger ethical concerns, so were they for the other republican writers of seventeenth-century England. However much those writers may have learned from Machiavelli, they had none of the Florentine's sense of the moral autonomy of politics. Milton's political thought may appear to us never more distinctive than in his repeated insistence that reformation of the state begins with reformation of the soul and reformation of the household: as he warned in 1654, if the English people were now to succumb to the allurements of luxury and to deviate from the path of reformation, then 'the tyrant, whom [during the civil wars] you imagined was to be sought abroad, and in the field, you will find at home, you will find within'.[8] Yet that conviction reflects, admittedly in a more intense form, the Aristotelian assumption common to his fellow republicans that public conflict between law and will is a projection of a struggle waged within every man between the liberty of reason and the slavery of passion. If that battle could be won – if political idolatry could be rooted out – then the question whether to admit a 'single person' might be a mere detail.

Even Milton's religious preoccupations were less eccentric to republicanism than they may initially look.[9] His Arminianism – that 'great argument' of *Paradise Lost* which justifies the ways of God to men by emphasising the

---

[8] *Ibid.*, viii. 241.

[9] For this resemblance, and for the other resemblances noted in this essay, between Milton's beliefs and those of the republican mainstream, see the chapter to which I refer in n. 1, above.

dependence of men's salvation upon the free exercise of their reason and choice – belongs to a reaction against Calvinist orthodoxy which is a unifying characteristic of seventeenth-century republicans. Just the same can be said about his Socinianism, his daring anti-trinitarianism; just the same can be said about his commitment to religious toleration; just the same can be said about his anticlericalism and his conviction that the clergy were to blame for that 'low dejection and debasement of mind' which he saw reflected in Englishmen's worship of kings (iii. 344). Sometimes historians regard the republican challenge to conventional theology as a secularising force, and of course the label of secularity cannot be plausibly attached to Milton. Yet the charge levelled against the clergy by Milton's fellow republicans, as by Milton himself, was not that they had promoted religion but that they had perverted it. To them as to him, politics was a supremely religious activity, in which the common-wealth was 'a minister of God upon earth', and in which the achievement of a perfect state would fulfil a divine instinct in man – a theme especially dear to Harrington, whose political thought has, like Milton's, its apocalyptic dimension.

In republican minds, and in Milton's mind, the relationship between civic and religious virtue is a close one. Milton is at one with his fellow republicans in his emphasis, at once Puritan and Machiavellian, on frugality, industry and sobriety, on 'honest poverty', on the fundamental distinction between liberty and licence, and on the evils of luxury and of sloth. And when we look at his profound if temporary attraction to religious presbyterianism in 1641–2, we find, at its heart, a preoccupation with 'discipline' that has its civic as well as its ecclesiastical dimension. Discipline is the 'very nurse and guardian' not only of 'piety' but of 'virtue'; for

He that hath read with judgement of nations and commonwealths, of cities and camps . . . will readily agree that the flourishing and decaying of all civil societies . . . are moved to and fro as upon the axle of discipline. (i. 751, 841)

Most radical Puritans referred to men with whom they found a sense of fellow-feeling as 'saints'. Milton, I think, never uses that term in that way. Instead – like his fellow republicans – he calls the Englishmen he admires 'citizens'.[10] He described the service of the gospel as 'rational, manly and utterly free' (vi. 548): he could equally well have applied the phrase to his conception of political service. He may have wanted to divorce church from state, but he did not think religion divisible from politics. He knew that the causes of civil and religious liberty were 'inseparably knit together' (i. 923); that beneath 'tyranny' and 'false religion' lay 'very dark roots' which 'twine and interweave' (iii. 509, 570); that

---

[10] *Complete Prose Works*, i. 812 (*cf. ibid.*, ii. 286, vii. 306, viii. 447; *Columbia Milton*, ix. 177, xii. 61, xviii. 164). Milton's application of 'saint' to politics is customarily ironic: *Complete Prose Works*, i. 851, iii. 343, 367.

'the idolising their kings' reflected the people's proneness 'not to a religious only, but to a civil kind of idolatry' (iii. 343). No government, he declared in 1660, came 'nearer' to the 'precept of Christ, than a free commonwealth' (vii. 366). The gospel speaks 'much of liberty, a word which monarchy and her bishops both fear and hate, but a free commonwealth both favours and promotes' (vii. 458).

There is a sound rule for the study both of the religious and of the political radicalism of Milton: we should begin not with his published but with his unpublished writings, where he could express himself more freely. Just as the proper guide to Milton's religious heresies is the unpublished *de Doctrina Christiana*, so the clues to his political heresies lie in his private compositions. The republicans, Milton among them, published in order to influence events. Their choices of argument and of emphasis were influenced by the requirements of persuasion. More often than not, those requirements obscured the extent of Milton's radicalism. In 1641–2, when he demanded the abolition of episcopacy, he addressed a parliament readier to countenance radical ideas in religion than in politics, and eager to work with rather than against the crown to dismantle the Laudian Church. In 1649–50 he wrote for a regime, the Rump, which had declared against monarchy only in gingerly and ambiguous terms and which was not anxious to encourage searching republican speculation. In 1654 he wrote for Cromwell, who had overturned the 'free state' of 1649–53 and had restored a semi-monarchical element to the constitution. To assess the extent of Milton's republicanism we should start not with those occasional pamphlets but with his unpublished commonplace book, which has been surprisingly little used by students of his political thought.[11] Admittedly Milton makes only brief comments there on the passages he transcribes from his reading, and an author does not necessarily subscribe to every opinion he notes in the works of others. Even so, the direction of his selections and observations is consistently radical, and even when they tell us nothing conclusive about his beliefs they are at least a guide to his preoccupations.

The commonplace-book shows how Milton's reading, and the intimacy it brought him with minds distant from his own time and place, freed him from the conceptual limitations of contemporary political debate. The Church fathers, historians and thinkers whom he cites might have been startled by the subversiveness of the selections he made and the conclusions he drew from their writings. If his editors have dated the entries correctly, then that radicalism developed remarkably early. In 1637–8 he noted during his reading of Sulpicius

---

[11] Christopher Hill (e.g. in *Milton and the English Revolution* (London, 1977)) is eager (i) to establish Milton's radicalism and (ii) to explain that the apparent limitations to the radicalism of his published writings are to be explained by the shadow of censorship. The logic of Hill's claims ought to, but does not, direct him to the commonplace book, which does indeed illustrate Milton's radicalism – but where the sources of his radicalism are not those which Hill seeks.

Severus 'that the name of kings has always been hateful to free peoples'.[12] Between 1639 and 1642, while the Puritan parliamentary leaders struggled to contain their messianic religious aspirations within the conventional political vocabulary of the ancient constitution, Milton was displaying a precocious interest in the binding power of the coronation oath and in the lawfulness of resistance to tyranny, and quoting Machiavelli to suggest 'that a commonwealth is to be preferred to a monarchy'. The pertinence of these reflections to current events is clear from Milton's pamphlets of 1642, which, although outwardly loyal to the king and blaming his troubles not on him but on his bishops, do nevertheless accuse those bishops of 'reducing monarchy to tyranny'.[13] Later, in 1649, Milton would publicly recall that under the personal rule of the 1630s, the time when, at Horton, the foundations of the poet's scholarship had been laid, 'all men, except court-vassals, opposed [the king] and his tyrannical proceedings' (iii. 344) a claim which, whatever its exaggeration, surely reflects something of Milton's own youthful opinions. And perhaps not his alone: by 1640 Hobbes had already concluded that the reading of Aristotle was persuading men of the legitimacy of resistance,[14] a statement we can set beside John Aubrey's observation that Milton's 'being so conversant in Livy and the Roman authors, and the greatness done by the Roman commonwealth' had produced his anti-monarchical sentiments.

It is in 1651–2 that the commonplace book shows Milton's absorption in Machiavelli to have been deepest: that heady period when the newly confident republic embarked on an aggressive policy designed to secure the absorption of Scotland, Ireland and the United Provinces into England; when its endeavours were hailed by the editorials of Milton's friend Marchamont Nedham, which sought, with the aid of Machiavelli's language, to educate Englishmen in the virtues and the policies of the classical republics; and when, as Milton would write, it seemed that England's rulers might build 'another Rome in the west' (vii. 423) – thanks not least to the parliamentary leader Sir Henry Vane, Milton's sonnet to whom in 1652 alludes to Machiavelli.[15] In the references to

---

[12] The commonplace book is translated, edited and indexed in vol. i of the *Complete Prose Works*. For the original text see *Columbia Milton*, xviii.

[13] *Complete Prose Works*, i. 732; cf. i. 572, 705, 769–70, 924, 925. It is true that at one point in 1642 Milton does seem to indicate that England has not been afflicted with tyranny ('if it should happen that a tyrant (God turn such a scourge from us to our enemies) should come to grasp the scepter . . .': *ibid.*, i. 852), but such tongue-in-cheek phrasing was an old dodge, designed to draw attention to the phenomenon which it superficially denied. The same ruse had been used, for example, by Antoine Muret in 1581 (see Peter Burke, 'Tacitism', in *Tacitus*, T.A. Dorey, ed. (London, 1969), p. 161); see too Algernon Sidney's *Discourses concerning Government* (London, 1772), p. 350.   [14] Hobbes, *The Elements of Law*, pt. ii, chs. 8, 9

[15] *The Poems of John Milton*, ed. J. Carey and A. Fowler (London, 1968), p. 328. For the republican aspirations of the early 1650s see B. Worden, 'Classical republicanism and the Puritan revolution' in *History and Imagination*, H. Lloyd-Jones, V. Pearl and B. Worden, eds. (London, 1981), pp. 190–1, and 'The Commonwealth Kidney of Algernon Sidney', *Journal of British Studies*, 24 (1985), 4.

Machiavelli in the commonplace book for 1651–2, and even in the pamphlets, we can glimpse Milton's interest in Machiavelli's arguments about the evils of hereditary rule; about the greater willingness of republics to honour virtue; about the appropriateness of armed resistance to tyranny; about the role of political and military participation in the fulfilment of citizenship; about the military benefits of frugality, the domestic consequences of military expansion, the benefits of tumults (cf. iii. 388, 564–5, iv. 390), the advantages of constitutional renewal.

Yet even in the early 1650s Milton's republican optimism is not unqualified. Throughout his work there runs a doubt, not about the healthiness of republican rule, but about the fitness of the English people to sustain it. It is a doubt which helps to explain why the principle of consent figures less in Milton's thought than in that of other republicans – and less than it logically ought to have done, given his belief that all legitimate power is entrusted by the people and given his conviction that man fulfils his capacity for 'reason' through the exercise of his 'choice' (*Complete Prose Works*, ii. 527; *Paradise Lost* III. 108). The doubt is a portentous one, 'for stories teach us that liberty sought out of season in a corrupt and degenerate age brought Rome itself into further slavery' (v. 449). That passage comes from another underexplored composition, unpublished by Milton, of telling interest to the student of his political beliefs, the digression to the *History of Britain*. The *History* dwells on the contrast between the civilising influence of the Roman occupation of the island and the monkish barbarism which had followed it. Why, after the departure of the Romans, had the opportunity to establish native liberty – 'such a smooth occasion given them to free themselves as ages have not afforded' – been lost: a failure which had cost more than a millennium of political health and happiness? It is a problem, Milton explains, with a pressing modern parallel: now that the Stuart tyranny has been defeated, will the English prove themselves any better qualified to create 'a just and well amended commonwealth to come' than they had been then (v. 441)?

Milton's gravest anxiety about the aptitude of his countrymen concerns not, as we might expect, their moral or spiritual shortcomings. It derives from the deficiencies of their political education. In common with his fellow seventeenth-century republicans, Milton believed political education to be essential to national political health. He is particularly dismayed by Englishmen's ignorance of the wisdom and the virtue of the Mediterranean past. In the Digression to the *History* he laments the nation's shortage of men with 'the happy skill to know what is grievance and unjust to a people, and how to remove it wisely'. 'To know those exquisite proportions' of constitutional felicity, he argues, requires a 'heroic wisdom' beyond the capacities of

narrow politicians . . . For Britain (to speak a truth not oft spoken) as it is a land fruitful enough of men stout and courageous in war, so is it naturally enough not over-fertile of men able to govern justly and prudently in peace; trusting only on their mother-wit, as most men do, and consider not that civility, prudence, love of the public more than of money or vain honour are to this soil in a manner outlandish . . . For the sun, which we want, ripens wits as well as fruits; and as wine and oil are imported to us from abroad, so must ripe understanding and many civil virtues be imported into our minds from foreign writings and examples of best ages: we shall else miscarry still. (v. 449–51)

Here was a recurrent anxiety to Milton, who as early as 1641 warned parliament that 'in the guidance of a civil state to worldly happiness, it is not for every learned or every wise man . . . to invent or frame a discipline' – to be a Lycurgus or a Numa (i. 753). In a private comment of 1652 he lamented the insularity of most of the republic's rulers, who were 'entirely ignorant of public political matters', and of whom no more than three or four had been abroad – a select group that included Milton's fellow republicans Algernon Sidney and Henry Nevile, like him pre-war travellers to Italy.

To grasp the full significance of Milton's lament for the opportunity missed after the withdrawal of the Romans from Britain, and of his plea for the adoption of Mediterranean political principles, we need to ask when the Digression was written. Milton states, in precise terms, that he wrote the earlier part of the *History of Britain*, to which the Digression belongs, in the weeks following the execution of the king in January 1649: that is, when the new rulers had yet to resolve on a form of government or to declare England a commonwealth and free state. His assertion has been widely disbelieved, on unconvincing grounds. It has been assumed that he could not have written so quickly, and that his memory must have been at fault.[16] Yet the rate of composition required, a few pages a day – rather flat pages at that, which draw

---

[16] *Complete Prose Works*, v. xxxvii–xli. I am not persuaded by the argument of Professor Austin Woolrych, carefully and elegantly proposed as it is, that the Digression was written many years after the text from which it digresses ('The date of the digression in Milton's *History of Britain*' in *For Veronica Wedgwood These*, R. Ollard and P. Tudor-Craig, eds. (London, 1986), pp. 217–46), and I do not accept his supposition that Milton was unlikely, at any of the points in the later 1640s when the poet might be thought to have written the Digression, to have experienced the despair which the Digression reflects. The suggestion that Milton wrote the earlier part of the *History* at a point between the execution of the king in January 1649 and the setting up of the Commonwealth in May seems to me to derive additional support – more indeed than has been conceded – from Milton's reference, at the beginning of Book Three, to the present 'interreign'. It is true that, as the *Oxford English Dictionary* shows, the word 'interreign' or 'interregnum' did not always bear the modern meaning of a vacancy between governments. It could simply mean a state of affairs in which the ruling power had broken down, a definition which would have made the term applicable at any point after 1642. Yet in all the seventeenth-century instances that I have noted outside the *OED*, the term has the narrower meaning: see e.g. *Mercurius Politicus*, 8–15 March 1655, p. 5189; Michael Hawke, *The Right of Dominion and Property* (London, 1656), p. 154; *A Copy of a Letter written to an Officer of the Army* (London, 1656 or 1657), p. 34. On the dating of the *History* and of the Digression I owe an exceptional debt to Mr Nicholas von Maltzahn, who discusses the problem in a forthcoming book on the *History of Britain* to be published by Oxford University Press. It is a pleasure too to acknowledge, as so often, a debt to Professor Woolrych, that most perceptive and constructive of critics, who commented most helpfully on a draft of this essay – but who, like Mr von Maltzahn, carries no responsibility for its assertions.

heavily on the chronicles which are their sources – was well within the customary pace of that voluminous writer. If Milton wrote when he said he wrote, then the passage must be read as his reflection on the constitutional position that followed the execution of Charles I. At that crisis the parliamentary leaders, those insular figures who lacked classical political prudence, clung to existing parliamentary forms, shunned constitutional experiment, and produced the improvised regime of the Rump. Milton, by contrast, saw in the regicide a Machiavellian *occasione* – a 'smooth occasion' – when the future happiness of the nation depended on its ability to break free of the insular ancient constitution and to follow the principles of Mediterranean wisdom. The chance was to be missed, just as the opportunity following the Roman departure had been missed. In 1650 Milton acknowledged that 'Our constitution is what the dissensions of the time will permit, not such as were to be desired',[17] and in 1660 he would complain that 'when monarchy was dissolved' in 1649

the form of a commonwealth should have forthwith been framed, and the practice thereof immediately begun, that the people might have soon been satisfied and delighted with the decent order, ease and benefit thereof; we had been then by this time firmly rooted past fear of commotion or mutations, and now flourishing. This care of timely settling a new government instead of the old, too much neglected, hath been our mischief.

Yet even now, in the months preceding the Restoration, when others realised that the republic was collapsing around them, Milton could see in the chaos another *occasione*: 'Now is the opportunity, now the very season wherein we may obtain a free commonwealth, and establish it for ever in the land' (vii. 430).

That dream was to be quickly shattered. With the restoration of monarchy Milton returned from the prose he had written 'of the left hand' to his poetic vocation, and completed *Paradise Lost*. Yet we should hardly expect a writer who had dedicated two decades of his life and creativity to a political cause, and who had proclaimed that 'poets truly so called', from Homer to Buchanan, were 'the sworn foes of tyrants',[18] to have suddenly lost his political interests. It is no news that in *Paradise Lost* the devil has the best lines; but is it realised how republican those lines are? Is it realised, in particular, how close is Satan's republicanism, which is accorded its most ample documentation in Book v, to the language of *The Ready and Easy Way to Establish a Free Commonwealth* early in 1660, the year when, as far as we can tell, Milton is likely, during the succeeding months, to have written Book v?[19] Satan's enemy is the God who 'sole reigning

[17] *Columbia Milton*, vii. 29.   [18] *Ibid.*, viii. 77–9.

[19] Of course, we cannot be sure about the timing, or even the order, of Milton's composition. But if the concluding lines of Book v have an autobiographical reference, it is surely to Milton's constancy to the collapsing Puritan cause. Books v and vi seem likely to have been written together. By the time Milton has written the opening of Book vii, when the poet has 'fallen on evil days', the Restoration is secure.

holds the tyranny of heaven' (I.123); and the monarchical qualities of 'heaven's high king', of 'heaven's matchless king', are underlined again and again (I. 637–40, II. 751, 992, IV. 41, 960, 973, V. 220, VIII. 239). Amidst the ambrosial fragrance and the golden pavements of heaven, behind its frequently mentioned towers, those recurrent symbols of monarchical oppression in Renaissance literature, are unmistakable features of a seventeenth-century court. First there is obsequiousness. Milton's pamphlets are full of the contrasted physical postures of freedom and slavery – a theme inevitably common throughout the imaginative writing which addressed itself to the rise of the Renaissance court, but nowhere more persistent than in Milton. In the prose works, free peoples are 'erect' – like Adam and Eve when we first meet them (*Paradise Lost* IV. 289) – 'bearing high their heads'.[20] By contrast the bishops of the pamphlets of 1641 are distinguishable by their 'servile crouching' (i. 522, 853), while in *Eikonoklastes* the English people reveal their 'low dejection and debasement of mind' by their readiness to 'fall flat' before 'the image and memory' of Charles I (iii. 344). The 'base necessity of court-flatteries and prostrations' is a target of *The Ready and Easy Way* (vii. 428), and it is there that Milton scorns 'the perpetual bowings and cringings of an abject people, on either side deifying and adoring' a king (vii. 426). Just so, in *Paradise Lost*, does Satan warn his fallen angels against the 'abject posture' with which they seem ready to 'adore' their conquering God (I. 322–3). Why, asks Satan, should the defeated angels 'bow and sue for grace with suppliant knee, and deify' heaven's monarch (I. 111–12)? Why should they offer 'knee-tribute' and 'prostration vile' (V. 782)? Satan, with his Roman constancy, his 'fixt mind/And high disdain' (I. 97–8), has a sound republican contempt for the servile courtier-angels who remain in heaven, 'Whose easier business were to serve their lord', and who 'cringe, not fight' (IV. 943–5). The archfiend had supposed that 'liberty and heaven/ To heavenly souls had all been one; but now/ I see that most through sloth had rather serve' (VI. 163–6). At least the expulsion of the rebellious angels has given them the chance of 'preferring' – as Mammon has it, and as Milton so often urged his countrymen to prefer – 'Hard liberty before the easy yoke/Of servile pomp' (II. 255–7).

Like the new monarchies of the Renaissance about whose evils the republicans had so much to say, the monarch of heaven has brought off a fundamental transition in the balance of power. Milton, like most of his fellow republicans, had mixed feelings about medieval kingship, but again like most of them he evidently thought it preferable to modern monarchy, whose rise across Europe in the later fifteenth and earlier sixteenth century was held by republicans to parallel the extinction of republican liberty and of senatorial independence under the Roman empire. Belonging in this respect to the

---

[20] *Complete Prose Works*, iii. 236, 237 (*cf. ibid.*, ii. 559); *Columbia Milton*, viii. 9.

aristocratic and nostalgic strain within seventeenth-century republicanism, Milton gratefully recalled the exertions of 'those faithful and courageous barons' of medieval England who had made 'glorious war against tyrants for the common liberty', and who, as the king's peers, had enjoyed at least a measure of 'equality' with him (*Complete Prose Works*, iii. 219, 343–4). Their effeminate successors had been corrupted and broken by the early modern courts: courts which had come to regard the hereditary succession, hitherto bestowed on monarchs by the people merely for reasons of what Milton called 'courtesy or convenience' (iii. 203), as an inherent right.[21]

The process which has corrupted early modern England and early modern Europe proves to have had celestial parallels. Satan reminds his fellow barons that they had been 'Equally free' until God had ventured to 'assume' and 'introduce' novel powers (*Paradise Lost* v. 792–7). Now God, 'whom reason hath equalled, force hath made supreme/ Above his equals' (i. 248–9). The coup which has altered the balance of heavenly power has been suddenly sprung. God's monarchy, like the medieval English monarchy as republicans saw it, had owed its authority, we learn, to 'Consent or custom' (i. 640). Now it has become a tyranny which imposes 'new laws', 'new commands', 'new subjection' (II. 239, v. 679–80, 691): how like the Renaissance monarchies, whose aspirations to absolutism were invariably charged by their opponents with 'innovation'! Of course God, again like the Renaissance monarchs, is careful to dress his novel claims as ancient rights. In the war in heaven, Father and Son resolve to 'hold what anciently we claim/ Of deity or empire' (v. 723–4), but Satan grasps that God means to 'extend/ His empire' (II. 315, 326–7). God's appeal to antiquity usurps an argument which properly belongs to Satan – just as, in Stuart England, the sanction of the ancient constitution was believed by the crown's opponents to be their political property. And just as the republicans believed the independence of the medieval nobility to have been immemorial, so in heaven the rebel angels 'know no time when we were not as now;/ Know none before us, self-begot, self-raised' (v. 859–60). The claim is powerless before God's legions, which expel the 'Natives and sons of heaven possessed before/ By none' (v. 790–1). Not only has God's empire been established in heaven: it is expanding territorially too. Now his sovereignty will extend to hell, where his power will be 'arbitrary' (II. 334), and to earth, whose creation his statecraft has 'long' been secretly 'contriving', and whose inhabitants, as Satan warns them, God will keep in fear of death, to 'awe' them and 'to keep ye low and ignorant' (IX. 138–9, 702–4).

---

[21] Milton is not always so aristocratic; and although in the passage quoted here he invokes the names of great noblemen, he believes the medieval nobility to have been a much broader class than the titular nobility of more recent times – a conviction that once more aligns him with Algernon Sidney: *Complete Prose Works*, iv. 423; Worden, 'The Commonwealth Kidney of Algernon Sidney', p. 23.

The decisive moment of the celestial revolution has been God's elevation of his Son, 'heir of all my might', the hereditary ruler to whom 'shall bow/ All knees in heaven' (v. 607–8, 720; cf. III. 321, 350). In *Paradise Regained* (I. 87–8) Satan observes that God 'obtains the monarchy of heaven/ And what will he not do to advance his Son?' In *Paradise Lost* we hear repeatedly that the Father has 'transferred' power to his Son, power which, in Satan's eyes, is not God's to transfer (v. 854–5, VI. 678, X. 56). For like the Renaissance monarchs, God (the Father) has come to treat his kingdom as a possession rather than a trust. The Son, in the manner of hereditary rulers, has quickly acquired the same proclivity, for he has 'engrossed/All power' at the expense of the baronial angels, whom he has 'eclipsed under the name/ Of king anointed', and from whom he will claim 'honours new' (v. 775–80).

As in Milton's Europe, so in Milton's heaven, the revolution in political power has been accompanied by a revolution in political theory. 'Strange point and new!' protests Satan when God claims that the angels are obliged to obey his Son; 'Doctrine which we would know whence learnt' (v. 855–6). Just so did seventeenth-century republicans remonstrate against the novel 'points' and 'doctrines' that supported the development of absolutism – like the corrupt and servile 'doctrines' of tyranny attacked by Milton in 1642 (i. 851, 925) or the 'new' 'doctrine' and 'new' 'precepts' detected by Sidney in the patriarchalism of Sir Robert Filmer.[22] Sidney portrayed the Stuart monarchy in Tacitean terms, as a Tiberian tyranny. Milton's heaven has likewise a Tiberian character. There, as in Tiberian Rome – and as in Post-Reformation England – mere words can be treasonous, so that Satan cuts short his incitement of the angels to rebellion because 'more in this place/To utter is not safe' (v. 682–3). Tiberianism has spread to Paradise, where Eve, having tasted of the apple, can only hope – in vain – that God's 'spies' will not have witnessed her transgression (IX. 815).

And yet . . . and yet it is, of course, a fallen Eve that speaks thus. Only between the fall of our first parents and their subsequent repentance are there affinities between their view of God's sovereignty and Satan's. Satan's rhetoric is fallen rhetoric. It is born, as we know from the outset, of the 'pride' (what we later learn to be 'monarchal pride') that has 'cast him out from heaven', and of his 'ambitious aim/ Against the throne and monarchy of God' (I. 36–42, II. 428, IV. 40). During the war in heaven his exhortations to his fellow rebels – so close to Milton's own arguments against earthly tyranny – are called 'blasphemous' by the outraged Abdiel, the most sympathetically (not to say autobiographically) drawn of Milton's angels. 'Shalt thou give law to God', Abdiel asks Satan, 'shalt thou dispute/ With him the points of liberty?' It is 'just', Abdiel protests, that 'every soul in heaven/ Shall bend the knee' (v. 809–24; cf. VI. 171ff.). The loyal angels appropriately bow low to God in a heaven 'where honour due and reverence none neglects' (III. 736–8), just as Adam and Eve, both before their

---

[22] Sidney, *Discourses concerning Government*, pp. 53, 356.

fall and after their repentance, bow spontaneously, reverently, and fittingly in their orisons (v. 144–5, XI. 249). We have seen Satan warning his fellow rebels, and Milton in *The Ready and Easy Way* warning his countrymen, against 'adoration' and 'prostration': yet we learn of Adam and Eve that before their fall 'Lowly they bowed adoring' and that after their repentance they 'prostrate fell' (v. 144, X. 1099–1100). Satan's warning that God aims to 'awe' man proves groundless, for we learn that Adam, when 'bowing low' to Raphael with 'reverence meek', is 'not awed' (v. 358–60). Similarly Satan complains of God's 'yoke' (v. 786; cf. v. 882), but the repentant Adam and Eve acknowledge the 'just yoke/ Laid on our necks' (x. 1045–6) – in the same way that Milton's pamphlets of the early 1640s had condemned the 'yoke of prelates and papal discipline' while welcoming 'the yoke of prudent and manly discipline' (i. 704, ii. 230).

'Yoke', 'discipline', 'awe', 'bow', 'adore': in Milton's writings each of those words – like many others – carries a clear good meaning and a clear bad meaning. The good meanings belong to men who have walked Milton's strenuous path to liberty, the bad to those who, like Satan, remain slaves to their lusts and passions. In the truly free man, deferential outward gestures of worship are at one with a manly uprightness within: in the corrupted man, physical self-abasement merely reflects spiritual self-abasement. We would not describe Milton's double uses of words as 'ambiguous', the term with which he characterises Satan's use of language (v. 703, VI. 568), for Milton's moral stance is never left in doubt. But ambivalence – the quality of looking two ways – is essential to his method. 'Equal' and 'obey' are other words which mean either well or badly according to the spiritual health or corruption which they reflect. Another is the noun 'tower', which is a symbol of earthly tyranny and pride and folly but which in heaven is (for all Satan's misunderstanding) a proper extension of God's majesty – a contrast made vivid when in Book XII (44, 51–2) the tower of Babel suddenly threatens to 'Obstruct heaven-towers'.

Of all Milton's two-faced words, none carries a greater argumentative burden than 'submit' or 'submission'. In the prose tracts Milton condemns the forced or craven 'submission' of subjects to unworthy kings. 'That all men should submit themselves to one man as superior to the law,' he declares, 'no law ever did enact or ever could.' How', he asks, 'can we submit as free men' to 'any civil power unaccountable', or 'yield subjection' to men 'most commonly not being the wisest or the worthiest . . . of those whom they govern?'[23] The indignant rhetorical question is Algernon Sidney's device too: why should we 'submit to his will, who is subject to the same frailties, passions, and vices, with the rest of mankind?'[24] It is Satan's device as well: 'Who can think submission?', he asks (I. 661). 'Will ye submit your necks', he challenges his rebel army, 'and

[23] *Columbia Milton*, vii. 215 (*cf. ibid.*, vii. 211, 283); *Complete Prose Works*, iii. 209, 486.
[24] Sidney, *Discourses concerning Government*, p. 107.

choose to bend/ The supple knee?' (v. 787–8). Having 'courage never to submit or yield' (I. 108), Satan cannot bring himself to retract from his rebellion, because no way 'is left but by submission', a prospect his 'disdain' and 'dread of shame' cannot bear (IV. 79–85, 96). Yet Adam's submission to his maker is endorsed by the poet both before the fall and after Adam's repentance. Adam greets Raphael with 'submiss approach' (v. 359), and later tells him how, discovering the glory of creation, he 'fell/ Submiss' 'with awe/ In adoration' (VIII. 314–16). Once the resistance waged by his passions against God's justice has subsided, Adam 'submits' to the 'just' punishment imposed by God's 'absolute decree' (x. 768–9, XI. 311–14, 372, 526).

Even Satan's republican or Aristotelian claim to rule by 'merit', and his 'sense of injured merit' (I. 98), are turned against him. It transpires that his 'merit' has raised him to a 'bad eminence' (II. 5–6), whereas the Son, whose authority has looked to be merely hereditary, proves to reign 'by right of merit' and 'by merit more than birthright', 'worthiest to be heir' (VI. 43, 707–8, 888; *Paradise Regained* I. 166). The Son, not Satan, proves to be the true Aristotelian king, ruling by virtue of distributive justice: as Abdiel explains, there is no 'servitude' 'When he who governs is worthiest, and excels/ Them whom he governs' (VI. 175–80). Satan's republicanism is humbug. He has wished to 'seem' a 'Patron of liberty' (IV. 957–9), but his 'high words', here as always, have 'Semblance of worth, not substance' (I. 528–9). Satan, indeed, embodies the very qualities he affects to despise. The angel Gabriel can deride him with the question 'who more than thou/ Once fawned, and cringed, and servilely adored/ Heaven's awful monarch?' (IV. 958–60). For Satan, as much as the 'Court parasites' of the Caroline court (*Complete Prose Works*, i. 670, iii. 204), is a 'fawning parasite' (*Paradise Lost* IX. 526; *Paradise Regained* I. 452). God had created him 'upright', only for Satan to deprive himself of that 'shape' (IV. 835–7). And although Satan uses the vocabulary of tyranny and equality to sway the rebel angels, that 'pretence' is 'Too mean' for him, for his true aim is a 'glory sole' which will make him not God's equal but his 'master' (VI. 421, IX. 125, 135).

Why has Milton taken such pains both to implant his republicanism in *Paradise Lost* and to expose the falsity of Satan's application of it? The likely modern answer, perhaps, is that the exposure is incomplete or unconvincing: that Satan's arguments against the tyranny of heaven have a good deal to commend them. Ever since William Empson went to school at Winchester and decided that the God he met in the classroom there was 'very wicked',[25] the failure of the Old Testament deity to accommodate himself to the moral requirements of twentieth-century liberal agnosticism has been a problem to Milton's readers. But Milton's God is not Empson's God. He is defined by a theological system

---

[25] W. Empson, *Milton's God* (London, 1961), p. 10.

which is thickly argued in the poem, and to which Empson is resolutely deaf. Far from subscribing to the Calvinist scheme with which Empson identifies Milton, the poet argues tirelessly against it: against a predestinarian theology which, he believes, makes God the author of sin and turns him into (what Satan and Empson take him to be) a tyrant. Milton's Arminianism, his certainty that men's salvation rests upon the free and rational exercise of their choice, is spelled out in those passages of *Paradise Lost* where, as Pope complains, 'God the Father turns a school-divine'.[26] There it is that the 'great argument' is articulated, the argument of which the poem is a celebration. Later generations, reading *Paradise Lost*, have been altogether less alert to the differences than to the similarities between the Calvinist and the Arminian systems of salvation, and it may well be a limitation of the poem, in one sense a bar to timelessness, that its intellectual coherence can be evident only to a reader conversant with its seventeenth-century theological position.[27] But to concede that point is one thing: to repeat that Milton was of the Devil's party without knowing it is another. Milton did very little without knowing it, and the exactness with which Satan's republican credentials are proclaimed and undermined requires us to give more credit to the poet's intelligence.

Readers have found in Milton's Satan a reflection of two figures: Oliver Cromwell, and Milton himself. The poet's decision, apparently around 1657, to return from prose to poetry is likely to have been related to his disenchantment with the protectorate, which had failed to achieve the substance of godly reformation and which had become increasingly monarchical in style. By 1659 he was ready to look back on the Cromwellian regime as 'a short but scandalous night of interruption'.[28] Although the evidence for the development and the depth of Milton's personal hostility to Cromwell is thin, the poet is certainly capable of having come to share the belief of other republicans that the protector had sacrificed the revolution on the altar of his own ambition. But whether or not Milton had Cromwell particularly in mind – whether or not Satan's invocation of 'necessity, the tyrant's plea' (IV. 393–4) is meant to recall the Protector himself – the 'scandal' of the protectorate was the product not merely of an individual's betrayal but of a deeper malaise of the Puritan Revolution. As 'the first/ That practised falsehood under saintly show' (IV. 121–2), Satan is the type, as Cromwell in republican eyes is the most eminent

---

[26] Pope's 'First Epistle to the Second Book of Horace', l. 102. The school-divine is at his most elaborate in *Paradise Lost*, III. 95ff.

[27] The school-divinity had lost its force well before Pope, for the controversy over predestination, which so exercised Milton's generation, had much less hold on the succeeding one. William Denton, in plagiarising in 1681 the passage in *Areopagitica* which foreshadows the Arminian argument of *Paradise Lost*, subtly eliminates its Arminian essence: see the quotations on p. 63 of G.F. Sensabaugh, *That Grand Whig Milton* (Stanford, 1952, repr. 1967).

[28] *Complete Prose Works*, vii. 274. The significance of the phrase is illustrated by Austin Woolrych, 'Milton and Cromwell: "A short but scandalous night of interruption"' in *Achievements of the Left Hand*, M. Lieb and J.T. Shawcross, eds. (Massachusetts, 1974), pp. 185–218.

and most destructive example, of the Puritan hypocrite. During the protectorate Puritan divines had anxiously noticed that many men now 'only took up religion' because the Roundheads' accession to power had made 'godliness . . . the easiest step to preferment'.[29] 'Hypocrisy', observed those divines, had enabled 'much profession of godliness' to become 'common in these days, wherein men have learned the art of looking one way and rowing another; pretending one thing and doing the quite contrary'.[30] The triumph of that art was held by Puritan divines to be Satan's triumph, for they knew that in the last times, the times which the Puritan Revolution appeared to have inaugurated, there would flourish 'false prophets (which are Satan's ministers)': 'the hour is coming and now is, that Satan in a more than ordinary manner doth transform himself into an angel of light', an angel that will strive to 'deceive the very elect . . . by fair shows of holiness, and excellent postures of piety . . . Therefore . . . a Christian-like outside may be, in some, but a cover for an Antichristian spirit.'[31]

The events of 1659–60, when republicans and radical Puritans were deceived by the mirage of political recovery and then saw their cause turned to destruction, sharply tested the integrity of the elect and found it wanting. During that time the language of radical politics – what Milton in *The Ready and Easy Way* calls 'the language . . . of the good old cause' (VII. 462) – becomes ever more self-righteous, ever more hackneyed, on ever more distant terms with the truth of men's motives and conduct. As the Puritan squabbles for power yielded to the royalist reaction, so Puritans were left to reflect that their own sins and divisions were alone to blame for the Stuarts' return.

The failures of the later 1650s – first the failure of the protectorate to answer the hopes of reformation that had led Milton to support and write for it, and then the humiliating collapse of the revolution itself – produced a rash of self-examination among the Roundheads. However bitterly they blamed each other, they, or at least the more honest of them, felt impelled to search into their own hearts too. Milton's Satan was created during that period of Puritan self-reassessment, and we can surely say that it reflects something of it. But though Milton's Satan is no doubt, at some level, a portrait of Cromwellian or Puritan hypocrisy, it must also have a more autobiographical application. Satan's 'ambiguous words' are not, in general, the words of Cromwell or of Puritan divines. They are Milton's words: precisely the words in which, in *The Ready and Easy Way* early in 1660, he urged his countrymen to shun the temptation of political idolatry and to keep to the austere path of true liberty. Why does Milton give Satan those words? We can say, of course, that in creating the

[29] Preface by George Griffith to William Strong, *Heavenly Treasure* (London, 1656). *Cf. The Life of George Trosse* (London, 1714), pp. 81–5.
[30] John Beadle, *The Journal or Diary of a Thankful Christian* (London, 1656), p. 33.
[31] Matthew Caffyn, *The Deceived and Deceiving Quakers Discovered* (London, 1656), Preface.

character of Satan the poet was bound to draw on those resources of his mind which fitted his dramatic purpose, and that the vocabulary of republicanism was perfectly suited to that purpose. We can point out that there is no drama without evil and that a writer who dramatises evil must possess a capacity to identify with it. But if Milton – of whom Dr Johnson's claim that he 'hated all whom he was required to obey' has struck a chord in too many readers to be discounted – in some sense identifies with Satan, he manifestly does not approve of him. With what feelings did the poet adapt his own political language to the characterisation of evil?

Milton is a writer to portray for us only his certainties, never his doubts; to advertise only his constancies, never his changes of mind; to criticise only others, never himself. His self-education and self-correction are kept private. If he recognises an error – as when he drops his commitment to religious presbyterianism in the 1640s or to the protectorate in the 1650s – we are left to detect the inconsistency for ourselves. Yet inconsistency there is, and there is self-education too.[32] In the years during which Milton appears to have written *Paradise Lost*, 1657–63, that self-education is likely to have been profound.

The hypocrisy of Milton's Satan differs in one essential respect from that of the Satan whom the Puritan divines saw 'transform himself into an angel of light'. The Satan of *Paradise Lost* has made himself an angel not of Christianity but of republicanism. It is the archfiend's false application of political vocabulary, not of religious vocabulary, that the poet exposes. Satan has presumed to apply the language of earthly politics to heavenly ones. As Milton explains in *de Doctrina Christiana*, Christ's kingdom has 'preeminent excellence over all others' because he rules 'chiefly by an inward law and spiritual power'.[33] It is a difference and a superiority of which Milton has long been conscious. In the commonplace book he notes the distinction between the 'worship' that is appropriate to God and the 'willing service' that kings must earn.[34] In *Of Reformation* he contrasts 'earthly tyrannies' with the 'mild monarchy' of heaven (i. 616); and in *Eikonoklastes* he hopes that the English people have learned to 'reject a king' precisely in order to make Christ 'our only leader and supreme governor' (iii. 236). The contrast between earthly monarchical pretensions and the Son's true claim to kingship is a theme to which Milton warms in the *First Defence*, where the Aristotelian argument that 'He is not fit or worthy to be king that does not far excel all the rest' is turned to support the contention that Christ alone 'is worthy to hold on earth a power that shall resemble the divine power'.[35] In the pamphlets, however, the error of confusing earthly with heavenly politics is a royalist, not a Puritan error. Royalists had made their king into a god. Satan's error is of a still greater magnitude: he can envisage God only

---

[32] Woolrych, 'Milton and Cromwell', confronts Milton's inconsistency admirably.
[33] *Columbia Milton*, xv. 297–9. [34] *Ibid.* xviii. 173. [35] *Ibid.* vii. 127, 279.

as a royalist king. Milton had not made that mistake. But had he claimed too much for the language of secular politics? And had his own sacrifice of two decades of major poetry to compositions 'of the left hand' – compositions that had exercised so little influence on the character of his countrymen or on the course of events – been vindicated?

For in 1657–63 it was the turn of the Puritans themselves to confront the lesson in which Milton had instructed the royalists: the lesson of the measureless difference of proportion between temporal politics and eternal verities. In those years, I suggest, Milton does not merely return to his right hand, from prose to poetry: he withdraws from politics into faith. The pain and complication of that process are characteristically kept hidden from us. That the process was not unbroken is evident from his return to pamphleteering between the fall of the protectorate and the Restoration. Yet even in the urgent pleading of *The Ready and Easy Way*, political language is beginning to yield to religious language. When in the past Milton has reflected on his countrymen's moral failings, he has assured himself that 'some few', even if 'so very few', retain the virtue which may yet be communicable to the rest (*Complete Prose Works* i. 944, 974, iii. 344, v. 174, 403). Those 'few' have been distinguishable by their political wisdom and virtue. Yet in *The Ready and Easy Way* the 'few' have acquired another name: they have become a 'remnant' (vii. 363) – a term which in this instance, and in the Puritan literature of the Restoration, denotes spiritual rather than political virtue. The 'fit audience though few' envisaged in *Paradise Lost* is likely to have been a Dissenting rather than a republican one (VII. 31; cf. XII. 480–1 and *Paradise Regained*, III. 59).

At the Restoration, as Milton feared they would, the English people chose 'a captain back for Egypt' (*Complete Prose Works*, vii. 463). The providentialist expectations and reforming ambitions of the early 1640s, and the thrilling heroism of regicide, had led only to bitter and disastrous failure, which in the 1660s was to be followed by persecution and oppression. Amidst the cataclysm the defeated Puritans were driven towards a profound re-evaluation of the providential meaning of the Revolution and of its place in the divine scheme of history. In its earlier stages it had seemed that, in the words of *Areopagitica*, 'God is decreeing to begin some new and great period in his church, even to the reforming of reformation itself: what does he then but reveal himself to his servants, and as his manner is, first to his Englishmen?' (ii. 553). The writing of Milton's pamphlets had seemed a compelling and imperative task to a poet confident of his divine vocation and of his national mission. But the God who had revealed himself to his Englishmen in the 1640s seemed in the 1660s, like the God of *Samson Agonistes*, 'to hide his face' from his chosen people. Confident interpretations of his purpose must yield to patient submission to it.

That recognition is present, I believe, in *Paradise Lost*. By the time of *Paradise Regained*, a poem written at the prompting of a Quaker, the retreat from politics is complete. For now it is clear that Christ's kingdom is not of this world – a text about which Puritans had had little to say during their years of power. In his prose of the Puritan Revolution Milton had again and again urged the Puritan leaders to 'deliver' their countrymen from tyranny. Time and again he had praised the 'deliverers' who had overthrown Charles I and the 'deliverers' who had defeated tyranny in other ages and other lands.[36] Yet in *Paradise Regained* Christ refuses successive invitations to 'free' and 'deliver' his people from the 'servile yoke' of Rome (*Paradise Regained* II. 48, III. 175, 374, 404, IV. 44, 102, 131). The Son knows – what Satan cannot learn, and what Milton, though he has often said it, has perhaps now come to hold in a more uncompromising spirit – that the only true liberty is to be found within: 'What wise and valiant man would seek to free/ These thus degenerate, by themselves enslaved,/ Or could of inward slaves make outward free?' (IV. 143–5). If the language of political resistance has become unfitting, so has the language of republicanism. Already in *Paradise Lost* Satan had cozened Eve in the manner of 'some orator renowned/ In Athens or free Rome' (IX. 670–1). Now, in the later poem, Satan reserves for the ultimate temptation the vision of 'great and glorious Rome' and of 'Athens the eye of Greece, mother of arts/ And eloquence' – only to be told by Christ that political virtue has nothing to learn from pagan sources, from 'all the oratory of Greece and Rome' (IV. 45, 240, 353, 360). How far we have come from the Milton who in the wake of regicide had recommended Mediterranean political wisdom as the cure to his country's ills, and who had looked to his fellow Englishmen to build 'another Rome in the west'!

[36] *Complete Prose Works*, i. 615, 706, 729, 925, ii. 539, 606, iii. 191, 346, 442, 511, 580, 581, v. 174, 200, 449, vii. 275, 424; *Columbia Milton*, vii. 65, viii. 3, 5, 245.

12

A controversial republican:
Dutch views on Machiavelli in the seventeenth and eighteenth centuries

ECO HAITSMA MULIER

In recent times many studies have been dedicated to the fortunes of Machiavelli and his works. They have examined the sometimes fierce reactions to his opinions and they have elucidated the slow process by which his realistic views on the exercise of power in the state were assimilated into the political thought of early modern Europe. Little by little nearly every country has received its due attention as for instance in Felix Raab's admirable book on England.[1] Whereas more generally oriented interest in Machiavelli's theories for a long time concentrated on what might be called the literature of the *raison d'état*, we are now, thanks especially to the work of J.G.A. Pocock, able to discern too how important and profound Machiavelli's influence as a republican has been in Europe and America.[2] It is remarkable, however, that, at least until recently, nowhere in the surveys of Machiavelli's reputation as *old Nick* or as a republican has the Dutch Republic been taken into account.

We must ask ourselves why this has been the case. Did one of the most important republican states of Europe in the seventeenth and eighteenth centuries abstain from the discussion about Machiavelli? Did the special features of the Dutch state, so often emphasised by Dutch scholars, or the rather orthodox character of Calvinism practised in the country, perhaps prevent an open reaction? Of course, in Dutch historical studies Machiavelli turns up now and then, but usually only to be cursorily mentioned before one passes on to the order of the day.[3] So even the Dutch side provides no solution to the problem.

I wish to thank Arthur Mitzman for his assistance in the English translation.

[1] F. Raab, *The English Face of Machiavelli. A Changing Interpretation 1500–1700* (London, 1965).

[2] J.G.A. Pocock, *The Machiavellian Moment. Florentine Political Thought and the Atlantic Republican Tradition* (Princeton, NJ, 1975).

[3] The only study (as far as I know) dedicated exclusively to Machiavelli in the Low Countries is not very useful for our purposes: V. Brants, "'Le Prince' de Machiavel dans les anciens Pays-Bas' in *Mélanges d'histoire offerts à Charles Moeller à l'occasion de son jubilé de 50 années de professorat à l'université de Louvain* (2 vols., Louvain and Paris, 1914), II, pp. 87–99. For remarks on Machiavelli see also the works of J.D.M. Cornelissen, for instance his 'De trouw der katholieken tegenover "ketters"' (1930) in Cornelissen, *De eendracht van het land. Cultuurhistorische studies over Nederland in de zestiende en zeventiende eeuw* (Amsterdam, 1987), pp. 271–83; P.H.J.M. Geurts, *Overzicht van Nederlandsche politieke geschriften tot in de eerste helft van de 17e eeuw* (Maastricht, 1942) and P.A.M. Geurts, *De Nederlandse opstand in pamfletten 1566–1584* (Utrecht, 1978; first edn 1956).

We are confronted with the fact that the chapter on the Dutch face of Machiavelli has not yet been written. Here, after outlining the opinions expressed in the Dutch republic on Machiavelli as a political thinker I shall concentrate on his role in shaping Dutch republicanism and discuss briefly the relation between the Dutch and the European reactions to Machiavelli.

In 1632 the greatest Dutch historian of the seventeenth century, Pieter Corneliszoon Hooft, expressed his satisfaction at the arrival of Machiavelli's *Istorie fiorentine*: 'At last the long-desired *Histories* of the secretary are here. I have looked for them in vain so often but now I have this sly dog's work complete'.[4] These lines may be called very significant for the situation of Machiavelli's work and reputation at that moment. On the one hand we observe the opprobrium in which he was held and consequently the difficulty one had in obtaining some of his works. On the other hand, a well-educated and tolerant man like Hooft, who in his youth had travelled in Italy, considered the study of Machiavelli's history and thought a necessity and thus wanted to obtain his works for his library.

We do not know how Machiavelli became known in the Netherlands, but it is certain that the emperor Charles V, born in Ghent, read his *Principe*. Also at Louvain, in those years the intellectual centre of the country, a group of Spaniards in the 1550s studied the work of the Florentine. In their treatises on government they tried to connect religious considerations with administrative practicalities. Here Machiavelli gave them a lead. Thus it comes as no surprise that Fox Murcillo and Furió Ceriol shared a reformist attitude towards the religious issues of their time. Unfortunately we know nothing about their contacts at the university with natives of the area. In the meantime the first warnings against Machiavelli's observations had led to a clear condemnation by men of the Church. The result was a stream of repetitively hostile treatises.[5] natives of the area. In the meantime the first warnings against Machiavelli's observations had led to a clear condemnation by men of the Church. The result was a stream of repetitively hostile treatises.[5]

Soon the Protestants too condemned Machiavelli for his amoral teachings and in the wars of religion both parties accused each other of machiavellianism. In the pamphlet wars that raged during the successive stages of the Dutch Revolt the same pattern appeared. For the insurgents peace seemed impossible

[4] *De briefwisseling van Pieter Corneliszoon Hooft*. H.W. van Tricht, ed. (3 vols., Culemborg, 1976–9), II, p. 274, no date [shortly after 19 December 1631]. He calls him 'dien lidsaert'.

[5] In general see Q. Skinner, *The Foundations of Modern Political Thought* (2 vols., Cambridge, 1978), I, pp. 250ff.; also Raab, *The English Face of Machiavelli*, pp. 30ff. for the first English reactions and G. Procacci, *Studi sulla fortuna del Machiavelli* (Rome, 1965), pp. 211ff. For the sixteenth-century Netherlands, Brants, '"Le Prince"' and R.W. Truman, 'Spanish responses to Machiavelli in the mid-16th century Netherlands' (Unpublished paper, European University Institute, Florence, 1983) and his 'Sebastián Fox Morcillo's *De regni regisque institutione* (Antwerp, 1556): humanist approaches to empiricism' in *Acta conventus Neo-Latini Sanctandreani. Proceedings of the fifth International Congress of Neo-Latin Studies*, I.D. McFarlane, ed. (Binghamton, NY, 1986), pp. 283–91, especially p. 287.

because the Spaniards, who followed the maxims of the pope and Machiavelli, would not keep a treaty, because for them, 'haereticis non est servanda fides'. The Spaniards, above all the Duke of Alba, were all 'Machiavelliques'. The Duke had even had a statue of him erected in the castle of Antwerp, that symbol of tyranny. William of Orange too had answered the accusations made against him by Philip II by stressing the fact that the king exercised a tyranny worthy of Machiavelli. In these debates his famous words about the lion and the fox were often heard. No wonder the other camp reversed the argument: there the Prince of Orange was seen as a machiavellian. Considering his transition from the Roman Catholic Church to Protestantism they accused him of using religion as a cloak for his political purposes.[6]

When the Dutch republic had established itself, the use of Machiavelli as a symbol for everything bad in politics and for amoral political action continued. The general opinion was that his prince lusted only after fame and an outward appearance of well-being. The mathematician and counsellor of the stadholder Prince Maurice, Simon Stevin, commented at the end of the century that a ruler ought never to mingle virtue with wickedness. Daniel Heinsius, professor of history at the university of Leiden, deplored the fact that in political science some now turned to Machiavelli, a man of sharp intellect but far inferior to the incomparable wisdom of Aristotle. Heinsius lived in the orthodox cradle of science in Holland, but on the periphery of the Dutch republic as well, an ex-pensionary of the northern city of Groningen (dismissed for drunkenness), he warned against the intrigues learned in the Tuscan school to gain admission to government posts. Scathingly he declared that sincerity had vanished, and concluded the wisest behaviour to adopt was that of the chameleon.[7]

The other end of the religious spectrum also expressed criticism on Machiavelli. Caspar Barlaeus, who because of his moderate remonstrant convictions left Leiden for Amsterdam, where he became a professor at the Athenaeum Illustre, even wrote a whole *oratio* against Machiavelli's *Principe*. This speech from 1633 contains all the traditional elements in this field. Although Barlaeus praised Machiavelli for his sharp intellect (probably a topos, since Heinsius also used the same characterisation), he viewed the Florentine's work as pernicious because in it words like 'virtue' and 'prudence' had lost their meaning. Machiavelli's arguments were deceitful, he changed a pious, virtuous

[6] Geurts, *Pamfletten*, pp. 179, 269, 272. Also by the present writer 'Willem van Oranje in de historiografie van de zeventiende eeuw' in *Willem van Oranje in de historie 1584–1984. Vier eeuwen beeldvorming en geschiedschrijving*, E.O.G. Haitsma Mulier, A.E.M. Janssen, eds. (Utrecht, 1984), pp. 32–62. G. Wells, 'The unlikely Machiavellian: William of Orange and the princely virtues' in *Politics and Culture in Early Modern Europe. Essays in Honor of H.G. Koenigsberger*, Ph. Mack, M.C. Jacob, eds. (Cambridge, 1987), pp. 85–94.

[7] For Stevin see Geurts, *Overzicht*, p. 139. D. Heinsius, 'Oratio VII de civili sapientia' in *Orationes* (Lugduni Batavorum, 1615), pp. 132–156. B. Alting, *De politycke kuyper onses tydts; ofte sin-rijck tractaet, handelende, (door in-voeringe eenes sprekenden vaders) van het ambacht der huydendaegsche kuypery* (Groningen, 1710; first edn. 1647), p. 20 and *passim*.

prince into 'a fox clad in purple' and the worst thing was that 'religion for him meant mere merchandise to be used for the benefit of what he considered to be the best for himself and the commonwealth'. The pessimistic and melancholic professor repeatedly stressed how dangerous it was for princes to follow Machiavelli's advice not to maintain treaties when they were not useful any more or to remain a realist whilst retaining every appearance of being devout. For Barlaeus this way of behaving was clearly as old as the world: Philip of Macedonia, Ferdinand of Aragon and Louis XI – as one could gather from Guicciardini – had shown themselves eager disciples of the politics of power. He even quoted from Machiavelli's *Discorsi* where the Florentine stated that the people take their lead in wickedness from the prince. If that was the case, Barlaeus asked rhetorically, why not put an honest and devout prince before their eyes? Finally he rebutted those who had stated that Machiavelli had only intended to show the meanness of princes: he 'is not a writer of history, but a teacher, who mixes honest and dishonest words with the intention so as not to be thought cunning and impious'. We will return to the fact that some people expressed themselves more positively about this subject.[8]

The way Barlaeus discussed Machiavelli's *Principe* was repeated by a professor from Groningen who wrote a programmatic speech in 1664 called *Politicus pius*. On another occasion the same scholar indignantly declared that of all political writers Machiavelli was the only one to think the state benefited from the struggles of factions.[9] Though the ban on free discussion and use of Machiavelli began – as we will see – to give way in these years, till the end of the eighteenth century, Schoockius and others repeated the condemnations of Machiavelli's ideas concerning religion and the use of power in the state. Thus one anonymous author considered him a follower of the pagan Polybius because of his conception of religion as a holy fraud. Another stated that Machiavelli had instructed the regents of the Dutch republic not to stick with the official religion but to admit many other creeds with detestable results for the republic. A third, very orthodox author quoted the dictum that the first machiavellian had been the devil himself.[10] In these years the origins of the expansionist politics of Louis XIV, which were threatening the republic, were found by some in the works of the Florentine. The prolific publicist of

---

[8] C. Barlaeus, *Dissertatio de bono principe, adversus Nic. Machiavelli Florentini scriptoris suasorias . . .* (Amsterdam, 1633). I use the Dutch translation 'Een redening of dissertatie, noopende een goet, rechtschapen en vroom prins . . .' in *Oratiën* (Amsterdam, 1662), pp. 48–89, cit. pp. 51 and 84. *Discorsi*, III, p. 29. For Barlaeus' life and illness see F.F. Block, *Caspar Barlaeus. From the Correspondence of a Melancholic* (Assen/Amsterdam, 1976).

[9] See Geurts, *Overzicht*, p. 137. M. Schoockius, *Politicus pius* (Groningae, 1664) and his *De seditionibus, seu discordiis domesticis libri tres* (Groningae, 1664), Praefatio.

[10] *Vrye politijke stellingen en consideratien van staat, gedaen na der ware Christenens Even gelijke vryheits gronden . . .* (Amsterdam, 1665), p. 25n.; P. Valkenier, *'t Verwerd Europe . . .* (Amsterdam, 1675), pp. 6 and 227; S. de Vries, *De geheele weereld (. . .) Kronijck der kronijcken* (Amsterdam, 1686), Voor-beright.

Huguenot descent, Jean le Clerc, who lived for over forty years in Amsterdam, made this quite clear at the turn of the century in his *Parrhasiana* when he expounded his ideas about the ideal political society. In his Lockean universe the law reigned supreme and people enjoyed the fruits of their industry. He deplored the growing strength of absolutism and, of course, alluded in his diatribe against the influence of Machiavelli to what he saw as the despotic tyranny of Louis XIV.[11]

Machiavelli did not appear so often in the eighteenth-century political literature of the Dutch republic – at least as far as we know now. Nevertheless the old view of him as a man who had taught princes how to reign without morality persisted. These utterances were sometimes accompanied by protestations of surprise because most authors interested in his work, as we will see, looked for the particular aspect of his observations that they wanted to use in their polemics on the history and conditions of the institutions of the republic. The difference between the old view and a more lenient attitude may be summed up in a comparison of the two Dutch translations of Machiavelli's works. The first dated from 1615 and featured first the *Discorsi* and at the back of the volume the *Principe*; it was reissued in 1625 and 1652. The second was printed between 1703 and 1705 and also included the *Istorie fiorentine*. It is noteworthy that both editions were published in periods when the position of the most eminent functionary in the state, the stadholder, was being challenged. And it is a pity that we know nothing about the translators who, however, in their forewords give some observations on their motives in translating the works. In 1615 it was still necessary to excuse oneself for a translation by saying that Machiavelli was more experienced in matters of state than Plato and Aristotle. Moreover, dialectics, medicine and even theology always presented good and bad, so why not read the Florentine secretary who excelled in the presentation of both sides? A poem followed next in which the Dutch were admonished not to dance to the tune of the Florentine flute. In 1704 the edition of the *Discorsi* alone was accompanied by an explanation in which all accusations against the author were attributed to prejudices fomented by the Catholic clergy. The translator stated without further ado that on the contrary Machiavelli feared God, and loved harmony, order, justice and discipline in the state, and that his intention was to rid mankind of idleness and voluptuousness. It was precisely Machiavelli who showed the activities of eminent persons in the 'honest affairs of a republic'.[12]

The reason for this increased self-confidence was the fact that in the Dutch Republic at the beginning of the eighteenth century Machiavelli had already

11 *De Fransche Machiavel, of hondert Fransch-politique staetsregelen* . . . (Utrecht, 1675), J. le Clerc, *Parrhasiana* . . . (Amsterdam, 1699), I, pp. 212–16.
12 *De discoursen van Nicolaes Machiavel Florentijn* . . . Tr. A. van Zuylen van Nievelt (n.p., 1615), 1625 and Leiden, 1652 and *De historische en politieke werken van Nicolaas Machiavel*. Tr. Daniel Ghys (5 vols., The Hague, 1703–5), IV.

been approached in a more positive way, especially where he was considered as a republican. So far I have explained just one part of the story. Not only were numerous editions of Machiavelli's works in various languages published in the country, they were also used in political treatises as scholars did elsewhere in Europe. Coping with practical political reality made discussion of the problems he had approached so forcefully inevitable. So the resistance of traditional Aristotelians or the aversion of the religiously orthodox had been neither powerful nor convincing enough. Sometimes Machiavelli's writings were quoted openly, at others they were referred to surreptitiously. A famous example of the first is the work by Justus Lipsius *Politicorum sive civilis doctrinae libri sex* from 1589. In this work on government and the state he referred by name to Machiavelli as a sharp intellect, but immediately added a warning that his prince had taken the wrong road. Nevertheless Lipsius' notion that prudence was sometimes mixed with fraud touched a Machiavellian chord. Although neo-Stoic influences and the effect of his reading of Tacitus also made themselves felt, behind Lipsius' machiavellian advice was his concern with concord and peace. Most notorious was his remark that the ruler is obliged to use religion to ensure unity. A prince was even justified in killing rebellious heretics. And Lipsius' most ardent critic, Coornhert, a staunch advocate of freedom of religion, did not hesitate to write down what many thought: 'ille machiavellisat'.[13]

For Lipsius, who wrote in the troubled times of the Revolt, hereditary monarchy was clearly the best system of government. Many at that time and later would agree with this opinion. Some however, less outspoken, preferred to use the Roman historian Tacitus for lengthy discussions of machiavellian problems without mentioning the Florentine's name. In this way the historian Hooft, Grotius and others (at Leiden university, for instance) mingled their political observations with historical examples.[14] The surprising fact in all this is – as has already been pointed out elsewhere – that political theory in the new republic of the first half of the seventeenth century focussed almost exclusively on monarchy and its institutions. That was one of the reasons why it was considered worthwhile proceeding with attacks on Machiavelli's *Principe*.[15]

[13] G. Oestreich, *Neostoicism and the Early Modern State* (Cambridge, 1982), pp. 39–56; M.E.H.N. Mout, 'Ideales Muster oder erfundene Eigenart. Republikanische Theorien während des niederländischen Aufstands' in *Republiken und Republikanismus im Europa der Frühen Neuzeit*, H.G. Koenigsberger, E. Müller-Luckner, eds. (Munich, 1988), pp. 169–94.

[14] See by the present writer: 'Grotius, Hooft and the writing of history in the Dutch Republic' in *Clio's mirror. Historiography in Britain and the Netherlands. Britain and the Netherlands VIII. Papers Delivered to the Eighth Anglo-Dutch Historical Conference*, A.C. Duke, C.A. Tamse, eds. (Zutphen, 1985), pp. 55–72 for some Dutch examples. The general aspects in E-L. Etter, *Tacitus in der Geistesgeschichte des 16. und 17. Jahunderts* (Basle/Stuttgart, 1966).

[15] E.H. Kossmann, *Politieke theorie in het zeventiende-eeuwse Nederland* (Amsterdam, 1960) and his 'The development of Dutch political theory in the seventeenth century' in *Britain and the Netherlands I*, J.S. Bromley, E.H. Kossmann, eds. (London, 1960), pp. 91–110.

No real republican theory emerged during the Revolt from which the Dutch republic originated. After the States-General had renounced Philip II in 1581 political writers were very reluctant to acknowledge that they went beyond the bounds of legality. Their main preoccupation was to show the admissibility of what had happened. The continuously changing political circumstances also increased a reluctance to reach high levels of abstraction. Thus for many years their preoccupation was more with the legality and the analysis of the existing situation than with the question of how the republic ought ideally to function.[16] So in his *De antiquitate reipublicae Batavicae* Grotius gave a kind of historical legitimacy by explaining that the origins of the new republic were to be found in Batavian times. In his opinion no important change had taken place since then. Nevertheless, how was one to explain in republican terms the anomalous features of the new situation: seven small provinces, which each had its own supreme institutions of government: the States, composed of representatives of the nobility and the cities; its stadholders from the House of Orange (often the same person in more than one province): a prince restricted in the use of his power but always trying to expand his competence; endless bickering and repeated consultations home when a decision had to be reached in the States-General at The Hague since the States were sovereign; one province – Holland – good for providing half the financial funds of the union, but which identified little with the Seven Provinces as a whole. How in these circumstances could one draw inspiration from Machiavelli?

Attempts were made to clarify the undefined and sometimes tense relationship which existed between the stadholder and other parts of the state structure. Apart from general remarks on the relationship between official persons and institutions accompanied by the observation that a republic showed great advantage over a monarchy, this could be done by superimposing the model of the Aristotelian mixed state upon the existing institutions. In this way it was possible to 'translate' them into the threefold division that ideal presupposed. Another way of explaining the situation was to make a comparison with other republics from the past, like Rome or Sparta, or present times. As has been shown elsewhere the influence of what has been called the myth of Venice, the idealised image of the history and the institutions of that republic, made a strong impact where institutions and administration were to be defined more precisely. It is evident that Machiavelli would have a part to play when classical republicanism made its appearance in the Dutch republic. An early exponent of some of these ideas, Paulus Busius, a professor from the Frisian city of Franeker,

---

[16] See E.H. Kossmann, A.F. Mellink, eds., *Texts Concerning the Revolt of the Netherlands* (Cambridge, 1974) 'Introduction', *passim*, also Mout, 'Ideales Muster', p. 183. I do not altogether share the conclusions of M. van Gelderen, 'A political theory of the Dutch revolt and the "Vindiciae contra tyrannos"', *Il Pensiero Politico*, 19 (1986), 163–81, who postulates the revolutionary and republican purposes of the Dutch protagonists at that moment.

read and quoted from Machiavelli but only from his *Principe* and in a negative way.[17]

However, one gets the impression that the *Discorsi* and the *Istorie fiorentine* – as far as one may conclude from this rapid survey – soon met with a much better press. The first Dutch translation of a work by Machiavelli, preceded by elaborate excuses, was of the *Discorsi* (followed by the *Principe*). The discrepancy in the acceptability of Machiavelli's works becomes clear in Barlaeus' speech of 1633, which I have already discussed, where he adduced a passage from the *Discorsi* to blame the Florentine for advice given elsewhere. After 1650, no stadholder was nominated in Holland or in other parts of the republic until an attack by four neighbouring states in 1672 revived the institution in the person of William III of Orange. Political theory and historical discussion were then dominated by the question of whether this functionary was indispensable to the constitution of the republic. It is interesting to note how partisans on both sides of this question made indiscriminate use of these two works by Machiavelli. Those in favour of a stadholder cited the Florentine's views on republics of the past and on the importance of their temperate mixed governments. They also picked up his warnings that a republic would decay when sudden changes were introduced into its constitution. Machiavelli thus provided them with an opportunity to stress the traditional importance of the function of the Prince of Orange.[18]

At the same time the first unequivocal expression of republicanism, based among other things on what Machiavelli had said, appeared in the Dutch republic in the works of the De la Court brothers and Spinoza. They did not hide their admiration for Machiavelli. The great philosopher called him wise and 'acutissimus', an expression which, we will remember, had already been employed by both friend and foe to characterise the Florentine. Johan (who died in 1660) and Pieter de la Court were the sons of an immigrant from the southern Netherlands. Pieter was a cloth manufacturer in Leiden who also published works on economic subjects. Their works, prepared for the press by Pieter, went through a large number of editions and evoked sharp reactions. The *Politike Discoursen* (Political Discourses, 1662) was particularly indebted to Machiavelli. From the title on, the whole structure of the work is machiavellian in its observations on government, war and defence, the relation of Church and state, and morals. Large parts were taken word for word from the *Principe*. Here no apology was given for using this work. On the contrary, in the preface the consultation of political writers from Italian republics (a plain reference to

---

[17] P. Busius, *Illustrium disquisitionum politicorum liber* . . . (Franekerae, 1613), IV, XV, XXXII.

[18] See f.i. *Apologie tegens de algemeene, en onbepaelde vryheyd, voor de oude Hollandsche regeeringe* . . . (Middelburg, 1669), pp. 11, 96 and *Consideratien ende redenen, daer by de nootsaeckelijkheyt vande stadthouderlijcke regeringe in desen staet en republique wordt aengewesen* . . . (The Hague, 1677) pp. 4, 16, 18.

Machiavelli) was expressly recommended. Like his *Discorsi* the work was divided into books and each chapter got a title sounding like a *maxime*. Short examples from history explained how by a comparison of matters of state past and present a republic ought to conduct its affairs. The world of Machiavelli, with the support of Tacitus' and Boccalini's experience, became elaborated and integrated in a republican vision of politics, related to a realistic and pessimistic *raison d'état*.[19]

In the *Politike Weegschaal* (Political Balance, 1660), enlarged and refined by Pieter in 1661 and again in 1662, the influence of Machiavelli strengthened the myth of Venice. The De la Court brothers wished to apply their theory to Holland or to the cities of Holland in particular. The 'popular' form of the state, the form of institutions, rotation of office and government were the ingredients of the classical republicanism they recommended. They associated their view of man (derived from an undifferentiated understanding of Cartesianism which gave it neo-Stoic overtones) with the form of the state. Men were, they claimed, always subject to passions which reason was seldom able to dominate successfully. Only through the creation of a condition of balance could the emotions be rationally controlled. That condition could only be achieved in the state which owed its existence to a contract. The brothers derived their contractualism from Hobbes, but in contrast with his opinion the De la Courts emphatically guaranteed every citizen the possibility of exercising his individual rights within the state. Whereas in monarchy and aristocracy the passions of one or more persons would very likely come to dominate, in the 'popular' state, by contrast, the passions of men could be kept in balance with each other. This, they argued, was therefore the best state.

Their defence of this 'popular' state was based on Machiavelli's *Discorsi*. Like Machiavelli they did not ascribe a political role to the entire population of a nation but only to those who were citizens: the 'people' had a political voice, but the *plebs* did not. At the same time, in order to strengthen the position of the States, then without a stadholder, they rejected the idea of the mixed state that Machiavelli had so arduously defended. The sovereign assembly of all the citizens in a city or a country must, they claimed, be given as much power as possible. The objective of the De la Court brothers was not a state in which all inhabitants were involved but one in which the line of division between the 'people' and the regents was not sharply drawn. In later editions of the *Political*

---

[19] For details of this and the next paragraphs which follow, see my 'The language of seventeenth-century republicanism in the United Provinces; Dutch or European?' in *The Languages of Political Theory in Early-modern Europe*, A. Pagden, ed. (Cambridge, 1987), pp. 179–195) I refer to my *The Myth of Venice and Dutch Republican Thought in the Seventeenth Century* (Assen, 1980). See also E.H. Kossmann, 'Dutch republicanism' in *L'età dei lumi: studi storici sul settecento europeo in onore di Franco Venturi* (2 vols., Naples, 1985), I, pp. 455–86, reprinted in his *Politieke theorie en geschiedenis. Verspreide opstellen en voordrachten* (Amsterdam, 1987), pp. 211–33 to which all references will be made.

Balance Pieter diluted the 'popular' state by adding an aristocratic element to his schema. Perhaps, just as in his admiration for Machiavelli, English influence played its part. He stipulated that no one who had received poor relief, or had worked in the service of another, was entitled to citizens' rights. Such persons were, in his opinion, unlikely to be capable of independent judgement.

After examining the situation in Venice and Genoa the De la Courts came to the conclusion that the ideal republic should have a dense population and be made prosperous through commerce and industry. It should not be expansionist as the Roman republic had been and as Machiavelli had recommended (although the De la Courts did take over his idea of a citizen-army). In this peace-loving ideal state with a general council open to new members, an assembly of more than 200 men was to be elected every year. Their decisions were to be taken by secret balloting, after the Venetian example, so that no parties threatening the 'virtue' of the autonomous and free participating individual would be allowed to develop. The rotation principle could be maintained, because members were to be re-elected only once. And a constitutional 'dictatorial' power of the kind described by Machiavelli would control the supreme council. 'Zindicatori' or 'Fiscalen' would see to the proper functioning of the institutions of government and, because their offices also rotated, there was no danger they might abuse them.

In his *Tractatus theologico-politicus*, on which he worked in the mid-1660, and the *Tractatus politicus*, incomplete at the moment of his death (1677), Spinoza incorporated the work of the De la Courts into a superior philosophical system concerned with the spiritual welfare of mankind. It is not easy, therefore, to discuss his political writings in isolation from his metaphysics. However, we know that Spinoza took a keen interest in the political events of his time. Inspired by Hobbes in his view of the origin of the state he took as his point of departure the notion that in order for any government to possess real power it was necessary for it to be supported by as many of its citizens as possible. For that reason he, like the De la Court brothers, rejected the mixed state. Following Machiavelli he preferred a state where freedom, maintained in the law, was to be secured by the people. Like the brothers from Leiden he excluded all 'servants' (and women), by which he meant all those who were not financially and socially self-sufficient, from citizenship. In his aristocracy the regular admittance of new members to the ruling elite was determined by the same criteria. Thus for Spinoza, in agreement with the De la Courts on this point as well, nobility was a matter of ability not of blood.

His constitutional claims went much deeper than those of the *Political Balance*. The terminology and the abiding concerns of classical republicanism are immediately evident. Spinoza was also anxious about the formation of parties. For that reason in a state governed by an aristocracy the numerical relationship between the patriciate and the rest of the population was to be examined by means of an annual census. All election procedures should everywhere follow the Venetian example in order to guarantee personal autonomy and the victory of reason over the passions. Spinoza showed himself less hostile to monarchy than the De la Courts but naturally there was no head of state in his ideal republic. The great lawgiver that Machiavelli had suggested to arrange the institutions of the state nevertheless figured in his treatises. To control the proper functioning of the councils and the rotation of offices Spinoza also introduced the now familiar constitutional 'dictator' that Machiavelli had judged necessary. This council of 'Syndici', the size of which was dependent on the number of patricians, performed some of the functions of the Venetian Council of Ten and of the Doge who supervised the drafting of all legislation.

The exceptional character of Spinoza's and the De la Courts' republicanism (only rapidly sketched in here and with emphasis given to its machiavellian links) becomes clear when we consider the unique way they used the Florentine's works. We do not know exactly why Machiavelli was so attractive to them. Their urge to do without a stadholder and to criticise the mighty position of Grand Pensionary John de Witt had perhaps made them look to contemporary England. There Machiavelli had inspired James Harrington when he composed his *Oceana* and the Dutch books show similarities with this work. But the different circumstances in which they lived made the Dutch political thinkers remain more or less independent from the mainstream of European classical republicanism. This stream of republican thought was merged with elements of their own political tradition. On the other hand, when one looks at the only Dutch contemporary who in 1665 propagated the idea of a 'popular' state without mixed government one realises too the distance that separates his work from theirs. The anonymous writer, probably related to radical religious groups, mentioned Machiavelli as his source but every mention was followed by an apology and the treatise was embedded in a religious context where the people was described as the guardian of freedom.[20]

However, this kind of republicanism was without an echo. The declaration of war in 1672 had put an end to the aspirations it embodied. There was no question any more of breaking up the regent oligarchy in the Dutch republic by reforms such as those the De la Courts and Spinoza had proposed. Their realism and cynical observations made it embarrassing even to mention their names let alone use their work.[21] In contrast to developments in England and America

---

[20] See *Vrye politijke stellingen* . . . (note 10), *passim.* A survey in G.O. van de Klashorst, H.W. Blom, E.O.G. Haitsma Mulier, *Bibliography of Dutch Seventeenth-century Political Thought: An Annotated Inventory* (Amsterdam/Maarssen, 1986).

[21] For the reputation of the De la Courts, I.W. Wildenberg, 'Appreciaties van de gebroeders De la Court ten tijde van de Republiek', *Tijdschrift voor Geschiedenis*, 98(1985), 540–56 and his *Johan en Pieter de la Court (1622–1660 and 1618–1685). Bibliografie en receptiegeschiedenis* (Amsterdam/Maarssen, 1986) with a summary in English.

this brand of machiavellian and classical republicanism had no real heirs in the Dutch eighteenth century. That Dutch attitudes towards Machiavelli were back to normal can be gauged from the republican ideas of Lieven De Beaufort, a regent from the province of Zealand. His *Verhandeling van de vryheit in den burgerstaet* (Treatise on liberty in a civil society) was published posthumously and anonymously in 1737, at a moment when, at least in Holland and Zeeland, there had been no stadholder since 1702. In all those years the regents had ruled the country developing their network of family connections into a closed oligarchy which no outsider could penetrate.[22]

De Beaufort defended the existing situation by postulating an ideal republic based on commercial and cultural activities. In this republic citizens showed their 'virtue' by participating actively in government institutions. Between the extremes of the really virtuous and the ambitious an inactive middle group must be won for the good cause. Then a kind of liberty would reign that automatically guaranteed security within the boundaries of law and reason. No pure aristocracy or even democracy but a mixture of both represented the ideal form of government for De Beaufort. Fortunately, to his mind, this mixture already existed in the States of Holland. Moreover, in his view no magistrature was in hereditary possession of one family as was the case in Venice and Genoa. The regent thus defended his ruling oligarchy against the danger of the possible return of a stadholder. The presence of this man, like Julius Caesar, could signify the end of the republic. Indeed, many of De Beaufort's examples of how liberty came to its demise were taken from the history of Rome. All this is very reminiscent of what Machiavelli had warned against and of classical republicanism. However, they remain just that, reminiscences.[23]

The De la Courts were never mentioned by De Beaufort, who, unlike them, had confidence neither in institutional mechanisms (be they of Italian origin or not) nor, understandably, in reforms. De Beaufort's attitude towards Machiavelli is also very dubious. On the one hand he wrote with hesitant approval of his *Discorsi*, in which he 'left us, here and there, some good remarks', especially on the danger for a republic of politically ambitious individuals and the way to block their ascent to power. His history of Florence also offered many examples of how they tried to satisfy their aspirations. On the other hand, the Dutch patrician was pessimistic and did not share Machiavelli's confidence in the force of the law. One gets the impression that De Beaufort gradually

---

[22] [L.F. De Beaufort], *Verhandeling van de vryheit in den burgerstaet* (Lieden/Middelburg, 1737).

[23] On De Beaufort see I.L. Leeb, *The Ideological Origins of the Batavian Revolution. History and Politics in the Dutch Republic 1747–1800* (The Hague, 1973), pp. 54ff. Kossmann, 'Dutch republicanism', p. 223 and W.R.E. Velema, 'God, de deugd en de oude constitutie. Politieke talen in de eerste helft van de achttiende eeuw', *Bijdragen en mededelingen betreffende de geschiedenis der Nederlanden*, 102(1987), 476–97.

became frightened of what he probably saw as his own audacity. Again and again he warned of Machiavelli's pernicious and unChristian remarks on how a prince should employ his power. That was the way kings were accustomed to rule nowadays, he observed, and concluded his book with a peroration which stated that only by preserving its official reformed religion would the Dutch republic save its liberty.[24]

Some years later, in 1741, on the occasion of the appearance of a Dutch translation of the *Anti-Machiavel* by Frederick the Great, a defence of the Florentine was written by an unknown Dutch author: *Machiavel republicain*. Significantly, however, for the direction interest in Machiavelli was to take, this work leaned heavily on a ten-year-old German tract. Nevertheless, a comparison between the two shows that large interpolations have been made in the Dutch version. There is no doubt that the purpose of *Machiavel republicain* was again to emphasise the advantages of republican government and to rescue Machiavelli for this cause. Voltaire in particular, who collaborated on the *Anti-Machiavel*, was blamed for his attacks on Machiavelli. And the eulogy on liberty that followed implicitly contained an elaborate reasoning in favour of the existing stadholder-less government in the country. Thus the writer stated that, as could be seen from the experience and political science of the past, only in a republic would arts and sciences flourish. But, clearly referring to the controversies of the *querelle*, he maintained that in his view this search for republican examples ought not to be limited to the great classical authors.

Therefore Machiavelli's *Principe* was important in that it showed the ruses of princes and this was done the better because it created a confrontation with his *Discorsi* which described 'a free government in an unparalleled way'. The Florentine was unjustly accused of nearly everything bad in the world. Why was he reputed to have been the *auctor intellectualis* of the theories of the monarchomachs in France? The fact too that Hobbes had misunderstood his intentions had done much to identify his work with that of the Englishman, a defender of absolutist kingship. Subsequently a large part of *Machiavel republicain* is taken up with telling the history of antimachiavellism with the intention of refuting all these accusations. But two last points must be taken note of. First, the efforts it makes to deny that Machiavelli was an irreligious man. These parts did not appear in the German example. Matched by a satisfied rendering of Machiavelli's attacks on the Roman Catholic Church they were typical of the preoccupations with religion constant in Dutch history. Remarkably, no conclusion concerning any detail of the institutional frame-

---

[24] Quoted in *Verhandeling*, p. 439. He referred to *Discorsi*, I, chs. 50 and 52 Against Machiavelli, *Verhandeling*, pp. 172, 203, 234. See also his *Het leven van Willem de I* (3 vols., Leiden/Middelburg, 1737) lxii, and III, 476.

work of the Dutch republic was reached, except perhaps the acceptance of its aristocratic character. Machiavelli here had become a *republicain* pure and simple.[25]

As already noted, apart from these two books Machiavelli was not quoted as an authority or even referred to very much in the political discourse of the Dutch eighteenth century. A reference is to be found here and there but evident pains have been taken to avoid the really dangerous passages. Among other things, of course, this was due to the slow penetration and acceptance of new enlightened authors in the field of political thought. We have seen that before 1747 a republican interpretation of his work was associated with a defence of the ruling oligarchy. The serious condition of the republic in the Austrian War of Succession in that year caused the return of the Prince of Orange as a stadholder in all seven provinces just as in 1672. In the ensuing pamphlet wars about the position of the stadholder in the Dutch constitution, Machiavelli was generally not mentioned. Neither did the fate of the other existing republics in Europe serve any more as a useful example or arouse any feeling of republican solidarity.[26] Nor was Machiavelli referred to in the noisy squabble of the 1750s on the great contemporary of the De la Courts and Spinoza and antagonist of William III, John de Witt. Orangists and adversaries of the stadholder respectively accused and defended the symbol of the period. This historical dimension of the pamphlet discussion is typical of the way the Dutch expressed their opinions on the institutions of the republic.[27]

In the 1770s and 1780s, when economic problems and internal dissent shook the foundations of the republic, treatises concentrated on the phenomen of decline. They discussed the old commercial glory of the Dutch republic, now endangered by English rivalry, as an ideal to be regained. A reform movement of regents and citizens at first favoured only a restoration of the constitution but gradually developed into a battle against the oligarchic rule of the patrician families. Unofficial assemblies of elected representatives of the people that would advise and control the regents in their tasks were requested. The stadholder, who was pro-British, now became the target of the anti-Orangist and pro-French opposition. These *Patriots*, as they were called in their

---

[25] *Anti-Machiavel, of oordeelkundig onderzoek, van den vorst, van Machiavel geschreeven door een' voornaam' monarch in 't Fransch uitgegeven door den Heer Voltaire* . . . (Amsterdam, 1741). *Machiavel republicain, tegens den Anti-Machiavel verdedigt. Waer achter bygevoegt is Machiavel boekdrukker* (Utrecht, 1741). This work follows I.F. Christius, *De Nicolao Machiavello libri tres* . . . (Lipsiae, 1731), see Velema, 'God, de deugd ed de oude constitutie', 495–6. The interpolations, on Machiavelli's religion, pp. 57–61 and 81ff. The anti-Roman Catholic remarks on pp. 230, 233. His rejection of the mixed state in a reaction to Algernon Sidney's *Discourses on Government* (1698), quoted in a French translation, pp. 79–80, note d.

[26] Se my 'Genova e Amsterdam 1746–1748: il caso del repubblicanesimo nel Settecento' in *Atti del II congresso internazionale di studi storici rapporti Genova–Mediterraneo–Atlantico nell'età moderna*, R. Belvederi, ed. (Genoa, 1986), pp. 195–210.

[27] For this 'war of the De Witts' see P. Geyl, *De Witten-oorlog. Een pennestrijd in 1757* (Amsterdam, 1953).

programmes, expressed themselves in a more or less democratic way and at last urged a republic without a stadholder. Whereas the books written by the De la Court brothers in these years did not meet with a favourable reception, those by Machiavelli, whose raw realism was not very different from that of the brothers from Leiden, sometimes fared better.[28] References to Machiavelli, however, remain scant and nearly always take second place to the preferred authors of the English and French Enlightenment. Moreover the great expectations of Enlightenment were really only more or less applicable to Machiavelli the republican. The reception of the *Principe* was a more difficult subject.

When in 1785 the Orangist professor of history at Leiden, Adriaan Kluit, defended the sovereignty of the States of Holland against those in favour of popular government he considered first the nature of sovereignty. To avoid an absolutist interpretation he warned never to identify utility with justice: to do so would be to enthrone Hobbes and Machiavelli again. Kluit now wanted to demonstrate how this kind of well-defined sovereignty in the course of the centuries had devolved from the courts of Holland to the States. In the existing constitution (including the stadholder) these States *were* the people and no one had the right to attack their supreme authority. This version of what had happened rejected the traditional view of Grotius, which implied the States' continuous sovereignty from the oldest times.[29] Curiously that same year an anonymous author in a patriot weekly attacked Kluit for his point of view. In an extensive article this man had previously denounced the *Principe* of Machiavelli. Of course, he wrote, one could interpret the work just as a warning but he considered it self-evident that all honest and religious men would find its message detestable. A not very benevolent extract from Machiavelli followed to call attention to the fact that the ruses of the Italian princes in the enlightened age had spread over the whole world. Seven issues later, the same writer, in the conviction that he had now sufficiently indicated the danger of the stadholderian regime, confessed himself to be surprised to see how Kluit had used Machiavelli to denounce the claims of popular sovereignty. In Kluit's lecture, he wrote, it was not, as might have seemed logical, the stratagems of princes which were the target. On the contrary, the English theorists Price and Priestley who tried to defend the rights of the people against monarchs were the victims of this unjust assault. Indeed these writers were very popular in patriot circles. Together with Fletcher's defence of a citizen-army they inspired, for instance, the writings of the patriot protagonist Van der Capellen. At this point we must stress again the fact that the way Machiavelli's ideas were employed in all this

---

[28] Wildenberg, *Johan en Pieter de la Court*, p. 50.

[29] [A Kluit], *De souvereiniteit der Staaten van Holland, verdedigd tegen de hedendaagsche leere der volks-regering* . . . (Groningen, [1785]), p. 61, a second edition was published in 1788 with his name after the Prussian army had put an end to the patriot movement. See also Leeb, *Ideological Origins*, pp. 198 ff.

was the usual one. The *Principe* was seen as a symbol of the ruthless use of power without detailed application to the Dutch situation.[30]

The same remark applies to the *Discorsi*. In these years some references indicate how Machiavelli was also used as a support in a plea for a well-ordered republic. One author, Schimmelpenninck, who would later occupy a very high position in Napoleonic Holland, gave the people a sovereign position in his state, but only within the bounds of the law and in respect of those who ruled. With this in mind he repeatedly analysed stipulations from American constitutions. For him too Machiavelli was 'acutissimus', a characterisation we remember was used from the beginning of the seventeenth century.[31] As happened in revolutionary France, Machiavelli evidently experienced a certain revival in the Dutch republic. In 1793 (after the restoration of the stadholder in 1787 to his former powers and two years before the advent of the Batavian Republic) another patriot and soon active participant in the political life, S.I. Wiselius, rendered public his ideas on how democracy in reality ought to be defined. Political equality for him was indispensable and no politically privileged group must be given any rights. The government, moreover, was obliged to promote the causes of religion and morality for the well-being of the people. In the historical part of his work Machiavelli is paid honour to as a forerunner. Wiselius praised the independence of Italian thinkers and philosophers from tyranny of the Church of Rome and then wrote:

He did immense service to the science of government by writing works which give testimony on every page of his profound mind, and which will remain worthy of the attention of intelligent men for all times. For he was the first to indicate the foundations on which civil society, if it be worthy of the qualification 'well-ordered', ought to rest. His extensive reading was incredible, his political observations mark a noble mind; and, if the lessons he gives to princes, in case they are to be taken seriously, really must be qualified as detestable, his love of liberty is worthy of an ancient Roman.

This was the moment when Machiavelli himself was seen as a historical person, a man who in the past had changed the nature of political science. On the one hand his work was now integrated into a historical process and thus looked upon from a distance with more detachment than before. On the other hand a kind of commitment to the example of ancient Rome still made Wiselius prefer to see him in classical republican garb.[32]

---

[30] See L.J.B. in *De Post van den Neder-Rhijn*, 5(1785), 505–12 and 565–72. Kluit's oration was published in 1787 *Academische redevoering, over het misbruik van 't algemeen staatsrecht, of over de nadeelen en onheilen, die uit het misbruik in de beoefeninge voor alle burgermaatschappijen te wachten zijn* (Leiden, 1787).

[31] R.J. Schimmelpenninck, *Dissertatio de imperio populari rite temperato* (Lugduni Batavorum, 1784), pp. 38, 44, 47, 67. References to *Discorsi*, I, chs. 4, 31, 58.

[32] Wiselius' writings were conceived in 1793 but published only in the nineteenth-century *Proeve Ver de verschillende regeringsvormen in derzelver betrekking tot het maatschappelijk geluk* (Leiden, 1831), p. 57 and *De staatkundige verlichting der Nederlanderen, in een wijsgeerig-historisch tafereel geschetst (een geschrift van den jare 1793)* (Brussel 1828, 2nd edn.) quoted p. 114.

We have now followed the traces of Machiavelli through more than two centuries of Dutch history. The reception of his work, as I have tried to show, was not an easy one. Hesitation, defence and condemnation were paramount. But the identification of the history and fate of the Dutch republic with the religious cause made this inevitable. Everywhere in Europe the attitude towards Machiavelli's work raised the question of whether considerations of a moral and religious nature were still to be maintained in political thought. Perhaps in this respect the persistence of Dutch writers in their condemnation of Machiavelli is typical of the situation in the Dutch republic. The second point that remains to be discussed is the relation of Machiavelli to Dutch republicanism. Recently an eloquent argument has emphasised that there was no such thing as a peculiarly Dutch intellectual republican tradition, a Dutch paradigm. This statement was made after an elaborate discussion of the difficulties of integrating Dutch republicanism as a whole into the Atlantic republican tradition as defined by J.G.A. Pocock in his *magnum opus*.[33] After this *tour d'horizon* of Machiavelli's career in the Dutch republic I must come to the same conclusion.

Dutch republicanism was eclectic to a high degree and the opposite of monolithic. Because of that the fact that men like the De la Courts and Spinoza diverged in some sense from the standard view of Machiavelli must be considered a kind of miracle. They had no inhibitions about recognising Machiavelli as a source of inspiration. That is why they entered the field of European republicanism. Overall, however, it is clear that for the most part Machiavelli was treated with great indifference. It is impossible to know whether there was a more profound influence at work. It seems unlikely. The attention of Dutch educated men was focussed on the history of the institutions of their own republic. For them this history was a school for political experience. Even at the end of the eighteenth century historical argumentation was closely related to politics in questions concerning the right competences of institutions or interpretations of privileges. Of course, natural law and juridical expositions had their place, but only insofar as they were useful. In the seventeenth century Machiavelli had been an integral part of a still invigorating classical tradition in which the De la Courts and Spinoza participated, in spite of their resistance and fundamental originality. The next century saw Dutch republicans more and more receptive to other authorities on the question of community and state. Machiavelli was relegated to the background.

[33] Kossmann, 'Dutch republicanism', pp. 224ff.

13

Montesquieu and the new republicanism

JUDITH N. SHKLAR

Montesquieu did for the latter half of the eighteenth Century what Machiavelli had done for his century, he set the terms in which republicanism was to be discussed. It goes without saying that it was a significantly different republicanism, not so much because of Montesquieu's doubts about Machiavelli's scholarship, but because their aims were not the same.[1] To be sure, like all republicans they shared at least one polemical object, hostility to the Roman Catholic Church, but even here the reasons for their respective hatred were quite different. Machiavelli objected to the papacy's interference in Italian politics, and Christianity's lack of martial spirit. Montesquieu hated the Church for the cruelty of its persecutions, its intolerance, its obstruction of scientific learning and its superstitious practices and prejudices. Paganism did not therefore seem like an attractive alternative to him and he had no more use for political than for theological religiosity. This was thus not an aspect of Roman republicanism that was significant for him, as it certainly was for Machiavelli.

The two authors also had different political enemies, even though republicanism might stand as a reproach to all of them. Machiavelli's contempt was directed at the incompetence of the petty rulers of the Italian city states, while Montesquieu excoriated the absolute monarchy created by Louis xiv. His great fear was not political impotence, but despotism, a regime to which Spain was rapidly descending and to which even France might fall prey. This had an extremely important bearing on the character of his republicanism. Indeed most republican ideologies after the Reformation found their inspiration and structure in revolts against monarchy, rather than in an unbroken adherence to the Florentine tradition. Montesquieu, however, was to present a wholly new case against the political mores of the monarchical order. Among the several ideologies which sustained the *ancien régime* there was what one might call the Augustan charade. It was certainly used by Augustus himself, and eventually by Seneca in *De Clementia*. It consisted in simply transferring the ancient Roman virtues to the new ruler and his court. He and his successors continued to

---

A version of this essay was presented as the Samuel Paley Lecture in the Hebrew University of Jerusalem in 1987.

[1] *Dossier de L'Esprit des Lois, Montesquieu. Oeuvres complètes*, ed. Roger Caillois (Paris, 1951), vol. II, p. 996.

distinguish themselves drastically from the primitive kings of Rome, and posed as the saviours of the republic. Something analogous was, surely, perpetrated by the panegyrists of the monarchy of Louis xiv and certainly by the fascist ideologies that flourished in the years between the two wars in our century. In the seventeenth-century version of the Augustan pretence, a good prince not only possessed all the great stoical and republican virtues of selfless patriotism, abnegation of all personal inclinations in favour of the public good, stern repression of all ambitions other than public ones, impartial justice for all, and so on, but the courtiers also displayed republican virtues by just serving him as selflessly as he serves the state. For he is the republic now. That is what the young were taught as part of the classical curriculum and that was what the finest drama put on the public stage. Consider Corneille's *Cinna*, where Augustus not only gives up justifiable personal vengeance and weariness as well, because he now *is* Rome. In Racine's *Berenice* Titus gives up a woman he loves because she is a queen and Roman republican mores do not allow a marriage to a princess, it is just too monarchical. And Nero's unlucky tutor in *Britannicus* tries to persuade the young emperor to restore the practices and mores of the republic under his absolute, omnipotent rule. As a determined critic of that monarchy, Montesquieu's first task was to delegitimise this ideology by exposing it as essentially fraudulent. To this end he had to demonstrate that republican virtue was possible only in genuinely popular non-monarchical republican regimes and that political virtue had never been the effective ideology of any monarchy, whose 'principle', that is, active political ethos, was that of personal honour, and not virtue.[2] That is, in fact, one of the main themes of *The Spirit of the Laws*. Moreover, even on purely scholarly historical grounds, he would show that the republic was a political form that had no place in the modern age. It was a thing of the past. It had been admirable, in its time, but now it was an object of scientific historical study and curiosity, not of emulation. Unlike Machiavelli he did not for a moment dream of a new Roman republican order to replace the monarchy, and that is, of course a very great difference. Even though Montesquieu eventually wrote two different accounts of the character of ancient republics, he never wavered in his conclusion that they were utterly remote from the political world of modern Europe. The differences between then and now were numerous, but they could be summed up in one word, size. The modern state was large, its culture diffuse, while the ancient republic had to be small and governed by a shared civic ethos. If a republic tried to expand, it simply lost its soul and decayed as Rome had. That meant that if the republican past was not to become irrelevant it would have to be imaginatively recreated or to be explicitly replaced by a new expansive

[2] *De L'Esprit Des Lois*, Bk iii, chs. 5–7. (I do not cite pages here since there are so many scholarly editions and as the chapters are very brief.)

republicanism to fit the modern political world. Rousseau responded to the first of these intellectual possibilities, while the authors of *The Federalist* pursued the second one. Both were deeply indebted to Montesquieu.

The opening sentences of Montesquieu's first published work on classical antiquity, *Considérations sur les causes de la grandeur des romains et de leur décadence*, tell us that Rome was not even a city in the modern sense of the word. Its private dwellings were insignificant, because it was a place of public structures for public activity.[3] In *The Spirit of the Laws* we are reminded that with the discovery of the compass, the symbolic significance of which did not escape him, Europe was so transformed that it had become wholly unlike anything that had ever existed in the past.[4] New directions, communications, discoveries, new wealth and above all new power, had made it completely unlike the earlier world. The great danger in this, Montesquieu thought, was that it tempted princes to strive for a world monarchy, like the Roman empire. They could not achieve it, but their efforts would certainly ruin Europe.[5] Empire was on the agenda of every European state and Montesquieu meant to deglamorise it. The Roman empire was to serve as an awful example and the republic that had preceded it and led to it could, therefore, not be painted in altogether glowing colours. We are never allowed to forget the inveterate bellicosity of the Romans. Rome was always bent on war and conquest was its only passion.[6] And so he took the story right up to its bitter end, the fall of the Eastern empire. Machiavelli, while he does mention later events, wisely quit with the Punic Wars. But as part of this debunking enterprise Montesquieu went all the way to the final decline and fall. Also his naturalistic approach to history, so unlike Machiavelli's, led him to brush aside that staple of heroic republican history, the great military and political hero. In his history great men were insignificant except at the very beginnings of cities. Later they scarcely mattered. If it had not been Caesar some other general would have done the republic in.[7] Fortune therefore plays no part at all, since it is not required to account for the failures of great leaders, as it does in Machiavelli. History is about deep, determining causes and immediate precipitating ones. To know them is to explain the past.[8]

In other respects Montesquieu's history of Rome is more conventional. Martial virtue is appreciated for its civic qualities and it is not denied that the republic was a free and popular state. Nor did the people fail. It is leaders who corrupt the people, not the other way around, so that we are not led to believe that the popular basis of republican rule was at fault.[9] Military success was itself, however, bound to lead to corruption, and it is conquest that led to the influx of wealth and avarice, and to luxury and effeminacy. But these were not in themselves the most serious causes of decline. Rather, it was the independence

---

[3] *Oeuvres* vol. ii, p. 69.   [4] *Esprit*, Bk xxi, ch. 21.
[5] *Romains*, pp. 193–4; *Esprit*, Bk ix, ch. 8.   [6] *Romains*, pp. 70–4, 80, 122.
[7] *Ibid.* pp. 70, 124–32.   [8] *Ibid.* p. 173.   [9] *Ibid.* p. 139.

of local military commanders and their rivalries that were the real cause of the fall of the republic. The scenario is one in which the martial vigour that had made the city virtuous also killed its spirit and freedom, as it succeeded in its objective, the conquest of the known world. Rome was bound to commit civic suicide because it was first and foremost an expansionist military state. A tragedy of character, not of fate, in short.[10]

The analysis of republican government in *The Spirit of the Laws* is far less harsh and more traditional. Even the Polybian cycle is resurrected though it was not, in fact, Montesquieu's only theory of political decline. The purpose of that work was in any case far more scientific than polemical. The great question was to determine what made various regimes survive or fail, and to construct a comprehensive theory of comparative law. The positive features of republics are therefore stressed, especially their equality. Virtue is the love of equality, and while it does create a dreadful danger of anarchy that is not inevitable. The account of Athens in *The Spirit of the Laws*, the most democratic of cities, is especially notable, for Montesquieu attributed all the commercial virtues to its citizens, as well as the normal republican ones of patriotism, in this case love of equality itself. Frugality, prudence, honesty, caution, these are the commercial traits of character, and a democratic republic needs them especially.[11] Athens' failure was military, because its citizens had too good a life to sacrifice themselves to the demands of war. A federation of small republics should in principle have rendered them more secure, Montesquieu thought, but the evidence was discouraging.[12] Like a martial republic, an egalitarian one, requires intense education, a small face-to-face society, and inviolable traditions, mores and personal habits, all directed towards public objectives. Censors must reinforce the informal restraints that citizens impose on each other, and if small size is a military liability, republics can always federate. However, the demands of the virtuous, egalitarian republic seemed overwhelming, and Montesquieu thought that they were very frail and likely to slip into other forms. The aristocratic republic depends on the moderation and intelligence of its ruling class, and with the example of Venice before him, Montesquieu did not rate its chances of success very highly. What is most significant in this picture of republicanism is the stress on equality and the sense that these regimes were not very durable. At no time did Montesquieu present them in such a way as to make them appear as anything but irretrievable memories of the past, objects of historical understanding.[13] They acted as contrasts, not examples to be copied. And there was no nostalgia at all here. Let us recall that the celebrated Eleventh Book of the *Spirit of the Laws* is not merely about England, but a *comparison* between England and Rome, and that Rome is

[10] *Ibid.* pp. 116–20, 151. [11] *Esprit*, Bk v, ch. 6; Bk xxi, ch. 7.
[12] *Ibid.* Bk ix, chs. 1–3.
[13] *Ibid.* Bk ii, ch. 2; Bk iii, ch. 3; Bk v, chs. 2–7; Bk viii, chs. 2–4, 16.

presented as less self-correcting and less just than England.[14] For while the life of every citizen was precious and capital cases were very carefully tried, Rome did not have an independent judiciary. The people, the Senate and the magistrates, all three, had judicial functions, and that made the separation of powers and its cornerstone, a wholly independent judiciary, impossible. It was England's achievement to have such a judiciary which alone could secure the personal, as well as the political liberty of its citizens. The Romans enjoyed only the latter. The classical republic was, in sum, not only gone forever, it was for all its many remarkable qualities not to be regretted. The model for Europe now was a commercial, extensive, non-military representative 'democracy disguised as a monarchy', England, ruled by legislation, not mores.

In the Thirteen Colonies of North America this was a tune that was going to play extremely well. Not virtue, but interest, and not unchanging customs, but consciously made laws keep a modern free state like England going. It was certainly a more stable and less oppressive form of government than any other, even if it was less than edifying. Above all it raised the prospect of an extensive republic that would not be a conquering imperial power. In 1787 no writer was quoted by all sides more often than Montesquieu.[15] It was his hour of vindication, for many French readers had not appreciated his doctrines. To some readers, indeed, Montesquieu's new political science was nothing but an intellectual obstacle, not because it was untrue, far from it, but because it seemed to eliminate republicanism from relevant modern political discourse. Democratic readers might well wonder whether he had succeeded in making equality and virtue politically obsolete ideas. Rousseau certainly feared that he had, and it forced him into a life-long struggle with the modern author whom he respected the most and quoted most often. That accounts for the otherwise incomprehensible and absurd remark in the Fifth Book of *Emile*, that only 'the illustrious Montesquieu' might have created 'the great and useless science' of political right, but that 'he was content to discuss the positive right of established governments'.[16] In short, he had chosen to discuss what is, rather than what ought to be, or to be exact, what Rousseau thought 'ought' should be. He did not disagree with Montesquieu about the prospects for republicanism in Europe, his pose as the citizen of Geneva did not last, and eventually, in his enraged *Lettres écrites de la montagne*, he reminded the citizens of that city that they were not Spartans, or even Athenians, but just a bunch of petty, selfish merchants and artisans.[17] Corsica, happily underdeveloped, was the last faint hope that some remote corner of Europe might remain uncorrupted by civilisation, but that did not amount to a refutation of Montesquieu's analysis of

[14] See also *Romains*, p. 116.
[15] Donald S. Lutz, 'The relative influence of European writers on late eighteenth-century American political thought'. *American Political Science Review*, 78 (1984), pp. 189–98.
[16] J.-J. Rousseau, *Oeuvres complètes*, (Paris, 1969), vol. IV, p. 836.   [17] *Oeuvres*, III, p. 881.

the modern world. On the contrary, it only proved how far Europe had strayed from the republican ideal.[18] The problem for Rousseau was therefore to find a way to bring the egalitarian ethos of republican regimes back into modern political theory, if not into practice.

In some ways the distance that Montesquieu had created between ancient and modern politics served Rousseau very well. It allowed him to condemn modernity by comparing it to an idealised republican antiquity. It was only when he wanted to construct a model of a truly just egalitarian society that Montesquieu became a threatening presence. Nevertheless, Rousseau was able to work his way around his predecessor and to use him for his own purposes. It was done in three ways: first, by using Montesquieu's version of the egalitarian republic as a critical mirror for modern society as a whole, secondly, by showing that the old republic, especially Sparta, was the only fit model for a just society and finally, by universalising republicanism as a preventive psychotherapy for the anguish created by inequality and indeed by all social encounters. It comes as no surprise, therefore, that Rousseau admired Machiavelli without reservations, and probably wished that it were possible to return to his relatively simple stance.[19]

To illustrate these three uses of republicanism one need consider only three of Rousseau's works: *The Discourse on the Arts and Sciences*, his first published essay, 'Political economy', written for the *Encyclopédie* and in some ways a first draft for the *Social Contract*, and lastly the first chapter of *Emile*. In the *First Discourse* the classical republic is a mixture of Sparta and Rome and it is seen as a culture, as what Montesquieu would have called the spirit of a people. Physically and morally healthy, the republican citizen endures hardship joyfully. Virtue, 'the sublime science of simple minds' flourishes, as there are no arts, no sciences and no scepticism. Cato had thrown out the Greek intellectuals, and Spartans were taught only courage in war, religion, physical fitness and to repress cupidity. Virtue is first and foremost anti-intellectual. It must be so, since the difference in human talents has been the origin of 'the sinister inequality' that has ruined European society. Sparta, in stark contrast, was a wholesomely mindless, single-value society. In their happy ignorance the Romans, who shared this virtue, conquered the world. Their forced marches cannot be repeated in the modern world which consists of happy slaves, whose arts disguise their chains, who live in a divisive inequality, racked by vanity, curiosity and doubt, which have as debilitating an effect on their moral as on their physical well-being.[20] It is a clear answer to the question of whether art and science improve us, but it is so colossal a critical over-kill, that no hope for any recovery for modern Europe is imaginable. The effect of the distance between

---

[18] *Du Contrat Social*, Bk II, ch. 10.

[19] 'Le Prince de Machiavel est le livre des républicains', *Contrat Social*, Bk III, ch. 6. *Oeuvres*, III, p. 409, can stand for many similar remarks.   [20] *Oeuvres*, III, pp. 6–30.

republican virtue as health and modern vice as terminal decay is so great as to leave no plausible way of making the ancient republic politically relevant except as a blunt instrument of moral aggression. It also put Rousseau in a very equivocal position to Montesquieu, because he praises everything the latter found most questionable in classical republicanism, especially the spirit of conquest, but yet stays within the confines of Montesquieu's historical paradigm.

In *Political Economy* we discover that the ultimate moral justification of the republic is that in it 'man is not in contradiction with himself', because the laws succeed in making his personal wishes identical with the just aims of society.[21] The personal self is utterly absorbed by the public self in a genuine republic. Indeed all erotic energies are directed towards the republic as the citizens do not just obey the laws, they *love* them. There are no partial societies, for these would tend to divert love and loyalty from the state. The education of the young is not left to the family, but conducted by retired magistrates and soldiers who have already proven themselves in the service of the republic. The children 'do not perceive their own existence except as part of the state'. This would not be possible if this were not a just society, whose laws exist to protect the life, the goods and the freedom of the citizens. Their freedom, moreover, is based on both material and political equality. The government administers the laws and makes them conform to the 'general will', a phrase drawn from Montesquieu but given a new meaning. It was Montesquieu's assumption that the British House of Commons spoke for the general will, while Rousseau did not think that it could be represented, that indeed representative institutions made a mockery of republican freedom.[22] The effect is that the socially informed consent of all prevails and both the spirit and actuality of social equality are maintained by a system of graded taxation. Here the republic is more Spartan than Roman and the dangers of a policy of conquest are stressed, because the whole purpose of republican government is to create a small, cohesive community whose citizens will be almost identical. If there is competition here it is athletic, both in the physical and moral sense, as men compete for public approbation, which depends on displays of public not of personal qualities. The magistrates of the republic have basically only one task, to maintain equality, by the laws and by education. The laws being loved are spontaneously followed, and it is they that are 'the miracle' of the just society, because they treat all citizens identically, and indeed see to it that they in fact *are identical*. As he was to say in the *Social Contract*, liberty cannot prevail without equality, because the dependence of one person upon another is inevitable in all unequal relationships. And such dependence 'est autant de force ôtée au corps de l'Etat'.[23]

---

[21] *Discours sur l'économie politique, Oeuvres*, III, pp. 241–78, *passim*.
[22] *Contrat Social*, Bk III, ch. 15. [23] Untranslatable. *Contrat Social*, Bk II, ch. 11, p. 390.

Whatever the liberty within the body of the state might be it was not the individualism that prevailed in Montesquieu's idealised England.

To see the full implications of the specifically republican institutional order that Rousseau favoured one must turn to the last section of the *Social Contract*. These pages are directed not just against modern practices in general, but against Montesquieu in particular. Because representation was no substitute for democratic participation, Rousseau had to show that a large population might be able to govern itself directly, after all. He therefore set out to show that the Romans proved that 200,000 citizens could be assembled to legislate for themselves. In the synopsis of this section of the *Social Contract*, in the section 'On Travel', in *Emile*, Rousseau said that one of the questions he dealt with there was whether the democratic Roman republic was a large state.[24] In fact he never tells us whether 200,000 citizens are or are not a large population. 200,000 people are obviously quite a crowd, but by eighteenth-century standards it was clearly a small state, which would prove Montesquieu right, which was very troublesome. If republics must remain small to function as politically egalitarian regimes, then they have no place in modern Europe, and it is not at all clear that this is the conclusion Rousseau wanted his readers to draw at this point. He certainly wanted to embellish the picture of Roman institutions that Montesquieu had so convincingly drawn. So in the last part of the *Social Contract* what he first of all set out to deny was that block voting was weighted in favour of the rich in Rome, as Montesquieu had argued, but it was not the main issue for him. The heart of the matter was that as long as tribunes and censors and other magistrates saw to the virtue of the Romans, they had governed themselves more directly and perfectly than Montesquieu had suggested.[25] Finally, there was the matter of religion, which more than any other part of the *Social Contract* was meant to speak to contemporary Europe. For the civil religion not only completes the institutional design of the just and virtuous republic, it also presents a modern substitute for paganism.[26] Rousseau had first presented this notion in a letter to a horrified Voltaire, and we can be sure that Montesquieu would have been even more repelled by it.[27] As is entirely clear, the civil faith is a religious programme for a post-Christian society, not a simple reversion to paganism. In his view of religion Rousseau was very close to Machiavelli, but unlike the latter he could imagine a modern alternative to both a lost paganism and a decadent Christianity. Its effect would be to emulate the republican martial ethos by removing the deepest source of our inner division. Rousseau often said that we are what we believe, that opinion makes us. Give Europe a new civic religion of public loyalty, and maybe it could yet attain a republican future.

---

[24] *Émile. Oeuvres*, IV, p. 843. [25] *Contrat Social*, Bk IV, chs. 4–7.

[26] *Contrat Social*, Bk IV, ch. 8.

[27] *Lettre à Voltaire*, August, 1756. *Correspondance complète de Jean-Jacques Rousseau*, ed. R.A. Leigh (Geneva, 1967), vol. IV, pp. 37–50.

A revival of republicanism, especially in the absence of a new Lycurgus–Moses figure was not likely. And for Rousseau as for his Plutarchian models, everything depends on great, creative authority figures, from Moses to Calvin and his own vision of a Great Legislator. That such a miracle should recur was not likely and psychologically little could be hoped for without him. The *Discourse on the Origins of Inequality* had given such a harrowing account of the depth of the psychological damage that we suffer in any society and of the encompassing deformity we suffer at its beginning, at the most primitive level of our experience, that inequality and all its vices seem wholly insuperable. Health is not possible, even in those rustic societies where people see each other very rarely and only in order to quickly conduct their public business. The republican regime in the face of this disastrous psychological reality acts as a possible preventive psychotherapy. It denatures us to such an extent that we lose all our natural instincts and respond only to social stimuli. In Rome a man was neither Caius nor Lucius, he was only a citizen, and Spartan mothers rejoiced in military victories in which they had lost all their sons. What they do not suffer from is the dreadful inner tug of war between nature and culture that renders civilised humanity so neurotic and distraught. In a republic early and complete training avoids it. The citizen does not 'float between inclination and duty', he has been wholly denatured.[28] It is not a plausible defence of republicanism on Rousseau's own showing. Our corruption is rooted so deeply in our psyche that no amount of patriotic fervour or civic reinforcement can really touch it. If the very proximity of others arouses our *amour propre*, our tendency to see ourselves through the eyes of others and to torment ourselves because in *no* society can our natural differences fail to lead to a degree of inequality, then republicanism cannot repair the pain of *all* association. It might be palliative at best.

Such then were the uses of republicanism for Rousseau. He was not able to make a contemporary programme out of republicanism in the way that Machiavelli had been able to do, because he could not and did not wish simply to discard the historical confines within which Montesquieu had placed that model. What he did recover was the absolute primacy of the idea of virtue, of egalitarian patriotism, as the essence of the republic. It gave his theory of equality its most characteristic feature and restored it to a second life in the vocabulary of modern radicalism. He thus opened a new chapter in its uses. First it became a weapon against modernity, especially against scepticism and modern intellectuality. Secondly, it could be used as a way of highlighting the psychological tensions inherent in all social life, but especially in complex, stratified and inegalitarian societies. And, most fatefully of all, in the most directly political of his essays, one sees republicanism as a new and powerful ideology for modern Europe. It was to offer both a democratic and a spiritual

---

[28] *Emile*, Bk I, pp. 249–50; Bk II, p. 311.

regeneration. We should not, however, place him too hastily. We ought to remember that Rousseau never lost sight of the ordinary individual for whom the republic exists. The best test of a good society, we are told in the *Social Contract*, is to see whether people have big families. If they do, it means that they are secure and content. That is why Rousseau's republicanism is popular and not heroic in its ultimate character, even if he resorted to all the Plutarchian myths of great men. For all their divergences, and they are very great, Rousseau accepted more of Montesquieu's theories than he rejected. He certainly turned them to unexpected and utterly new uses; not those of Machiavelli after all, but of a new democracy with a will to equality.

The bridge that leads from the republicanism of Machiavelli to that of the French Revolution does not stand alone. There is another one that ends in the United States Constitution of 1787. After a heated debate about the possibility of an extensive republic Americans discovered that they were actually living in such a polity and that they needed to explain it to themselves. That was the task that Alexander Hamilton and James Madison, writing under the name of Publius, accomplished in their celebrated *Federalist Papers*. Their first object, however, was to reply to the numerous critics of the proposed constitutional plan. Many democratically inclined Americans shared Rousseau's fears, and one journalist in Newport, RI even quoted him correctly to demonstrate that representation on the English model was not freedom, but a charade.[29] Other less original anti-federalists argued, quoting Montesquieu copiously, that no large territory could be a republic, that the government was so remote from the people that it must soon degenerate into a distinct political class, and become despotical. The electoral districts were so large that only the rich and clever could ever be elected to the House of Representatives, and that they would certainly not speak for the general will. The culture of the North, with its industrious traders was wholly unlike that of the slave-owning, idle planters of the South. Had not Montesquieu said all there was to say about the differences created by the climate? No government could possibly suit such diverse populations and one must dominate and oppress the other, soon there would be Georgian militiamen in New England and Pennsylvania. Finally the separation of powers was not as complete as was required by Montesquieu, nor did the provisions for a safe criminal law and jury trials meet his or their standard for a free government.[30] As we know, half the amendments of the Bill of Rights are about the rights of the accused in criminal cases, so the point was well taken. For us the most relevant issue is, however, about republican government. The

---

[29] *A Newport Man*, Newport Mercury, 1788, *The Complete Anti-Federalist*, ed. Herbert J. Storing (Chicago, 1981), vol. IV, pp. 250–4.

[30] See especially, *Essays of John DeWitt*, and *Letters of Agrippa* for New England anti-federalism, and for Pennsylvania, *Essay by Montezuma* and, most important of all, *The Address and Reasons of Dissent of the Minority of the Convention of Pennsylvania to their Constituents, The Complete Anti-Federalist*, vol. IV, pp. 15–40 and 68–116; vol. III, pp. 53–7 and 145–67.

radical Pennsylvanians clearly believed that the individual states were small societies in the classical pattern, and that egalitarian virtue could survive only under democratic political arrangements in which the sovereignty of the people expressed itself in fairly direct, participating ways, and the distance between voter and representative was slight. It should be added that there was no trace of martial breast-beating among the Pennsylvanian anti-federalists, some of whom were, of course, Quakers.

Such were the arguments Publius had to answer. He was, however, determined to do more than merely assuage the fears of his opponents; he meant to show that the new constitutional order would be in every way superior to all other republican governments, especially those of classical antiquity. It was intrinsically better because it would offer its citizens stability and freedom such as no city-state had ever known. Moreover, it would be a real republic, not in spite but because of its size. Without a monarch, or a hereditary nobility, or a mixed regime it would be an entirely popular state based on the consent of the governed. The very divergences among its many citizens would, moreover, create a system in which no party would impose its will upon the public to destroy the republic in the suicidal manner of the ancient city states.[31] To that end Publius had to put the greatest possible distance between modern America and classical antiquity. The illusion that any of the thirteen states resembled republican Rome or Athens was to be dispelled once and for all. They were simply far larger already. However, the old city-states were in any case an unworthy example to follow. Publius had far less affection for them than Montesquieu had displayed. Their main use for him was negative, as awful examples of political failure. The only time Rome is mentioned with full approval in *The Federalist* is to demonstrate that two concurrent taxing authorities are compatible with achieving greatness. The power of both the states and the Federal Government to tax the same citizenry does not, therefore, have to lead to any dire consequences at all.[32] With that exception, the institutions of antiquity were treated as suggestions to be discarded or as examples of everything that was to be avoided.

The rejection of the example of antiquity begins very early on, with a reminder of their endless wars. Unlike Montesquieu and most liberal political theorists Publius did not think that commercial states were particularly peaceful. Commercial republics he noted, pointing to Athens and to Carthage, were inclined to go to war. And they did so for no good reason. War is always an option. Pericles apparently dragged Athens into war in order to please a prostitute.[33] There was no need to dwell on the conduct of military republics, since they were completely irrelevant to the civilian ethos of America.[34] The

---

[31] See especially *Federalist*, 10, 39 and 51. Because there are so many editions of *The Federalist Papers*, and since the individual papers are so short, I shall cite them only by number.

[32] *Federalist*, 34.   [33] *Ibid.* 6.   [34] *Ibid.* 8.

message of antiquity was, however, clear. Unless the states accepted the proposed constitution and united under it, they would sooner or later go to war against each other. That was not the only classical disaster that would be averted. The internal divisions of the ancient republics had been a perpetual invitation to foreign intrigue and to treachery on the part of the very men to whom the people had entrusted the powers of government.[35] 'It is impossible to read the history of the petty republics of Greece and Italy without feeling a sensation of horror and disgust at the distractions with which they were continually agitated, and at the rapid successions of revolutions by which they were kept in a state of perpetual vibration between the extremes of tyranny and anarchy', wrote Publius. All of this could be avoided only if the states were to be united into a modern extended republic, built on principles of an improved political science that was unknown to the ancients, for the latter knew nothing of self-correcting representative federal government that was both energetic and free. Should the constitution be rejected, however, the states would also become 'little, jealous, clashing, tumultuous commonwealths, the wretched nurseries of unceasing discord and the miserable objects of universal pity and contempt'. Just like the classical republics. A genuine federal republic would avoid all that, for it would have the resources to quell any uprising in any of the States as well as to provide for the common defence.[36]

When one considers the scorn that Publius heaped upon the endemic disorders of the republics of antiquity, one might suppose that unity was his highest political aim, which would scarcely be compatible with his ardent championship of liberty. That was not the case, however. It was his view that America could overcome the tension between freedom and unity thanks to the practices of representative government. In this it was again ahead of the ancient republics, for although the Athenians had understood representation, they did not use it fully, and so fell prey to personal tyrants.[37] There was far too much direct participation by the entire body of citizens in every branch of the government, and especially in Athens' popular assemblies. 'Had every Athenian citizen been a Socrates, every Athenian assembly would still have been a mob.' Such a crowd is bound to give way to unreasoning passions and is invariably manipulated by some wholly unprincipled leader.[38] In contrast to this lamentable spectacle, 'is it not the glory of the people of America' that 'they have not suffered a blind veneration for antiquity?' Though they have shown 'a decent regard for the opinions of former times', they have now embarked upon 'the experiment of an extended republic' and posterity will be grateful for this innovation. 'Happily for America, happily we trust for the whole human race' they have rejected the past and 'pursued a new and more noble course'.[39] To legislate for one's own needs as they arose and to favour political change, rather

---

[35] *Ibid.* 22.   [36] *Ibid.* 9.   [37] *Ibid.* 63.   [38] *Ibid.* 55.   [39] *Ibid.* 14.

than merely to preserve one's institutional patrimony, was clearly one of the greatest departures of Publius from classical political theory and even from Montesquieu's caution. Above all, it reversed the belief that republics had to be bound by ancient mores, rather than by innovative legislation. Publius had, after all, absorbed the lessons of a successful revolution, and if his faith in human nature was not great, he certainly had a lot of confidence in modern science, not least the political science learned from Montesquieu. That science had taught him that freedom and virtue were not necessarily tied to each other. The English, as they make their second appearance in *The Spirit of the Laws*, are presented as selfish, irrational, debauched and devoid of any religious beliefs whatever. Yet they will bear any taxes and give their lives for their freedom.[40] Joined to what he had said about the excellences of the British constitution, Montesquieu's American readers, who thought of themselves as the last true Englishmen, could now understand just how different their world was from that of ancient Sparta and its like. The political qualities that they had to cultivate did not in any way depend on the educative forces of the small, watchful city. They appreciated virtue, but its requirements were not those of Rousseau. A respect for the property and rights of all citizens and a willingness to do one's best for one's constituents was all that was required of those who ruled. Nor should one rely on great men. Even 'enlightened statesmen' were a rarity, and a good constitution was built on their absence or political insignificance. What counts is to get reasonably able representatives into office, and here the larger the constituency, the greater the pool of able people who might be candidates for election. Extensive republics are simply 'more favorable to the election of proper guardians of the public weal'.[41] Moreover, as long as elections are popular the essence of republicanism is preserved, for it is not size or immediacy that counts, but the ultimate source of authority, which remains the people. This was no monarchy or aristocracy, but a republic, that realised the permanent will of the people because both the states and the proposed federal republic had constitutions that were designed to preserve their liberty and property.[42] The new extended republic, unlike the little republics of antiquity would, moreover, be able to protect the public against the local factions that threatened freedom and property precisely because it was both large, powerful and overtly grounded in the consent of the entire American people, 'the only legitimate fountainhead of power'.[43] After all, the constitution Publius was defending does begin with the words, 'We the People' and it did not mean the plebs of Rome or the Commons of England or the Third Estate of France. It was everybody. The mixed constitution had, in fact, died early on in the Convention, when Charles Pinckney got up and said what everyone knew, that there was nothing to mix in America, the difference between the rich and

---

[40] *Esprit*, Bk XIX, ch. 27.   [41] *Federalist*, 10.   [42] *Ibid.* 36.   [43] *Ibid.* 49.

poor was not so great as to require any institutional recognition. Neither Polybius' Roman constitution, nor its equally mixed feudal successor had any relevance. Even England, was not to be treated with the reverence that Montesquieu had heaped upon it.[44]

If the mixed constitution was gone, direct democracy and its ethos were even more irrelevant. Modern representative government in an extended republic was a vast improvement because, unlike classical democracy, it has a built-in remedy against the ruinous conflicts of factions. Far from having to crush differences of interest or political and religious opinion, diversity was encouraged to flourish in an extended republic. The greater the multiplicity of religious sects and of more tangible property interests, the more likely these groups are to form changing and flexible electoral coalitions, none of which has a motive for crushing the others.[45] Bargaining replaces the tumult of popular assemblies, as order and freedom are reconciled pre-politically just as among free sects, in society generally. As every group has a chance of being part of a majority at some time, but also in the minority at others, none have an interest in oppressing their opponents. The representatives of the people act according to the same expectations. They can, moreover, deliberate calmly and save the people from occasional follies, and still remain close enough to the electorate to maintain their trust. Any temptation to behave despotically must die as they remember that they must face the voters soon and eventually become ordinary citizens again. With federalism the need for what Montesquieu called 'intermediary powers' is satisfied, and together with the separation of powers, any concentration of authority in too few hands becomes impossible. Indeed the separation of powers in the federal government was greater than Montesquieu, with his English model, had prescribed. Not only was the judiciary given all the independence it needed, the balance of powers was psychologically perfectly equilibrated; 'ambition had been made to counteract ambition'. To be sure, in a republic the legislature must predominate, but in an extensive republic the multiplicity of interests will be reflected there as well, and 'the security for civil rights must be the same as that for religious rights', which were in principle at least fully protected.[46] Finally, as a trump, Publius recalled the military inefficiency of small republics which would now be overcome in a federation that really worked. That was more than all those ancient leagues had been able to do. The latter only showed the costs of smallness, an awful warning to the States.[47]

Turning from the general structure to the specific institutions of the ancient city-states Publius found that they also failed to pass muster. Rome had so feeble an executive that it had to resort to dictators in moments of danger, which was a

---

[44] *The Records of the Federal Convention of 1787*, ed. Max Farrand (New Haven, 1966), vol. I, pp. 396–404. [45] *Federalist*, 10 and 51. [46] *Ibid.* 51. [47] *Ibid.* 17 and 18.

dangerous expedient.[48] The consuls who made up its plural executive, were often at odds and would have been so more often if, as patricians, they had not been united by their fear of the people.[49] And finally, worst of all, ancient politicians did not really know how to put a constitution together. They had to find individual legislators who were driven to resort to violence and superstition to impose a basic law upon their republics. The men who together had written the proposed constitution of the United States were in every way their intellectual and ethical superiors. They had managed to introduce stability and energy into a limited republican government designed for a free people.[50] And they had done this by 'quitting the dim light of historical research' and following 'reason and good sense'.[51] Antiquity had very little to teach them, except to remind them of its many errors.

This then is the second bridge from Montesquieu to a wholly new notion of republicanism. Clearly Publius used Montesquieu's account of republican government to suit his own purposes. He had to denigrate the old republics far more than Montesquieu was inclined to do, and while the latter did constantly speak of legislators, the very idea of a constitutional assembly writing out a future scheme of government had not occurred to him. Cromwell's failed attempt was, after all, the only predecessor of this American political practice. Nevertheless, the extensive republic, short on virtue and dedicated to securing 'the blessings of liberty' was deeply indebted to him. If Rousseau was able to rescue the virtuous, small republic from the assaults of modern politics, Publius managed to make the expansive republic respectable and to devise a model of government that was neither oppressive nor given to the militaristic Augustan ideologies which Montesquieu set out to unmask and destroy. In either case republicanism survived thanks to him even though in forms that were notably different from the Renaissance version and its classical archetype.

[48] *Ibid.* 69.   [49] *Ibid.* 70.   [50] *Ibid.* 37 and 38.   [51] *Ibid.* 70.

PART IV

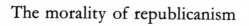

The morality of republicanism

14

The ethos of the republic and the reality of politics

WERNER MAIHOFER

THE REALITY OF POLITICS

The famous speech which Thucydides places in the mouth of Pericles, which we usually regard as his political testament, summarises the basic features of the constitution of a polis. These are what Aristotle later called *Politeiai* and Cicero *res publicae*, and their survival and resumption in Renaissance republicanism, not least in Machiavelli, is one of the principal concerns of this volume. 'Love of freedom', 'respect for the law', 'equality before the law', 'rule through agreement' of the ruled, and government through the consent of the governed, are the decisive characteristics of Attic democracy at the very birth of Europe's political culture, as opposed to the Asiatic despotism that faced it on the other side of the Aegean. Rejection in principle of despotism, of rule through the enslavement of the ruled as a possible constitution of a state, is something that continues to operate even in Montesquieu's opposition to despotism, and it echoes throughout the republican tradition of the Italian Renaissance.

Whilst we have been concerned with reconstructing the origins of this tradition of the republic, a tradition that includes Machiavelli and from which, as Quentin Skinner has so impressively shown, he decisively departs in relation to both *pax* and *iustitia*, what concerns us also is the future of this conception of the republic, in an extrapolation, as it were, of the stimulus Machiavelli gave to political thought at the threshold of the modern era. This stimulus resulted, at the end of that era, in revolutions in both thought and government that continue to define and motivate political thinking in our own period.

The fact that this 'revolution in thought', in what we call the Enlightenment, starts specifically from thinkers who explicitly saw themselves as Machiavelli's successors – which is why Jean Jacques Rousseau in his *Contrat social* calls Machiavelli's *Il principe* a textbook for republicans – is no coincidence. Nor is the fact that in our own time nowhere in his conception of the republic has Machiavelli met with such intellectual resonance as in the case of the thinker who, inspired by Machiavelli, converted Rousseau's republicanism into political philosophy. I am referring of course to Immanuel Kant; and it is again no coincidence that his study in far-off Königsberg contained only one picture: Rousseau's.

In his philosophy of politics we find all the questions that occupy this volume. These range from such ultimate objectives as 'peace' and 'justice' to such decisive preconditions for the constitution and ethos of a republic as 'participation' and 'representation'. They also include the relation between *vivere politico* and *vivere libero*, or the basic contradiction in Machiavelli himself between *amore della parte* and *amore della patria*.

In Rousseau, and again with unrivalled acuity in Kant, the contrast and contradiction brought out by Machiavelli between the reality of politics and the ethos of the republic becomes the central theme of political philosophy. The reality of politics is described by Machiavelli, with incomparable outspokenness and steadfastness for his time, in these words:

You must be clearly aware that there are two kinds of conflict, those which involve the law and those which involve violence. The former corresponds to man, the latter to animals. Since the former often fails to achieve its aims, it is necessary to have recourse to the latter . . . accordingly, one must be a fox to scent the nooses, and a lion to frighten the wolves.

Giving his reasons for this conclusion, Machiavelli adds:

Between man as he actually is and man as he ought to be there is such a fundamental difference that anyone who pays attention only to what ought to happen and not to what does happen will bring about his ruin rather than his survival. One man seeking to act purely morally among many who do not needs must perish.

Accordingly, the question is not only how this kind of analysis of politics can still be combined, even for Machiavelli, with a conception of the republic, since that can only involve 'conflicts involving the law' (and therefore not violence). It is also whether a new conception of the republic might not secure a new relationship with reality and a new truth-content precisely by not starting from the reality of society, determined as it is by *diversità naturale* and *discordia civile* of the *umori* and *sette*, rather than by *harmonia* and *concordia*.

First, though, we must ask ourselves if this reality of politics as described by Machiavelli at the threshold of the modern era is, in principle, still the same three centuries later in the present republican system. After all, in a bizarre conceptual reversal, we like to call it 'Machiavellian', and talk about machiavellianism in politics.

Let us look for an answer not in abstract speculation but in a concrete analysis of the reality of politics, as Kant did, during the time of enlightened despotism, in the first part of the Appendix to his essay 'On eternal peace'. He describes a number of 'sophisticated maxims' of practical politics which, he says, are determined purely by tactics and expediency – and does so in formulations that might all have come from Machiavelli himself. The fact that they are in Latin should not prevent us from asking the question that reaches beyond Kant's own time of how far they apply to the reality of politics today.

Fac et excusa: do what you need to, and then make your excuses. This is the first of the mottoes that Kant explains in his essay on peace, in the following fine words:

Seize a favourable opportunity to gain possession for yourself . . . the justification can be presented much more readily and prettily after the fact, and the violence glossed over . . . the boldness itself will give a certain impression of internal conviction as to the justness of the deed; and the God *bonus eventus* is the best advocate afterwards.

This tried and tested recipe for a politics of the *fait accompli* has been followed, on a large and a small scale, to the present day. It robs one's opponent of any positional advantage and reduces him merely to reacting. True masters of this are easy enough to find; they even manage to get the reaction, and not the prior aggression, to appear in the proper light – a bad one – in both the great world and in everyday life.

Si fecisti nega: whatever you have done, deny it, wherever it harms you. This political slogan is still applied today in all those categorical denials that belong to the rituals of practical politics, even when no one believes them.

But that is not all: as experience shows, it allows an extremely 'beneficial' policy of disloyalty to be pursued at the expense of others, interpreting any statement that causes offence as a regrettable 'misunderstanding' after the fact; and any underhand machinations as groundless 'fabrications' by others. And, as we see on all sides, a no less 'beneficial' policy of leaks can be pursued, followed by convincing denials from the adepts of political ritual who originated them.

Divide et impera: divide and rule is the third all too familiar slogan. It has been around since time immemorial not only in large-scale politics but in petty everyday politics, known to all those who know how to set their political competitors against one another and their political opponents fighting among themselves.

This proven pattern can be used not only to set up a 'balance of power' among states, always to gain greater advantage – one's own. It can also be used by individuals both to place the weak where they can do no harm, and by the strong to eliminate others, where that may be of benefit.

Thus, with a bit of nous and judgement, one need never lose a fight, i.e. a majority decision. If this is combined with making the same promises to all important competitors, so as to keep others in the race whatever happens, then one really cannot help winning.

There are other no less proven and successful political slogans, of the kind that take on their special value only with majority rule. One of them is: 'keep yourself covered' (as we hear in today's political jargon) 'until you see which side has the biggest guns'.

Another slogan, equally successful in daily life, is: always put responsibility for decisions of doubtful success on several shoulders. This is another recipe for successful survival, for it allows success to be immediately taken on one's own shoulders, but failure to be fobbed off on to others. This may run counter to the old legal adage that he who stole the wine should pay the fine, but who gives a damn for some sententious old saying anyway!

One could go on endlessly juggling political slogans, old and new. They define the practice of politics better than anything else, where that means getting and keeping a majority and thus holding back or if need be shutting out competitors from that majority, whether it be a majority of the representatives of an institution, members of a party, electors at the so-called grass-roots level or whatever.

It is hardly surprising if observation of political reality, today as in the past, albeit with more moderate forms and the subtler methods of an advanced political civilisation, reveals essentially the same features. Untruthfulness, not truthfulness, prevails: the subtle division of truths into simple, pure and mere truths, as in Adenauer's famous and cynical dictum. But, as was said in the great memorial speech for Carlo Schmid by that authoritative source, Willy Brandt, 'ruthlessness rules politics too'. He knew what he was talking about: the need to oppose the growing frigidity of a politics dehumanised and overgrown by party calculation and party interest.

Thus, it does not seem mere coincidence that there is so much talk of morality in politics. For, after all, that is part of a politician's image, today as in the past: in acting politically, he always acts morally. And yet morals come into the reality of politics so seldom that even after years you can count on the fingers of one hand the situations where morality was really called for, was really the deciding factor rather than the opportunism I have mentioned.

Not that I am complaining; I wish merely to point out that this is the reality of politics today too. That means that the same question presents itself to us today as it did to Machiavelli: how can we, given this sobering political reality, make law and morality rather than violence and trickery prevail? Bringing this about is what the constitution of the republic is for. So how can we venture to maintain that the republic does have something to do with morality, even if only in some strange, yet to be explained, fashion?

THE CONSTITUTION OF THE REPUBLIC

By a morally oriented action we mean conduct guided no longer one-sidedly, solely from the standpoint of the advantage or disadvantage of the actor, but taking account also of other viewpoints, others' advantage and disadvantage, be they individuals or society as a whole.

This guidance of one's own conduct in the light of its effects on the advantage and disadvantage of others is pointed out for us, in a kind of self-referential reflection, by the two fundamental rules of morality we call the Golden Rule and the Categorical Imperative, as ways of orienting our actions towards the principle of reciprocity or even the principle of universality.

'Do as you would be done by.' Or, in the proverbial, negative version: 'Unto others do not do what you don't want them to do to you.' This requires us to determine our own conduct simultaneously from the viewpoint of the advantage and disadvantage of the other, i.e. according to the principle of reciprocity.

'Act in accordance with a rule that you could wish to be a universal law for all others.' Or in another well-known negative version: 'Where would we be if everybody acted that way?' This requires us to determine our own conduct simultaneously (both mutually in social action, but also universally in the social system) according to the advantage and disadvantage of all others, i.e. according to the principle of universality.

If, then, moral conduct by human beings in principle means and requires nothing more than conduct oriented no longer unilaterally towards one's own advantage and disadvantage but mutually and universally according to the corresponding advantage and disadvantage of others, then the republic too has to do with precisely this morality. Its government is no longer to be for the advantage of the rulers but for that of the ruled. Or, as Rousseau explicitly said, government is no longer to be in the private interest of the rulers but in the general interest of the governed. But this means not a *bonum commune* over and above the actual interest of real individuals, but the *utilitas civium*: the real interests of existing individuals.

This maxim of political morality is taken by Rousseau in his *Political Economy* as the basis of what he calls a 'just government of the people', where there is 'unity of interest and of will between rulers and the ruled'. That means that the 'general will', governing people through the laws, is nothing less than the expression and the instrument of the 'common interest'.

About this 'common good', towards which all republican politics must morally be oriented, Rousseau later makes the following unequivocal statement in his *Contrat social*:

If the conflict of private interests (*intérêts particuliers*) has made necessary the establishment of societies, it has nevertheless made possible the harmonisation of those very interests. What is common to these various interests constitutes the social bond; and were there not some point at which all interests agree, no society could exist. It is solely and entirely according to this common interest that society must be governed.

It is not, then, some sort of ill-understood, surreal *volonté générale* that rules in the sort of commonwealth, *res publica*, that Rousseau calls the republic and that we today call democracy. For Rousseau too, this *volonté générale* is nothing but the expression of the *intérêt commun* in the sense just set forth. And therefore Rousseau says of this, very significantly:

It must be understood that it is less the number of votes that generalises the will than the general interest that unifies them, for with this institution each subjects himself to the conditions that he imposes on others. An admirable harmony of interest and of justice prevails.

If it is morality, according to the common view of both Greek philosophy and Christian theology, expressed since time immemorial in the Golden Rule, that guarantees mutuality in human conduct, it is therefore the only law which will ensure that mutuality of advantages and disadvantages within society will prevail in the conduct of the citizens towards each other: with the 'general will for the common interest' made into law it is no longer the 'personal advantage' of the rulers but the general advantage of the ruled that prevails. Otherwise it would be, as Rousseau says, 'A great folly to hope that those who are in fact the rulers pursue any other interest than their own.' As he emphasises, 'Machiavelli proved this with great clarity.'

It is only, then, when the law is the guarantor of the reciprocity and universality of the relationships arranged by it and the conduct governed by it that it becomes the foundation of a just society of free and equal people. The society will then be based on that fundamental concordance of the common interest: *le point d'accord de l'intérêt commun*, where utility comes into harmony with justice, as Rousseau so finely says.

On the other hand, this also means that justice in such a society of free and equal people can be brought about only through the mutuality of the law. Again, this was clearly seen by Rousseau:

Undoubtedly there is a general justice proceeding only from the reason; even if only to be recognised by us, this justice must be mutual. If things are considered only from the human standpoint, then the laws of justice are, lacking natural confirmation among men, not binding; they serve only for the profit of the bad and to the disadvantage of the just, if the just observe them towards everyone whereas none observes them towards the just. Accordingly, certain agreements and laws are required in order to reconcile rights with duties and bring justice back to its object.

Thus in a free society a 'government of the people by the people' must be founded on rules of conduct and an ordering of relationships which, in contrast with previous political systems, have as their sole goal political morality in the public sphere, based on principles of reciprocity and universality. In a republic, these principles are no longer merely appeals to a personal sense of mutual behaviour, but also to the legality of external conduct in accordance with mutual laws.

This means that in its constitution the republic becomes reduced to institutionalised morality, but at the same time to a morality that is reduced to legality. With this step, already sketched out by Rousseau – namely perceiving the law as guarantor of the reciprocity and universality of all orderings of relationships and guidance of conduct – Kant combines a second and decisive step: that of perceiving the republic as sanctioned rationality.

The decisive weakness in the constitution of the republic as seen by Rousseau and Machiavelli is its declared foundation in the last instance upon 'civil religion'. In other words, on a moral or even religious appeal to the reasonable individual. Even in Rousseau the dubious nature of the ultimately value-based legitimacy of the constitution of a republic becomes apparent. Kant therefore replaced it by a purposive legitimation, related solely to man as understanding subject (*Verstandessubjekt*). In the first 'Amendment' to 'on eternal peace' he says this about it:

Now the republican constitution is the only one fully adequate to the rights of man, but also the hardest to found, and still more to maintain, so that many assert [he means Rousseau] that it would require a nation of angels, because men, with their selfish inclinations, would not be capable of a constitution of such sublime form. But now nature comes along to help the general will grounded in reason – which is honourable but through those very selfish inclinations in such a way that it depends only on the good organisation of the state (which is within human capacity) to direct the forces of each in such a way that one restrains or removes the destructive effect of the other: so that for reason the outcome is as if neither were there at all, so that the individual, even if not a morally good individual, is nevertheless compelled to be a good citizen. However incredible it may sound the problem of creating a state is soluble even for a race of devils (as long as they have reason).

This decisive idea has been repeatedly formulated (for instance by Radbruch): the law must suit even a race of devils, as long as they have reason. From this rational calculation of advantage and disadvantage, based on the viewpoint of prudence and utility and the resulting (purposively) rational appeal to the reasoning subject, the constitution of a republic is efficacious even with regard to a subject who cannot be approached as a reasonable being (*Vernunftperson*).

But over and above this, how is the relationship between politics and the republic, which is described even by Kant as a 'mismatch between politics and morality', to be converted into a 'concordance of politics and morality', by making the ethos of the republic prevail also in the politics of the republic?

THE ETHOS OF THE REPUBLIC

The first attempt at an answer to this difficult question, left open by Machiavelli and Rousseau, is given by Kant in Part II of the Appendix to his essay 'On eternal peace', the section 'On the compatibility of politics and morality in accordance with the transcendental principle of public law.'

Kant is as free as we are today of the illusion that politics is always determined by those pragmatic slogans of tactics and strategy that we have cited. But he makes the consistent requirement of a constitutional state founded upon freedom and equality, which he calls the republic, by contrast with a state of unfreedom and inequality, that politics too must take on a different quality in self-determination and self-control. Kant here sets up a moral concept of law in opposition to the previous pragmatic concept of politics developed in Part I of the Appendix (*Staatsklugheit*) based on considerations of pure intelligence as a 'theory of maxims' (i.e. rules) 'to choose the most serviceable means for one's aims calculated with regard to advantage'. This moral concept of politics, what he calls the 'applied theory of law', expresses nothing less than his fundamental views of the position and role of politics in a republic.

Kant declares the principle of this moral politics to be a requisite of democracy:

That a people should combine into a state in accordance with the sole legal concepts of freedom and equality; this principle is founded not upon prudence but upon duty. But however much political moralists may pontificate about the natural mechanisms of a mass of people entering into a society that will undermine these principles and frustrate its end, or about examples of badly organised constitutions (e.g. democracies without representative systems) in attempting to prove what they say against it, they do not deserve a hearing.

What Kant therefore requires is a politics founded not only upon the intellect, upon 'prudence' and 'utility', but also upon reason, law and morality. In a republic, there should be neither a politics of the pure moralist nor one of the pure politician, but a politics of the moral and legal politician who understands the 'principles of political wisdom' and how they can in every case 'co-exist with morality and with the law'.

But how is the concordance of politics and morality to be achieved in the case of conflict between the pragmatic and moral motivations in politics, not merely theoretically but in practical terms too, and despite all the discordances between morality and politics described and certainly not underestimated by Kant?

Kant's surprising answer is that this can be achieved in accordance with the 'principle of publicity', which calls in every democracy for the broadest possible disclosure of all political acts. For Kant, this follows from the so-called 'transcendental formula of public law' that underlies any free order of society. He formulates it thus: 'All acts relating to the rights of other men, the maxims of which are incompatible with publicity, are unlawful.'

In other words, this means that every measure, every decision taken by a politician for which the true reasons cannot be disclosed, since otherwise there would be a 'public uproar', is unlawful.

Since in a republic the bearers of the function of the state may not decide things that are in line only with the particular will of an individual or few, but only things that are in line with the general will, every politician in a republic has to accept the reasons for his political actions being analysed not only in Parliament, but also in public. Moreover he can, if necessary, be compelled to disclose them, since only in that way does the public have, as Kant requires, the possibility of checking the 'rightfulness of a political act' to see if it is 'in harmony with the rights of the public'.

If a politician takes a measure but cannot stand up for it before the public, he is acting against the ethos of the republic and his action is therefore immoral. Whilst reasons need not be disclosed in every case, the principle of publicity requires that they could in every case have been disclosed in advance without meeting with the disapproval of the generality.

Kant therefore regards it as no less than the basic principle of political morals and moral politics in a republic that the reasons for a political act should not only be disclosed to as many people as possible, but that the 'moral politician' himself should be able to assure his own conscience of the 'agreement of the generality', even in the case of political acts which cannot be made public in good time or in full detail for reasons of 'political wisdom'.

If, then, in a republic every political act must be open to verification by the public and can ultimately arrive at 'rightfulness' only through their 'consent', then the broadest possible publicity for all political acts becomes the essential precondition for this necessary 'agreement or disapproval' by the generality, for whose purposes alone every political act should serve.

Accordingly, even for Kant, although he was living in the political reality of enlightened despotism, the 'freedom of the pen' is nothing less than the 'palladium of the people's rights', since it is only if the state 'allows the spirit of freedom, so deserving of honour in its origins and in its effects, to express itself' that the citizen can form an opinion of what 'concerns the general duty of man', of which he asks to be convinced through reason. Government can in this way become open, in turn acquiring the knowledge that promotes its own end, notwithstanding all political wisdom, even that of the legality of its politics, i.e. ensuring the consent or disapproval of the public.

This means that the office-bearer, the deputy in Parliament, is 'representative of the whole people'; so also is a government minister, who has an obligation to 'ward off harm from the people and promote their well-being'. The principle of publicity applies to all politics in a republic as the special commitment to the ethos of representation.

This requires, in a representative system founded (as Rousseau says) upon the 'concord of interest and will between rulers and ruled', the constant identification of the representatives not with the immediate interests and will of their group or party, but with the actual interests of those represented by them in the state.

It is only in this way that the state can, in our eyes, fulfil its mission, which is the representation of every individual: not only those who share one's own interests and convictions but also those more remote from them and indeed opposed to them, especially the disadvantaged and neglected, whose representation is of more not less importance than all the others.

It is only on the basis of this ethos of representation that the constitution of a republic can be realised through a government in harmony with the governed in 'will and interests', thus complying with the high goal that the state's end is man and nothing else. This is the republican formula, following the 'Copernican revolution' in our political thinking.

CONCLUSION: THE ETHOS OF THE REPUBLIC AND THE PARTY STATE OF THE PRESENT DAY

The ethos of publicity and representation takes on a new importance in the party state of today, whether in one-party states or multi-party systems. Invariably the danger arises of a prevailing orientation of politics towards the interests of the ruling majority and towards the career interests of professional politicians whose election and re-election depends entirely on their own 'clientele', the delegates in their own party's rank-and-file.

If, then, we see a decline in the ethos of representation today, with representatives being said to act no longer in the interests of the republic but as representatives acting merely in line with party interests; if in politics, whether on this side or on that, 'my party right or wrong' is starting to become the ill-omened successor to 'my country right or wrong' and politics today threatens to become no less denatured by 'raison de parti' than it was earlier by 'raison d'état', then this changed political reality seems to call for some fundamental change in our thinking. What we should be concerned about is how the constitution of the republic is to deal with these laws in securing and maintaining majority rule in a party state, without distorting the ethos of representation.

What is needed, at long last after so many failed attempts, is a political system for a modern republic with a 'representative constitution'. It was on this that Kant placed his hopes for further 'progress towards the good' in the 'internal governmental relationships' of 'civil society'. It is also the hope for the 'cosmopolitan society' (*weltbürgerliche Gesellschaft*) emerging in our world today, in the 'external governmental relationship' between 'major political entities' in accordance with the same constitutive principles of an all-embracing 'legal community' and 'ethical community' so movingly evoked by Kant.

15

The republican ideal of political liberty

QUENTIN SKINNER

I

'The crucial moral opposition', Alasdair MacIntyre has recently claimed, 'is between liberal individualism in some version or other and the Aristotelian tradition in some version or other.[1] Part of the significance of the republican tradition analysed in this book lies in suggesting that this is a false dichotomy. I should like to end by underlining this point, seeking to do so by way of concentrating on the 'republican' theory of political liberty. I want in particular to focus on two distinctively 'republican' claims about liberty which are apt to be dismissed as paradoxical or merely confused, but which ought I think to be seen as constituting a challenge to our received views on the subject.[2]

First a word about what I mean by speaking, as I have just done, about our received views on political liberty. I have in mind the fact that, in recent discussions of the concept among analytical philosophers, one conclusion has been reached which commands a remarkably wide measure of assent. It can best be expressed in the formula originally introduced into the argument by Jeremy Bentham and recently made famous by Isaiah Berlin.[3] The suggestion is that the idea of political liberty is essentially a negative one. The presence of liberty is always marked by the absence of something else; specifically, by the absence of some element of constraint which inhibits an agent from being able to act in pursuit of his or her chosen ends, from being able to pursue different options, or at least from being able to choose between alternatives.[4]

[1] Alasdair MacIntyre, *After Virtue* (London, 1981), p. 241.
[2] The ensuing argument constitutes an adapted and extended version of my article 'The paradoxes of political liberty' in *The Tanner Lectures on Human Values*, vol. VII, 1986, ed. Sterling M. McMurrin (Cambridge, 1986), pp. 225–50.
[3] See Douglas G. Long, *Bentham on Liberty* (Toronto, 1977), p. 74, for Bentham speaking of liberty as 'an idea purely negative.' Berlin uses the formula in his classic essay, 'Two concepts of liberty', in *Four Essays on Liberty* (Oxford, 1969), at p. 121 and *passim*.
[4] For freedom as the non-restriction of options, see, for example, S.I. Benn and W. Weinstein, 'Being free to act, and being a free man', *Mind*, 80 (1971), 194–211. Cf. also John N. Gray, 'On negative and positive liberty', *Political Studies*, 28 (1980), 507–26, who argues (esp. p. 519) that this is how Berlin's argument in his 'Two concepts' essay (cited in note 3 above) is best understood. For the stricter suggestion that we should speak only of freedom to choose between alternatives, see, for example, Felix Oppenheim, *Political Concepts: A Reconstruction* (Oxford, 1981), ch. 4, pp. 53–81. For a defence of the even narrower Hobbesian claim that freedom consists in the mere absence of external impediments, see Hillel Steiner, 'Individual liberty', *Proceedings of the Aristotelian Society*, 75 (1975), 33–50. This interpretation of the concept of constraint is partly endorsed by Michael Taylor, *Community, Anarchy and Liberty* (Cambridge, 1982), pp. 142–6, but is criticised both by Oppenheim and by Benn and Weinstein in the works cited above.

Hobbes bequeathed a classic statement of this point of view – one that is still repeatedly invoked – in his chapter 'Of the Liberty of Subjects' in *Leviathan*. He begins by assuring us, with typical briskness, that 'liberty or freedom signifieth (properly) the absence of opposition' – and signifies nothing more.[5] Locke makes the same point in the *Essay*, where he speaks with even greater confidence. 'Liberty, 'tis plain, consists in a power to do or not to do; to do or forbear doing as we will. This cannot be denied'.[6]

Among contemporary analytical philosophers, this basic contention has generally been unpacked into two propositions, the formulation of which appears in many cases to reflect the influence of Gerald MacCallum's classic paper on negative and positive freedom.[7] The first states that there is only one coherent way of thinking about political liberty, that of treating the concept negatively as the absence of impediments to the pursuit of one's chosen ends.[8] The other proposition states that all such talk about negative liberty can in turn be shown, often despite appearances, to reduce to the discussion of one particular triadic relationship between agents, constraints, and ends. All debates about liberty are thus held to consist in effect of disputes either about who are to count as agents, or what are to count as constraints, or what range of things an agent must be free to do, be, or become (or not be or become) in order to count as being at liberty.[9]

I now turn to the two claims about political liberty which, in the light of these assumptions, are apt to be stigmatised as confused. The first connects freedom with self-government, and in consequence links the idea of personal liberty, in a seemingly paradoxical way, with that of public service. The thesis, as Charles Taylor has recently expressed it, is that we can only be free within 'a society of a certain canonical form, incorporating true self-government'.[10] If we wish to assure our own individual liberty, it follows that we must devote ourselves as wholeheartedly as possible to a life of public service, and thus to the cultivation

[5] Thomas Hobbes, *Leviathan*, ed. C.B. Macpherson (Harmondsworth, 1968), Bk. ii, ch. 21, p. 261. (Here and elsewhere in citing from seventeenth-century sources I have modernised spelling and punctuation.)

[6] John Locke, *An Essay Concerning Human Understanding*, ed. Peter H. Nidditch (Oxford, 1975), ii.21.56.

[7] Gerald C. MacCallum, Jr., 'Negative and positive freedom' in *Philosophy, Politics and Society*, Peter Laslett, W.G. Runciman, and Quentin Skinner, eds., 4th ser. (Oxford, 1972), pp. 174–93.

[8] This is the main implication of the article by MacCallum cited in note 7 above. For a recent and explicit statement to this effect, see for example J.P. Day, 'Individual liberty' in A. Phillips Griffiths, ed., *Of Liberty* (Cambridge, 1983), who claims (p. 18) 'that "free" is univocal and that the negative concept is the only concept of liberty'.

[9] This formulation derives from the article by MacCallum cited in note 7 above. For recent discussions in which the same approach has been used to analyse the concept of political liberty, see, for example, Joel Feinberg, *Social Philosophy* (Englewood Cliffs, NJ, 1973), esp. pp. 12, 16, and J. Roland Pennock, *Democratic Political Theory* (Princeton, NJ, 1979), esp. pp. 18–24.

[10] Charles Taylor, 'What's wrong with negative liberty' in *The Idea of Freedom*, Alan Ryan, ed. (Oxford, 1979), pp. 175–93, at p. 181.

of the civic virtues required for participating most effectively in political life. The attainment of our fullest liberty, in short, presupposes our recognition of the fact that only certain determinate ends are rational for us to pursue.[11]

The other and related thesis states that we may have to be forced to be free, and thus connects the idea of individual liberty, in an even more blatantly paradoxical fashion, with the concepts of coercion and constraint. The assumption underlying this further step in the argument is that we may sometimes fail to remember – or may altogether fail to grasp – that the performance of our public duties is indispensable to the maintenance of our own liberty. If it is nevertheless true that freedom depends on service, and hence on our willingness to cultivate the civic virtues, it follows that we may have to be coerced into virtue and thereby constrained into upholding a liberty which, left to ourselves, we would have undermined.

II

Among contemporary theorists of liberty who have criticised these arguments, we need to distinguish two different lines of attack. One of these I shall consider in the present section, the other I shall turn to discuss in section III.

The most unyielding retort has been that, since the negative analysis of liberty is the only coherent one, and since the two contentions I have isolated are incompatible with any such analysis, it follows that they cannot be embodied in any satisfactory account of social freedom at all.

We already find Hobbes taking this view of the alleged relationship between social freedom and public service in the course of his highly influential attack on Renaissance republicanism in *Leviathan*. In Chapter 21 he tells us with scorn about the Lucchese, who have 'written on the turrets of the city of Lucca in great characters, at this day, the word LIBERTAS', in spite of the fact that the constitution of their small-scale city-republic placed heavy demands upon their public-spiritedness.[12] To Hobbes, for whom liberty (as we have seen) simply means absence of interference, it seems obvious that the maximising of our social freedom must depend upon our capacity to maximise the area within which we can claim 'immunity from the service of the commonwealth'.[13] So it seems to him merely absurd of the Lucchese to proclaim their liberty in circumstances in which such services are so stringently exacted. Hobbes' modern sympathisers regularly make the same point. As Oppenheim puts it, for

---

[11] For a discussion that moves in this Kantian direction, connecting freedom with rationality and concluding that it cannot therefore 'be identified with absence of impediments,' see, for example, C.I. Lewis, 'The meaning of liberty', in *Values and Imperatives*, John Lange, ed. (Stanford, 1969), pp. 145–55, at p. 147. For a valuable recent exposition of the same Kantian perspective, see the section 'Rationality and freedom' in Martin Hollis, *Invitation to Philosophy* (Oxford, 1985), pp. 144–51. [12] Hobbes, *Leviathan*, Bk. II, ch. 21, p. 266. [13] *Ibid.*

example, in his recent book *Political Concepts*, the claim that we can speak of 'freedom of participation in the political process' is simply confused.[14] Freedom presupposes the absence of any such obligation or constraints. So this 'so-called freedom of participation does not relate to freedom in any sense'.[15]

We find the same line of argument advanced even more frequently in the case of the other claim I am considering: that our freedom may have to be the fruit of our being coerced. Consider, for example, how Raphael handles this suggestion in his *Problems of Political Philosophy*. He simply reiterates the contention that 'when we speak of having or not having liberty or freedom in a political context, we are referring to freedom of action or social freedom, i.e., the absence of restraint or compulsion by human agency, including compulsion by the State'.[16] To suggest, therefore, that 'compulsion by the State can make a man more free' is not merely to state a paradoxical conclusion; it is to present an 'extraordinary view' that simply consists of confusing two polar opposites, freedom and constraint.[17] Again, Oppenheim makes the same point. Since freedom consists in the absence of constraint, to suggest that someone might be 'forced to be free' is no longer to speak of freedom at all but 'its opposite'.[18]

What are we to think of this first line of attack, culminating as it does in the suggestion that, as Oppenheim expresses it, neither of the arguments I have isolated 'relate to freedom in any sense'?

It seems to me that this conclusion relies on dismissing, far too readily, a different tradition of thought about social freedom which, at this point in my argument, it becomes important briefly to lay out.

The tradition I have in mind is essentially the Aristotelian one, which may be said to be founded on two distinctive and highly influential premises. The first, developed in various subsequent systems of naturalistic ethics, claims that we are moral beings with certain characteristically human purposes. The second, later taken up in particular by scholastic political philosophy, adds that the human animal is *naturale sociale et politicum*, and thus that our purposes must be essentially social in character.[19] The view of human freedom to which these assumptions give rise is thus a 'positive' one. We can only be said to be fully or genuinely at liberty, according to this account, if we actually engage in just those activities which are most conducive to *eudaimonia* or 'human flourishing', and may therefore be said to embody our deepest human purposes.

I have no wish to defend the truth of these premises. I merely wish to

---

[14] Oppenheim, *Political Concepts*, p. 92.

[15] *Ibid.*, p. 162. For a recent endorsement of the claim that, since liberty requires no action, it can hardly require virtuous or valuable action, see Lincoln Allison, *Right Principles* (Oxford, 1984), pp. 134–5.

[16] D.D. Raphael, *Problems of Political Philosophy*, rev. edn (London, 1976), p. 139.

[17] *Ibid.*, p. 137.   [18] Oppenheim, *Political Concepts*, p. 164.

[19] See, for example, Thomas Aquinas, *De Regimine Principum*, Bk. 1, ch. 1, in *Aquinas: Selected Political Writings*, A.P. D'Entrèves, ed. (Oxford, 1959), p. 2.

underline what the above account already makes clear: that if they are granted, a positive theory of liberty flows from them without the least paradox or incoherence.

This has two important implications for my present argument. One is that the basic claim advanced by the theorists of negative liberty I have so far been considering would appear to be false. They have argued that all coherent theories of liberty must have a certain triadic structure. But the theory of social freedom I have just stated, although perfectly coherent if we grant its premises, has a strongly contrasting shape.[20]

The contrast can be readily spelled out. The structure within which MacCallum and his numerous followers insist on analysing all claims about social freedom is such that they make it a sufficient condition of an agent's being at liberty that he or she should be unconstrained from pursuing some particular option, or at least from choosing between alternatives. Freedom, in the terminology Charles Taylor has recently introduced, becomes a pure opportunity concept.[21] I am already free if I have the opportunity to act, whether or not I happen to make use of that opportunity. By contrast, the positive theory I have just laid out makes it a necessary condition of an agent's being fully or truly at liberty that he or she should actually engage in the pursuit of certain determinate ends. Freedom, to invoke Taylor's terminology once more, is viewed not as an opportunity but as an exercise concept.[22] I am only in the fullest sense in possession of my liberty if I actually exercise the capacities and pursue the goals that serve to realise my most distinctively human purposes.

The other implication of this positive analysis is even more important for my present argument. According to the negative theories I have so far considered, the two claims I began by isolating can safely be dismissed as misunderstandings of the concept of liberty.[23] According to some, indeed, they are far worse than misunderstandings; they are 'patent sophisms' that are really designed, in consequence of sinister ideological commitments, to convert social freedom 'into something very different, if not its opposite'.[24] Once we recognise, however, that the positive view of liberty stemming from the thesis of naturalism is a perfectly coherent one, we are bound to view these claims in a quite different light.

There ceases, in the first place, to be any self-evident reason for impugning the motives of those who have defended them.[25] Belief in the idea of 'human

---

[20] For a fuller exploration of this point see the important article by Tom Baldwin, 'MacCallum and the two concepts of freedom', *Ratio*, 26 (1984), 125–42, esp. at 135–6.

[21] Taylor, 'Negative liberty', p. 177.   [22] *Ibid.*

[23] See, for example, the conclusions in W. Parent, 'Some recent work on the concept of liberty', *American Philosophical Quarterly*, 11 (1974), 149–67, esp. 152, 166.

[24] Anthony Flew, '"Freedom is slavery": a slogan for our new philosopher kings' in *Of Liberty*, Griffiths, ed., pp. 45–59, esp. at pp. 46, 48, 52.

[25] At this point I am greatly indebted once more to Baldwin, 'Two concepts', esp. pp. 139–40.

flourishing' and its accompanying vision of social freedom arises at a far deeper level than that of mere ideological debate. It arises as an attempt to answer one of the central questions in moral philosophy, the question whether it is rational to be moral. The suggested answer is that it is in fact rational, the reason being that we have an interest in morality, the reason for this in turn being the fact that we are moral agents committed by our very natures to certain normative ends. We may wish to claim that this theory of human nature is false. But we can hardly claim to know *a priori* that it could never in principle be sincerely held.

We can carry this argument a stage further, moreover, if we revert to the particular brand of Thomist and Aristotelian naturalism I have singled out. Suppose for the sake of argument we accept both its distinctive premises: not only that human nature embodies certain moral purposes, but that these purposes are essentially social in character as well. If we do so, the two claims I began by isolating not only cease to look confused; they both begin to look highly plausible.

Consider first the alleged connection between freedom and public service. We are supposing that human nature has an essence, and that this is social and political in character. But this makes it almost truistic to suggest that we may need to establish one particular form of political association – thereafter devoting ourselves to serving and sustaining it – if we wish to realise our own natures and hence our fullest liberty. For the form of association we shall need to maintain will of course be just that form in which our freedom to be our true selves is capable of being realised as completely as possible.

Finally, consider the paradox that connects this idea of freedom with constraint. If we need to serve a certain sort of society in order to become most fully ourselves, we can certainly imagine tensions arising between our apparent interests and the duties we need to discharge if our true natures, and hence our fullest liberty, are both to be realised. But in those circumstances we can scarcely call it paradoxical – though we may certainly find it disturbing – if we are told what Rousseau tells us so forcefully in *The Social Contract*: that if anyone regards 'what he owes to the common cause as a gratuitous contribution, the loss of which would be less painful for others than the payment is onerous for him', then he must be 'forced to be free', coerced into enjoying a liberty he will otherwise allow to degenerate into servitude.[26]

III

I now turn to assess the other standpoint from which my two opening claims about liberty have commonly been dismissed. The theorists I now wish to discuss have recognised that there may well be more than one coherent way of

[26] Jean-Jacques Rousseau, *The Social Contract*, tr. Maurice Cranston (Harmondsworth, 1968), p. 64.

thinking about the idea of political liberty. Sometimes they have even suggested, in line with the formula used in Isaiah Berlin's classic essay, that there may be more than one coherent *concept* of liberty.[27] As a result, they have sometimes explicitly stated that there may be theories of liberty within which the two seemingly paradoxical contentions I have singled out no longer appear to be paradoxical at all. As Berlin himself emphasises, for example, several 'positive' theories of freedom, religious as well as political, seem readily able to encompass the suggestion that people may have to act 'in certain self-improving ways, which they could be coerced to do' if there is to be any prospect of realising their fullest or truest liberty.[28]

When such writers express doubts about the two claims I am considering, therefore, their thesis is not that they are incapable of being accommodated within any coherent theory of liberty. It is only that they are incapable of being accommodated within any coherent theory of negative liberty – any theory in which the idea of liberty itself is equated with the mere absence of impediments to the realisation of one's chosen ends. To put the argument in the form in which my opening quotation from MacIntyre appears to advance it, the suggestion is that the two claims I began by isolating can *only* be rendered coherent within an essentially Aristotelian structure of thought.

This appears, for example, to be Isaiah Berlin's view of the matter in his 'Two Concepts of Liberty'. Citing Cranmer's epigram 'Whose service is perfect freedom', Berlin allows that such an ideal, perhaps even coupled with a demand for coercion in its name, might conceivably form part of a theory of freedom 'without thereby rendering the word "freedom" wholly meaningless'. His objection is merely that, as he adds, 'all this has little to do with' the idea of negative liberty as someone like John Stuart Mill would ordinarily understand it.[29]

Considering the same question from the opposite angle, so to speak, Charles Taylor appears to reach the same conclusion in his essay, 'What's wrong with negative liberty'. It is only because liberty is *not* a mere opportunity concept, he argues, that we need to confront the two paradoxes I have isolated, asking ourselves whether our liberty is 'realisable only within a certain form of society', and whether this commits us 'to justifying the excesses of totalitarian oppression in the name of liberty'.[30] Taylor's final reason, indeed, for treating the strictly negative view of liberty as an impoverished one is that, if we restrict ourselves to such an understanding of the concept, these troubling but unavoidable questions do not arise.[31]

What are we to think of this second line of argument, culminating in the

---

[27] This is how Berlin expresses the point in the title of his essay, although he shifts in the course of it to speaking instead of the different 'senses' of the term. See *Four Essays*, esp. p. 121.

[28] *Ibid.*, esp. p. 152.   [29] *Ibid.*, pp. 160–2.   [30] Taylor, 'Negative liberty', p. 193.

[31] See Taylor, *ibid.*, insisting (p. 193) that this is 'altogether too quick a way with them'.

suggestion that the two claims I am considering, whatever else may be said about them, have no place in any ordinary theory of negative liberty? This brings me to the main point I am concerned to bring out. For it seems to me that this conclusion depends on ignoring another whole tradition of social thought, the Renaissance republican tradition with which this book has been concerned. The view of social freedom to which this tradition gave rise is one that has largely been overlooked in recent philosophical debate. But it seems well worth trying to restore it to view, for the effect of doing so will be to show us, I believe, that the two paradoxes I have isolated can in fact be accommodated within an ordinary theory of negative liberty. It is to this task of exposition, accordingly, that I now turn, albeit in an unavoidably promissory and over-schematic style.[32]

Within the classical republican tradition, the discussion of political liberty was generally embedded in an analysis of what it means to speak of living in a 'free state'. As I have tried to show in chapter 6 of the present volume, this approach was largely derived from Roman moral philosophy, and especially from those writers whose greatest admiration had been reserved for the doomed Roman republic: Livy, Sallust, and above all Cicero. Within modern political theory, their line of argument was first taken up in Renaissance Italy as a means of defending the traditional liberties of the city-republics against the rising tyranny of the *signori* and the secular powers of the Church. Many theorists espoused the republican cause at this formative stage in its development, but the greatest among those who did so, as Professor Viroli emphasises in chapter 7, was undoubtedly Machiavelli in his *Discorsi* on the first ten books of Livy's History of Rome. Later we find a similar defence of 'free states' being mounted – with acknowledgements to Machiavelli's influence – by James Harrington and other English republicans of the seventeenth century, among whom, as Dr Worden shows in chapter 11, John Milton must undoubtedly be numbered. Still later, we find something of the same outlook – again owing much to Machiavelli's inspiration – among the opponents of absolutism in eighteenth-century France. As Professor Shklar indicates in chapter 13, many elements of the theory recur in a mutated form in Montesquieu's account of republican virtue in *De L'esprit des Lois*.

---

[32] I cannot hope to give anything like a complete account of this ideology here, nor even of the recent historical literature devoted to it. Suffice it to point to the earlier chapters of the present volume, and to add that the classic general study is J.G.A. Pocock, *The Machiavellian Moment* (Princeton, NJ, 1975), a work to which I am much indebted. I have tried to give a fuller account of my own views in two earlier articles: 'Machiavelli on the maintenance of liberty', *Politics*, 18 (1983), 3–15, and 'The idea of negative liberty: philosophical and historical perspectives', *Philosophy in History*, Richard Rorty, J.B. Schneewind, and Quentin Skinner, eds., (Cambridge, 1984), pp. 193–221. The present essay may be regarded as an attempt to bring out the implications of those earlier studies, although at the same time I have considerably modified and I hope strengthened my earlier arguments.

By this time, however, the ideals of classical republicanism had largely been swallowed up by the rising tide of contractarian political thought. If we wish to investigate the heyday of classical republicanism, accordingly, we need to turn back to the period with which this book has mainly been concerned, the period before the concept of individual rights attained that hegemony which it has never subsequently lost. We need, that is, to turn back to the moral and political philosophy of the Renaissance, as well as to the Roman republican writers on whom the Renaissance theorists placed such overwhelming weight. It is from these sources, therefore, that I shall mainly draw my picture of the republican ideal of liberty, and it is from Machiavelli's *Discorsi* – perhaps the most compelling presentation of the case – that I shall mainly cite.[33]

IV

I have said that the classical republicans were mainly concerned to celebrate what Marchamont Nedham later described in a resounding title as 'the excellency of a free state'. It will be best to begin, therefore, by asking what they had in mind when they predicated liberty of entire communities. To grasp the answer, we need only recall that these writers take the metaphor of the body politic as seriously as possible. A political body, no less than a natural one, is said to be at liberty if and only if it is not subject to external constraint. Like a free person, a free state is one that is able to act according to its own will, in pursuit of its own chosen ends. It is a community, that is, in which the will of the citizens, the general will of the body politic, chooses and determines whatever ends are pursued by the community as a whole. As Machiavelli expresses the point at the beginning of his *Discorsi*, free states are those 'which are far from all external servitude, and are able to govern themselves according to their own will'.[34]

There are two principal benefits, according to these theorists, which we can only hope to enjoy with any degree of assurance if we live as members of free states. One is civic greatness and wealth. Sallust had laid it down in his *Catiline* (7.1) that Rome only became great as a result of throwing off the tyranny of her kings, and the same sentiment was endlessly echoed, as I have tried to show in chapter 6, by later exponents of classical republican thought. Machiavelli also insists, for example, that 'it is easy to understand the affection that people feel for living in liberty, for experience shows that no cities have ever grown in power or wealth except those which have been established as free states'.[35]

---

[33] All citations from the *Discorsi* refer to the version in Niccolò Machiavelli, *Il Principe e Discorsi*, ed. Sergio Bertelli (Milan, 1960). All translations are my own.

[34] *Ibid.*, i.ii, p. 129.   [35] *Ibid.*, ii.ii, p. 280.

But there is another and even greater gift that free states are alone capable of bequeathing with any confidence to their citizens. This is personal liberty, understood in the ordinary sense to mean that each citizen remains free from any elements of constraint (especially those which arise from personal dependence and servitude) and in consequence remains free to pursue his own chosen ends. As Machiavelli insists in a highly emphatic passage at the start of Book II of the *Discorsi*, it is only 'in lands and provinces which live as free states' that individual citizens can hope 'to live without fear that their patrimony will be taken away from them, knowing not merely that they are born as free citizens and not as slaves, but that they can hope to rise by their abilities to become leaders of their communities'.[36]

It is important to add that, by contrast with the Aristotelian assumptions about *eudaimonia* that pervade scholastic political philosophy, the writers I am considering never suggest that there are certain specific goals we need to realise in order to count as being fully or truly in possession of our liberty. Rather they emphasise that different classes of people will always have varying dispositions, and will in consequence value their liberty as the means to attain varying ends. As Machiavelli explains, some people place a high value on the pursuit of honour, glory, and power: 'they will want their liberty in order to be able to dominate others'.[37] But other people merely want to be left to their own devices, free to pursue their own family and professional lives: 'they want liberty in order to be able to live in security'.[38] To be free, in short, is simply to be unconstrained from pursuing whatever goals we may happen to set ourselves.

How then can we hope to set up and maintain a free state, thereby preventing our own individual liberty from degenerating into servitude? This is clearly the pivotal question, and by way of answering it the writers I am considering advance the distinctive claim that entitles them to be treated as a separate school of thought. A free state, they argue, must constitutionally speaking be what Livy and Sallust and Cicero had all described and celebrated as a *res publica*.

We need to exercise some care in assessing what this means, however, for it would certainly be an oversimplification to suppose that what they have in mind is necessarily a republic in the modern sense. As Professor Maihofer makes clear in chapter 14, what the republicans take themselves to be describing is any set of constitutional arrangements under which it might justifiably be claimed that the *res* (the government) genuinely reflects the will and promotes the good of the *publica* (the community as a whole). Whether a *res publica* has to take the form of a self-governing republic is not therefore an empty definitional question, as modern usage suggests, but rather a matter for earnest enquiry and debate. It is true, however, that most of the writers I have cited remain sceptical about the

---

[36] *Ibid.*, II. ii, p. 284. [37] *Ibid.*, I.xvi. p. 176. [38] *Ibid.*, I.xvi, p. 176; cf. also II.ii, pp. 284–85.

possibility that an individual or even a governing class could ever hope to remain sufficiently disinterested to equate their own will with the general will, and thereby act to promote the good of the community at all times. So they generally conclude that, if we wish to set up a *res publica*, it will be best to set up a republic as opposed to any kind of principality or monarchical rule.

The central contention of the theory I am examining is thus that a self-governing republic is the only type of regime under which a community can hope to attain greatness at the same time as guaranteeing its citizens their individual liberty. This is Machiavelli's usual view, Harrington's consistent view, and the view that Milton eventually came to accept.[39] But if this is so, we very much need to know how this particular form of government can in practice be established and kept in existence. For it turns out that each one of us has a strong personal interest in understanding how this can best be done.

The writers I am considering all respond, in effect, with a one-word answer. A self-governing republic can only be kept in being, they reply, if its citizens cultivate that crucial quality which Cicero had described as *virtus*, which the Italian theorists later rendered as *virtù*, and which the English republicans translated as civic virtue or public-spiritedness. The term is thus used to denote the range of capacities that each one of us as a citizen most needs to possess: the capacities that enable us willingly to serve the common good, thereby to uphold the freedom of our community, and in consequence to ensure its rise to greatness as well as our own individual liberty.

But what *are* these capacities? First of all, we need to possess the courage and determination to defend our community against the threat of conquest and enslavement by external enemies. A body-politic, no less than a natural body, which entrusts itself to be defended by someone else is exposing itself gratuitously to the loss of its liberty and even its life. For no one else can be expected to care as much for our own life and liberty as we care ourselves. Once we are conquered, moreover, we shall find ourselves serving the ends of our new masters rather than being able to pursue our own purposes. It follows that a willingness to cultivate the martial virtues, and to place them in the service of our community, must be indispensable to the preservation of our own individual liberty as well as the independence of our native land.[40]

We also need to have enough prudence and other civic qualities to play an active and effective role in public life. To allow the political decisions of a body-politic to be determined by the will of anyone other than the entire membership of the body itself is, as in the case of a natural body, to run the gratuitous risk that the behaviour of the body in question will be directed to the attainment not

---

[39] See Z.S. Fink, *The Classical Republicans*, 2nd edn (Evanston, 1962), esp. pp. 103–7, on Milton and Harrington. For Machiavelli's equivocations on the point see Marcia Colish, 'The idea of liberty in Machiavelli', *Journal of the History of Ideas*, 32 (1971), 323–50.

[40] This constitutes a leading theme of Book II of Machiavelli's *Discorsi*.

of its own ends, but merely the ends of those who have managed to gain control of it. It follows that, in order to avoid such servitude, and hence to ensure our own individual liberty, we must all cultivate the political virtues and devote ourselves wholeheartedly to a life of public service.[41]

This strenuous view of citizenship gives rise to a grave difficulty, however, as the classical republican theorists readily admit. Professor Bock touches on the point in chapter 9, in the course of analysing Machiavelli's views about civic discord. Each of us needs courage to help defend our community and prudence to take part in its government. But no one can be relied on consistently to display these cardinal virtues. On the contrary, as Machiavelli repeatedly emphasises, we are generally reluctant to cultivate the qualities that enable us to serve the common good. Rather we tend to be 'corrupt', a term of art the republican theorists habitually use to denote our natural tendency to ignore the claims of our community as soon as they seem to conflict with the pursuit of our own immediate advantage.[42]

To be corrupt, however, is to forget – or fail to grasp – something which it is profoundly in our interests to remember: that if we wish to enjoy as much freedom as we can hope to attain within political society, there is good reason for us to act in the first instance as virtuous citizens, placing the common good above the pursuit of any individual or factional ends. Corruption, in short, is simply a failure of rationality, an inability to recognise that our own liberty depends on committing ourselves to a life of virtue and public service. And the consequence of our habitual tendency to forget or misunderstand this vital piece of practical reasoning is therefore that we regularly tend to defeat our own purposes. As Machiavelli puts it, we often think we are acting to maximise our own liberty when we are really shouting, 'Long live our own ruin'.[43]

For the republican writers, accordingly, the deepest question of statecraft is one that recent theorists of liberty have supposed it pointless to ask. Contemporary theories of social freedom, analysing the concept of individual liberty in terms of 'background' rights, have come to rely heavily on the doctrine of the invisible hand. If we all pursue our own enlightened self-interest, we are assured, the outcome will in fact be the greatest good of the community as a whole.[44] From the point of view of the republican tradition, however, this is simply another way of describing corruption, the overcoming of which is said to be a necessary condition of maximising our own individual liberty. For the republican writers, accordingly, the deepest and most troubling question still remains: how can naturally self-interested citizens be persuaded to

[41] Book III of Machiavelli's *Discorsi* is much concerned with the role played by great men – defined as those possessing exceptional *virtù* – in Rome's rise to greatness.
[42] For a classic discussion of 'corruption' see Machiavelli, *Discorsi*, I.xvii–xix, pp. 177–85.
[43] *Ibid.*, I.liii, p. 249.
[44] See, for example, the way in which the concept of 'the common good' is discussed in John Rawls, *A Theory of Justice* (Cambridge, MA, 1971), pp. 243, 246.

act virtuously, such that they can hope to maximise a freedom which, left to themselves, they will infallibly throw away?

The answer at first sounds familiar: the republican writers place all their faith in the coercive powers of the law. Machiavelli, for example, puts the point graphically in the course of analysing the Roman republican constitution in Book I of his *Discorsi*. 'It is hunger and poverty that make men industrious', he declares, 'and it is the laws that make them good.'[45]

The account the republican writers give, however, of the relationship between law and liberty stands in strong contrast with the more familiar account to be found in contractarian political thought. To Hobbes, for example, or to Locke, the law preserves our liberty essentially by coercing other people. It prevents them from interfering with my acknowledged rights, helps me to draw around myself a circle within which they may not trespass, and prevents me at the same time from interfering with their freedom in just the same way. To a theorist such as Machiavelli, by contrast, the law preserves our liberty not merely by coercing others, but also by directly coercing each one of us into acting in a particular way. The law is also used, that is, to force us out of our habitual patterns of self-interested behaviour, to force us into discharging the full range of our civic duties, and thereby to ensure that the free state on which our own liberty depends is itself maintained free of servitude.

The justifications offered by the classical republican writers for the coercion that law brings with it also stand in marked contrast to those we find in contractarian or even in classical utilitarian thought. For Hobbes or for Locke, our freedom is a natural possession, a property of ourselves. The law's claim to limit its exercise can only be justified if it can be shown that, were the law to be withdrawn, the effect would not in fact be a greater liberty, but rather a diminution of the security with which our existing liberty is enjoyed. For a writer like Machiavelli, however, the justification of law is nothing to do with the protection of individual rights, a concept that makes no appearance in the *Discorsi* at all. The main justification for its exercise is that, by coercing people into acting in such a way as to uphold the institutions of a free state, the law creates and preserves a degree of individual liberty which, in its absence, would promptly collapse into absolute servitude.

Finally, we might ask what mechanisms the republican writers have in mind when they speak of using the law to coerce naturally self-interested individuals into defending their community with courage and governing it with prudence. This is a question to which Machiavelli devotes much of Book I of his *Discorsi*, and he offers two main suggestions, both derived from Livy's account of republican Rome.

He first considers what induced the Roman people to legislate so prudently

---

[45] Machiavelli, *Discorsi*, I.iii, p. 136.

for the common good when they might have fallen into factional conflicts.[46] He finds the key in the fact that, under their republican constitution, they had one assembly controlled by the nobility, another by the common people, with the consent of each being required for any proposal to become law. Each group admittedly tended to produce proposals designed merely to further its own interests. But each was prevented by the other from imposing them as laws. The result was that only such proposals as favoured no faction could ever hope to succeed. The laws relating to the constitution thus served to ensure that the common good was promoted at all times. As a result, the laws duly upheld a liberty that, in the absence of their power to coerce, would soon have been lost to tyranny and servitude.

Machiavelli also considers how the Romans induced their citizen-armies to fight so bravely against enslavement by invading enemies. Here he finds the key in their religious laws.[47] The Romans saw that the only way to make self-interested individuals risk their very lives for the liberty of their community was to make them take an oath binding them to defend the state at all costs. This made them less frightened of fighting than of running away. If they fought they might risk their lives, but if they ran away – thus violating their sacred pledge – they risked the much worse fate of offending the gods. The result was that, even when terrified, they always stood their ground. Hence, once again, their laws forced them to be free, coercing them into defending their liberty when their natural instinct for self-preservation would have led them to defeat and thus servitude.

V

By now, I hope, it will be obvious what conclusions I wish to draw from this examination of the classical republican theory of political liberty. On the one hand, it is evident that the republican writers embrace both the paradoxes I began by singling out. In a manner that contrasts sharply with modern liberal individualism, they not only connect social freedom with self-government, but also link the idea of personal liberty with that of virtuous public service. Moreover, they are no less emphatic that we may have to be forced to cultivate the civic virtues, and in consequence insist that the enjoyment of our personal liberty may often have to be the product of coercion and constraint.

On the other hand, these writers are equally far from being Aristotelians, and never appeal to a 'positive' view of social freedom. They never argue, that is, that we are moral beings with certain determinate purposes, and thus that we are only in the fullest sense in possession of our liberty when these purposes are

---

[46] *Ibid,* 1.ii–vi, pp. 129–46.   [47] *Ibid.,* 1.xi–xv, pp. 160–73.

realised. As we have seen, they work with a purely negative view of liberty as the absence of impediments to the realisation of our chosen ends. They are absolutely explicit in adding, moreover, that no determinate specification of these ends can be given without violating the inherent variety of human aspirations and goals.

Nor do they defend the idea of forcing people to be free by claiming that we must be prepared to reason about ends. They never suggest, that is, that there must be a certain range of actions which it will be objectively rational for us to perform, whatever the state of our desires. It is true that, on their analysis, there may well be actions of which it makes sense to say that there are good reasons for us to perform them, even if we have no desire – not even a reflectively considered desire – to do so. But this is not because they believe that it makes sense to reason about ends.[48] It is simply because they consider that the chain of practical reasoning we need to follow out in the case of acting to uphold our own liberty is so complex, and so unwelcome to citizens of corrupt disposition, that we find it all too easy to lose our way in the argument. As a result, we often cannot be brought, even on reflection, to recognise the range of actions we have good reason to perform in order to bring about the ends we actually desire.

Given this characterisation of the republican theory of freedom, my principal conclusion is thus that it must be a mistake to suppose that the two paradoxes I have been considering cannot be accommodated within an ordinary negative analysis of political liberty.[49] If the summary characterisation I have just given is correct, however, there is a further implication to be drawn from this latter part of my argument, and this I should like to end by pointing out. It is that our inherited traditions of political theory appear to embody two quite distinct though equally coherent views about the way in which it is most rational for us to act in order to maximise our negative liberty.

Recent emphasis on the importance of taking rights seriously has contrived to leave the impression that there may be only one way of thinking about this issue. We must first seek to erect around ourselves a cordon of rights, treating these as 'trumps' and insisting on their priority over any calls of social duty.[50] We must then seek to expand this cordon as far as possible, our eventual aim

---

[48] Although those who attack as well as those who defend the Kantian thesis that there may be reasons for action which are unconnected with our desires appear to assume that this must be what is at stake in such cases.

[49] I should stress that this seems to me an implication of MacCallum's analysis of the concept of freedom, cited in note 7 above. If so, it is an implication that none of those who have made use of his analysis have followed out, and most have explicitly denied. But cf. his discussion at pp. 189–92. I should like to take this opportunity of acknowledging that, although I believe the central thesis of MacCallum's article to be mistaken, I am nevertheless greatly indebted to it.

[50] See, for example, Ronald Dworkin, *Taking Rights Seriously* (Cambridge, MA, 1977), p. xi, for the claim that 'individual rights are political trumps held by individuals', and pp. 170–7 for a defence of the priority of rights over duties.

being to achieve what Isaiah Berlin has called 'a maximum degree of non-interference compatible with the minimum demands of social life'.[51] Only in this way – as Hobbes long ago argued – can we hope to maximise the area within which we are free to act as we choose.

If we revert to the republican theorists, however, we encounter a strong challenge to these familiar beliefs. To insist on rights as trumps, on their account, is simply to proclaim our corruption as citizens. It is also to embrace a self-destructive form of irrationality. Rather we must take our duties seriously, and instead of trying to evade anything more than 'the minimum demands of social life' we must seek to discharge our public obligations as wholeheartedly as possible. Political rationality consists in recognising that this constitutes the only means of guaranteeing the very liberty we may seem to be giving up.

VI

My story is at an end; it only remains to point the moral of the tale. Contemporary liberalism, especially in its so-called libertarian form, is in danger of sweeping the public arena bare of any concepts save those of self-interest and individual rights. Moralists who have protested against this impoverishment – such as Hannah Arendt, and more recently Charles Taylor, Alasdair MacIntyre and others[52] – have generally assumed in turn that the only alternative is to adopt an 'exercise' concept of liberty, or else to seek by some unexplained means to slip back into the womb of the polis. I have tried to show that the dichotomy here – either a theory of rights or an 'exercise' theory of liberty – is a false one. The Aristotelian and Thomist assumption that a healthy public life must be founded on a conception of *eudaimonia* is by no means the only alternative tradition available to us if we wish to recapture a vision of politics based not merely on fair procedures but on common meanings and purposes. It is also open to us to meditate on the potential relevance of a theory which tells us that, if we wish to maximise our own individual liberty, we must cease to put our trust in princes, and instead take charge of the public arena ourselves.

It will be objected that this attempt to enlist the traditions of Machiavellian republicanism as a third force amounts to nothing more than a nostaligic anti-modernism. We have no realistic prospect of taking active control of the political processes in any modern democracy committed to the technical complexities and obsessional secrecies of present-day government. But the objection is too crudely formulated. There are many areas of public life, short of

---

[51] Berlin, *Four Essays*, p. 161.

[52] For Arendt's views see her essay 'What is freedom?' in *Between Past and Future*, rev. edn (New York, 1968), pp. 143–71. For Taylor's, see 'Negative liberty', esp. pp. 180–6. For MacIntyre's, see *After Virtue* (London, 1981), esp. p. 241.

directly controlling the actual executive process, where increased public participation might well serve to improve the accountability of our *soi disant* representatives. Even if the objection is valid, however, it misses the point. The reason for wishing to bring the republican vision of politics back into view is not that it tells us how to construct a genuine democracy, one in which government is for the people as a result of being by the people. That is for us to work out. It is simply because it conveys a warning which, while it may be unduly pessimistic, we can hardly afford to ignore: that unless we place our duties before our rights, we must expect to find our rights themselves undermined.

INDEX

Ideas in Context

Edited by Richard Rorty, J.B. Schneewind, Quentin Skinner and Wolf Lepenies

14) DAVID LIEBERMAN
The Province of Legislation Determined
Legal theory in eighteenth-century Britain

15) DANIEL PICK
Faces of Degeneration
A European disorder, c.1848–c.1918

16) KEITH BAKER
Approaching the French Revolution
*Essays on French political culture in the eighteenth century**

17) IAN HACKING
The Taming of Chance*

18) GISELA BOCK, QUENTIN SKINNER and MAURIZIO VIROLI (eds.)
Machiavelli and Republicanism

Forthcoming titles include works by Martin Dzelzainis, Mark Goldie, Noel Malcolm, Roger Mason, James Moore, Dorothy Ross, Nicolai Rubinstein, Quentin Skinner, Martin Warnke and Robert Wokler.

Titles marked with an asterisk are also available in paperback.